MINE EYES HAVE SEEN THE GLORY

MINE EYES HAVE SEEN THE GLORY

A Journey into the Evangelical Subculture in America

25th Anniversary Edition

RANDALL BALMER

OXFORD
UNIVERSITY PRESS

OXFORD

UNIVERSITY PRESS

Oxford University Press is a department of the
University of Oxford. It furthers the University's objective
of excellence in research, scholarship, and education
by publishing worldwide.

Oxford   New York

Auckland   Cape Town   Dar es Salaam   Hong Kong   Karachi
Kuala Lumpur   Madrid   Melbourne   Mexico City   Nairobi
New Delhi   Shanghai   Taipei   Toronto

With offices in

Argentina   Austria   Brazil   Chile   Czech Republic   France   Greece
Guatemala   Hungary   Italy   Japan   Poland   Portugal   Singapore
South Korea   Switzerland   Thailand   Turkey   Ukraine   Vietnam

Oxford is a registered trade mark of Oxford University Press
in the UK and certain other countries.

Published in the United States of America by
Oxford University Press
198 Madison Avenue, New York, NY 10016

Library of Congress Cataloging-in-Publication Data
Balmer, Randall Herbert.
Mine eyes have seen the glory : a journey into the evangelical
subculture in America / Randall Balmer. — 25th Anniversary Edition.
pages   cm
Includes bibliographical references and index.
ISBN 978-0-19-936046-8 (pbk. : alk. paper)
1. Evangelicalism—United States—History—20th century.
2. Fundamentalism—History—20th century.
3. Pentecostals—United States—History.
4. United States—Church history—20th century.   I. Title.
BR1642.U5B35   2014
277.3'0828—dc23   2013040031

1 3 5 7 9 8 6 4 2

Printed in the United States of America
on acid-free paper

For Christian

Contents

Preface to the Fifth Edition   *ix*

Acknowledgments   *xiii*

A Word about Words   *xv*

PROLOGUE   3

CHAPTER 1   California Kickback   13

CHAPTER 2   Dallas Orthodoxy   32

CHAPTER 3   On Location   48

CHAPTER 4   Phoenix Prophet   71

CHAPTER 5   Adirondack Fundamentalism   90

CHAPTER 6   Georgia Charismatics   107

CHAPTER 7   Bible School   127

CHAPTER 8   Campaign Journal   146

CHAPTER 9   Mississippi Missions   176

CHAPTER 10   Bible Bazaar   193

CHAPTER 11   Episcopal Indians   209

CHAPTER 12   Camp Meeting   226

CHAPTER 13   City Crusade   246

CHAPTER 14   Oregon Jeremiad   258

CHAPTER 15   Prime Time   278

CHAPTER 16   Sound Check   295

CHAPTER 17   Kinkade Crusade   312

CHAPTER 18   Purpose Driven   326

CHAPTER 19   Latino Evangelicals   339

EPILOGUE   351

AFTERWORD   Twenty-five Years Later   360

Notes   379

Index   393

Preface to the Fifth Edition

A QUARTER OF A CENTURY AGO, the chair of my department warned me against writing this book. I was a fledgling assistant professor in the late 1980s, and I was concluding the revisions to my dissertation about the time that the televangelist scandals were breaking: Jim Bakker's tryst with a church secretary from Long Island, Jimmy Swaggart's voyeuristic adventures in Louisiana motel rooms, and Oral Roberts's declaration that God had, in effect, taken him hostage and would dispatch the evangelist unless God's people ponied up a ransom of several million dollars.

It was great fun, of course, watching the televangelists get their comeuppance. But I soon tired of the media's assumption that all evangelicals were the moral equivalent of the televangelists, so I devised this crazy idea to travel around the country and write about American evangelicalism at the grass roots. As a student of American religious history and as someone reared in the evangelical subculture, I thought I could offer a more textured portrait of evangelicalism in all of its diversity.

My department chair thought it was a terrible idea, tantamount to professional suicide. It might be construed as too popular, he said, and besides, no reputable scholar combined history with ethnography, much less bundled the two into a narrative. What was I thinking?

Had I not been told at my hiring, repeatedly and in no uncertain terms, that I would never—*never!*—be tenured at Columbia University, I might have taken the prudent course and heeded his caution. But I had little to lose, so I embarked on my travels into evangelical America. The first edition of *Mine Eyes Have Seen the Glory* appeared in June 1989, three weeks after the publication of the book based on my dissertation. Slowly, stealthily this book won a following that exceeded all expectations: four editions (this is the fifth) and a three-part companion documentary for PBS. The book has been used in history, sociology, religion, anthropology, and writing courses as well as in journalism schools. One of the chapters appeared in the venerable Norton anthology.

When I approached Cynthia Read, my superb and trusted editor, about a Twenty-fifth Anniversary Edition, she was enthusiastic. We talked over several possibilities and decided on the addition of another chapter, this one on Latino evangelicals, together with updates on some of the people and places I encountered in earlier editions. I was unable to revisit all of them, but as my travels have taken me to various places over the past couple of years, I've tried to take detours whenever possible to visit some of those people and places.

Detours, of course, provide the best stories, and I offer them here.

I'D LIKE TO ADD, IF I MAY, a personal note. Most professors become accustomed to spending years and years on scholarly projects, shepherding them through, finally, to publication, and then encountering a deep silence. Aside from a couple of pedantic reviews, they rarely hear from people who read their books.

I've endured my share of pedantic reviews, and some of the books I've written have failed to engender extended conversations. But I count myself fortunate to hear from those who have read my books and responded in one way or another. I'm grateful for that, truly grateful. Nothing I have written has elicited more response than *Mine Eyes Have Seen the Glory*. Over the past twenty-five years, and as recently as a couple of weeks ago, I've received letters and e-mails, too many to count. Sometimes, people will collar me after a lecture somewhere. A few want to quarrel with some interpretation or another (which is fine), but most want simply to express appreciation for the book and for telling "their" stories, for understanding them, even though we'd never met. The most gratifying responses have come from those who, on the verge of abandoning their faith, choose to reconsider. Belief is a rare and precious gift, especially in a culture inebriated with Enlightenment rationalism, and if something I might have said, done, or written helps to sustain faith, I couldn't be happier.

So, thank you. And keep the faith!

Wilder, Vermont
Feast Day of St. Philip the Evangelist
October 11, 2013

Acknowledgments

A NUMBER OF PEOPLE contributed to this book in myriad ways. John Wilson, Yoma Ullman, Albert Raboteau, Mark Noll, and Frederick Borsch all provided advice and encouragement at the formative stages of this project; Don Haymes, Marvin Bergman, Sue Anne Morrow, and Stephen Stein led me to believe I might be on to something. Several colleagues at Columbia—Robert Somerville, Wayne Proudfoot, and Jack Hawley—gave an early draft of the manuscript the benefit of their scrutiny, as did Grant Wacker and Elena Garella. Peter Awn got me thinking about the meaning of modernity to fundamentalists, and Harry Stout suggested several interpretations which I have tried to develop in various places. Stephen Warner, a true sociologist, corrected some of the mistaken notions that fell from the pen of a shade-tree sociologist. Jack Fitzmier is both a good friend and a trenchant critic, and he manages somehow to keep one role from compromising the other.

Others contributed in ways less tangible but no less important. Countless late-night conversations with Jerome and Kay Iverson over the years have helped me understand the psychology of growing up fundamentalist. Also, I owe a debt of gratitude to my parents, whose gentleness, faith, and piety I have always deemed worthy of emulation, even as I fell so abysmally short of those standards.

I know that many of the people I've just named will disagree with some, much, and perhaps all of this book, so I hasten to add the following disclaimer: I alone bear responsibility for what follows. Far too often in their history evangelicals have judged people guilty by association. That verdict, I emphasize, should not be rendered in this case.

Several others made possible the completion of this volume. A grant-in-aid from the American Council of Learned Societies helped to defray the costs of travel. The Columbia University Council for Research in the Humanities also provided a stipend, for which I am most grateful. Paul Schlotthauer and Cynthia Read made this a better manuscript than it would have been without their steady editorial hands.

The most timely encouragement, however, came from this latter source. After several fruitless approaches to foundations and publishers, I had virtually given up on my quixotic idea to travel around America and write about popular evangelicalism. Then an envelope arrived from Cynthia Read, religion editor at Oxford University Press. Responding to a letter I had written in the *New York Times,* she asked if I was working on any projects that Oxford might find interesting. Figuring I had nothing to lose, I dusted off an old prospectus, and soon thereafter, armed with a contract and fueled by a modest advance, I set off to explore the evangelical subculture in America.

At times, my absence as half-time homemaker necessitated complicated arrangements for the care of Christian and Andrew. On the morning of one of my final trips, I informed Christian, not yet three years old, that I would be leaving again for several days. "You know what, Daddy?" he said. "You sure do leave a lot."

Well, son, after two years of airports, rental cars, cheap motel rooms, and enough bad sermons to last a lifetime, I'm home.

New York
March 1989

A Word about Words

FOR OUR PURPOSES, any discussion of the terms *evangelical, fundamentalist, charismatic,* and *pentecostal* should steer a middle course between an extended, technical treatment and the kind of dismissive description suggested by Potter Stewart's attempt to define pornography a few years back. "I can't define it," the Supreme Court justice acknowledged, "but I know it when I see it."

The term *evangelical* has been bandied about a lot in recent years. The *Oxford English Dictionary* defines it simply: "Of or pertaining to the Gospel" of the New Testament, especially the gospels of Matthew, Mark, Luke, and John.[1] Historically, the term often refers to the theology of the Protestant Reformation in the sixteenth century, when Martin Luther "rediscovered the gospel" after its eclipse in the scholastic theology of the Middle Ages. Luther believed that Roman Catholic theology, particularly the thought of St. Thomas Aquinas, had compromised the *evangel* or gospel, the "good news" of the New Testament, by substituting a theology of works (the notion that you effectively earn your salvation by good works, avoiding sin, and remaining in communion with the Church) for the New Testament theology of grace (God, through Jesus Christ, bestows a saving grace without regard to human merit). For Luther, this discovery, based on his study of St. Paul's letters to the Galatians and to the Romans, liberated him from responsibility for his own salvation.

Ostensibly at least, modern-day evangelicals still subscribe to the rudiments of Luther's theology, although they rejected his ideas about polity and worship as too formal and "papist," and their theology emphasizes human volition in salvation far more than Luther would have countenanced. *Evangelical* has picked up other connotations in the four-and-one-half centuries since Luther challenged the papacy and launched the Protestant Reformation. Evangelicals generally believe that a spiritual rebirth, a "born again" experience (which they derive from John 3) during which one acknowledges personal sinfulness and Christ's atonement, is necessary for salvation. While Luther certainly took the Scriptures seriously—they formed the basis for his attacks on Roman Catholic accretions to Christian theology—many successive evangelicals have insisted on a literalistic hermeneutic for understanding the Bible. In the nineteenth century, amid challenges from Darwinism and the discipline of higher criticism emanating from Germany, this insistence on literalism led to an emphasis on the inerrancy of the Scriptures. Evangelicalism has also been characterized by a proselytizing zeal that, at various points in its history, particularly in the eighteenth and nineteenth centuries, has erupted into large-scale revivals or spiritual awakenings.

Part of what defines an evangelical, however, transcends mere doctrine or belief; in greater or lesser degrees, evangelicals place a good deal of emphasis on piety. On May 24, 1738, John Wesley attended a religious gathering on Aldersgate Street in London. There, as someone read Luther's preface to his commentary on the book of Romans, Wesley felt his heart "strangely warmed" and felt an assurance that Christ "had taken away *my* sins, even *mine*, and saved *me* from the law of sin and death."[2] Wesley's evangelical experience has served as a model for many American evangelicals. They, like him, point to some sudden, instantaneous, datable experience of grace, and they aspire to the kind of warm-hearted piety so characteristic of Wesley's spiritual life.

In the years since the Iranian Revolution, the term *fundamentalist* has been applied to many religions to denote literalistic, moralistic, pietistic, and even militant impulses within the larger tradition. However, the word has its origins in American evangelicalism and derives from a series of pamphlets entitled *The Fundamentals,* published early in the twentieth century to turn back the theological challenges of Protestant liberals or "modernists." These pamphlets, financed by California tycoons Lyman and Milton Stewart of Union Oil, set forth a series of doctrines their authors regarded as essential to evangelical Christianity. Those who subscribed to these doctrines, which included belief in the virgin birth of Jesus, the infallibility of the Bible, and Christ's imminent return to earth, became known as *fundamentalists*. Many within the fundamentalist camp, moreover, chose to separate from denominations that harbored modernist ideas, and their general suspicion of "worldliness" issued in strict codes of personal morality and taboos against such worldly evils as cosmetics, card-playing, dancing, movies, and alcohol.

Pentecostals, members of such denominations as the Church of God in Christ, the Assemblies of God, and Aimee Semple McPherson's International Church of the Foursquare Gospel, comprise another camp of evangelicals. Rising out of the holiness movement in the nineteenth century and the pentecostal revivals in the early years of the twentieth century, pentecostals believe that the spiritual gifts bestowed upon the early church in the book of Acts are available to modern-day believers. Pentecostals insist that a spiritual experience of baptism or filling by the Holy Spirit, often marked by *glossolalia* or "speaking in tongues," constitutes the mark of a true Christian. Other spiritual gifts include the word of knowledge (an ability to discern the needs and spiritual condition of another) and divine healing.

Like pentecostals, *charismatics* believe in the spiritual gifts (*charismata*), but this term generally refers to those affiliated with non-pentecostal denominations. Pat Robertson, a charismatic, is a member of the Southern Baptist Convention, a denomination that generally shies away from dramatic, emotive outpourings of the Holy Spirit. Charismatics, moreover, have been active among the Episcopalians since 1959, and since the mid-1960s the charismatic movement has taken root within Roman Catholicism and other denominations.

If all this sounds neat and compartmentalized, it isn't. Southern Baptists, for instance, squirm in the face of attempts to force them into categories. For years, evangelicals and fundamentalists have looked askance at pentecostals and charismatics. Many evangelicals resist the label fundamentalist. Jerry Falwell, on the other hand, styles himself a fundamentalist, not an evangelical, although he pulled off a minor miracle in the late 1970s and early 1980s by uniting hitherto diverse elements of American evangelicalism under the political banner of Moral Majority. I can think of several people in the pages that follow who would be embarrassed, even outraged, to appear in the same book as some of the others treated here.

Such is the unwieldly nature of evangelicalism in America. But its breadth and diversity, I think, only add to its allure. All of the terms above appear in the following pages; the context should make the meaning clear. Moreover, I shall use the word *evangelical* as an umbrella term to refer broadly to conservative Protestants—including fundamentalists, evangelicals, pentecostals, and charismatics—who insist on some sort of spiritual rebirth as a criterion for entering the kingdom of heaven, who often impose exacting behavioral standards on the faithful, and whose beliefs, institutions, and folkways comprise the evangelical subculture in America.[3]

MINE EYES HAVE SEEN THE GLORY

Upon my arrival in the United States, the religious aspect of the country was the first thing that struck my attention.

ALEXIS DE TOCQUEVILLE, 1835

...I can see no reason, but the most deceitful one; for calling the religion of this land Christianity. I look upon it as the climax of all misnomers, the boldest of all frauds, and the grossest of all libels.... I am filled with unutterable loathing when I contemplate the religious pomp and show, together with the horrible inconsistencies, which every where surround me.

FREDERICK DOUGLASS, 1845

Heave an egg out of a Pullman window and you will hit a Fundamentalist almost anywhere in the United States today.

H. L. MENCKEN, 1925

Glibness is the great danger in answering people's questions about religion.

FLANNERY O'CONNOR, 1958

Prologue

I n Bay City, Michigan, on a rainy day during my childhood, I finally mustered the courage to "witness" to Stanley Strelecki, my next-door neighbor and playmate. Though not yet in my teens, hundreds of hours of sermons, Sunday school lessons, revival meetings, and Bible study had prepared me for this moment.

"Stanley," I began, my voice quavering. "Are you a Christian?" There. The opening gambit, everyone said, was the toughest. After that initial exchange, I had been promised, witnessing would get easier.

"Yes," he answered.

None of the coaching, none of the role-playing in church youth meetings or pep talks at Bible camp, had prepared me for that response. I was ready with reasoned arguments about the existence of God, the sinfulness of humanity, and every person's need to accept Christ as his or her savior. But how do you deal with someone who lies about his spiritual condition? Stanley, I knew, was a Roman Catholic, not a Christian, a plight in some respects worse than outright paganism, I had been told, because it lulled followers into a deadly complacency. But *Christian?* Certainly no Catholic, no matter how benighted, would dare call himself a Christian.

"Are you sure?" I asked meekly, beating a hasty retreat.

He was sure. Once the rain cleared, we resumed playing catch and fantasizing about our futures in professional baseball.

I've long since lost track of Stanley Strelecki, although I know he never became a pitcher for the Detroit Tigers. I never became a second baseman for the Tigers, nor did I follow my father's footsteps and become the preacher and evangelist that my parents so fervently wanted.

It would be years beyond college before I realized why that exchange with Stanley Strelecki was so peculiar, why I as an evangelical, a fundamentalist, simply spoke a different language from Stanley. *Christian,* in the vernacular of my evangelical subculture, was an exclusive, elitist term reserved for someone who had "prayed the prayer," had acknowledged personal sinfulness and the need for salvation, and "accepted Jesus into his heart."*

Christian also meant a good deal more. It meant immersing oneself in the evangelical subculture, affiliating with a local church (not just any church, but a church that "preached the Bible"), eschewing "worldliness" in its many insidious forms, hewing to strict codes of personal morality, sending the kids off to Sunday school, youth meetings, Bible camps, and, eventually, to a Bible school or a Christian college. It meant establishing a daily "quiet time," a period of personal devotions characterized by reading the Bible, meditation, and prayer. Being a *Christian* meant witnessing, "sharing your faith" with non-Christians—that is, anyone who did not fit this definition.

It also meant feeling very guilty if you failed to do any of the above, or if you failed to do it with sufficient rigor or enthusiasm, for there were always spiritual athletes around to shame you—pastors, traveling evangelists, godly matriarchs in any congregation whose personal piety served both as examples worthy of emulation and implicit rebukes to your own spiritual lethargy.

THIS IS A BOOK about popular evangelicalism, a kind of travelogue into the evangelical subculture in America, a subculture that encom-

---

*Semantics are quite important on this issue. Some evangelicals draw a careful distinction between being (merely) Christian and being *a* Christian; therein lies the difference between hell and heaven. Most evangelicals, moreover, bristle at being called *religious* because identifying their faith as a *religion* implies that there may be other, equally valid faiths, a concession most evangelicals are reluctant to grant.

passes fundamentalists, charismatics, and pentecostals. It was born of the suspicion that many Americans, and certainly the media, really did not have much of a clue about who evangelicals were, what they believed, or what motivated their recent forays into the political arena. The sudden surge of evangelicals into national prominence in the mid-1970s was treated as a kind of curiosity, with little acknowledgment of evangelicalism's history or its broad—and growing—popularity. The media relied far too heavily on the shopworn stereotypes that Sinclair Lewis and H. L. Mencken perpetrated in the 1920s, caricatures that depicted evangelicals as country bumpkins and their leaders as venal, disingenuous opportunists. As both a student of American religious history and a product of the evangelical subculture, I knew better.

But what began as an exploration of the variegated forms of American evangelicalism quickly turned into a personal odyssey of sorts. Although I was reared within the subculture, a series of personal circumstances, including impatience with a political agenda that I found (now, as then) reprehensible, prompted my withdrawal from the evangelical subculture in the late 1970s, a distancing born not so much of a resolve to reject my past, but of a curiosity about what lay beyond the citadel of evangelicalism, which I found more and more confining. After more than twenty years within the protective cocoon of this subculture, it was time for a breather, time to escape the censoriousness I had known much of my life.

I found in the ensuing years the joy of friendships uncluttered with the guilt and repressiveness that often come with growing up fundamentalist. I discovered the beauty of worship in a liturgical, "high-church" setting. I found that many of the theological liberals I had been taught to despise had a good deal to teach me about tolerance and compassion, even as I became convinced anew of the theological bankruptcy of Protestant liberalism. To the extent that I thought about evangelicals at all in those years, I regarded their theological quarrels as silly and churlish, if not irrelevant. The strict parietal rules they placed on children struck me as petty and mistrustful.

My subsequent forays into the evangelical subculture, then, provided a fresh look at a phenomenon I had all but ignored for the
better part of a decade. My travels quickly triggered a personal
agenda that included attempts to come to terms with what it meant
to grow up fundamentalist, to sort out the many ways that the evangelical subculture had shaped me and continues to define who I am.
After years of self-conscious withdrawal from evangelicalism, I also
became interested in reacquainting myself with the revolutionary
force of the evangelical gospel, those kernels of truth and insight
into the human condition that had, in my judgment, become lost in
the ephemera of modern evangelicalism and squandered in a kind
of Faustian bargain by evangelicalism's assimilation to contemporary
American culture, even as it purported to maintain a critical distance from "worldliness."

My purpose in undertaking this project, however, was neither to
vilify nor to vindicate American evangelicalism, and the reader will
early on detect my own ambivalence toward the subculture and all
it represents. On the one hand, I felt something of a compulsion to
defend evangelicalism against its many detractors who dismiss it
without troubling themselves to understand it. On the other hand,
I could not readily disguise my own discomfiture with all the nonsense that parades as the New Testament gospel of Jesus Christ.

What puzzled me even more was how much of my own reflec-
tions I should integrate into the narratives. No historian worthy of
the name can claim utter objectivity, but in the early version of this
manuscript I sought to maintain a scholarly detachment. After I had
drafted a few chapters and sent them to my editor and to trusted
advisers, however, I received a nearly unanimous response: "All well
and good, but what do *you* think?" I stammered out some answer
or another, but the question of how much (or how little) of myself
I had invested in the narrative continued to haunt me. I have become
convinced in recent years that one of the birthrights of Midwestern-
ers is a sense that your opinions don't really matter, so I found it
difficult to believe that anyone would truly be interested in my views

or my reactions to the various phenomena I had described. Half of the blood that courses through my veins, moreover, is Swedish, and we Scandinavians are rather chary about tipping our hands. Finally, one of the things that has irked me over the years is the tendency of evangelicals to pontificate on anything from codes of behavior to politics to eschatology. They define *their* position as "Christian" or "biblical," and every other view as somehow less so. I am not a theologian, either by training or by temperament, and I emphatically did not want simply to dispense gratuitous judgments.

One day near the end of the project, an imaginary interlocutor appeared in the chair on the other side of my desk. "Why did you write this thing in the first place?" he asked.

"I was pretty sure that the press had missed the story, that they had bunched all evangelicals together and failed to appreciate the spectrum of evangelicalism in America."

"What else?"

"Well, I wanted to say something about the evangelical subculture that defines and nurtures and sometimes suffocates those who consider themselves born-again Christians."

"Anything else?" The interlocutor's eyes bore down on me.

"Well, I suppose I wanted to exorcise a few demons of my own."

"Aha!" he said. "I figured as much. Besides," he added wryly, "those demons need exercise. Tell us what *you* make of all this."

From that point onward, I began extemporizing. I wasn't always comfortable with this feet-on-the-desk analysis, but whenever I lapsed into the reportorial mode, my interlocutor turned me back to the task.

Some of what follows, then, is self-disclosure; I abandoned the detached and dispassionate analysis I had originally envisioned. But it is not autobiography. I have tried as much as possible in this ethnographic study to allow people to tell their own stories and thereby render a portrait—or at least a collage—of evangelicalism, America's folk religion, in all its variation and diversity. Whereas sociologists try to find commonalities among apparently disparate phenomena,

I wanted to show variations within a subculture generally regarded as monolithic.

As a historian who holds an appointment in a research university, this project entailed other, professional perils beyond the risk of self-disclosure. I have tried to produce a book that might appeal both to scholars interested in popular religion in America and to the public in general—including, certainly, evangelicals themselves—curious about a phenomenon that has received a good deal of attention in the past decade.

At an early planning stage, I decided that this book would not be about the powerful evangelical bigwigs—Jerry Falwell, Billy Graham, Oral Roberts, and locally renowned pastors—who exert such a large influence over popular evangelicalism. That is not to say that these people are not important, although I do think that their influence is overrated. I've long believed, in fact, that evangelicalism in America, lacking the confessional emphasis and liturgical rubrics that bind other religious groups, has been susceptible to the cult of personality, a weakness only magnified in recent years by the widespread use of television.

Several factors loomed in my decision to avoid these stars. First and most important, I wanted to write a book about *popular* evangelicalism, to examine the ways evangelical theology and morality shaped individuals within the movement, how their participation in the evangelical subculture defined who they were and shaped the way they viewed the world. As a cultural historian, I was curious to see how evangelical theology functioned in various social contexts. Whatever contemporary evangelicalism has to commend it lies not in its media stars but in the sincerity and ingenuousness of the ordinary folk who consider themselves evangelicals.

I remain convinced, moreover, that the attention paid to the televangelists is disproportionate to their influence within the evangelical subculture. There are good reasons for this, of course. For nonevangelicals, the televangelists are the most conspicuous element of evangelicalism, and their bizarre antics in recent years make for good copy and tantalizing footage on the six o'clock news. But for many evangelicals themselves, the televangelists are more of a nuisance and an embarrassment than a substantive influence (even though many local churches have imitated their style). I confess to no little amusement at the media's coverage of recent scandals, because the formula was always the same. After a lead-in about the scandal itself, a reporter would ambush an unsuspecting churchgoer at some Baptist church in Tennessee to ask whether Jimmy Swaggart's latest indiscretion would affect his or her faith. For anyone familiar with evangelicalism, that question misses the point. The faith of American evangelicals is shaped by many forces—their own reading of the Scriptures (which in turn is affected by what translation or study Bible they choose), their local church and pastor, the kinds of devotional materials they use, and, perhaps least of all, by Jimmy Swaggart or Jim Bakker or Oral Roberts.

Finally, I had another, more personal reason for steering clear of well-known evangelical leaders. As a product of the evangelical subculture, I knew that such people are especially adept at that parlance of piety known as "God talk," and I suspected it would be very tedious, perhaps impossible, to penetrate this verbal veil in order to tease out useful answers.

"How, Reverend Jones, do you account for the success of your church?"

"It's just the work of the Lord. I can't explain it any other way. The Lord has blessed our ministry here."

There's nothing wrong with such answers, I suppose, and I have no reason to question the sincerity of those responses. It's just that I have the same reaction to them as I have to weather forecasters on television. No matter how firmly I resolve to hear them out, my eyes glaze over after about twenty seconds.

I heard my share of platitudes from the people I talked with during my travels. But I found that if I pressed a bit further, repeated the question in a slightly different way, or simply allowed people to elaborate, they often gave more satisfying answers. Such comments form the core of this book.

The travel motif seemed especially appropriate, not only because of its discursive possibilities and because evangelicalism in America extends to every region of the country, but also because Americans themselves have always been on the move, migrating from one place to another in search of economic opportunity, personal fulfillment, and even religious contentment. Frequently, moreover, the genre of American travel literature has included observations about religion. Captain John Smith's comments on the natives of colonial Virginia come to mind, as do Alexis de Tocqueville's assertions about the relationship between American religiosity and the function of democratic institutions, Charles Nordhoffs examination of nineteenth-century utopian experiments, and Robert Pirsig's tortuous spiritual journey, *Zen and the Art of Motorcycle Maintenance*. America's persistent religiosity has elicited comment in other travel narratives as well: John Steinbeck's *Travels with Charley*, Jonathan Raban's *Old Glory: An American Voyage,* and *Blue Highways: A Journey into America* by William Least Heat Moon.

All these pilgrims discovered religion of one sort or another in the purlieus and beyond the back roads of America. I did too.

CHARTING THE PILGRIMAGE was, in some respects, as perilous as the journey itself. Several criteria came into play: geographical balance, a thematic approach to various chapters, and a desire to portray the spectrum of evangelicalism. It would have been easy (and, I confess, a good bit of fun) to confine myself to the strange-and-wacky world of American evangelicalism, but I was more interested in reaching the heart of the subculture rather than perpetuating common stereotypes. Accordingly, then, I gave up on fire-breathing evangelists and the born-again motorcycle gang down in Arkansas; those with a taste for the bizarre will have to content themselves with Neal Frisby, the "Phoenix Prophet," who will not disappoint.

At Calvary Chapel in southern California I wanted to assess the maturation of a church that had its genesis in the Jesus movement of the early 1970s. In Mississippi I found several groups of people struggling against both the entrenched racism of the old Confederacy and the social apathy that still grips American evangelicals. Word of Life Island in the Adirondacks evoked in me the memories of summers long past and showed me anew the quandary that evangelical parents face in trying to ensure that their children claim the evangelical faith for their own. Dallas Theological Seminary provided a look at the theology that undergirds much of American fundamentalism, but it also offered a glimpse of the sexism that persists within the evangelical subculture.

If there is any one thing that has brought evangelicalism to the attention of the broader public in recent years, I suspect it would be the fundamentalist involvement in politics, beginning in the mid-1970s. I knew that over the long range of American history there was nothing novel about evangelicals asserting themselves in the political sphere, but I wasn't certain why such passion had been invested in a certain, rather narrow range of issues. So I headed off to Iowa for the precinct caucuses and then to New Hampshire prior to the first primary of the 1988 presidential campaign. I was interested to see how evangelicals, especially evangelical women, were learning the political process, and I came away convinced that they will be a force for many campaigns to come.

My search for an old-fashioned revival reminiscent of the holiness camp meetings of the nineteenth century took me to St. Petersburg, Florida, but I might just as easily have ended up in Arkansas or Ohio or Virginia. In the Dakotas I found a marked contrast in the mission strategies of different Protestant groups. Donald Thompson, an evangelical filmmaker whose best-known movies depict life on earth during the apocalypse, is also an extraordinary individual whose unblinking optimism and faith in God represent the kind of piety that many evangelicals aspire to. My editor suggested attending the annual convention of the Christian Booksellers Association, which turned out to be a huge, bewildering bazaar of Bibles, video, music, books, and kitsch.

I think I first heard the term *subculture* applied to evangelicalism from Douglas Frank when I was a college student in the mid-1970s. A visit with him in Oregon gave me the excuse to rekindle an old friendship, catch up on his thinking, and try to unravel the contradictions that afflict twentieth-century evangelicalism.

Such are the contours of my pilgrimage into the evangelical subculture in America. But the most arresting dimensions of any journey are the detours, the wrong turns, the unexpected vistas along the way. In many cases, what I saw and heard by chance or indirection was more interesting than what I'd expected to find.

Herewith, then, the journey.

CHAPTER 1

California Kickback

I'VE ALWAYS SUSPECTED that you can tell a lot about a church (or any voluntary association, for that matter) by looking at the automobiles in its parking lot. In car-crazed southern California, that suspicion seems almost axiomatic. Herewith a sampling of bumper stickers, license-plate frames, and other paraphernalia on cars in the parking lot of Calvary Chapel in Santa Ana, California:

PEACE RULES WHERE GOD REIGNS

JESUS

I ♥ JESUS

I ♥ GOD

INVITE JESUS INTO YOUR ♥

PRAISE THE LORD

ROBERTSON '88

DONT BE CAUGHT DEAD WITHOUT JESUS

GET BACK TO BASICS. READ THE BIBLE

I'M INTO GOD

JESUS TAKES GOOD CARE OF ME

HAPPINESS IS BEING BORN AGAIN

HAPPINESS IS BEING SINGLE

JESUS LIVES

MY HEART BELONGS TO JESUS

GOD WILL BLESS AMERICA WHEN AMERICA BLESSES GOD

SMILE, JESUS LOVES YOU

GOD ALREADY MADE MY DAY!

TO KNOW ME IS TO LOVE ME

BEGIN YOUR DAY WITH NUTRITION. READ THE BIBLE

JESUS ON BOARD

BEAM ME UP, JESUS!

JESUS IS AWESOME

Some of the automobiles sport vanity plates. One California tag reads ADONAI, a Hebrew name for God. Another: DIED 4U2, presumably a reference to Jesus. Another: COM LORD. A car in the space reserved for the pastor reads CALVARY. The vehicles themselves range from a Rolls Royce, several Mercedes Benzes, Lincoln Continentals, and Cadillac Eldorados to old Ford Mavericks, motor scooters, and Volkswagen vans stuffed with junk, so dilapidated as to appear unroadworthy.

Inside on this Sunday morning, a quintessentially California crowd gathers, wearing anything from three-piece suits to beachwear—and everything in between: knit polo shirts, denims, madras, miniskirts, tee-shirts. Hairstyles range from the meticulous and coiffed to the insouciant and sun-bleached. Outside the auditorium, some worshipers lounge on the grass in lawn chairs, listening to the service on speakers located at various points around the grounds. Some listen from their automobiles as security guards on ten-speed bicycles patrol the parking lot. Virtually everyone totes a large Bible with some sort of casing—suede, hand-tooled leather, homemade quilting, vinyl with pictures of a cross and a dove. The woman in front of me carries one with PARTNER EDITION PTL CLUB emblazoned on the cover.

By eleven-fifteen, starting time for the third worship service of the morning, the huge auditorium is full, and four men file onto the stage beneath a stylized rendering of a dove to begin the service. A large man in a light-colored suit comes to the pulpit. "It's good to be back," he begins. I quickly surmise that this cheerful, avuncular man just short of his sixtieth birthday is Chuck Smith, senior pastor of Calvary Chapel and known to his large congregation as "Pastor Chuck."[1] As his bald, evenly bronzed head indicates, Smith has just returned from a two-week vacation in Hawai'i. "It was total kick-back," he said. "God brought the surf up. It was really great." He recounts days of golf and swimming and surfing and concludes, "We thank the Lord for the privilege of just total kickback for a couple of weeks."

The service itself at Calvary Chapel is simple, even spartan. After an opening prayer, Smith leads the congregation in singing "Holy! Holy! Holy! Lord, God Almighty." Another man on the platform comes to announce some of the many activities available throughout the week. A second congregational hymn follows the offering, which is followed in turn by special music from five women, members of the Joyful Life Bible Study. Smith then returns to the pulpit, reads the morning's Scripture text, and begins his sermon.

Smith projects an air of competence in his preaching, but the style itself won't make anyone forget Jimmy Swaggart, Billy Graham, or even Chuck Swindoll, who preaches in nearby Fullerton. He demonstrates a good deal of knowledge and dexterity, moving easily from one text to another. On this Mother's Day, he talks about "children in rebellion" and extols the value of "persistent and prevailing prayer." At the end of the sermon, the congregation stands as Smith recites—from memory—a poem that concludes, "The hand that rocks the cradle / Is the hand that rules the world." As the congregation sings the benediction, Smith walks down the center aisle and out the rear of the auditorium.

Calvary Chapel, a large, sprawling complex of buildings surrounded on all sides by a huge parking lot, lies at the corner of Fairview and Sunflower in Santa Ana, just beyond the limits of Costa Mesa. The architecture loosely resembles the Spanish mission style ubiquitous in southern California, and its modest scale contrasts with the ostentation of Robert Schuller's Crystal Cathedral down the road in Garden Grove. The rear of the auditorium opens out into a courtyard surrounded by other buildings, which house the fellowship hall (complete with huge closed-circuit television screens to serve overflow crowds), various church offices, and a warren of classrooms used for Sunday school and throughout the week for Calvary Chapel's grammar school, Maranatha Christian Academy. When the services end, thousands of people spill into the courtyard and the adjacent parking lots. Amid this flurry of activity, church-goers socialize. From a table in the courtyard, a girls' youth group sells sweatshirts to raise money, and young parents (of which there are many) retrieve their children from nurseries or Sunday school classrooms. In the parking lot just outside one of the exits, a gray pickup truck containing two large bins of avocados sports a hand-painted sign that reads:

CALVARY CHAPEL FARM
THIS IS YOUR FARM! PLEASE HELP YOUR SELF.
IF YOU CAN, LEAVE A DONATION. THANK YOU FOR YOUR
SUPPORT!

Pastor Chuck had announced earlier, in what seemed to me at the time a spontaneous gesture, that each mother in the congregation could grab an avocado in celebration of Mother's Day, instead of the usual carnation offered by other churches. Avocados are moving briskly.

The Sunday evening service is even more casual. Once again, the auditorium, which seats about twenty-three hundred, is filled. After a brief opening prayer, a large group of people—mostly young, but not all—leave their seats and come to the platform. They sing several songs, each separated by only a few guitar chords. The congregation joins in freely, without prompting. The music alternates between lively and joyful on the one hand and solemn and devotional, almost lugubrious, on the other. The melodies are simple, rather folksy, and everyone seems to know the words.[2] After half an hour or more, Pastor Chuck reappears and launches into a casual sermon, almost conversational in tone, about Second Samuel 3–5, an exposition that continues about ninety minutes.

Over most of his pastoral career, Smith has emphasized the systematic study of the Scriptures. And there on a Sunday evening in May, talking easily about one of the more recondite passages of the Bible, he is in his element, doing what he does best. For most preachers, Second Samuel is deadly, hardly the stuff of great oratory; yet Smith, in his workmanlike way, makes sense of the various Hebrew dynasties and the courtly intrigues, examining them as earnestly as a sports fan would study box scores. He digresses casually, calling on personal experience or, more often, other passages of Scripture (which he often recites from memory) to illustrate a point.

What is even more striking than Smith's deft handling of an obscure passage is his ability to hold this young audience's rapt attention for so long. Looking around the congregation, I find little evidence of impatience, and virtually the only sound is the rustling of pages. The auditors try in vain to keep up with Smith as he jumps from book to book, chapter to chapter, testament to testament.

Smith repeats the performance the following evening to another packed house with an exposition of Revelation 14 and again on Thursday night in his series on the Gospel of Luke. On Monday, after the obligatory half hour of singing led by several young people with guitars, Smith simply sits on the edge of the platform with a lapel microphone clipped to his pink polo shirt and talks extemporaneously about Revelation and the impending apocalypse. "We are living in the last days, when Satan is running amok in this world," he says at one point. "My heart goes out to you kids," he concludes. "In living for Christ today you have to go against the world." He exhorts them to a life of holiness and purity amid a world careening toward God's judgment.

MANY YEARS AGO, during revival meetings in Fairmont, Minnesota, I heard a pastor comment that Saturday evening was "the devil's night out." He explained that few churches conducted services on

Saturday, and that gave the devil free rein to work his mischief, even among putative Christians.

If so, the devil doesn't have much of an opening among the faithful of Calvary Chapel. Pastors there estimate that up to twenty-five thousand people pass through their twenty-one-acre campus every week, including a thousand students at Maranatha Christian Academy (kindergarten through eighth grade), Sunday school pupils, and worshipers at the three morning services on Sunday that fill the auditorium to capacity (the overflow for the latter two services also fills the seven-hundred-seat fellowship hall).[3] But that's just the beginning. A full range of other programs (or ministries, as the folks here prefer) round out the weekly schedule. Services and Bible studies are held for the deaf and in Korean, Spanish, and Arabic. The church sponsors ministries to high school and to junior high school youth. I counted fifty-one events scheduled for the week of my visit, including three prayer breakfasts and eleven Bible studies. The Working Women's Joyful Life Bible Study (not to be confused with the Women's Joyful Life Bible Study) meets on Monday evening, as does the Proverbs Class for Men, in addition to Smith's study of Revelation in the auditorium. A fellowship of ex-convicts meets on Friday night. Single parents gather on Wednesday night, singles on Friday, and the High School Mothers' Prayer Meeting convenes Tuesday afternoon. New Spirit, an alcohol and drug recovery program, meets Wednesday and Friday evenings. On Friday night, Calvary's Messianic Jewish Fellowship celebrated thirty-nine years of Israel's independence. Saturday evening, the Radical Street Ministry convenes opposite the Outreach Program, a weekly gathering for young people that features music by various Christian recording artists, a short devotional message, and an invitation to come forward and accept Jesus as savior.

In addition, the church runs a radio station, KWVE ("K-wave"), and a conference and retreat center in Twin Peaks, California. A tract of land near San Diego awaits development as another conference center. Through weekly gatherings for Bible study and prayer, thirty Home Fellowships scattered throughout the southern California area offer a more intimate sense of community than that available in larger assemblies at the church.

Some experts refer to a church like Calvary Chapel as a phenomenon or a "megachurch," a species that thrives here in southern California.[4] But the success of Chuck Smith and Calvary Chapel is all the more remarkable because of its genesis in the mid-1960s as a congregation of twenty-five contentious people, and because of its identification with a larger cultural phenomenon, the Jesus movement.

In the early 1960s, Chuck Smith, a pastor in the International Church of the Foursquare Gospel, a pentecostal denomination begun by Aimee Semple McPherson in the 1920s, began to tire of church-growth schemes propagated by the denominational hierarchy. Typically, these notions (quite common in evangelical circles) involve dividing the congregation into two or more teams that compete against one another to rack up the most points for filling up their assigned pews or inviting the unsaved to church. Churches within a denomination then compete against one another for the largest growth during the contest period. When promotional materials for still another contest began arriving at his church, Smith discarded them. "I couldn't face another Blues against the Reds," he said, resolving instead simply to teach the Bible.[5] In compliance with the requirements of the contest, however, the church secretary filed periodic reports about attendance, and at the conclusion of the contest Smith received a letter congratulating him as the winner— the church with the greatest increase—and inviting him to a rally to collect his trophy, even though his congregation had known nothing about the contest.

Disillusioned with denominational officiousness, Smith soon accepted a call to a nondenominational congregation in Corona, California, where he enjoyed similar success by continuing his emphasis on Bible teaching. Then, in 1965, he received an invitation from Calvary Chapel in Costa Mesa, a congregation of twenty-five, deeply divided and on the verge of disbanding. Smith accepted, even though he was forced to supplement his income by cleaning carpets several days a week. Under his ministry, this tiny church, growing at a rate of five percent a week, soon had to look for new quarters.

The largest increase came from an unlikely source. At that time, the height of the counterculture movement, the beaches of southern California fairly swarmed with hippies, and Smith later confessed that "these long-haired, bearded, dirty kids going around the streets repulsed me." Still, he felt a calling to them: "My wife and I used to go over to Huntington Beach and park downtown to watch the kids and pray for them. We wanted somehow to reach them, but we didn't know how."[6]

Through the friends of his college-age daughter, Smith soon began to meet hippies, many of whom had discovered in Christianity an answer to their intellectual searchings, and a cure, sometimes instantaneous, to their drug dependencies. Smith's house became a "hippie pad," where "Jesus freaks," as they became known, found both physical shelter and, in Smith's teaching of the Bible, spiritual sustenance.

Oden Fong, now a staff member at Calvary Chapel, was an early convert. "I came out of mysticism. I used to study religions, and at the time I learned about Calvary Chapel I was living down in Laguna Beach where there was a different representative of every faith on just about every corner. You could walk down the street and talk to a Zen Buddhist, walk a bit further and see a Krishna, a little farther and see a Satanist. It was a real hodge-podge of different faiths. I spent years in metaphysics, trying to attain perfection—fasting and that type of stuff, eating nothing but pure foods, meditating for hours and days, sitting in the same position for days. When I was doing yoga and things like that, I was just trying to get perfect. And there was just no way. I studied under the hierarchy of Tibetan Buddhism, Krishna Consciousness. A lot of my friends had gone up to Calvary Chapel, and they invited me one day. I went, reluctantly, and it was just so real. It was so much more real than anything I had seen. I found compassion and love. There was a fullness in the hearts of the people I met—the Jesus people—and I wanted that, too." Fong found the answer to his searching in the grace of God. "There's no perfect man. By Jesus' simple act, we have the power to change and not to fall."[7]

Smith's message, his acceptance and compassion, caught on. L. E. Romaine, a retired military man and a longtime associate of Smith's, remembers that in the early 1970s "not more than five or ten percent of the crowd was over twenty-five. Everybody wore granny dresses and carried fur-covered Bibles and jeans and biboveralls and tie-died shirts and long hair and beards," he said. "They were so wild it was scary. The news media couldn't understand it. Other churches couldn't understand it; some of them spoke against it."[8]

Fong remembers that when he first came to Calvary Chapel, it met in a small building down the street from its present location. "I think the most they could pack in there if they filled up all the seats and filled up all the aisles—which they did, it was standing room only in those days—was about three hundred people. We ripped down the walls, tore down the side walls, and had people sitting outside. Even in the rain people would be sitting out there. It was just a great, massive revival; there was a great movement of people into Christianity at the time. Every month or so, the church would double."[9]

To accommodate the crowds, the congregation bought a parcel of land at the intersection of Fairview and Sunflower (their present site), put in a parking lot, and purchased a big, second-hand circus tent as temporary quarters while they constructed an auditorium. The night before their first service in the tent, Smith and others set up sixteen hundred chairs and planned double services. "I looked out at that sea of folding chairs," Smith recalled. "I had never seen so many folding chairs in all my life!" He asked an associate: "How long do you suppose it will take the Lord to fill this place?" The associate looked at his watch and answered, "I'd say just about eleven hours."[10]

He was right. The next morning every seat was filled and people stood around the perimeter of the tent—for both services.

FROM ALL APPEARANCES, Chuck Smith seems like an improbable guru. What's the attraction? I put that question to many people during my visit to Calvary Chapel. Predictably, the answers ranged from the spiritualized to the philosophical.

Richard Cimino, an earnest young pastor at Calvary Chapel, waxed almost rhapsodic. "This balding, old guy taught the Word of God to the most bizarre hippies imaginable, and these people's lives were so changed by Jesus that they brought their friends, who brought their friends, who brought their friends. Now, people are here because they love to be taught the Word of God. They like coming to a place where they can wear Levi's, shorts, tennis shoes, bare feet, whatever, and sit and listen to some guy teach the Word of God in a way that they can understand it. I think Chuck Smith is Everyman's teacher. If I wanted to read a sermon, I'd probably read Chuck Swindoll's sermons before I'd read Chuck Smith's sermons. But there's a tremendous authority that God has given him in the pulpit, and yet it's something that everyone can understand. He's at ease. He's quick to confess his own faults. There are no pretenses about him. People respond to that. When they designed the church, he said 'I don't want anything big or flashy,' and as you can see it's major low profile. Everything about him is casual. He doesn't like structure. I just know that when I talk to him, I'm going to be a wiser man when I walk out."

More recent arrivals share similar impressions. When I checked into the motel in Costa Mesa and asked the woman at the desk if she could direct me to Calvary Chapel, she looked up and smiled. "That's my church," she said brightly. "Well, I've only been going there a little while. But I love it! I feel at home, and the people are really on fire for the Lord. There's good, solid Bible teaching there, and God has really been doing some radical things in my life since I started going to Calvary Chapel."

I met Tony when I sat in on the Single Parents Fellowship on Wednesday night. Tony moved to southern California from Brooklyn two years ago. "I just love it here," he said. "When I first started coming to Calvary Chapel I was struck by how real the place was, how real the people were. And I said, 'This is the place for me.'"

According to Oden Fong, the end of the 1960s found people "totally disillusioned with the counterculture revolution, the 'peace,' 'love,' 'flower power' movement, LSD, and so forth. All the heroes of that time—the musical heroes of the youth and political leaders of the youth—were all dying off, either by heroin overdoses or suicide or assasination. People were turning on one another, turning each other in. You had Timothy Leary turning state's evidence against the Black Panthers. It caused a lot of people to be extremely disillusioned with the counterculture revolution. But it was still a time of searching. The sixties was a time of looking inward and outward. We were trying to figure out who we were, what we were, where we were going as a human race." Fong paused and gathered his thoughts.

"Just about that same time, there was a spiritual awakening in Christianity where the walls of the traditional churches that had not allowed certain elements of the society to enter—I'm thinking of the so-called hippies—began to crumble. Christians began to concern themselves with living for Jesus Christ on a day-to-day basis, rather than simply adhering to the dogmas of the Church. There were also incredible manifestations of spiritual power. I have seen people's legs grow out. I've seen blind and deaf people healed. These miracles added a lot of excitement to the movement, too. Calvary Chapel and Chuck Smith were just part of that broader movement. A lot of them, thousands of them, were hippies, people coming out of the drug culture. It was kind of like one hobo telling another where he can get a good meal. We got the name Jesus people or Jesus freaks from the media, primarily because of our baptisms."

PIRATE'S COVE AT CORONA DEL MAR STATE BEACH lies at the entrance of Newport Bay, just across from the Balboa Peninsula. Protected from the waves by two jetties that guard the entrance to the channel, the sand in the cove slopes gently upward toward a large formation of rocks that fan out in a semicircle. Here in the early morning hours, at low tide beneath an overcast sky, the beach is empty save for a few seagulls and sandpipers. The surf thunders in the distance. A small fishing trawler sputters by. The mood is serene, peaceful.

But in the early 1970s a bit of history took place here, history involving Calvary Chapel and the baptism of Jesus people in the Pacific Ocean. On those occasions, Corona del Mar was anything but serene.

"Dope addicts, panhandlers, and just regular kids who were confused have come through here and accepted Christ," Smith explained to a reporter at the time. "Baptizing is the symbol of this acceptance."[11] Fong remembers the chaos. "You pushed and shoved to get either into the parking lot or somewhere above the beach area. You'd walk all the way down over the rocks. You'd see this mass of humanity, thousands of people sitting on the rocks and down on the beach and all around the outsides of the cove. And then down by the water itself would be the pastors and hundreds of people lined up to be baptized—usually three hundred or more."

Romaine, Smith's associate, also remembers the huge crowds. "The first big baptism down at Corona del Mar took place in 1970. We got down to Pirate's Cove on a Saturday around nine-thirty, ten o'clock, and there were thousands and thousands of people waiting there. These so-called Jesus freaks are climbing all over the rocks and into the adjacent residential area. They're knocking on doors and telling people about Jesus and hugging them. People were out there drinking iced tea in their swings, and these kids would just sit down and talk to them about the Lord. They had no pretenses whatsoever. They just loved the Lord, and if you'd sit still they'd tell you about the Lord.

"These kids are climbing all over the place, and the residents called the police; they thought it was another Woodstock or something. They're scared. They see two or three thousand young people, and they don't know what to think. So here come four or five police cars. The police got out, and these young people—I don't like to use the term hippies, but that's what they were—they were hugging the policemen and telling them about Jesus Christ. They wanted to know if the police would accept Jesus Christ. These policemen were scared to death. I watched them; I stood right there and watched their faces. Their eyes flew wide open. They looked as though someone had just stabbed them with a pin.

"When we started the baptisms, the kids sitting on the rocks surrounding the cove started singing. I'll tell you, I've never run into anything like that in my life. Four of us were baptizing people, and it took us two-and-a-half hours to baptize everyone who wanted to be baptized. I was so stupefied, I couldn't see straight. It was more than I could understand, more than I could handle."[12]

Baptisms in the Pacific took place about once a month. They're less frequent now, but still well attended. At the Monday night study of Revelation, Smith announced: "The next baptism will be June 26 at Corona del Mar. A Friday night. We'll play volleyball, eat some hot dogs, and then baptize anyone who wants to identify with the death, burial, and resurrection of Jesus."

THERE IS SOMETHING COMFORTABLE, almost beguiling, about the services at Calvary Chapel. The mood is relaxed, the singing alternately joyful and dolorous. There is also an appealing naiveté about Smith and his approach to the Bible, an approach that might be characterized as, "Here is what it says, so this is what it means." When Martin Luther posted his *Ninety-five Theses* on the cathedral door at Wittenberg, he declared, in effect, that he would be guided by his own understanding of the Bible and not by the teachings of the Roman Catholic hierarchy. Luther's sentiments created a demand for Scriptures in the vernacular, and Protestants ever since have stubbornly insisted on interpreting the Bible for themselves, forgetting most of the time that they come to the text with their own set of cultural biases and personal agendas.

Underlying this insistence on individual interpretation is the assumption (which received explicit sanction in the philosophy of

Common Sense Realism in the nineteenth century) that the plainest, most evident reading of the text is the proper one. Everyone becomes his or her own theologian. There is no longer any need to consult Augustine or Thomas Aquinas or Martin Luther about their understanding of various passages when you yourself are the final arbiter of what is the correct reading. This tendency, together with the absence of any authority structure within Protestantism, has created a kind of theological free-for-all, as various individuals or groups insist that *their* reading of the Bible is the only possible interpretation.

Chuck Smith clearly interprets Scripture literally and in its plainest sense, with the presumption of inerrancy, but he is remarkably undogmatic by nature. In the past decade or so, virtually every evangelical and fundamentalist congregation in America has had to address the issue of the charismatic or pentecostal movement. Pentecostals believe in a "second blessing" of the Holy Spirit (after the first, which is conversion) that makes the believer a "Spirit-filled" Christian. This blessing is often accompanied by *glossolalia*, or "speaking in tongues," where the believer, in a state of spiritual ecstasy, babbles in an unfamiliar language, just as the early Christians did on the original day of Pentecost.[13] Other "spiritual gifts" include the gift of healing and the gift of interpreting tongues. Many pentecostals (such as the Church of God or the Assemblies of God or the International Church of the Foursquare Gospel) regard this spiritual blessing as an essential mark of a true Christian. Fundamentalists and most evangelicals, on the other hand, acknowledge the spiritual gifts described in the New Testament, but they insist that these supernatural phenomena were confined to the first-century Christians and no longer apply to the modern Church.

This controversy, based on divergent interpretations of the Bible, has occasioned acrimonious battles among conservative Protestants in recent years, with many a congregation torn asunder over the validity of spiritual gifts. Pentecostal worship tends toward spiritual ecstasy and emotionalism, while fundamentalists emphasize teaching and preaching—a more rationalistic faith. Pentecostals value "the leading of the Spirit," and they are known for long meetings punctuated by healings, speaking in tongues, and by people lifting their hands in reverence or throwing up their arms in joyful abandon.[14]

During the services at Calvary Chapel, especially during the singing that opens the meetings, it's not uncommon to see some people close their eyes and lift up their hands in a gesture of worship and devotion (in fact, most people—leaders and congregation—close their eyes while singing). A few will even stand up and lift their arms high in the air. In some churches, such gestures would spark a theological controversy over spiritual gifts. But Smith seems unperturbed. Calvary Chapel's statement of faith reads, in part: "We believe worship of God should be Spiritual. Therefore we remain flexible and yielded to the leading of the Holy Spirit to direct our worship."

I asked Oden Fong to what extent pentecostal theology and practice influences Calvary Chapel. "We believe in the gifts of the Holy Spirit in this day—divine healing, prophecy, word of knowledge, speaking in tongues—but we differ from pentecostals in that we do not believe in emotionalism. In fact, we shy away from emotionalism. We believe that a faith grounded in emotions is rather shallow, that it will dissipate when the emotions disappear."

Chuck Smith's latitudinarianism, his unwillingness to engage in theological battles that he views as irrelevant, has defused many of the controversies that afflict other evangelical churches. Smith also retains his suspicion of denominations. "We are not a denominational church," the statement of faith reads, "nor are we opposed to denominations as such, only their overemphasis of the doctrinal differences that have led to the division of the Body of Christ." Still, Calvary Chapel of Costa Mesa has inspired others. There are over three hundred congregations around the country—and the world—that maintain a loose association or fellowship. These Calvary Chapels (some have different names) are all autonomous; they elect and ordain their own pastors. Typically, someone who has attended Calvary Chapel and then moves elsewhere will begin a Bible study in the new community. As this gathering expands, the congregation will contact Calvary Chapel for a pastor, whereupon Smith encourages one of his staff members to take the position. In this way, characteristically informal and uncalculated, Calvary Chapel has expanded its influence well beyond Costa Mesa.

Sociologists who study voluntary associations generally agree that a religious group goes through several phases in its development. During the first phase a group coalesces around a charismatic leader, who defines the group largely through the force of his personality. After a time, however, a process sociologists call "routinization" sets in as patterns of behavior and association become rationalized and institutionalized. This phase in the life of a religious group is generally associated with a dissipation of the religious fervor that characterized the organization in its formative period. I was eager to see how much routinization had affected Calvary Chapel in the last twenty years.

Saturday night was Outreach Night, geared especially toward the young people. From seven-thirty to nine-thirty this group, most of them in their early twenties, gathered in the auditorium to listen to a Christian recording artist and a sermon from a young preacher who earlier in the meeting had invited everyone in attendance to go down to Balboa Pier in Newport Beach afterward for witnessing. "It's a heavy spiritual battle down there," he announced. All hands were needed.

As the meeting drew to a close, he repeated the announcement and offered some coaching. "When I begin preaching at the entrance to the pier," he said, "it's very important that you all pay close attention, that you look at me as if you've never seen me before. That's the key, because people walking by will look at the audience and see how interested they are before deciding whether or not to stop and listen." He advised the people to avoid arguments and confrontations. It's better, he said, "to just share the love of Jesus." Anyone interested in witnessing, he concluded, could pick up some tracts at the front of the auditorium. A good number, perhaps fifty or sixty, came forward after the service. One man in his late twenties or early thirties, who introduced himself as Mark, fidgeted nervously while paging through the tract he had collected. "I haven't done this for three or four years," he said. 'I'm kinda out of practice."

The group reassembled in Newport Beach a little after ten o'clock, and for about an hour thereafter the entrance to the pier buzzed with activity. There was an almost palpable sense of expectation and excitement. People were milling about, floating in and out of conversations. "Jesus loves you. He's the only way to heaven." "He's real. I know He's real because I can feel Him in my heart." "Jesus delivered me from drugs, and He can do the same for you." Some spectators climbed atop cars in the adjacent parking lot to hear the preacher. Nearly everyone passing by stopped to listen, at least for a time; some of them took on an air of bemusement, others disgust, still others curiosity.

But the mood wasn't quite right—too contentious. Things got off on the wrong foot when a rather boisterous young man began taunting the "Jesus freaks," as he called them, and then, feeling surrounded, grew rather defensive and argumentative. "I don't need no God; I'm happy the way I am," he protested. That confrontational style spread as the eager evangelists circled their prey. One passerby, seeing all the commotion, said, "What's this, a brawl? Make a circle and let them go at it." When informed that they were talking about God, he elbowed his way in and joined the fray.

In all, there were too many graphic descriptions of the torments of hell. One woman complained: "I haven't even opened my mouth, and four people have told me I'm going to hell." Another woman was involved in Wicca, a kind of feminist neopaganism often associated, mistakenly, with Satan worship. "But Satan is the prince of lies!" one evangelist shouted in exasperation. The youth of Calvary Chapel had their hands full. Quite frequently, several of them would step aside and huddle in prayer over some prospect who was particularly obdurate. The young preacher had been right; the forces of righteousness were engaged in a "heavy spiritual battle" at Balboa Pier.

And yet, here, just a short distance from Pirate's Cove, the scene was strangely evocative of decades past: the briny scent of the ocean mixing with the smell of campfires on the beach, the restless waves—and, sure enough, a few people who looked for all the world like hippies, with long hair in pony tails, mutton-chop sideburns, denim shirts, necklaces made of turquoise, wide leather watchbands, sunglasses at eleven o'clock in the evening. One of them, sitting on a park bench at the periphery of the crowd, crouched over a guitar and belted out songs about Jesus in a throaty, insistent whine.

By eleven forty-five the crowd had dissipated and it was time to conduct a post-mortem. I asked Mark about the experience. "It went pretty well," he said. "I witnessed to a Catholic." I asked another woman, Carol, to assess the evening. "I'm really stoked," she said. "I ran into this guy I had talked to the last time we were out witnessing. He wanted me to meet his friends, and one of them said he wasn't sure whether he was a Christian or not. So we prayed, and when we finished tears were rolling down his face."

Not everyone reported successes, so it was important to close ranks and bolster sagging morale. "I had this guy so close, and then his friend came and pulled him away," one man said, shaking his head. "He didn't want to go either." Friends consoled him that a "seed had been planted," that "God's word does not return unto Him void."[15] Someone else opined that the people who resisted most vociferously were the ones most interested in the gospel. "Take my word for it," he said, "in six months they'll be Christians."

Toward the end of the evening, one man who appeared to be in his late twenties had launched into a long, desperate harangue. "Salvation is in every man's hand. Jesus loves you, man, He loves you with all his heart. And I love you. The truth is here. And people's lives have been changed: marriages coming together, alcoholics being renewed, drug addicts being changed. Man, this is the real stuff! And it's the Spirit of God, the Holy Ghost. God has changed my life. I walked as a heathen. I partied with the best of them.

"There's hope out here," he continued, his voice growing more forceful, his hands beating the air. "There really is hope. There really is God, and you really are going to be accountable for your sins. I guarantee you'll be accountable for your sins. Receive the love of Christ. All you have to do is say, 'Yes, Lord, I know I've sinned against You, and I know I haven't walked with You, and I know I don't know You, man. But help me. Help me!' All you have to do is be sincere, because God is merciful."

His cadence grew faster, his tone more plaintive. "It's getting worse in the world. There's people dabbling in mystics, man, and witchcraft, and they're loving it, man, they're pushing it. And it's going to get worse. I'm not going to contend with people about this and that, because I don't come to preach religion. I preach reality. Jesus is real, and He loves you. He loves you and He cares. He loves you so much that, like I said, if you come to Him with a sincere heart and tell Him, 'Hey Lord, I've sinned against you,' He'll forgive you and square you away, I tell you, He'll square you away. He'll change your life around. You've got free will, man, you've got a choice. Repent, and your life will change; I guarantee your life will change."

Most of his auditors had drifted away. "I'm willing to put myself on the line right here. I'll pray with anyone who wants to accept Jesus."

No takers. When he learned later that many of the people he preached to in the thinning crowd were from Calvary Chapel, he threw up his hands and chuckled at the incident. "Here I am preaching my heart out, and all these people are already Christians," he said in mock despair. "What a drag, man!"

"That's okay," someone assured him quietly as waves crashed in the distance. "The Spirit was moving."

1987

CHAPTER 2

Dallas Orthodoxy

FLUSHED WITH OIL MONEY of the seventies and prompted in part by the arrival of Northerners to the Sun Belt, Dallas, Texas, has recast its skyline with a building boom that only now, in the unaccustomed austerity of the late 1980s, shows any sign of abating. The results are impressive: a passel of post-modernist structures that represents a wholesale assault on the canons of modernist and international-style architecture dominating much of the twentieth century.

The pleasant, well-manicured campus of Dallas Theological Seminary, just a couple of miles from the center city, will never win acclaim for architectural distinction, but the people of Dallas Seminary have sustained their own quarrel with a different sort of modernity for more than half a century. Since its founding in 1924 to combat the theological modernism then popular with American Protestants, Dallas Theological Seminary has, in its view, held down the fortress of evangelical and fundamentalist orthodoxy against the sundry assaults of twentieth-century theological liberalism. My visit to Dallas Seminary, then, was a kind of inspection tour of these doctrinal ramparts, or (to shift the metaphor) an examination of the theological infrastructure of American evangelicalism. The intellectual case for evangelical theology, people here believe, rests to a remarkable degree on the twin pillars of biblical inerrancy (the conviction that the inspiration of the Holy Spirit rendered the Scriptures errorless in the original autographs) and a nineteenth-century doctrine that goes by the rather ponderous name of dispensational premillennialism.[1]

IN THE 1830S A BRITISH STUDENT of the Bible, John Nelson Darby, came up with a novel interpretation of the Bible. All of human history from creation through the present and into the coming millennium, Darby decided, could be divided into seven periods or dispensations. These different ages also largely coincide with successive covenants between God and humanity. In the Noahic covenant, for instance, God had promised Noah that the world would never again be destroyed by a flood. The covenant of works between God and ancient Israel obligated the Hebrews to strict moral and dietary standards. Since the day of Pentecost in the New Testament book of Acts, Darby argued, humanity has lived in the covenant of grace, under the terms of which Christ offers salvation and deliverance from the judgment of God to anyone who acknowledges Jesus as savior.

Darby's ideas, grounded in a literalistic interpretation of Scripture, also led him to posit that we are living now in the sixth and final dispensation before the return of Christ to take the true believers out of this world to their reward in heaven. The prophecies of the Bible—principally the books of Daniel in the Old Testament and Revelation in the New Testament—have been fulfilled and we can look for this "second coming" at any moment. We are poised at the end of human history, Darby believed, waiting for the apocalypse prophesied in the Bible. Although the notion of imminence was not new in Christian theology, this doctrine, known as premillennialism, held that Christ would return to claim (or rapture) His Church (the true believers) before the millennium, one thousand years of theocratic rule on earth predicted in Revelation 20.

Darby was not the first to predict the imminent end of human history. Ever since Jesus admonished His followers that "this generation will not pass away" before the coming of the Son of Man, Christians have speculated about the future and taken a strong interest in eschatology, the doctrine of the end times. Enigmatic passages about the seventy weeks in the book of Daniel and the elaborate apocalyptic imagery in Revelation have fueled the imagination of everyone from St. Augustine in his classic *The City of God*, written in the fourth century, to Swedish filmmaker Ingmar Bergman, in his movie *The Seventh Seal*, released in 1957. The early Christians, taking Christ's words at face value, prepared for their immediate translation into heaven, while Martin Luther dismissed the book of Revelation as irrelevant to Christian life and theology and urged that it be excluded from the canon of Scripture.

Darby's interpretive scheme of seven ages or dispensations caught on in Great Britain, especially with the Plymouth Brethren (among whom Darby numbered himself), but his ideas found especially fertile soil among evangelicals in nineteenth-century America. When Darby came to the United States in 1862, he found that his premillennial views fit the evangelical temper perfectly. Although the New England Puritans had been decidedly premillennial in their theology— that is, they expected the return of Christ at any moment—most evangelical eschatology in the eighteenth and nineteenth centuries had veered toward postmillennialism, the belief that Christ was even now establishing His kingdom on earth and that He would return for His Church *after* the millennium.

Postmillennialism implied a certain optimism about the perfectibility and progress of both humanity and society. It inspired, for example, such diverse utopian communities as the Society of Believers in Christ's Second Appearing (better known as the Shakers) and the Oneida Community in western New York, John Humphrey Noyes's experiment in "complex marriage." The Second Great Awakening, an evangelical revival early in the nineteenth century that engulfed three geographical theaters of the new republic—New England, western New York, and the Cumberland Valley—prompted breathless predictions about the millennial age already under way in America. More important, this optimism about the amelioration of society energized countless evangelical reform movements—abolitionism, temperance, education, prison reform, the female seminary move-ment—all grounded in the conviction that Christ was even then, through the efforts of His people, constructing a millennial kingdom.

By the time John Nelson Darby arrived, however, much of this evangelical ebullience had dissipated. The sectional rivalries of the Civil War had fractured evangelical unity, and among Northerners the Emancipation Proclamation removed the one cause that, more than any other, had united them. The industrialization and urbaniza-tion of the latter half of the nineteenth century, moreover, together with the influx of immigrants (most of them Roman Catholic) engendered doubts about the progress of godly rule in America. Squalid tenements and rowdy taverns hardly resembled the pre-cincts of Zion. Nineteenth-century evangelical orthodoxy also reeled from the assaults of two alien ideologies: The German discipline of higher criticism called into question the veracity of scriptural texts, and Charles Darwin's publication of *The Origin of Species* in 1859 challenged the Genesis account of creation and, pressed to its log-ical conclusions, undermined all literal interpretations of the Bible.

At the moment when evangelical leaders sensed the need for an adjustment to their theology, Darby arrived with his dispensational premillennialism. His claim to strict biblical literalism constituted part of Darby's appeal, but his elaborate schemata for understanding human history made even more sense. Darby convinced evangelicals that they had been mistaken to suppose the millennium already un-derway. In fact, such a supposition misconstrued biblical prophecies entirely, and he proceeded to recast the sequence of eschatology. The millennium would not begin before Christ returned for His Church. After this rapture, Darby said, a seven-year tribulation (predicted in Matthew 24) would occur, followed *then* by the millennium.

This premillennialism, the doctrine that Christ would return to rapture the Church before the millennium, had broad implications for the social ethics of evangelicals. Society, this new rubric insisted, was careening toward judgment; it could never be reclaimed for Christ, short of His return to establish the millennium. Despite the continuation of some evangelical reform efforts, this notion relieved evangelicals of the obligation to labor for the amelioration of social ills. Evangelicals increasingly stood in judgment of culture and awaited its destruction, which would follow their translation into heaven. "I don't find any place where God says the world is to grow better and better," evangelist Dwight L. Moody, a premillennialist, said in 1877. "I find that the earth is to grow worse and worse, and that at length there is going to be a separation." That separation of godliness from sinfulness, righteousness from worldliness, Moody believed, would take place at the rapture, when Christ came to translate the true believers out of this world.[2]

Historically, the adoption of this new eschatology coincided with the splintering of American Protestantism. At the same time that evangelicals began to neglect social reform efforts and exhorted anyone who would listen to prepare for the second coming by confessing faith in Jesus Christ, some of the more liberal theologians such as Washington Gladden and Walter Rauschenbusch articulated what they called the Social Gospel, a theology that sought first to understand the social conditions that lay behind the wretchedness of the urban dwellers and then worked toward their deliverance from the sinful social institutions that perpetuated their enslavement to poverty. As Protestant conservatives retreated to an otherworldly theology, liberals became convinced that the gospel mandated efforts to reform social institutions.

Even a century later, the twain still have not met. While evangelicals engage in internecine quarrels over eschatology—columns of the faithful have mustered over such issues as whether Christ will return before, during, or after the seven-year tribulation—mainline Protestants, for the most part, reject this dispensational scheme altogether. Grace Presbytery of Texas, for instance, whose bailiwick includes Dallas, has declared dispensationalism a heresy and "out of accord with the system of doctrine set forth in the Westminster Confession of Faith."[3]

Although John Nelson Darby formulated this dispensational premillennialism, a whole network of individuals and institutions disseminated these notions. Dispensationalism caught on with such evangelical preachers as Moody, Reuben A. Torrey, A. J. Gordon, James M. Gray, and A. C. Dixon, among many others. Those leaders, in turn, organized prophecy conferences to advance these views. Schools such as Moody Bible Institute and the Bible Institute of Los Angeles (now Biola College) further promoted dispensationalism.

The one man responsible more than any other for popularizing this new gospel was Cyrus Ingerson Scofield, a Congregational minister from Dallas. Scofield sponsored a series of Bible institutes around the country and established the *Comprehensive Bible Correspondence Course*, the Scofield School of the Bible in New York City, and Philadelphia College of the Bible to propagate dispensational premillennialism.[4] His most enduring contribution to the evangelical subculture, however, was the *Scofield Reference Bible*, and edition of the Scriptures, first published by Oxford University Press in 1909, that included elaborate glosses and cross-references to guide the reader in his or her understanding of dispensationalism. For generations of fundamentalists ever since, the Scofield Bible has served as a kind of template through which they read the Scriptures. Although superseded in many ways by the *Ryrie Study Bible*, compiled by a former member of the Dallas Seminary faculty, the *Scofield Reference Bible* continues to sell briskly.[5]

Scofield passed the mantle on to a protégé, Lewis Sperry Chafer, a graduate of Oberlin College and an evangelist who had met Scofield at Dwight Moody's Bible conference center in Northfield, Massachusetts. Chafer, who in 1923 succeeded Scofield as pastor of the First Congregational Church in Dallas (promptly renamed Scofield Memorial Church), began to explore the possibility of addressing what the World Christian Fundamentals Association called "one of the greatest needs of the hour," namely, "the establishment of a great evangelical premillennial seminary."[6] On October 1, 1924, thirteen students assembled for classes offered by the new Evangelical Theological College (later renamed Dallas Theological Seminary).

From the beginning, Chafer, president of the institution which now bills itself as "the largest independent evangelical seminary in the world," insisted that the curriculum emphasize the biblical languages, especially Greek and Hebrew.[7] At a time when theological liberalism (or modernism) and the Social Gospel prompted some of the older seminaries in the United States to abandon their emphasis on languages in favor of courses in psychology, philosophy, and sociology, Dallas held firm. Even today Dallas requires two years of Hebrew and three years of Greek, an exacting schedule that, coupled with all the other required courses, demands four years to complete, rather than the three years required for a divinity degree at most seminaries.[8]

My day in classes at Dallas Theological Seminary began early. A Protestant seminary is not supposed to be a monastery—the Reformation did away with that notion—but, at least by twentieth-century standards, the regimen here might draw grudging admiration even from St. Benedict, who required his charges to "rise at the eighth hour of the night" to engage in study, meditation, and prayer.[9] On Tuesday and Thursday mornings at seven forty-five, students choose among two sections of elementary Hebrew, two sections of elementary Greek, two sections of expository preaching, two sections called senior preaching, a course on pre-exilic and exilic prophets, and a course on eschatology.

I chose eschatology. Well in advance of seven forty-five, students toting briefcases and large, well-thumbed Bibles filed into the lecture hall. (The student population is overwhelmingly white, overwhelmingly male, and invariably dressed in jackets and ties, in compliance with the seminary's dress code. Despite an occasional lack of sartorial sophistication, students here look like they might be refugees from Wall Street: very clean, with closely cropped hair, conservative, very Republican.) When the professor, John A. Witmer, arrived, he grabbed a card from a lucite holder on the lectern and announced that today's prayer request concerned mission work in Bulgaria.

Witmer said that, unfortunately, Bulgarian religion was overwhelmingly Eastern Orthodox, that the number of Protestants there was less than one-half of one percent. He asked for someone to "remember these missionaries in prayer." Even at this hour, it seemed, there was no shortage of volunteers. After choosing someone in the front row, Witmer asked, "Any special requests?" Yes, said a young man. He asked for prayer to help him locate a volleyball and volleyball net for the church youth gathering he was organizing for Saturday night. After some sympathetic moans from the class, Witmer said, "Let's remember that youth meeting and the need for equipment." The man in the front row then prayed aloud for a volleyball and a net and asked God to "raise up the missionaries" in Bulgaria and to "send others to proclaim the Word."

The morning's lecture, midway through the semester, opened a section on "the imminent return of the Lord," an important tenet in dispensational theology. (Article XVIII of the seminary's doctrinal statement reads: "We believe that, according to the Word of God, the next great event in the fulfillment of prophecy will be the coming of the Lord in the air to receive to Himself into heaven both His own who are alive and remain unto His coming, and also all who have fallen asleep in Jesus, and that this event is the blessed hope set before us in the Scripture, and for this we should be constantly looking.")[10] This blessed hope, Witmer said, "is the next item on the prophetic agenda; it could take place at any time, without delay." He then recited a numbing litany of proof-texts that, he insisted, substantiate his view—and the view of the entire faculty here—that Christ will return at any moment and certainly before the tribulation. In the jargon of eschatology, this is pre-trib premillennialism, the belief that the rapture will precede the seven-year tribulation and the thousand-year millennium predicted in Revelation.

Perhaps it was the early hour or perhaps the soporific presentation, but the lecture prompted no dissent, just a friendly query from the back row: "Dr. Witmer, Christ spoke of the destruction of Jerusalem. How does that fit in?" "That does present a problem," the professor conceded. But it is a problem, his long, rambling answer implied, that can be finessed by juggling certain verb tenses and re-examining the context of the quotation.

A booklet published and distributed by the seminary insists that "Dispensationalism is an interpretive necessity," and that "Without this recognition of the different ways God has governed the world, consistent interpretation of the Bible becomes impossible."[11] Nevertheless, I found that many people at Dallas Seminary were eager to dispel the impression that dispensationalism was the most important tenet of the seminary's theology. "Some people have the idea that we live, think, and breathe dispensationalism around here," said Randy Gardner, a Master of Theology student who has also recruited students around the country for the past two years. He finds that dispensationalism is "the number one question I get from prospective students." Dispensationalism, Gardner acknowledged, is "an underlying philosophy" at Dallas, but what makes the seminary distinctive, he thinks, is a passion on the part of the faculty to "teach people to know and communicate the Scriptures." American evangelicalism, he said, has moved away from the Bible, and there's a need to reassert the importance of the Scriptures as the inerrant Word of God.

Norman Geisler, professor of systematic theology, agrees. "I think inerrancy is a test for evangelical consistency, for evangelical leadership, and it should be in our doctrinal statements. If you do not hold to inerrancy, that the Scriptures are errorless in the original autographs, you are not evangelical on that doctrine." How important is it? "I think it's crucial. It's a watershed. Almost everybody who is anybody in evangelicalism has affirmed this view."[12]

A greater attention to the dictates of Scripture, Geisler believes, would help evangelicals avoid the perils of what he calls experientialism, "an experiential test for truth." Accordingly, Geisler and others at Dallas Seminary take a dim view of even the modulated sort of pentecostalism at Calvary Chapel. Charismatics, Geisler said, are most culpable of relying on religious experience, but he sees other assaults on evangelical orthodoxy coming from Eastern or New Age spirituality, American pragmatism, and vestiges of existentialism. "All of these are experience-oriented epistemologies—it's true because you experience it—rather than a more rational, cognitive one," he said. "I think ultimately we could all drown in a cesspool of experientialism."[13]

This rationalistic approach to the Bible and theology, Geisler contends, implicitly refutes a neo-orthodox or Barthian view of Scripture. Karl Barth, an eminent twentieth-century Swiss theologian, believed that the Bible *becomes* the Word of God, an idea that lent dynamism to the reading of Scripture; the Bible, Barth argued, is not a static book meant to be treated as an ancient relic but is rather the *living* Word of God that, through the agency of the Holy Spirit, speaks afresh to the reader. But such a view, Geisler insists, undermines the whole process of hermeneutics or biblical interpretation. "When you finish your exegesis and you've found out, presumably, what the author meant—that's what exegesis is all about; what did the author mean?—you still have to ask the question, 'Hath God said?' You have to have an objective focal point that is hermeneutically determinable wherein rests divine authority."

ONE OF THE LONGTIME FIXTURES on the faculty at Dallas is J. Dwight Pentecost, the redoubtable professor of Bible exposition, now retired. I sat in on an elective course he still offers on Thursdays called "The Biblical Covenant." Pentecost, a genial, white-haired man who drives to work in a Mercedes-Benz sports coupe, opened the class with prayer and then said, "I think we're somewhere in the Davidic Covenant." The notion of successive covenants, a distinctive characteristic of dispensational theology, asserts that God has adopted different strategies for dealing with humanity through the successive dispensations. According to Pentecost, the Davidic covenant—God's covenant with David, king of ancient Israel—came to a close when the Jews rejected Jesus as their messiah. That apparently signaled a kind of interregnum, also known to dispensationalists as the

Church Age, between the Israelite kingdom of the Old Testament and the millennial kingdom predicted in Revelation. "The Davidic covenant was postponed," Pentecost said, "until Christ's return."

This covenantal understanding of the Bible has enormous implications for the relation of Christians and Jews. Pentecost and other dispensationalists believe that the Jews' rejection of Jesus as their messiah during His lifetime exempted them from God's favor and effectively transferred the Old Testament promises from the people of Israel to the Christian Church. Although the interests of Israel and the Church will be reconciled in the millennial kingdom, according to Pentecost, the very fact that we live now in the Church Age (or dispensation) implies that God has turned His back on the Jews for their rejection of His Son. "Israel is condemned by God," Pentecost said, "although individual Jews can escape judgment by acknowledging Christ and identifying themselves with the Church publicly, by baptism."

A student later elaborated this doctrine for me. "There's a future for Israel," he said, "but it's related to the messiah, to Christ. There's no salvation for Jews now, short of recognizing Jesus as the messiah." This conviction has prompted proselytization efforts (such as the organization called Jews for Jesus) among the Jews by fundamentalists. Although less rigid Christian theologians, following the lead of Reinhold Niebuhr in the late 1950s, have been willing to acknowledge that Jews, as God's chosen people, attain salvation through their own covenant, dispensationalists insist that Jews must become Christians in order to enter the kingdom of heaven.

But what does this interregnum between ancient Israel and the millennium mean for the present age or dispensation? The parables of the New Testament, Pentecost believes, reveal the essential features of "theocratic administration." In the present age God has assigned authority in four areas: in the civil realm, to magistrates to curb lawlessness; in employment, to the master or employer; in the Church, to elders; and in the family, to the husband and father. Moreover, according to Pentecost, "when God assigns authority,

He demands submission to authority. So that in the civil realm, we are to be subject to rulers. The wife is subject, the children subject, to authority. The employee is subject to the authority of the employer." And finally, in the Church, "the younger are subject to the authority of the elders."

Perhaps unwittingly, Pentecost provided an illustration. At one point during the lecture a student, one of only seven women in a lecture hall of ninety-four students, admitted some confusion about the configuration of the covenants. Pentecost responded: "Can I ask you to hold that until I go a bit farther? Maybe a light will go on. Prayerfully. Hopefully." He paused. "If not, can I fall back on Paul's injunction? Ask your husband at home." The classroom erupted in loud, sustained laughter and guffaws. If the instructor intended the remark as good-natured humor or a wry riposte, his expression betrayed no hint. He simply resumed the lecture.[14]

The mere presence of women here at Dallas has provoked some controversy. As biblical literalists, students and faculty point to St. Paul's injunctions against allowing women as teachers in the Church in order to justify their exclusion from the ordained ministry, even though many Protestant groups over the past two decades have abolished their proscriptions against women's ordination, citing the broader, inclusive demands of the New Testament.[15] At Dallas, however, the seminary's constitution bars women from serving on the faculty. Although they have been allowed into selected degree programs and permitted to take courses as non-degree candidates for several years, women were admitted as candidates for the Master of Theology (the seminary's basic divinity degree) for the first time in the fall of 1986. Women now make up thirteen percent of the student body (as against the national average in Protestant seminaries of twenty-six percent, a figure that is much higher, approaching fifty percent, in liberal institutions).[16] But even though they are enrolled in the divinity program at Dallas, women are not allowed to take homiletics courses, the expectation being that they would never have occasion to preach, that their activities would be limited to some sort of parachurch work, teaching in a Christian school, or perhaps, in less rigid fundamentalist churches, administration or Christian education.

Apparently, however, such restrictions do not concern the female students. During my visit the current issue of *Kindred Spirit*, the seminary's glitzy, four-color public relations magazine, contained an article by Barbara A. Peil, a Master of Arts student in Christian education. Entitled "A Seasoned Approach," the article urged older Christian women to tutor younger women in their proper roles: "Young women need to be taught a biblical view of their roles and relationships with their husbands in order to truly liberate them to be all that God intended them to be and to experience the best that He has for them." God measures a woman's success in life, the author wrote, "by her relationship with her husband and children." Extolling the virtues of purity and self-control, Peil urged younger women to learn "the oft-maligned delights of homemaking."[17]

In such a climate, even modest attempts by women to enlarge the scope of their responsibilities meet with resistance. Holly Hankins completed her studies for the Master of Arts in biblical studies in December 1986, but in April 1987 she was working part-time as a clerk in the seminary bookstore. She hopes to find a job in a church somewhere but, she said, "I'm having a hard time finding a job because I'm a woman." Still, she has no designs on ordination because she believes that would be a violation of biblical teaching. Hankins would like a job as head of a women's ministries program in a church, a kind of nonordained pastor to women in the congregation. "Women should be counseled by women," she said, and that would take some of the counseling burden off the pastor.

Hankins, an attractive, articulate woman, has been something of a pioneer at Dallas Seminary—the first woman to serve on the student council and the first woman to pray publicly in the seminary chapel. She insists that neither the professors nor the students have looked down on her, but the placement office has provided little help. The head of placement, she said, "definitely believes" that a woman has no place on a church staff. "It's slow," she said of her job search. "Even after receiving my resume, many churches tell me they have secretarial jobs available."

DEFENDING TRADITIONAL ROLES for women at Dallas Theological Seminary follows logically from both its epistemology and its cultural location. As biblical literalists, the faculty cannot maneuver around Paul's emphatic proscriptions against women in leadership positions.

Moreover, as the spiritual and intellectual descendants of fundamentalists who earlier in this century began dissenting from what they regarded as a secularizing society, their opposition to fuller roles for women coincides with their uneasiness with popular American culture. At a time when academic scholarship adopted the tenets of Darwinism and German higher criticism, and when the publicity surrounding the trial of John T. Scopes, a biology teacher from Tennessee, succeeded in portraying fundamentalists as rubes and anachronisms, fundamentalists began to perceive American culture as hostile. Whereas in the previous century evangelicals had shaped social and political agendas, in the twentieth century fundamentalists found themselves pushed to the periphery. Thus marginalized, they grew increasingly suspicious of the broader culture. Generations of children in fundamentalist households were instructed to eschew "worldliness" and to adhere to strict codes of morality that forbade card-playing, gambling, cosmetics, motion pictures, dancing, alcohol, and tobacco. Some of the proscriptions have eased somewhat in evangelical circles, but the suspicion of worldliness, of theological and cultural innovation, endures.

Norman Geisler, for instance, who describes himself as a "strong creationist," has testified in the courts in favor of permitting the Genesis account of creation to be taught along side of evolution in public schools. "I hold that God directly and immediately created every kind of thing, every form of life, and that there was no macroevolution between them," he insisted.[18]

Geisler along with other faculty and students at Dallas Seminary have also been active in the anti-abortion movement. A sign in the student center read:

> Join Drs Geisler and House
> and your Fellow Students to
> Protest the Destruction
> of Innocent Human Life
> at a Local Abortion Clinic
> Meet *each Wednesday right*
> *after chapel* in the parking
> lot by Academic 1

Several of the students I spoke with denied any necessary connection between conservative theology and conservative politics, although they acknowledged a correlation between the two. "I think there's something to be said for taking a conservative stance regarding abortion and subscribing to conservative Christianity," one man told me. "I think there's something to be said for taking a conservative stance against homosexuality and being a conservative Christian. I wouldn't vote for a politician who was for gay rights, because there you're dealing with morality."

I ASKED TWO STUDENTS, Herb Bateman, who had come to Dallas Seminary from Philadelphia College of the Bible, and Jimmy Carter, a Southern Baptist from Tulsa, what was at stake in the doctrine of dispensational premillennialism. How does one's adherence to pre-millennialist ideas affect the way you live? "The imminent return of Christ affects the way I approach each day," Bateman said, "because if I know that He can return at any moment I certainly want to make sure that my life on a daily basis is in accordance with what His will is, which is derived from the imperative statements of Scripture. Wherever I'm at, I'm to be living for Christ, and I know that with Him returning at any time I'll have to give an account for my life, and I'll be rewarded accordingly."[19]

Bateman added that a premillennialist interpretation of the Bible was "the best option available and the most consistent, but that's not to say that someone is any less a Christian because he believes that Christ will return *during* the tribulation rather than before. It's not an issue to die over."

Both Bateman and Carter felt more strongly about the inerrancy of the Scriptures. Bateman volunteered that he would "go to the wall" for the doctrine of inerrancy, and Carter said that he couldn't envision ever changing his views on that issue. I wondered if subscribing to the doctrine of inerrancy affected the way they read the Bible. "When you approach it as an inerrant text, it's not open to the subjectivity of man," Carter said. "By believing that the text is inerrant, we can go to it as the basis of our authority." Bateman concurred, adding that "if you throw that out, you lose some of your footing."

"We're taught a theological grid here, I won't deny that," Bateman acknowledged, a bit defensively, "but I don't think the Christian community is as closed-minded as the world would like to make us out to be. We're more than willing to open up and speak and dialogue. The closed-mindedness many times doesn't come from the Christian, it comes from the liberal." He paused. "If you've got the truth, what's there to fear in open dialogue?"

1987

CHAPTER 3

On Location

A 1969 CHEVROLET MALIBU careened down a country road, its headlights piercing the darkness. Soon the left front wheel veered across the yellow line. The car gathered speed and plunged off an embankment, landed on its nose in the ravine below, and then somersaulted onto its back in a creek.

A couple of beats after the rear tires stopped spinning, a voice yelled "Cut!" A company of onlookers burst into spontaneous applause. From the ravine the same voice inquired of his walkie-talkie, "Gloria, is Geoff okay?"

"Yes," another voice crackled, "we're okay, Don."

The operator of camera 1 invited the director to examine the final perspective. The automobile was framed squarely in the viewfinder. The director pronounced it perfect and exclaimed, "Jimmy, you're the best." He called across the creek to another cameraman: "John Leiendecker, how's it look?"

"Looks good, Don."

After acknowledging—and returning—the congratulations of his crew, the director allowed himself a little titter and muttered, almost under his breath, "God is good."

Indeed, the entire crew seemed to breathe a palpable sigh of relief. Unlike dialogue or interior shots, this scene could be shot only once; there would be no second take. It had to be perfect, and the consensus among the crew was that it was. All the hours, even days, of preparation had paid off. Gloria Fiorimonti, the stuntwoman, had drawn an imaginary X in the ravine, calculated speed and distances, and landed the nose of the car squarely on the X. The director of photography calibrated the camera angles according to Gloria's calculations. Pete Roseman, the gaffer, barked instructions to his lighting crew in order to carve the proper combination of light and shadow out of the September darkness. The sound man also captured the scene, the car roaring off the cliff and bouncing into the stream, then the eerie wash of water churning past the metal carcass.

"We'll dub a little more engine noise with that, Don, and it'll be real nice," he said.

"Good, Curt."

The euphoria and self-congratulation, however, passed quickly. The crew began preparing for the next scene, a shot of an empty beer can (which the driver of the car had tossed out the window during the previous night's shooting) meandering down the stream and colliding into the rear fender of the overturned automobile.

It is a poignant scene, even to the spectators gathered on the bridge watching take after take of the beer can rolling down the bank and swirling toward the car. The red and white container won't tumble down the bank in any predictable way, so the scene has to be shot again and again—one crew member tossing it into the water and another retrieving it downstream—until it's just right.

The man responsible for getting it just right is Donald W. Thompson, the director. He checks camera angles, inquires about the lighting and sound, rehearses the actors' lines for the next scene. People constantly pepper him with questions: Where do you want the spectators? Will the noise of the still camera intrude onto the soundtrack during the crash scene? What about the catering truck? Almost an hour ago Thompson instructed his associate producer to radio for the helicopter as soon as the car landed in the ravine. There's no time to lose; with a crew this size and a limited budget, delays are costly.

Yet Thompson finds time for a word of praise or encouragement. Late into the night he'll rub the shoulders of a weary colleague or offer coffee to an assistant. When Gloria Fiorimonti, the stunt-woman, announced she was returning to the West Coast, Thompson left the cameras and climbed out of the ravine to say farewell and offer his thanks. Amid their goodbyes Gloria asked if he had a minute to share something she'd read in the Bible the other day.

Yes, there's time. There's always time. (Earlier in the evening Thompson had informed me that Gloria, the first and only woman inducted into the stuntmen's hall of fame, was a new, a recently converted, Christian.)

Gloria, wearing tight denims, a tee-shirt from Jackson Hole, Wyoming, and a California tan, returned with a devotional booklet and began reading a meditation about God's strength, His ability to overcome adversity. She'd read that meditation the same day she first scouted this location. "I didn't tell you, Don," she confessed now, "but when I first saw this location I was terrified. I thought there was no way we could pull it off."

Apparently, sending an automobile off a cliff is not as easy as it looks. First, she needed a straight shot at the ramp, but the winding country road wouldn't allow it. She also had to thread the car into a narrow aperture between a tree on the left and the bridge abutment on the right, and all of this at a sufficient speed—thirty to thirty-five miles an hour—so that the automobile would sail off the cliff rather than just tumble into the ravine. God helped her overcome a difficult situation, she said, and in the process He taught her a valuable lesson about depending on Him.

Soon after Gloria headed home to California, the helicopter arrived. If this sleek, blue-and-white machine isn't exactly the star, it at least plays the title role in *Life Flight*, this movie about the genesis of helicopter ambulance service in central Iowa. Don Thompson's film dramatizes the early days of Life Flight, a program begun several years ago by Iowa Methodist Hospital in Des Moines and duplicated by hospitals elsewhere. Based on actual events, Thompson's screenplay depicts a series of accidents in remote areas whose victims survive because of the swift medical attention available by helicopter.

The screenplay also takes us into the lives of the people and families involved. The struggle of a veteran with memories of Vietnam and his fear of flying. An argument between a father and son just minutes before the angry, drunken son drives his car off the embankment. There are heroes aplenty in Thompson's screenplay: the helicopter, the veteran who overcomes his fears, the woman who pushes for Life Flight in the face of considerable bureaucratic resistance.

IN THE REAL WORLD, however, life doesn't always imitate art. One scene in the movie, based on an actual incident, shows two people on a snowmobile disappearing into an icy lake. The helicopter manages to pull both victims out of the water and drag them to safety. In reality, however, the rescuers lost grip of one of the victims, who plunged to an icy death. While I was in Des Moines for the filming, Justin Charles Cupples, thirteen years old, was struck repeatedly in the chest by an older boy on a school playground in Newton, Iowa, thirty miles east of Des Moines. The blows were severe enough to dislodge a plastic heart valve that Justin had received weeks earlier to correct a birth defect. He collapsed onto the ground. Blood poured into his lungs. As Justin was being loaded aboard the Life Flight helicopter, he looked at his father and said, "Please don't let me die." During the helicopter ride to Des Moines, however, his heart stopped altogether.[1]

In *Life Flight*, the helicopter offers hope, a kind of redemption. But the real redemption Thompson wants to depict in his films is deeper and, to him, infinitely more important. All his movies during the past fifteen years have mixed action, suspense, and drama with a very unsubtle evangelical message. At a crisis point in the plot, the main characters kneel and give their lives to Christ. In *Blood on the Mountain*, an escaped convict learns God's forgiveness and asks to be saved from his sins. In *All the King's Horses* (whose stars Grant Goodeve and Dee Wallace went on to play, respectively, the eldest brother in the television serial *Eight is Enough* and the mother in *E.T.*), the answer to a troubled marriage is conversion to Christianity.

The evangelical message in *Life Flight*, Thompson insists, is a bit more subtle—no longer the Scripture verses emblazoned on the screen, but rather a tear signifying repentance in place of the full-fledged conversion scene. It is a movie about God's will, a favorite topic for Thompson, but one he hasn't tackled before because it is so difficult to portray on screen. Discerning God's will, he believes, is central to the Christian life. "I really want to be where God wants me to be," he says. "It doesn't make your troubles go away, it's just that God is in control of your life. He takes care of you."

Thompson's formula for happiness and success boils down to "choosing God first, and the rest of it will fall into line." The choice of this crash scene provides a good example. After a month of searching for the right location, he said, "I got lost one day going home, and I came across this bridge and I thought, 'Holy smokes, it's perfect!' I went home and told my wife, 'God designed that river for this movie.'"

Don Thompson, a small, unprepossessing man who often wears cowboy boots and western-style shirts, fairly brims with such illustrations of God's providence, and he enjoys nothing more than telling how God delivered him from difficult situations, how God made the impossible possible. I have known Thompson since the early seventies (he still delights in introducing me as one of his Sunday school students), and I never cease to marvel at his indomitable spirit, his boundless energy, and his boyish grin as he weaves together story after story about how God taught him this lesson or another through difficult circumstances and insurmountable odds. Each episode has its own moral, which Thompson invariably supplies in the form of a tidy aphorism, but there is nothing tiresome or disingenuous about all this. Thompson is, quite simply, one of the most remarkable people I have ever known, a man utterly without guile or pretension who sweeps you along with his irrepressible optimism. He very nearly embodies, I think (though he would be the first to deny it), the qualities most evangelical preachers have in mind when they talk about a "godly Christian"—someone with a conviction that seldom admits of doubt, who professes an intimacy with God, and who is always willing, even eager, to share his faith.

Thompson's vocation as a filmmaker supplies grist for his anecdotal mill; it also provides ample opportunity for Thompson's God to work His "magic." But Thompson recognizes that such serendipitous deliverances are no substitute for hard work, and he is eager to dispel the notion that he regards the Almighty as some sort of superhero who routinely rescues him from his own blunders or lack of preparation. Thompson approaches his craft, he says, with the attitude that "I have to work as if it all depends on Don, but pray as if it all depends on God. I don't want anybody to get the idea that God does this and God does that. I work my tail off," he said emphatically. Then his eyes brightened: "But God comes through when I need Him."

This attitude allows Thompson to face adversity with equanimity, with the confidence that "God has something better in store," perhaps a spiritual lesson of some kind. When I phoned him to make the final preparations for my visit, he recited a litany of difficulties that had plagued his shooting schedule: two weeks of steady rain (unusual for this time of year), the unavailability of the helicopter at critical junctures of the filming, even the decision of Iowa Methodist Hospital's board to press ahead with a long-delayed construction project. "But God has been good," he added after a sigh. "The Lord has really made His presence known to me these past weeks."

When I caught up with him on location, he repeated the same refrain. As we sat on the side of the highway late at night waiting for the crew to prepare for the next scene, he said, "It's been raining for three weeks, and we've been shooting for three weeks, but, praise God, we're still on schedule. I don't know how He does it. I'm to the point now where I don't even worry about the big problems," he continued, "I just leave them in the Lord's hands. I know He knows what He's doing. I've gone home nearly every night after filming and just cried because of all the problems, but the Lord keeps reminding me to leave it in His hands.

"When the people at Iowa Methodist Hospital told me that the board of directors had decided to go ahead with the demolition of one of the facades we were using for the movie, even though they'd been five days late getting me the helicopter they'd promised, I just shrugged my shoulders and said, 'Lord, you've got to get me through this.' Here it was pouring outside, and I had a day's worth of shooting to do in just a few hours before they began tearing the place down the next morning. But I walked outside and, suddenly, the weather cleared. We got everybody outside and shot all the scenes we needed." He smiled. "God is good."

Thompson's "divine connections" have apparently attracted notice in film circles. Occasionally, he said, people on the set will remark, "'This is a Don Thompson picture; things always work out well.'" When I asked if he had that reputation in Hollywood, he lowered his voice, "Yeah, that's what I hear," obviously embarrassed, but also not a little pleased.

"One night we were in Gunnison, Colorado, filming a television special. I'd wanted snow and peaks and sunshine, and the locals told me, 'You won't get any sunshine up there in February. The snow will get about eighty inches deep up there. The cabin you want to use will be buried.' I told them to bring tractors in and keep it plowed out if they had to, but I wanted it to look virgin. And I was working with people from Hollywood who told me, 'You're crazy to come up here and shoot. This is the coldest place in the country. You've got scenes where this woman is supposed to be singing, but her lips will freeze.' I said, 'Well, I really believe this is where God wants me to do it.' And I don't know why, because usually when twenty or thirty people tell me I'm wrong I think, well, maybe I *am* wrong.

"It was a big company, a union shoot. We had twenty-two pieces of equipment, tractor-trailers, lining the road. And it was so cold that cables started to split. Peoples' leather script covers were splitting. It was so cold the generators wouldn't run. And I remember standing out there and these three guys, the union manager, the production manager, and the assistant director, walked towards me. All I could think of was Dodge City and *Gunsmoke*, and I thought, I'm dead.' One of them said, 'Do you know you just lost your client thirty thousand bucks because you picked this location?' I said, 'Well, the sun's out.' And then I said, 'I'm sorry, guys. I just feel we're supposed to be here.'

"Do you know what happened? The sun came out for four days in a row. The radio stations and newspapers said that had never happened in the history of that community. Never had there been sunshine all day long that time of year. One night we heard that a big blizzard would hit us the next day. I began to panic. But then one of the crew members—who wasn't a Christian, by the way, one of the most worldly women you'd ever want to meet—said, 'It won't come in. Not with this company. This is the company that moves clouds. I've seen it happen.'"

I may have seen it happen, too. During the early evening preparations for the crash scene Friday night, one of the sheriff's officers who had been assigned to block off the road and divert traffic announced over his loudspeaker that the Weather Service had just issued a thunderstorm watch until eleven o'clock that evening. Off in the distance to the west an ominous thunderhead, belching flashes of lightning, moved in our direction. Thompson and the rest of the crew seemed unperturbed, or at least preoccupied with other matters. When the car dropped into the ravine, the cloud had passed to the north, safely out of danger. It *really did*, I convinced myself at the time, appear to have changed course and veer north.

At the time, amid the elation over the successful stunt, no one had deemed the weather worthy of comment. The next evening, however, when I arrived at the location, Thompson immediately pulled me aside. "I've got to tell you what happened," he said. "When we finished shooting last night at three-thirty (which was a miracle in itself), we got in our cars, everybody lined up and ready to go, and it started raining. Huge drops. It came down in torrents—well, not torrents, but it was raining hard. I was so grateful that we had finished. I just said, 'Praise God.' I was so excited I cried all the way home." He paused, then giggled, recognizing the irony. "Maybe it wasn't raining as hard as I thought. Maybe it was just me."

If God monitors the weather, God also receives credit for Thompson's success, both as a director and as a screenwriter. When he thought he had completed the script for *Life Flight*, he reread it and panicked. There was too much talk and not enough action, he concluded. Some of the transitions were still rough. "With two weeks until we started shooting, I knew I had six or seven weeks worth of work to do on the screenplay. I went home and got to work, and at one point I fell into bed and said, 'Lord, I got a problem I can't solve. There are major structural difficulties here.' God gave me the answer the next morning. I mean He just gave it to me on a silver platter."

Thompson described the scene. "Inside a house a mother and father are asleep, and all of a sudden you hear something crashing. The mother says, 'There's somebody in the house.' So the father gets up, goes to the closet and takes down a shoe box. Inside the shoe box there's a thirty-eight revolver and two cartridges. He takes the cartridges and puts two of them in the gun. He walks out into the hallway into the dark, and all of a sudden he sees this shadow—it looks like one of those guys out of the thirties, with a cape—and the shadow turns and a little girl says, 'Daddy, I have to go to the bathroom.'

"Then we leave the shot. When we come back the little girl is playing house. This is incredible! This is good cinema! She's got her high heels on, her dresses, her beads, and she goes into the closet to get Mommy's purse. She takes a stick and pulls the purse out and the shoe box with the gun falls onto the floor. She puts the hammer back and looks into the barrel and is playing with it. It's very scary. We show the shoe box empty. She's playing with it. She even points it directly into the camera, and you see her rotate the barrel and pull the trigger. The suspense builds because you know there are two loaded cartridges in there somewhere and you never know when it's going to go off. It could go off at any time.

"She says, 'Mom, come see what I found.' And just before her mom comes in she throws down the gun, picks up the doll, and says, 'Would you find my dolly's head?' So the mother thinks she's playing with the doll; the gun's buried in the toy box. Later on—it's nighttime now, the little girl is sleeping—she gets up, yawns, and starts playing with the doll. She sees the gun, puts down the doll, and starts doing the same thing again, pulling the trigger, rotating the barrel. The same routine. Finally she says, 'Mom, I want a drink of water.'"

At that point Thompson's cadence, though never deliberate, quickened to convey the drama along with the camera angles. "Then you see the mother coming down the hallway. Dutch tilt. Feet. Face. Dutch tilt. Feet. 'Click.' Feet. 'Click.' Feet. Face. 'Click.' All of a sudden the mother opens the door and blam! The gun goes off and hits her right in the chest.

"That sets up the rescue by the helicopter. And it leads into a critical transition in the story." He paused, nearly breathless with enthusiasm. "God gave me that. I didn't work that out. It just came. It's like I had to work everything else out really hard, but when it came down to where I was out of time, God said, 'I know you're out of time. Here.'"

When I suggested at one point in our conversations that making Christian films allowed Thompson to combine his two passions in life, his faith and motion pictures, he smiled. Then, after a pause, he wondered if faith wasn't more a gift than a passion.

Even so, he is clearly passionate about his convictions, and he finds it impossible to separate his faith from his filmmaking. "When I'm invited to universities to lecture about motion pictures, I tell them I'll come only if I can speak about my beliefs in addition to my films. You know what these film students ask me when I'm done? No one ever asks me about movies. One day I took a guy who worked on *Star Wars* because he was working with me on a film. But the students don't ask me about movies afterwards. They ask about the Lord."

APART FROM HIS PERSONALITY, Thompson also strikes me as exemplary in his literalistic approach to the Bible and, specifically, the seriousness with which he takes the various biblical prophecies concerning the end of time. He illustrates, moreover, the extent to which dispensational premillennialism, with its insistence on the imminent return of Christ, pervades the evangelical subculture in America and lends a sense of urgency to evangelical proselytization efforts. Thompson's most successful films—and perhaps the most controversial—depict the apocalyptic prophecies in the Bible, especially the books of Daniel and Revelation. "Those prophecy films were kind of hard," Thompson acknowledged at one point in our conversations, but he remains unapologetic.

A *Thief in the Night,* his first apocalyptic movie, filmed in 1972, takes the form of a dream. It opens with the sound of a clock ticking against a black background. As a shot of the clock on a nightstand comes slowly into focus, a message appears on the screen:

> Keep a sharp lookout! For you do not know when I will come, at evening, at midnight, early dawn or late daybreak. Don't let me find you sleeping!
>
> JESUS CHRIST

A voice over the radio interrupts with a special bulletin. "To say that the world is in a state of shock this morning would be to understate the situation." The camera pans slowly from the clock on the nightstand to a woman obviously just awakening from a nightmare. The voice continues: "Suddenly and without warning literally thousands, perhaps millions of people just disappeared. The few eyewitness accounts of these disappearances have not been clear, but one thing is certainly sure: Millions who were living on this earth last night are not here this morning."

The woman climbs out of bed and searches for her husband. "Jim? Jim?" Down the hallway and into the bathroom. There she sees an electric razor, still buzzing, in the sink. She screams, realizing that her husband has just disappeared.

In the next scene a young preacher exhorts a small group of listeners: "The world will be at ease, banquets and parties and weddings, just as it was in Noah's time before the sudden coming of the flood. People wouldn't believe what was going to happen until the flood actually arrived and took them all away. So shall my coming be. Two men will be working together in the fields. One will be taken, the other left. Two women will be going about their household tasks. One will be taken, and the other left. So be prepared, for you know not what day your Lord is coming.

"What does all this mean? It means exactly what it says. Any minute, any second, could be the last chance that anyone has to give himself to Jesus, because when He returns it will happen that fast—the Bible says in the twinkling of an eye. Millions of people will suddenly disappear, leave this earth to meet their Lord. And a shocked world will discover suddenly that what the Bible said is true. This is no joke. This is not a fairy tale. It will happen, just as surely as you and I are here right now.

"So, Christian, be alert. And, friend, if you haven't given your life to Christ, do it, and do it now, because the rapture will come and Christ will return. It says in the Bible that He will come as a thief in the night."

The preacher then joins several other sober-looking young people in a mournful, haunting melody:

> Life was filled with guns and war,
> and everyone got trampled on the floor.
> I wish we'd all been ready.
>
> Children died, the days grew cold,
> a piece of bread could buy a bag of gold.
> I wish we'd all been ready.
>
> There's no time to change your mind,
> the Son has come and you've been left behind.

The black background, the insistent chords of a synthesizer, and the deliberate beating of a drum render the words into a kind of requiem.

A man and wife asleep in bed,
she hears a noise and turns her head, he's gone.
I wish we'd all been ready.

Two men walking up a hill,
one disappears and one's left standing still.
I wish we'd all been ready.

There's no time to change your mind,
the Son has come and you've been left behind.[2]

The music dies and the scene fades to black.

The plot itself begins on the midway of a state fair, and it follows the lives of several young people in their early twenties who
meet for the first time at the fair. One man, a rather devilish-looking
sort who often lapses into Humphrey Bogart impersonations, immediately gravitates to a tall, blonde woman in a miniskirt. Another
couple, Jim and Patty, the woman who awakens from the nightmare
at the opening, eventually fall in love and marry midway through the
movie. A third woman, the odd person out, wanders into an evangelistic tent and is born again, accepting Christ as her savior.

Although all the characters figure into the plot, Jim and Patty are
the focal points. After a brush with death following a bite from an
Indian cobra, Jim (a veterinary student) also is born again. But Patty
resists. "I'm a Christian," she says early in the movie. "I go to church
almost every week." Just any church, it turns out, isn't good enough.
Her minister, the Reverend Turner, a theological liberal who refuses
to interpret the Bible literally, debunks the Genesis creation account
as a myth and, more important, refuses to believe the apocalyptic
prophecies in the books of Daniel and Revelation.

If the Reverend Turner (played by Russell Doughten, the movie's executive producer and Thompson's partner) represents an evil,
corrupting force, several characters point out the path of righteousness. There are repeated exhortations to "take Christ into your life"
lest you be left behind when Jesus comes back to earth to remove

the true Christians in the rapture, predicted in the fourth chapter of First Thessalonians. "We're living in the end times," a preacher warns.

The inevitable occurs. Suddenly on a summer afternoon, people find that their friends, the true Christians, have disappeared, including Jim. To deal with the crisis an organization called UNITE, the United Nations Imperium of Total Emergency, takes command. This sinister one-world government soon demands that all citizens take the "mark of the beast" described in Revelation. The wizened Reverend Turner, left behind at the rapture because of his unbelief, now recognizes the literal truth of the Bible. Disconsolate, he asks, "How many have I misled? How many are still here because of me?" On the basis of his new appreciation for Revelation, he counsels Patty to resist the mark of the beast (a computerized rendition of the digits 666) because it is evil, and accepting it precludes any possibility of a "second chance" at salvation later in the apocalypse.

Patty, now a fugitive from UNITE, cannot purchase food without the computerized mark of the beast. Her friends betray her. She manages to elude a helicopter that searches for her in the woods; tired and frantic, she runs down a shimmering road. Then the music:

Life was filled with guns and war,
and everyone got trampled on the floor.
I wish we'd all been ready.

A voice reverberates: "There will be no place to hide. There will be no place to get away anywhere." Surrounded by UNITE agents atop a large dam, Patty is forced onto a landing just above the cascading water. While trying to elude her captors, she slips...and then wakes up from her nightmare.

But the film's opening scene repeats itself. She looks for Jim, her husband, while the radio reports the strange disappearance of millions of people. When she finds the shaver buzzing in the bathroom sink, just as the music repeats "The Son has come and you've been left behind," Patty lets out a scream. A Bible verse appears on the screen: "But of that day and that hour knoweth no man, no not the angels which are in heaven, neither the Son, but the Father. Take heed, watch and pray for ye know not when the time is..."[3]

This is good, effective drama. Even chilling. You needn't sympathize with the message to be moved by the story, and many viewers identify readily with Patty, a "good person" whose goodness, nevertheless, according to the film's producers, will still leave her shy of heaven.

If the plot is a bit obvious in places, it's also quite compelling, especially when shown in an evangelical setting to people reared to take the apocalyptic passages of the Bible literally. Since its release in 1973, *A Thief in the Night* has been translated into three foreign languages, subtitled in countless others, and its international distribution continues strongly a decade and a half later. Six or seven hundred prints now circulate, in addition to videocassettes. In the United States, where distribution is limited to church groups, camps, youth organizations, and the like, it is difficult to quantify the number of people who have seen the film. When I pressed Russell Doughten, Thompson's partner, for a figure, he reluctantly estimated that one hundred million people had seen *A Thief in the Night* in the United States, a figure, he hastened to add, that would include those who had seen it more than once. Even if you slash that number in half to account for hyperbole, fifty million is still a staggering figure, a viewership that would be the envy of many Hollywood producers.

For Doughten—and for Thompson—the more important statistic is the number of those who were converted as a result of viewing *A Thief in the Night*. Doughten estimated this figure in excess of four million, "a tremendous harvest of souls," especially for a movie that cost about $68,000 to produce (by the middle of 1984 the film had brought in $4.2 million in revenues). The film works best, they believe, when followed by an "altar call" or invitation to conversion. Typically, when the movie is over, a pastor, youth leader, or camp director will ask the audience to bow their heads in prayer. An organ might play softly in the background. The pastor will then ask people to examine their lives and ask themselves if they are ready for Christ's second coming. Have they invited Jesus into their hearts? "If Jesus should return tonight, or if you were killed on the way home this evening, would you be ready to meet God?" The movie's chilling ending, of course, sets this up nicely—Patty's abandonment, her growing horror as she realizes she's been left behind.

The success of any movie invites sequels, and Thompson has obliged. *A Distant Thunder, Image of the Beast*, and *Prodigal Planet* all depict life on earth after the rapture, after true Christians, the born-again believers, have ascended into heaven. The producers tout these films as a kind of pre-history—"a true story that is yet to happen"—portraying the brutality of existence during the tribulation prophesied in Revelation. Indeed, much of this is gruesome, replete with radiation sickness, blood-curdling screams, increased repression by UNITE, and stainless-steel guillotines. The events of the book of Revelation "could become a reality in your lifetime," the films warn. "Avoid these events by coming to Christ now."

Doesn't all this have the effect of frightening people into the kingdom of heaven? In the midst of her miseries in *A Distant Thunder*, Patty answers for the producers: "I would rather have been scared into heaven than have to go through this." I put the question to Doughten who, in contrast to Thompson, is soft-spoken and deliberate. His initial response was that "if they get into the kingdom through being scared, that's better than not making it at all." He continued: "Anybody who seriously reads the prophetic books or Revelation or Thessalonians or even Matthew 24 will be scared. There's some pretty heavy stuff in those prophecies. This is not for kindergarten. It's for those who are into the meat of the gospel. If you take seriously what's being said there, it's frightening. And it ought to be. All we've tried to do in the films is to put these things revealed in the Scripture into a dramatic setting. We're just trying to illustrate what's there. If it frightens you, then maybe it's your problem, because from our point of view that's what the Lord is telling you.

If we can convince you that the tribulation period is going to be filled with strong confrontation between God and the forces of evil, and this is going to affect mankind to the point that one-third of the population will be destroyed as the various vials predicted in Revelation are poured out, well, that's pretty frightening."

So the apocalyptic writings in the Bible have no value apart from a literal, dispensationalist reading—as comfort to the distressed and persecuted early Christians, perhaps, an assurance that God will avenge their sufferings? "When I was a young Christian," Doughten said, "I was frightened of the prophecies in Scripture. They seemed so remote to me. I could only look on them as figurative. I didn't have the inner strength to consider that these things were absolutely true. But after I'd been a Christian three or four years, I began to get drawn into those things, and I began to look into the prophetic writings and decided that if the Lord is really sincere about these things, then what's coming is absolutely staggering. It goes beyond human comprehension. And in working on the scripts for the prophecy films, I had to study these prophecies deeply and let them seep into my soul and psyche, so when it came out, it would be true and honest. We had the sense that we were dealing seriously with the Scriptures. People generally have one of two reactions to the prophecy films. Either people are scared to death and tell themselves it isn't real, or they say, 'Forget it, nothing like that could ever be.' But the Bible is true, and this is what the Bible says. We put a story around it in order to reveal these things to modern audiences, but the prophecy is true."

If Doughten, whose Hollywood credits include *The Blob*, provided the interpretive background for these apocalyptic films, it was Thompson's restless, frenetic energy that translated the ideas or messages into good, dramatic cinema, and herein lies his singular contribution to Christian filmmaking. For decades, evangelicals have shown movies at Bible camps or in Sunday evening services, and many, like Thompson's, warned of the impending apocalypse and implored viewers to repent. But almost invariably these were poorly produced, low-budget films exhibiting acting skills that bordered on the scandalous. One of them, *Missing Christians*, actually depicted Christians levitating by way of harnesses up into something that was supposed to be a cloud, or heaven, during the rapture. When Thompson turned his cinematic skills to the subject, he produced a film that, despite its low budget and some infelicities in acting, combined drama, action, and suspense into a convincing portrayal of the "end times." It is only a slight exaggeration to say that *A Thief in the Night* affected the evangelical film industry the way that sound or color affected Hollywood.

Thompson's work also belies the persistent myth that evangelicals are somehow anti-modern and suspicious of technology or innovation. The two issues must, I think, be separated. Yes, evangelicals are anti-modern, but only in the sense that the term *modernity* is invested with moral overtones. When modernity is defined as a flight from "traditional" values—as politically conservative evangelicals want to define it—then there surely are anti-modernist elements within the evangelical subculture. But that does not mean that evangelicals are chary about technology or innovation in general. Indeed, especially in the realm of communication, evangelicals historically have been pioneers in the use of media. In the eighteenth century, George Whitefield triggered the Great Awakening with his itinerant preaching, his oratorical skills, and his persuasive rhetoric, techniques that patriots used to rally support for the American Revolution several decades later. During the Second Great Awakening early in the nineteenth century, Charles Grandison Finney employed "new measures," including the use of newspapers, to publicize his revivals. The benevolent societies of the nineteenth century and the highly organized Methodist circuit riders who evangelized the frontier prefigured the grass-roots organizations of political parties. In the twentieth century, Charles E. Fuller and other evangelists used the radio to communicate the gospel long before Franklin Roosevelt discovered its utility as a political device.

None of this suggests a fear of technology or innovation, although it is certainly true that evangelicals were slow in catching on to the evangelistic possibilities of motion pictures, due at least in part to lingering doubts about Hollywood morality and its "communist" sympathies. Thompson may not have eradicated those suspicions, but his films provide an illustration of evangelicals' willingness to use new media for evangelistic ends.

Thompson's work, in fact, has attracted praise from both the Christian and the secular film industry. Harry Bristow, a film distributor in Ambler, Pennsylvania, and president of the Christian Film Distributors Association, told me that Thompson, whom he called "the finest director in the industry," singlehandedly "revolutionized the Christian film business." Others have tried to emulate Thompson, Bristow said, but he still has no peer: "Nobody else in the Christian field can match up with him."[4] Jack Thompson, a movie producer in California who has worked with Don Thompson (no relation) on several films, considers him "a good filmmaker" who would "stack up very favorably" with the directors working out of Hollywood. "I think the world of him," Jack Thompson added, an assessment shared universally by those on the crew of *Life Flight*. "There's no better guy to work for," according to James Berry, director of photography and Hollywood veteran, "not in this business."[5]

Although not diffident about discussing his accomplishments, Thompson readily credits God with his professional success. Since *A Thief in the Night* came out in 1973, Thompson's films have won seventeen "Christian Oscars" from the Christian Film Distributors Association, which also named Thompson "Director of the Decade" for the 1970s. One of his more recent successes, a motivational film called *The Miracle Man*, released in 1986, won the International Silver Screen Award, Thompson's second. James Manilla of New York University's film department called it "just about the best scripted, best acted, best produced motivational program that I'd ever seen."[6] When Thompson learned that *Miracle Man* won the *New York Times* Film Critics' Award, he said he wasn't surprised in the least. "I knew God was in that project, and if God is in something, it's going to be successful."

With all this praise, why doesn't Thompson head to California and ply his skills there? "Ever since I was nine I've wanted to do a theatrical movie," he confessed, but when the offers came recently, he turned them down. In 1984, after a partnership of twelve years that had produced twelve pictures, Thompson and Russ Doughten agreed to go their separate ways. Doughten remained with Mark IV Pictures, while Thompson sought other work. He remembers those months between jobs as a time of personal crisis, a testing of his faith.

While unemployed, Thompson received an offer to make family films in Hollywood, an offer that included a six-figure income and a percentage of the company. "I'd have a home in Oregon and work in California," Thompson said. "Everything the flesh could want." Still, he hesitated. Why, his wife asked one day, wasn't he taking the job? "It seems like everything I would want," he replied, "and I don't know why we're not taking it, but I don't think the Holy Spirit is in it."

After signing on with American Media in Des Moines as a kind of freelance producer-director, Thompson received another offer to direct a theatrical film. As negotiations with the producer in California grew more serious, however, Thompson began to have reservations. "I looked at the script one day and said, 'I can't do this.' But negotiations were well under way—they were talking deals and money and contracts and shooting schedules—and I felt myself getting sucked into this movie that had sex in it, and it was a bad script. I finally went to my boss and said, 'Art, I'm sorry. If you have to fire me, you have to fire me, but I just can't do this movie.' I was scared, but I decided that I'm going to stand up for my principles and let God take care of me."

Arthur Bauer, president of American Media and Thompson's boss, understood and respected Thompson's position. "So I had to call the producer—a man whose credits include *Rocky, Cabaret, The Right Stuff,* and a lot of other successful films—and let him know. I said, 'In all honesty, your script is a piece of junk.' He said, 'Who the hell are you to tell me that? I've been in this business for thirty years, and I've made literally millions of dollars on motion pictures. And you're telling me my script is no good?' And I said, 'Yes, sir, with all due respect to your talent and creativity, your script is lousy.' Well, we fought over the phone for weeks, then I took the initiative with another writer in Dallas to rewrite the script. We spent two weeks on it. I sent it to the producer, and he got even madder. He said, 'That's not even the same story.' I said, 'No, sir, but in my opinion it's a darn sight better than what you had. It's hard enough for me to do a movie I'm in love with, let alone do it just for dollars.' He called me back about a month later. He was very nice. He said, 'Don, it hit me kind of hard when some kid from Des Moines, Iowa, was telling me what's good and what's bad, but that treatment you wrote is good, it's very good. Would you direct it if we did that one?'"

Thompson promised he would think about it, would pray about it. "I said, 'Lord, all I want to do is what You want me to do. If You want me to make church movies for the rest of my life, then praise God, hallelujah, I'll make church films. I just want to do what You want me to do. I don't want to make theatricals if You don't want me to.' The time came when I had to make a decision, so I got down on my knees. In the end, it wasn't difficult. All I had to do was choose God first, and the rest would fall into line. I told them, No, I wouldn't do it."

Thompson paused. "The funny thing is that I just love those Panavision cameras. They're the elite, the best in the world. But they're hard to get. You just can't get them for a film like *Life Flight*. So God said, 'You want a Panavision camera? I'll get you one.' We got a Panavision camera for this film. It was a miracle, but it was God saying that I did the right thing in turning down that Hollywood movie."

How does God communicate? Only once in our conversations did Thompson catch himself using the phrase "God told me" or some variant. While recounting his decision to leave Mark IV Pictures, he said, "The Lord said to me—I hate it when people say that." He then continued with the phrase, "The Lord led me to believe...."

But Thompson clearly has a sense of divine guidance, a confidence that brooks no doubts or second thoughts.

Back in the mid-1970s, Thompson had visited a radio station in Des Moines for an interview. As he left, he became convinced that God was telling him to go back into radio. Thompson, who had spent many years as a disk jockey at KRNT in Des Moines, in what he called "big-time radio," resisted. "The Lord just kinda tapped me on the shoulder and said, 'I want you to do a Christian radio show.' And I remember saying out loud there in my car, 'Lord, no, I don't want to go back to radio.' But when the Holy Spirit talks to you, He never repeats Himself. He says it once, and you can choose to obey or not to obey, and I knew I'd be back on radio.

"I just kept driving. When I got back to my office that very morning I walked past the receptionist and told her, I'm going back into radio.' She said, 'Really? Where? When?' I said, 'I don't know.' I told the Lord, 'I'm not going to make one move to get back on radio. If You want me on, You'll have to do it.' Thirty minutes after I got back the manager from KWKY was in my office. As I had walked in the door, my assistant had been talking to him, and he told her he was looking for people who had been in radio to work for the station, a Christian station.

"As he sat in my office I told him I'd do it on one condition: I'm not going to take any orders from anybody. I know how to do this. At KRNT I had to take a lot of crap from a lot of people who didn't know what they were doing. If I go out to your station, I'm my own man, I do my own thing, and I'll pick the time.' He said, 'When do you want to go on?' I said, 'Ten to noon on Saturday.' He said, 'There are shows in that block that have been on for thirty years. What am I going to do?' He came back the next day and said, 'I cancelled all those shows.'

"So I went out there and thought, 'This is dumb. Who's going to hear me in this stupid little station?" But then I thought, 'This is where God wants you. Just do your best.' Pretty soon this little show became something of a classic; it's been on for eight years. I travel all around the state to speak and people come up and say, 'I listen to your show every Saturday.'"

Thompson's weekly radio show features music of the 1950s. He sees this program, like his films, as evangelistic. "People will listen to that radio show who aren't Christians, who couldn't care less about Christianity." Thompson intersperses the music with anecdotes, lighthearted shenanigans, and sound effects, and he concludes the program with a story or two about God's goodness, His provision in difficult situations, a feature of the program that listeners have come to call "Don's Storybook."

The program has become so popular that even when Thompson is off on location or traveling somewhere, the station runs tapes of previous broadcasts. One morning during the filming of *The Shepherd*, a movie about a military aviator, Thompson had reached the end of his rope with all the difficulties he had encountered with the weather and various technical problems. "I was driving to the set, and I started crying and said, 'God, I can't do this anymore. I just can't. I just don't know where to go.' It was eleven forty-five, and I thought I'd switch on the car radio and listen to some music and feel better. My show was on, and my 'Storybook' was on. And what I said was just what I needed to hear. I started laughing, because God really has a great sense of humor. I said, 'God, only You would use *me* to tell *me* it's going to be all right!'"

What's ahead for Thompson? "I don't know if God wants me to make theatrical features. There are people right now raising money for pictures they want me to direct. Big things are starting to happen for me, and they frighten me, they terrify me, because I can't live in the world of those people." He paused. Thompson, pensive now, sat cross-legged in the grass along the side of the road as the crew prepared for the next scene. "Someone asked me not long ago what my ultimate goal was. I hadn't thought about it before, but I knew immediately." He plucked a blade of grass and held it in his teeth. "My goal is when I get to heaven to have God walk up to me and say, 'You did a good job.' I want to be able to face Him and say, 'I did my best.'"

1986

CHAPTER 4

Phoenix Prophet

I T IS CURTIS FRISBY'S JOB to "warm up" the audience for his father, much the same way that Ed McMahon does for Johnny Carson or Ira Sankey did for evangelist Dwight L. Moody in the nineteenth century. Curt, a dark-haired man in his mid-twenties, struts onto the stage in shiny black trousers and a sportcoat with sleeves hiked up to his elbows. He grabs the microphone with a kind of practiced insouciance and exhorts the audience to "give God a clap offering." The congregation obeys. He then asks, "How many love the Lord with all your heart?" More applause. With the backup of an electric guitar, drums, several singers, and an electronic organ played in a way that suggests a skating rink rather than a cathedral, he croons several songs, all the while imploring the congregation to join in by singing and clapping in rhythm. Several in the audience have brought tambourines. "Let's give God a clap offering," he says again. Then: "Gimme a J-E-S-U-S!" The audience responds at the appropriate junctures. "ya' know," he says, "the more you praise God, the more happier you get." Another chant: "I'm saved." A lusty echo from the crowd, then: "By the blood of Jesus Christ."[1]

A large, amiable man in his late thirties, identified simply as Brother Max, steps to the microphone to announce the offering. There is no prolonged appeal, just a comment that a building like theirs isn't inexpensive. Indeed not. The Capstone Cathedral in Phoenix, Arizona, was built in 1971 at a cost well in excess of $1 million. Rising from the desert floor, the four walls of this square, concrete building slope upward at a gentle angle, and at the apex sits a steel-ribbed pyramid, forty feet square at its base and rising to a point thirty-one feet higher. The eighteen-ton pyramid is sheathed in a pattern of blue-green and red glass, and, from a distance, the effect is that of a large, gaudy jewel sitting atop some otherworldly launching pad.[2] To enter this Capstone Cathedral, you approach the building across a small berm that surrounds the structure and then step down into one of several entrances, small gashes in the foundation of the pyramid. Once inside, a huge space opens before you, unimpeded by structural supports. The floor slopes down toward the southwest corner where it meets the semicircular fronting of the stage, snuggled like a slice of pie into the corner. The sense of scale here is overwhelming. Row upon row of theater seats—enough for two thousand people—fan out from the stage and up to the far reaches of the building.

Except for the podium, which sits beneath a bank of television lights, the platform itself is ordinary enough, cluttered in the back with amplifiers, drums, a piano, and the electronic organ. As the wooden pulpit, fixed at center stage, rises from the floor, it becomes slightly broader at the top. A large, deep chevron is etched in the facing, beginning at the top two corners and extending almost to the floor. Toward the bottom of the chevron sits a white star within a circle. Inside of the two triangles formed by the upper parts of the chevron are red and blue stripes, overlaid by two bolts of lightning that begin near the top two corners and angle toward the star. Knowing that people at the Capstone Cathedral place a great deal of stock in symbolism, I asked one woman what this meant. "Wings of power," she replied matter-of-factly, in a tone that suggested any fool would know that. "It means the Lord's wings of power."

Back on stage, with the congregation now suitably prepared, arms flailing and clapping, Brother Max says, "And now, the watchman on our walls...Evangelist Neal Frisby!" From behind a curtain at the back of the platform a small, stocky man, wearing a spearmint-green sportcoat and a loosely knotted tie, rushes to the pulpit, waving a Bible to acknowledge his welcome.

"The Lord bless your hearts tonight," he begins. He then speaks about "the great things God is doing" in the crusade, this series of nightly revival meetings during the winter of 1987. Frisby launches into his sermon, which he delivers in clipped sentences and an uneven cadence. Much of it sounds like a stream of consciousness. He frequently concludes sentences—or fragments—with the phrase, "and so forth like that," as he hurries on to his next thought. In order to elicit a response from the congregation, he'll ask, "Amen?" or "How many of ya' believe that?" A sprinkling of applause or shouted affirmations follow each question. When Frisby wants to emphasize a thought, he tacks the inflection "ah" onto the end of his phrases: "There is coming a time-ah, when the glory of the Lord-ah, will appear to the faithful-ah." There is very little sustained argumentation here, just a random jumping from one thought to the next.

But the congregation of about one hundred people doesn't seem to mind. Tonight, Thursday evening, is Miracle Deliverance Night at the crusade, so Frisby's meditation centers around the spiritual power of healing, a phenomenon that accounts for much of his renown. At the conclusion of the sermon, he instructs those who seek healing or those who can attest to such healing to gather in two lines, one at either end of the stage. On his left are those who want some kind of healing—tumors, back troubles, stomach troubles, eye problems, respiratory problems, drug or alcohol dependency. "We'll get the drugs out and make the alcohol run," he promises. "There is nothing too big or too large for the Lord." On his right, are those who will come and testify about such healing, physical or spiritual, in the past. Queues of about twenty-five people gather at the steps on either side of the platform.

Frisby begins with the testimony line. A young black woman (perhaps one-third of Frisby's congregation, many of whom travel weekly from Los Angeles, is black), breathless and nearly incoherent with enthusiasm, says that she "became real" through Brother Frisby's ministry, "and that's where it's at," she continues. "God wants you to be real for Him." While she was pregnant several years ago, she said, "a force tripped me," and her son, now seven years old, was born mentally retarded. But now, praise God, through Brother Frisby's ministry, the boy is healed. "He's a genius. He's only seven years old, but he can read on a twelve-year-old level." This woman flies in from California every week, she says, "because this church is real."

Frisby then turns to the healing line. A young boy, perhaps eight years old, walks to the evangelist. (During this part of the service Frisby turned around in the pulpit, with his back to the audience, and the people who came up to face him were hidden behind Frisby and the large lectern.) "I can't breathe too good," the boy says. Frisby places his hand on the boy's forehead and asks Jesus to heal him. At the conclusion of the brief prayer, Frisby says, "Now take a deep breath. You couldn't do that before, could ya'?" The boy mumbles something, which apparently falls short of the wholesale affirmation Frisby was looking for, so he hedges: "As you obey, Jesus will keep on healing you." The boy heads off the stage and back to his seat. Frisby adds, "Sometimes the little fellas don't know how to say it, but it turns out okay."

He takes a few more from the healing line and then alternates between the two. A man who asked healing for arthritis testifies that God had healed his car. A young woman claims deliverance from "female problems." An elderly woman using a cane walks on stage. She says that Frisby has removed her bunions through prayer in the past, and she comes now for healing in her hips; one leg, she says, is longer than the other. Frisby touches her forehead and prays for healing. "Lord, heal this woman. By the power of your Spirit, adjust her hips. Take away the pain-ah!" The prayer completed, he asks, "What happened there? I really felt the Spirit adjust hips. Did one leg get longer? Walk around there. What do you feel?"

"It feels like it's getting even," the woman says, rather tentatively. "You don't need that cane anymore," Frisby announces. "Jesus has healed you!" Then to the audience: "Give the Lord a hand clap." The woman walks down the steps, across in front of the stage, and to her seat—using her cane. (The same woman returned to the healing line Sunday evening, the last day of the revival, this time without the cane. "I'd like a little more healing in my knees," she said.)

A teenager in denims and a dark tee-shirt approaches Frisby and asks for prayer. "I'm not doing too good in school," he says. Frisby grabs his forehead and unleashes a thunderous prayer calling on God to "give this boy some of Your special power-ah!" At the end of the prayer, the evangelist asks, "What happened there?" The young man looks a bit shaken, like he'd gotten more than he bargained for. He backs away, shakes his head, and answers, "I really felt the Spirit." Frisby sends him off and says, "Give the Lord a hand clap."

Another woman, one of Frisby's longtime followers in Phoenix, insists that "for eighteen years I haven't used a doctor. When I get sick I just call up and ask for Brother Frisby." Indeed, the evangelist dispenses healing as effortlessly as physicians write prescriptions. He treats coughs, colds ("I command the cold to go in the name of the Lord"), even toothaches ("Put the tooth back where it belongs, Jesus-ah"). Sometimes at the conclusion of the prayer, before Frisby invites a response, he'll say, "Oooh-wee. It really came out of me that time!" Or: "Did you feel that? The power really surges."

Frisby prays for everyone who comes onto the platform. Sometimes the prayer elicits no visible response. With others, however, it unleashes all manner of ecstatic behavior—tears, wailing, shaking arms and limbs, fibrillating voices (speaking in tongues), jumping up and down. People sometimes stagger away as though reeling from a jolt of electricity. "I feel good. I love ya', Lord. I feel great," one woman exclaims, waving her arms. Frisby clearly relishes such gyrations or outpourings of the Spirit. "Let's give the Lord a hand clap."

Frisby is not diffident about his healing powers. In the past he has claimed a ninety-nine percent success rate, and he frequently boasts that he has created ear drums and other body parts. These "creative miracles," as he calls them, date to the very beginning of his ministry in the 1960s. "Eardrums, one right after another, were created; legs were lengthened, one right after another," he wrote in his autobiography. "Backbones, nerves, and spinal parts were created. Hip sockets have been created, even when there was no ball." The list continues. "I have seen enamel put back on teeth. I have even prayed for corns and they have fallen off in people's socks, or just disappeared!"[3]

Unlike other pentecostal revival services that might continue long into the night, Frisby concludes his about an hour or an hour and a half after it begins. When the healings are over, he turns to the congregation, reminds them of the next meeting, and then invites them to "come to Jesus." "I'm going to pray a mass prayer here," he says. At that signal everyone leaves his or her seat and files to the platform. The music, now deafening, begins again, laced with a heavy beat. Frisby cups his hands around the microphone and emits a series of unintelligible, guttural sounds. As the congregation, gathered in front of him, claps in rhythm to the music, the evangelist gesticulates with his arms, sweeping them first to the left, then to the right, all the while barking strange noises into the microphone. The only word I could understand amid the banter was an emphatic, drawn-out "Jee-sus-ah." He leaves the pulpit briefly to dance to one side of the stage and then the other, sweeping his arms in a kind of ritualized motion. Coming back to the podium, he turns his back to the audience, now whipped into a frenzy, thrusts his arms into the air, throws back his head, and trots offstage behind the same curtain whence he emerged.

FRISBY'S ANTICS, especially in the surreal setting of his Capstone Cathedral, lend a kind of carnival atmosphere to his meetings. But the claims about his healing prowess are not terribly exceptional. Since the turn of the century, faith healers have abounded in America, and even in the nineteenth century various evangelicals propagated divine remedies for physical ailments. In the early 1830s, Sylvester Graham, a Presbyterian evangelist and temperance preacher, developed a cracker as a health and dietary aid; the Graham cracker is still popular today. Ellen Gould White, afflicted from childhood with various physical disorders, had several visions that revealed the secrets of good health. White, leader of the Seventh-day Adventists, founded the Western Health Reform Institute in Battle Creek, Michigan, under the auspices of which John Harvey Kellogg invented corn flakes and other health foods. Mary Baker Eddy believed that deliverance from physical affliction lay in the spiritual realm. Even the science of chiropractic, developed by D. D. Palmer in Davenport, Iowa, in the 1890s, grew to some extent out of religious impulses and convictions.

When the pentecostal or sanctified movement—grounded in the belief that the Holy Spirit anoints true Christians with special spiritual gifts—began to gather force in American evangelicalism early in the twentieth century, healing became one of the spiritual gifts that pentecostals claimed as evidence of sanctification. Later in the century, the media propelled some of the faith healers to prominence. Through radio, Kathryn Kuhlman of Pittsburgh built a national reputation out of her gifts of healing. Oral Roberts, whom Frisby admires, parlayed his into a huge empire centered in Tulsa, Oklahoma. Neal Frisby belongs in that tradition, though he is clearly on the fringes, but there is another dimension that sets him even farther apart from the pentecostal mainstream: He believes he is a prophet sent from God, the final prophet before the end of time.[4]

The Capstone Cathedral (also known as the Temple of Destiny, the Headstone, or the Great Pyramid), it turns out, is fraught with apocalyptic significance. Its construction in the early 1970s prefigures the rebuilding of the temple in Jerusalem.[5] Frisby claims that God designed it, and that the dimensions were revealed to Frisby (who then apparently relayed them to Ray Parrish, an architect in Scottsdale).[6] "He even told me where to build it," Frisby claims. The seven concrete layers that recede upward toward the cap represent the seven ages of the church or the seven thunders of Revelation 10.[7] The tiers also symbolize the seven great prophets or messengers of Christianity, beginning with Paul the apostle and concluding with the "Star Prophet," William Branham, a pentecostal preacher who claimed a visitation from an angel on May 7, 1946, and whom Frisby considers his mentor and predecessor.[8]

For an understanding of the top pyramid of green and red glass, the capstone, Frisby asks his followers to look at a one-dollar bill. "On the back side of a dollar and at the left corner is the sign of the PYRAMID and at the top we see the 'Capstone' separated forming a 'Capstone Eye' with glory around it, revealing the 'all seeing eye' of God was rejected!" The base of the pyramid, moreover, "depicts the large groups that started in the 7 Church Ages through history and as it gets closer to the top it shows how" the Lord narrows down a small group separated in the eye to take away!" Thus, the capstone depicts the true followers of God (the followers of Frisby) who will be taken in the rapture. The capstone also represents Frisby himself, who believes he is the final prophet, the culmination of history and revelation, God's mouthpiece in these last days.[9]

The symbolism continues inside. Every few rows the color of the seats extending from the platform changes. This spectrum of color symbolizes both Frisby, the "Rainbow Prophet" predicted in Revelation 10, and his followers, "the Rainbow Elect of God." The star on the pulpit represents Jesus, "the bright and morning star"; the blue stripes signify the bruises Jesus sustained before His crucifixion and the red stripes the blood He shed for the sins of humanity. The lightning bolts represent the power of God's revelation given to Frisby, who writes: "In Bible symbology when lightning cuts through the air this portrays a spirit message going forth."[10] A sign above an accordion door to the left of the platform, along the south edge of the building, reads THE VEIL in block letters. This is Frisby's inner sanctum, the last of a series of three chambers reserved for his use. In coming years, as the eschaton approaches, Frisby believes that the United States will pass laws against spiritual healing. The area behind the veil, then, will serve as a place of healing. Frisby, I was told, does much of his meditation and prayer here in the "chamber of revelation," but it is also used now, albeit infrequently, as a place for "special healings" or "special ministrations of the Spirit." Frisby says that just before construction workers covered the floor in the room behind the veil, "the Lord Jesus gave me some secrets and I put them underneath and I will not reveal them until later." This sanctum is the rough equivalent of the holy of holies in the Old Testament, a place reserved to the high priest and cordoned off from the people by the veil of the temple.[11]

HOW DID FRISBY come to his calling as a prophet? Born July 23, 1933, in Strong, Arkansas, Neal Vincent Frisby, a scrappy kid, had a troubled early life. "I always had a desire to be a conqueror, a champion," he confessed in his autobiography, without elaboration. After moving to California, he completed the ninth grade and then went to barber college. Following the birth of her second child, Frisby's wife, still in her teens, committed suicide, an action Frisby now attributes to possession by a demon, "a melancholy spirit from the devil." Shortly thereafter, he went to an Assemblies of God church and was converted. "When I was saved my heart was healed instantly," he wrote. "It was miraculous!" Later, he spoke in tongues and became convinced that "the Spirit of God bade me go preach and pray for the sick."[12]

Frisby, however, resisted that call. He began to drink heavily, neglecting his family and his barber shop. "After a year of hard drinking, and begging the Lord to just save me, but not call me to preach, I began to have convulsions, the last stage of alcoholism. I began to use dope. In my convulsions I chewed my tongue. My bones would come out of joint and have to be put back in." Frisby went to hospital psychiatric wards several times and entered the state mental asylum for treatment, where he witnessed all manner of demon possession. But his problem, he knew, was spiritual: "Sin brings on insanity and sickness." Frisby found deliverance only when he resolved "to have it out with the devil." "I told the Lord I would do what He wanted me to do," he wrote. "Instantly by the power of God, and I lie not, a light feeling hit me. The demons had departed. I had no craving to drink, no seizures or convulsions."[13]

Frisby embarked on a forty-day fast, consuming nothing but water, in the course of which God came to him on the seventh, twenty-first, and thirty-seventh days, and said, according to Frisby, "'There shall not anything stand before thee all the days of thy ministry. As I was with Moses I will be with thee! Be thou strong and full of courage!'"[14] God also endowed Frisby with the extraordinary power of "creative miracles" that at times, he insists, is so overwhelming that people find it frightening. "Even now," Frisby wrote in his autobiography, "I can't stay around anyone on the platform for very long because the anointing will wear them down. There is something strange about it." During this fast, he also became convinced of his prophetic calling: "The anointing is upon me. God spoke to me and said, 'The words I speak unto thee, write them and put them into a book.'" Frisby also declared, "I am a man given to prophetic visions [of] the glory of the Lord in a vision of white shekinah."[15]

How does this prophet interpret his calling? Frisby views himself as a messenger who "speaks by Divine Revelation and a Prophetic Spirit that goes beyond all gifts and utters the exact words of God to the Elect of his age and thunders the judgement of God on a nation!"[16] At irregular intervals since 1967, Frisby has issued prophetic scrolls to his followers. These scrolls, printed in two colors on a kind of parchment, contain his revelations from God. The introduction to a collection of the scrolls sets forth their importance: "Throughout the entire history of the world no work has been placed before the public which is as comprehensive revealing the fundamental truths of the Bible as this timely book on prophecy and its fulfillment!" As the end of time approaches, Frisby declared, "the Lord will release true wisdom unto His children through the dynamic scrolls"; furthermore: "One should carefully read this Literature in prayer because it is a written revelation by the supernatural wisdom of God! The writer does not claim infallibility, but we definitely believe the events, dates and symbols were placed in correct position close as humanly possible under divine inspiration!"[17]

Like many evangelicals, Frisby insists upon a literal reading of the Bible, from Genesis to Revelation. This hermeneutic, together with the conviction that he is a latter-day prophet, leads to a kind of fixation with apocalyptic prophecies in the Scriptures. Unlike other evangelical clergy who are content to study apocalyptic writings, discern the signs, and preach the importance of repentance, however, Frisby is eager to locate himself within God's prophetic scheme for the end of the world. He finds his niche, he believes, in Revelation 8. The apostle John, in the midst of his apocalyptic visions, sees a Lamb upon a throne (generally interpreted as Jesus Christ, "the Lamb of God who takes away the sins of the world"). In the sixth chapter, the Lamb opens the first six seals, one by one, and out come, in succession, four different colored horses, the martyrs, and, finally, various signs in the heavens—earthquakes, falling stars, a solar eclipse. After the sixth seal, chapter 7 records an interlude. "When the Lamb opened the seventh seal," Revelation 8:1 reads, "there was silence in heaven for about half an hour." In chapter 10, after the sounding of six trumpets, John records another interlude and the arrival of an angel, "coming down from heaven, wrapped in a cloud, with a rainbow over his head." "He had a little scroll open in his hand," John continued. "And when the seven thunders had sounded, I was about to write, but I heard a voice from heaven saying, 'Seal up what the seven thunders have said, and do not write it down.'"[18]

This silence, Neal Frisby believes, prevailed until recently, when God designated Frisby as this Rainbow Prophet or "the mighty rainbow cap angel" in the last days who would reveal the hidden messages of God and inaugurate a "great rainbow revival," replete with all manner of divine signs: "The dramatic flashing appearance on lightning and thunder miracles will occur! Tremendous anointing is coming to create parts of the body, at times all will be healed!"[19] This, Frisby believes, is his place in prophetic history: a source of divine healing and revelation who communicates the workings of God—and the contents of the unopened seventh seal—on parchment scrolls.

"In the scrolls Jesus isn't adding to the Bible or taking away," Frisby writes, "but a continuing work of the spirit revealing a highly inspired written key message to reveal the 7th seal that was opened." His scrolls, Frisby believes, contain the "Key to interpret the secrets to the book of Revelations!" Even the U.S. dollar bill confirms this. Beneath the pyramid on the reverse side is the inscription THE GREAT SEAL, which, Frisby believes, refers to the seventh seal, described in the book of Revelation.[20]

Frisby's prophecies, revealed on these scrolls, range from the predictable to the bizarre. He inveighs against such commonplace evangelical targets as rock music, drugs, alcohol, homosexuality, communism, and Roman Catholicism.[21] In the 1960s he predicted the emergence of a U.S. president who "does much for the poor and religion" and who would "move toward uniting church and state." "How quick this president rises I'm not certain," Frisby wrote, "but I will tell you who he is if I get permission from the Lord." He predicts the unification of the three Cs—communism, Catholicism, and capitalism—to form one kingdom that seeks to replace the "great C" (Christ).[22]

He also thinks that the ancient Hebrew prophet Nahum "saw the (last car) not the first one made! It was rocket turbin, electric or radar controlled."[23] Late in the 1960s he advised his readers that America's highways "will undergo vast changes in the 70's and radar controlling will come into view about the time Christ appears." Frisby worries about such issues as transportation during the millennium, in light of Zechariah's prophecy that people would go to Jerusalem to worship once a year. "This would be utterly impossible with out some kind of huge swift space craft, (possibly some new gravity free super sonic or atomic craft!)," Frisby wrote, but then he offered consolation: "Never the less the Lord may supply the transportation, 'He has supernatural craft.'" Some prophecies build on popular fears, such as the prediction in the 1960s that an earthquake would plunge much of California into the ocean. Back then he also predicted the rise of Ronald Reagan, "a man preordained and predestined," to national prominence. In Reagan's strategic defense initiative ("Star Wars") of the 1980s, Frisby doubtless found vindication for another vision of the late 1960s: "I am shown paralyzing rays of light far ahead of the atomic bomb are being invented. Cosmicide radiation which rends people helpless will be discovered and used from outer space and land!"[24]

All of Frisby's prophecies point to the imminent end of human history and the beginning of the apocalyptic events foretold in the Bible. Frisby welcomes the end. He already feels caught up in the inexorable sequence of events: "The cycles and dates converging and innerlocking together in astounding fashion prove we are in the hands of Divine Providence!"[25] Like other preachers who seek to interpret the signs of the times in order to predict the impending eschaton, Frisby has his own ideas about the sequence of events. First comes the rapture, when the *true* Christians—those who subscribe to his "Capstone Ministry"—are taken from earth and united with Christ in heaven. The tribulation, a time of trial and testing for those left behind, begins immediately, followed in three-and-one-half years by the Battle of Armageddon predicted in Revelation 16. The millennium directly precedes the great white throne judgment of Revelation 20, when those with names recorded in the book of life go to heaven and those not found there are cast into the lake of fire. Finally, according to the penultimate chapter of Revelation, "a new heaven and a new earth" appear.[26]

All of this, Frisby believes, is imminent. One of his scenarios reads like this: "If God should allow by Divine intervention that the Rapture should go past 1977, my feeling then in Revelation time cycles is the Tribulation will start in 1983, Armageddon in 1986. The Church would leave between 1977–83 or sooner. But this I know by divine wisdom Armageddon will not take place until after January 1976."[27]

Interwoven with all these calculations are the familiar evangelical intimations that the unsaved must be saved and the elect must live holy lives and eschew evil, for the apocalyptic moment is close at hand. "We can safely say it looks like He is pointing to the ending of things. Early or late 70's," Frisby says at one point in his transcription of God's messages. "However, if it goes past the 80's it will all totally end by 1986. AMEN! But I really feel the 70's will tell the complete story of the end." Elsewhere, commenting on the apocalyptic end of time predicted in Revelation, he wrote, "I definitely feel it will all be finished before 1986."[28] When I heard Frisby in February 1987, the dates had changed. He spoke obliquely about three five-year periods and said that the end would come before the conclusion of the third five years.

While he insists that "I am not writing an extra Bible only fulfilling it," Frisby is certainly convinced that the scrolls contain divine revelation. "I speak by the mouth of the Lord!" he declares in one scroll. Sentences often begin with phrases like, "The Lord told me . . ." or "God showed me that . . ."; elsewhere he writes, "I am sent with 'the angel of the Lord to warn you'" and "that great angel is standing by my side." At one point Frisby claimed to relive the visions of Daniel, the Hebrew prophet in the Old Testament. "I feel a strong anointing," he wrote at the beginning of Scroll 8, "taking me back to the days of Daniel, and entering a new depth of Revelation."[29]

He admonishes his readers: "Soon these Scrolls will be the most valuable possession you own. Remember the Bible will be changed by man soon or taken, but not these Scrolls. The wise will see what God is doing through me." The scrolls, according to Frisby, also contain supernatural powers. "Reading these scrolls," he wrote, "will relieve and protect against mental disorders."[30] Indeed, Frisby's followers take these scrolls quite seriously. I spoke with one man, a follower since the early 1970s, who told me that he studied the scrolls regularly and had marked his copy at home with glosses and cross-references.

To undergird his prophecies, Frisby turns to solar eclipses and astrology, numerology (most often relating to his birthdate), and photographs of his Capstone Cathedral, all interleaved into the volume of prophetic scrolls.[31] The captions under each photograph—and often the text of the scrolls themselves—explain some supernatural wonder revealed in the photograph, very often a cloud formation that shows the face of God perched above the capstone. "Now I am going to reveal something here that is going to dumbfound the world," he announced in Scroll 61. "The stone the builders rejected (Christ—Mark 12:10) was photographed on top of the building, and has become the head of the corner." Once he publishes this photograph, Frisby wrote, "there isn't anything anybody can do but just stand and fall back in awe!"[32]

Many of the photographs suffer from some sort of aberration caused by double exposures, lens flares from shooting into the sun, or poor developing. But rather than tossing these pictures into the wastebasket or firing off an angry letter to Eastman Kodak, Frisby believes they reveal some divine mystery. "The Lord has given us the most sacred and rarest photographs ever seen before," Frisby boasts. In these photographs, he sees angel wings, golden halos, pillars of fire, and, most often, shekinah glory.[33] The Capstone Cathedral itself, the central subject in all these photographs, plays a central role in the coming apocalypse, and Frisby enjoins his followers to visit the building before Christ's return.[34]

NEAL FRISBY, THIS STOCKY MAN with dark hair and a receding hairline who wears sportcoats of canary yellow and powder blue and spearmint green, looks like a truck driver or maybe a small-town insurance salesman, the kind of man you might expect to find at the local diner kibitzing with the guys. In truth, however, in recent years (for reasons I never learned) Frisby has grown increasingly reclusive and misanthropic. He and his family live on the church property in a two-story house surrounded by an eight-foot cinder-block wall. Brother Max, Frisby's assistant, told me that he had never had an extended conversation with Frisby; they had exchanged words only casually and in passing. When I made discreet inquiries about speaking with Frisby, I was told in no uncertain terms that he would not be available and that he rarely gave a personal audience. How do members of his congregation communicate with him? Apparently they don't, except for whatever contact they have in the healing or the praise lines during the services, although I was assured that Frisby would respond to a written note or question from a member of the congregation.

Frisby's day begins at four or five in the morning, when he goes into his private chambers and begins a regimen of prayer and writing that continues virtually all day. Frisby closets himself away in this "chamber of revelation" and writes his prophecies. From time to time, the text itself offers a few clues about this process. A parenthetical sentence in Scroll 40 reads: "while writing this late at night in my room I am also receiving something to do with the World Market and USA business exchange! It is important I am shown the years 1976–77."[35] Elsewhere, he writes: "I am lifted up above the world catastrophe (Armageddon) and All ages will be used in the last war. I saw children, young men and women and old men armed prepared to fight the last great war, as Russia and the Orientals came down on Israel."[36] Beyond that, there are remarkably few clues about this enigmatic prophet.

There are, however, some tantalizing glimpses. In searching through clipping files at a local library, I discovered several newspaper articles about Frisby and his nephews. In August 1984, his nephews exploded half a stick of dynamite in the back yard of the assistant police chief, claiming that the policeman's son owed them $600 for guns they had sold him. The nephews subsequently led an undercover agent from the Bureau of Alcohol, Tobacco and Firearms, posing as a gun buyer, to their cache of weapons. The agent purchased four hand grenades, eleven bombs, and several sticks of dynamite from Frisby's nephews; he passed on the submachine guns equipped with silencers, but stayed long enough to hear one nephew boast that he could blow up cars without a trace. "My dynamite is the strongest on the market," he said. "You put this under somebody's car, and you're going to lift it off the ground."[37] The case never came to trial. Frisby's nephews were granted probation after Frisby wrote a letter on Capstone stationery attesting to their regular church attendance. (After learning about this incident, and knowing about Frisby's passion for secrecy, I winced whenever I turned the ignition on my rental car.)

Apparently, Frisby's congregation remains unperturbed about such matters, although there has been a dramatic ebbing of his popularity in recent years. In his salad days of the early 1970s, several people told me, the crowds would begin arriving at four-thirty for an eight o'clock meeting. The line for healing sometimes extended from the platform, down through the auditorium, and out the front door, a distance of several hundred feet. I saw film clips of the building, seating two thousand, filled to capacity.[38] Along the walls of two sides of the pyramid sit banks of metal files containing Frisby's mailing list, which includes, I was told, the names of twelve million followers around the country and the world.[39]

The remnant of the faithful, down now to 100 or perhaps 150, is a mixed lot. During the first night of the crusade I sat near a woman, a member of the local Assembly of God, who was visiting the Capstone Cathedral out of curiosity. She expressed wonderment at both the service and the congregation. "This is really—I don't know how to say it—a lower-class crowd," she said, "which surprises me, because this is a well-to-do neighborhood." Indeed, most of the people hardly looked affluent. A sizable percentage of the congregation is black. I saw a good number of elderly people—some of whom arrived in wheelchairs, others with canes or walkers—hoping no doubt for some miraculous deliverance from physical suffering. I noticed prescription bottles in the side pockets of several purses. I asked one older woman, a kindly person who stood behind one of the tables selling literature, about the old days and why attendance at Capstone had slackened so badly. "People just don't want to do God's will," she said. "They come for healing, but they don't want to follow the teachings of the Lord." I suspected that the real answer was a bit less spiritual. Frisby is a good example of an evangelical figure who gathers a following because of his charisma and his claims of healing power. At the same time, Frisby, who elevated himself to the status of prophet, was accountable to no one; because of the increasingly freakish twists in his theology, moreover, erstwhile followers became disenchanted and fell away.

But those who remain faithful—the elect—will be rewarded, Frisby promises. "Now the 'Capstone' people (the Sons of God) is called in the Thunders! Like Enoch they walked with God and will be translated! This is the 'Rod iron elect', little is heard of them at first, but they are the most powerful group who ever came on the face of the earth!"[40]

The promise of power in the afterlife to compensate for suffering and powerlessness in this life? I wondered.

AS THE CRUSADE DREW TO A CLOSE, it became clear that I'd be unable to penetrate this veil of secrecy around Frisby. On Sunday morning, the final day of the revival, however, I conceived a plan. Several times Frisby had announced that on Sunday he would have a special prayer line for those who had come from out of town, giving them a chance to request healing either for themselves or for others. I figured that I qualified. The week before, moreover, a student had visited my office, and when the conversation came around to this impending trip, she volunteered that she had recently lost the hearing in one ear. This provided the perfect pretext, I reasoned, and as the line snaked forward, I rehearsed my appeal. Three women in front of me, all dressed alike and all from Los Angeles, went away crying, dancing, and shouting. Then came my turn.

"Brother Frisby," I began, feeling every bit the impostor, "I have a friend named Alexandra who recently lost the hearing in one ear. Could you heal her in the power of Jesus' name?" Frisby rose to the challenge, ears being something of a specialty. "Well, we'll pray for her right here," he announced. "Can she come to the meetings, or is she too far away?"

"She's too far away."

The Rainbow Prophet grabbed the back of my neck with his left hand and placed his right hand on my forehead. Having watched the prayer line several times now, I knew that the correct posture at this moment was to cast aside my inhibitions, throw my arms up in the air, and close my eyes. I don't recall all of Frisby's prayer, although I remember a few words and phrases: "don't know what has affected this girl's hearing," "let her feel the anointing of Your Spirit all through her body," "heal her," "name of Jesus." As the prayer continued, the evangelist began to shake me, while bearing down with increasing pressure on my forehead. When he finished, he let out a little "whooo-ee," released me from his grasp, and stepped away as though thrown backwards by the recoil of a rifle. He was looking for some sort of response, I realized later. Surely I disappointed him when I muttered "thank you," shook his hand, and walked away.

What did I feel? Nothing. Just a sweaty palm on my forehead, shaking and pushing.

AS THE PLANE LIFTED OUT OF PHOENIX on Monday morning after the revival, I searched the flat, barren landscape below for the Capstone Cathedral, the jewel atop the pyramid. Neal Frisby was, perhaps even now, I thought, scratching away at his latest prophetic scroll, or maybe flailing away at some private demon that retreats before him like a desert mirage. Like the city here in this desolate Valley of the Sun, I thought, Frisby was a kind of phoenix himself, rising out of the ashes of despair to become, of all things, the Rainbow Prophet.

The day after I arrived home, I phoned Alexandra. "How's the ear?" I asked. I tried to sound mischievous and conspiratorial, but I was genuinely curious.

"No change," she said.

1987

CHAPTER 5

Adirondack Fundamentalism

IN THE EARLY MORNING HOURS, Schroon Lake is gray and placid. Wispy clouds tumble over the pine-covered hillsides that surround the lake. Steam rises from the water. A lone canoe paddles by. For a brief moment, the sun pushes past the clouds but then settles back into exile.

When the receding glaciers carved Schroon Lake into the Adirondack mountains of upstate New York, they left a ninety-acre island at the north end of the lake. There, pine trees sprouted among the glacial rocks, and thus surrounded by frigid mountain water, the island became an ideal location for a youth camp.

Jack Wyrtzen, a fundamentalist Bible teacher from New York City, took possession in 1946, at about the same time that motor travel began to diminish the attractiveness of the resorts dotting the Adirondacks. He has since added an inn, a family campground, a ranch, and a Bible institute—hundreds of acres, all told—to his empire, the Word of Life Fellowship, in and around Schroon Lake. Word of Life also includes radio broadcasts on more than one hundred stations around the world, mission enterprises in places as diverse as Peru, Hungary, Israel, and New Zealand, various traveling evangelists, musicians, and drama troupes, and over a thousand Bible clubs held in churches throughout the country. All of this consumes an annual budget of about $12 million, but the youth camp, "for young people and college-career young adults aged 13 to 30," remains the centerpiece of Word of Life.[1]

I'M NOT SURE THERE IS ANY WAY I could document this, but I suspect that the greatest fear that haunts evangelical parents is that
their children will not follow in their footsteps, that they will not
sustain the same level of piety as their parents—stated baldly, that
they are headed for hell rather than heaven. Such themes as way-
wardness and redemption provide the grist for countless evangelical
sermons; the parable of the prodigal son, I am convinced, is one of
the most popular texts in the evangelical subculture. Prayer meetings
fairly reverberate with petitions for this or that son or daughter who
has wandered from the faith. In recent decades, many churches,
reflecting the concerns of parents in the congregation, have hired
youth pastors, whose job it is to keep children safely within the evangelical fold, to shield them from the perils of worldliness.

Indeed, there is ample cause for concern. What can be harder
than passing on religious verve and vitality from one generation to
the next, especially within a tradition that defines itself by the conversion process, that transition from darkness to light, from sinfulness to redemption? The Puritans of the seventeenth century faced
this problem and never fully resolved it. New England's founding
generation had forsaken fortune and family in England in order to
carve a godly commonwealth out of the wilderness of Massachusetts. By the time the second generation approached adulthood, the
spirituality of the founding generation had taken on heroic proportions, and when this next generation was asked as a requirement
for church membership to stand before their elders in the meet-
inghouse and give an account of their conversions, most of them
refused, knowing full well that their piety paled before that of their
parents. Before long, the Puritans discerned in their midst a spiritual
malaise that they called declension, and by the latter half of the seventeenth century the pulpits of New England reverberated with
calls to repentance.

In his novel *The Chosen*, Chaim Potok illustrates how this gen-
erational problem plays itself out within a different context. Reb
Saunders, a pious, learned man venerated by his Hasidic followers,

wants desperately to pass along the mantle of religious leadership to his eldest son, Danny, a precocious child who has studied the Talmud exhaustively all of his life and who regularly astounds his father's congregation with his grasp of even the most recondite Jewish sacred writings. Danny Saunders, the elders all agree, would be a worthy spiritual successor to his father.

But Danny Saunders's restless mind leads him in other directions, to intellectual pursuits outside the narrow confines of his father's calling and to friendships outside of his Hasidic community. When it finally becomes clear that Danny will not follow in his father's footsteps, Reb Saunders bids his son an anguished farewell, whereupon Danny Saunders, shorn of his earlocks and no longer dressed in black Hasidic hat and coat, walks down the street and toward a new life very different from the sheltered existence he has known.[2]

It doesn't take much imagination to appreciate the quandary of parents who want to pass along to their children the faith that has shaped their lives and solved for them the riddle of eternity. You want to shelter your children from the temptations that assail them at every turn. You want to school them in the Scriptures and in the theology that you know to be correct. And you also want them to be models of godliness, a credit not only to the faith but also to you as wise, godly parents.

Yet at the same time, such sheltering diminishes the drama of their own spiritual conversions when—and if—those conversions do occur. Whereas your embracing of the gospel had delivered you from a life of, say, alcohol or drugs or promiscuity, theirs serves merely as a ratification of the beliefs and lifestyle that you, their parents, have drilled into them since infancy. (The prodigal son's older brother who stayed at home, after all, never knew the contrast between the perils of the world and the security of home, and he envied the lavish party his father threw for his brother's homecoming.) On the other hand, neglecting your children's spiritual nurture will not suffice either, for that entails the considerable risk of trusting them (through God's leading, of course) to come to Christ of their own volition.

Ever since the 1925 Scopes Trial convinced fundamentalists that the broader American culture had turned hostile to their interests, fundamentalists have busied themselves devising various institutions to insulate themselves and their children from the depredations of the world. (In fact, the terms *worldly* and *worldliness* are probably the closest most evangelicals come to epithets; these words are often spoken sneeringly, in a tone at the same time condescending and cautionary.) First, the fundamentalists separated out of mainline denominations so that they could maintain a theology untainted by liberalism or, in the argot of the day, "modernism." Evangelicals then established their own mission boards, Christian schools, Bible institutes, colleges, and, eventually, seminaries. For children, Sunday school provided socialization and instruction in the rudiments of evangelical theology. Once the children had grown, you could ship them off to a Bible institute where they might prepare for the pastorate, missionary work, or some other kind of "Christian service."

But by the 1940s many fundamentalist parents recognized a gap in this system. How do you shelter your children from the onslaughts of the world during those critical teenage years when, with hormones swirling furiously, temptations reach their zenith?

About this time Jack Wyrtzen devised a summer Bible camp for teenagers, a sanctuary for fundamentalist parents to send their children, a place where strict parietal rules would be enforced and, more important, where some sort of religious commitment would be exacted.

A SMALL PONTOON PROVIDES FERRY SERVICE between the western shores of Schroon Lake and Word of Life Island. As you approach, a boat-house with the legend A VERY SPECIAL ISLAND comes into view. Once on the landing, a sign welcomes you to Word of Life Island and, beyond that, a second notice warns: ALL VISITORS MUST REPORT TO THE OFFICE AND SIGN IN! A winding pathway leads to a large frame building called the Pine Pavilion.

The Pine Pavilion is a squarish building constructed on a hillside, with terraces of long, wooden benches sloping down toward the stage. Flags and red-white-and-blue bunting festoon the interior. In the northeast corner, a large wooden sign reads:

CHRIST WALKS ON THIS ISLAND
WILL YOU MEET HIM HERE?

Green porcelain warehouse-style lamps hang from the rafters.

The evening service begins at seven, and several announcements over a public-address system warn campers to be on time. Soon, a torrent of energetic campers tumbles into the building. Most of them are white and dressed in standard teenage fashions—tee-shirts, denims, sneakers, large, oversized sweatshirts.

Ten minutes into the meeting, as the sun sets across Schroon Lake, the Pine Pavilion is rocking. It's military week on the island, and the campers have been divided into Army and Navy teams. A series of games, challenges, and good-natured rivalry has been devised by the camp directors to generate spirit, teamwork, and enthusiasm. Apparently they've succeeded. Some of the counselors wear camouflage fatigues, and not infrequently amid the singing of various evangelical songs and choruses, the pavilion erupts in rival chants of "Army! Army!" and "Navy! Navy!" Each team sings its fight song—" Anchors Aweigh" and "The Caissons Keep Rolling Along"—accompanied by spirited stomping, and soon, amid all this excitement, the building begins to smell faintly of adolescent sweat.[3]

The crowd reverts to rhythmic clapping and stomping when a middle-aged man in a plaid, open-necked shirt plays "When the Roll Is Called Up Yonder" on his trumpet, triple-tonguing the second verse. When he finishes, more applause, shouting, hooting, and stomping. The pavilion quiets somewhat as a pretty blonde woman in her late teens, wearing a khaki skirt and a navy blazer, mounts the stage. She sings several songs to the accompaniment of taped music played over the sound system. After one of the songs, she exhorts the audience in a kind of breathless whisper: "It's so important to keep your standards high. You know, it's a nasty world out there." The next song, "Build on Higher Ground," reiterates that theme:

Build your house above the ocean.
Build your house on higher ground.
Build above the world's commotion
And its mesmerizing sound.

The music finishes with a flourish, and after an announcement encouraging campers to purchase a *Ryrie Study Bible* and books by Chuck Swindoll at the bookstore, the young soprano joins the trumpet player for a duet, "I've Just Seen Jesus," a fitting complement, I thought, to the sign in the northeast corner of the pavilion.

Jack Wyrtzen, a snowy-haired man in white pants and a floral-print tropical shirt, comes to the podium. He reminds the campers about some of the rules that govern life on the island. Everyone must wear a robe or sweat clothes to the beach. Shorts must be at least fingertip length. Word of Life promotional literature has already spelled out these regulations in some detail. "Please keep modesty in mind regarding all clothing," the literature counsels, adding that campers should bring a Bible and "sportswear for daytime activities, dress-up clothes (dress shirt and slacks for guys, dress for girls) for Sunday and some evening meals, modest onepiece bathing suit (I Tim. 2:9) and beach robe."[4]

Wyrtzen is an old fashioned, unvarnished fundamentalist. An affable, bespeckled man, his photographs in Word of Life promotional materials invariably show him with a large, open-mouthed grin, wearing an expression that suggests he has just told you the funniest joke in the world and is awaiting your reaction. He opens with a prayer asking God that everyone in the building will be "born again by the Word of God." Immediately thereafter, he asks how many in the audience have Bibles. Virtually everyone thrusts a Bible high into the air. As he announces this evening's text, he tells the audience that he hopes "before the night is done you will come to the Lamb of God." For the first nineteen years of his life, he says, "nobody told me about Jesus Christ" in the liberal churches he attended. The United States Army, in fact, is "the greatest denomination in the U.S.," because that's where Wyrtzen became a Christian.

Fundamentalists are fond of belittling the pretensions of mainline, liberal churches, and Wyrtzen is no exception. He uses certain code words or phrases to indicate his derision of theological liberals. The one he employs most often is "First Church." He will tell of some member of "First Church" who came to one of Wyrtzen's rallies, heard the gospel for the first time, and went away born again. Or some worldly woman, also a member of "First Church," who "got saved" at Word of Life and now is "on fire for the Lord." The audience, many of whom have apparently heard this nomenclature before, picks up on this right away, snorting disapprovingly at the reference to theological liberals and the putative name of their churches.

But tonight Wyrtzen is not interested in preaching to the converted; he wants to bring more of the unsaved into the fold. After telling of various sinners—including a woman he refers to as the "blonde bomber"—whose lives have been transformed by Jesus, and after warning of the torments of hell, he asks, "Have you been to Calvary?" He implores the campers to come to Jesus and leads them in a slow, mournful chorus that evokes Jesus' death at Calvary:

> Dying there for me,
> Dying there for me.
> Jesus died, was crucified.
> Dying there for me.

"You need to confess you are a sinner and believe Jesus died for you," Wyrtzen says. "Invite Him into your heart right now." Wyrtzen makes it easy, providing a formula prayer for the wavering: "Dear Jesus, I confess that I am a sinner. Thank you for dying on the cross for me. Come into my heart and save me now. Amen."

All heads are bowed. All eyes closed. The meeting's raucous beginning is long forgotten. Wyrtzen asks for a show of hands from those who prayed the prayer. A few timid arms reach upward. Wyrtzen acknowledges each one. "Yes, I see that hand. Is there another?" He pleads a bit longer and then closes the meeting with this stark admonition: "If you leave this building without Jesus, you're guilty of His crucifixion."

THE HARVEST TONIGHT IS DISAPPOINTING, but it's still early in the week. Wyrtzen has a whole stable of speakers, Bible teachers, and counselors who will hammer the message home in the next few days. The entire schedule, in fact, is calculated to produce a maximum yield of converts and rededications, those who publicly reaffirm their conversions and resolve to live holier lives.

The day begins with breakfast at eight, followed by a morning of Bible study. After lunch, the campers have an afternoon of play—swimming, water skiing, basketball, volleyball—before supper and the evening meeting, either a rally in the pavilion or around a campfire. After the meeting, the counselors organize more competitive games between the Army and Navy teams. Even with lights out at ten-thirty, fatigue sets in, what with all the fresh air, sunshine, and just plain fun. But that's part of the scheme as well, for there is a certain rhythm the organizers are trying to impose. The religious appeals begin early in the week at the rallies and in the morning sessions. By Wednesday evening's campfire, a sense of camaraderie, of shared experience, has set in. Campers are beginning to see their friends profess conversions or rededications, and nothing motivates an adolescent better than the example of his or her peers.

Figuring unpredictably into this mix is that confounding, exhilarating phenomenon: the summer romance. The people at Word of Life Island tolerate such courtships and even encourage them with a special dinner on Wednesday night to which boys are encouraged to bring dates. Parents back home, who are praying fervently for their child's spiritual renewal, also tolerate the courting that takes place at teen camp. They figure that their child's chances of meeting a nice Christian girl or boy at Bible camp are certainly greater than back home in a public high school. They trust Jack Wyrtzen and his staff, moreover, to police such romances carefully, lest passions run awry.

I kissed a girl for the first time at Bible camp—and, come to think of it, the second, third, and fourth times—all of it quite innocent, of course. Somewhere along the shores of Rainbow Lake a tree still bears the initials "R.B. + C.S.," chiseled into the bark with a jack-knife. Word of Life Island bears the markings of similar romances and infatuations, flames that burn brightly, last through several exchanges of letters, but then generally flicker and die before the leaves fall:

Erika & Howard
I love Dave
Dawn & John
Kyle + Deanna
Leon and Joan

Some have thoughtfully included the date in their memorials, as if establishing a statute of limitations:

85 Denise -n- John
I ♥ Joel Hoffman '86

Adolescent love is a sweet and wonderful thing, and if your beloved is a good Christian girl—"wholesome" is the adjective my parents always favored—then your resistance to the gospel weakens further.

By the time the Friday night campfire comes around, you are tired to the bone. You've never played so hard, swum so far, or slept so little. You are sunburned and mosquito-bitten; you have several proud bruises to show your sister. A sense of melancholy sets in because you know that tomorrow you must say goodbye to all the friends you've made at camp that week: the cabinmates who put corn flakes and shaving cream in the bottom of your sleeping bag and who helped you ambush one of the girls' cabins, the counselor who listened and became a friend, and most of all the lovely girl with the cornflower-blue eyes seated next to you. You have been peppered

all week with invitations to receive Christ into your life and warnings about the fate of those who refuse. You may not have another
chance, you are told; Jesus may come at any time—before the week
is out, before morning, even before the campfire ends. Don't let Him
find you unsaved. It's easy. Come to Jesus. Just ask Him into your
heart and live for Him.

The counselors at Word of Life Island refer to the Friday
campfire as the "say so" meeting, taken from Psalm 107:2: "Let the
redeemed of the Lord say so." Other Bible camps have different
names. "Testimony service" or "afterglow" are rather common. Some
camps used to refer to the final campfire, quite seriously, as a "faggot
fire," a reference to the practice of grabbing the unburned end of
one of the embers and tossing it into the fire as you begin your testimony about what Jesus has done in your life that past week. There
is an illusion of spontaneity in these services, but for anyone who
has witnessed more than a couple of them at Bible camps across the
country, there is a remarkable uniformity to these gatherings. Having
stared into a few fundamentalist campfires myself, I well remember
the rhythms, the emotions, the ritualized adolescent behavior that
takes place around the fire.

The service at Word of Life Island opens with singing; one of the
counselors has supplied a guitar. The purpose of the say so meeting,
another counselor informs the gathering, is to provide a chance for
campers to tell what the Lord has done in their lives. He continues:
"I'd just like to begin by saying that I've grown a lot this week. Pastor
Jim's Bible studies have taught me a lot about what it means to be a
Christian and to live for the Lord. I don't know about the rest of you,
but I just praise the Lord for Pastor Jim and for the insight God has
given him into the Scriptures."[5]

A few appreciative murmurs follow and then a short silence as half
a dozen people sitting there in the encroaching darkness summon
the courage to stand and address the other campers. The fire is still
struggling to take hold. The sun has just disappeared beyond the

ridge at the west end of the lake, and all eyes are adjusting to the twilight.

There are no takers yet, the Spirit hasn't yet moved, so the guitarist begins strumming the chords for "Cum by Yah," and after the first few bars everyone joins in:

> Cum by yah, my Lord, cum by yah.
> Cum by yah, my Lord, cum by yah.
> Cum by yah, my Lord, cum by yah.
> O, Lord, cum by yah.

The plaintive, doleful melody functions as a kind of invocation: Come here, Jesus, and grace this gathering with Your presence.

Once the music dies, Joyce Johnson is ready. She rises confidently to her feet. All eyes move briefly from the fire to see who is talking and then, after a moment, settle back on the flames. There will be no dramatic confession here; Joyce Johnson, everyone at camp knows by now, is too good for that. Instead, this is a kind of homily disguised as self-disclosure. "I've been coming to camp ever since I was eight years old," she begins, "and once again the Lord has really worked in my life. He's shown me some new things out of His Word this week, and I know I'll be a better witness for the Lord during this next year." The tone then shifts from self-congratulatory to admonitory. "If anybody here isn't a Christian, my prayer is that you'll accept Jesus as your savior before tonight is over, before you leave this island tomorrow. You may never have another chance to receive Jesus into your heart."

After a decent interval, Candy Schroeder stands. "I'm not sure what I'm gonna say," she confesses with an uneasy chuckle, "but I wanted to tell you what the Lord has been doing in my life. For a while now I've been seeking the Lord's will for my life, and I've been praying for His guidance—especially to know what to do after I graduate from high school next year." She pauses, then wipes the corners of her eyes with the back of her hand. The length of the silence is uncomfortable for those seated around the fire, and only a few steal a glance at Candy, standing there in denims and a loose, gray sweatshirt. "I'm just so grateful to my parents," she continues between sobs, "and to everyone who has prayed for me. On Tuesday during the missionary hour, the Lord just spoke to my heart. When Reverend Hunt told about the millions of unsaved people down in Argentina, I just knew that the Lord was calling me to be a missionary to all those people who have never heard the gospel, to all those people—" she pauses again, biting her lower lip, "to all those people who are lost without Jesus." A dozen "amens" greet this happy news, and they are repeated sporadically as Candy Schroeder reveals her plans to attend a Bible institute after high school and then go to South America as a missionary.

Paul Snyder, a big, strapping kid of fourteen, is next. "I didn't grow up in a Christian home," he says. "In fact, my parents are members of the Lutheran church back in Easton, Pennsylvania, and they didn't want me to come. When my friend Mike here invited me to Word of Life, I wasn't sure, either, but then he told me how much fun it was, so I convinced my mom and dad to let me come." The fire is thriving now, shooting flames and sparks upward into the darkness like a kind of offering. The mosquitos have arrived, searching for patches of flesh. A small motorboat trolls by, its green and red lights slicing through the darkness. "I sure am glad I came, though, because on Thursday night after the rally I gave my life to Christ. I had always thought I was a Christian because I went to church with my parents. But when I asked Don, my counselor, if I was going to heaven, he told me that unless I asked Jesus into my heart I would go to hell when I died. Well," Paul continues, halting slightly, "I gave my life to Christ. I'm a new, baby Christian. I'm going to read my Bible every day and tell all my friends at school about the Lord."

The guitarist thinks it's time for another song:

Seek ye first the kingdom of God
and His righteousness
and all these things shall be added unto you.
Hallelu-hallelujah.

The sweet, soft words echo across the lake. Paul Snyder's testimony has stirred something inside of Amy Durkin, because last year at this time she, too, gave her life to Jesus for the first time. She remembers now the feeling, the euphoria, and also her resolve to live a Christian life.

"I became a Christian here at camp last summer," Amy says, almost apologetically. "But once school started I fell in with the wrong crowd. Many of my friends are worldly, and I thought I was a strong enough Christian to stand up to them—" she begins to cry, "but I wasn't. Pretty soon I was just as worldly as the rest of them— going to movies and dances and stuff like that." Amy stops to regain her composure. The mournful cry of a loon reverberates across the lake. "But this year is going to be different. I've rededicated my life to the Lord this week, and I'm going to live for Him and bring my Bible with me to school every day and witness to my friends."

There are countless subtle variations to this rededication soliloquy, but most of them recount a previous commitment to Christ and a resolve to maintain high standards of godliness in the midst of a sinful and decadent world. But somehow, something went wrong—perhaps the lack of parental support or the absence of a good church youth program. Most often, however, even the most resolute convert from Bible camp caves in to peer pressure. "It's not easy being a Christian in my high school," is a familiar refrain.

Indeed not. If being a Christian as the people here define it means abstaining from drinking, smoking, dancing, movies, and perhaps even bowling and roller-skating (because of their "worldly" connotations), it doesn't take long for an evangelical high school student to become a pariah among his or her peers—or, more frequently, a kind of cipher on the social scene. The options then become either finding a new support network—a church youth group, perhaps—or compromising your fundamentalist scruples in order to fit in with your peers. If your parents are evangelical Christians, they want you to do the former, of course, but doing so exacts a price. It's not easy turning your back on your peers, rejecting the companionship and approval of friends at school for the comparatively unfulfilling friendships of people your own age at church.

No, it's not easy being an evangelical in high school. Carl Watkins, I think, understands that. For some time now I had been watching him shift uneasily on the stony ground; he seemed to be summoning the courage to get up and speak. Now, finally, Carl unfolds his tall, gangly frame, shuffles his feet uneasily, and clears his throat.

"My father is a preacher," Carl begins, "so I was raised in a Christian home. But I haven't always lived a good Christian witness. I'm not even sure that the kids at school know I'm a Christian." Carl stares at his shoetops. "I mean, sometimes I go out drinking with my friends. I know that's not right. I know that's not what the Lord wants me to do, but, I don't know, I just do it."

As he continues his halting confession, I begin to see myself in Carl Watkins. I see a Little Leaguer who had to miss all his Wednesday games, even the all-star game, because Wednesday was prayer-meeting night. I see in Carl Watkins an eighth-grader forced to sit on the sidelines during square dances in gym class and a teenager who couldn't wear bluejeans to school because his parents thought they would damage his Christian testimony. I see a high school graduate who never overcame his sense of alienation from his peers.

"I don't mean to hurt my parents," Carl continues, his voice cracking now, "but I guess, I don't know, that I always feel like I'm supposed to be perfect, to be this super-Christian at church and at school. But I'm not." Carl thrusts his hands deep into his pockets and shrugs his shoulders. "I really love my mom and dad. And I'm so grateful to the Lord for allowing me to grow up in a Christian home."

I also see in Carl Watkins a teenager contemplating the consequences of his rebellion, recounting sermon illustrations about eternity—time utterly without end, going on and on and on. If a tiny sparrow flew around the world and took a sip from the ocean at each pass, so the sermon illustration goes, by the time the ocean was dry, eternity would only have begun. Eternity was an awfully long time to be burning in hell, that lake of fire and brimstone.

"I ask you to pray for me this year," Carl concludes, "as I try to live a good Christian life." His gaze rests on the flames for a brief moment, and then he sits down. The fire crackles and spits sparks into the air. Carl Watkins reaches back and turns up the collar of his jacket against the sudden autumn chill that whips across the lake. Off to the east, a new moon hangs in the late-August darkness. Carl shifts once more and squeezes the hand of the girl with the cornflower-blue eyes seated next to him.

IN ANOTHER ERA, IN ANOTHER CAMP, I sat next to a fire and shifted uneasily on the stony ground. My repeated attempts to appropriate the faith of my parents were desultory and imperfect, as I realized even then. Summer camp was where I tried annually to get it right, to conjure the same piety that my elders showed, to claim the elusive "victory in Christ" that they professed. More often than not, what I felt instead was defeat and inadequacy, a gnawing sense that the persistent doubts I harbored about God and Christianity or my occasional transgressions of the fundamentalist behavioral codes would consign me to damnation.

Therein lay the conundrum. What I did not see then—indeed, *could* not have seen—was that the "gospel" presented to me was really an adumbration of the New Testament "good news." Much of the news I heard was bad—that I deserved damnation for my sinfulness and that if I didn't do something about it quickly I would certainly receive my just deserts. The solution to the predicament, as I understood it, was not to rely utterly on the grace of God, as Martin Luther recognized in the sixteenth century; rather, the way of salvation seemed to lay in subscribing to a set of doctrines and then hewing to strict standards of morality, usually expressed in negative terms: Don't dance, drink, smoke, swear, or attend movies.

That differed, I suspect, from the message that brought my parents into the evangelical fold. They heard about their sinfulness, yes, but the complementary element of the law is God's grace, which saves us in spite of ourselves. Therein, as Luther realized, lies true freedom and liberation—not in the observance of tiresome moralistic schemes, but in the celebration of deliverance from sin in Christ. In time, first-generation evangelical converts learn the canon of evangelical taboos, but only *after* their experience of grace. For their children, however, the sequence often is reversed. As an evangelical parent, if you are concerned (understandably) about the spiritual welfare of your children, you will establish guidelines for them so they will grow up in the faith, or, more accurately, grow up with all the trappings of godliness. Their "conversions" then become adolescent (or pre-adolescent) rites of passage, often accompanied by fabricated emotions in order to convince their peers, their parents, and, most important, themselves of their sincerity.

The difficulty, however, is that Christianity has already been defined for them in behaviorial terms—do this, don't do that—rather than in terms that Luther would have approved: We all are sinners by dint of *who we are*, not *what we do*, and therefore we rely abjectly on God's mercy. For a child in a fundamentalist household, a second-generation evangelical who already adheres to most of the standards of "godly" behavior, it is difficult to grasp the significance of any such conversion, since it demands no alteration of behavior. Instead of assurance, very often they feel anger and resentment because their conversions failed to deliver the religious euphoria and freedom from doubt implied in their parents' promises.

What brings Carl Watkins and Amy Durkin back to Word of Life Island year after year, I suspect, is the same mixture of motivations that took me back to Rainbow Lake summer after summer during my teenage years. Our parents want us there, in the first place, not only because Bible camp offers a sheltered, protective environment, but also because of their abiding hope that we will someday, somehow claim their faith as our own. That's easier to do, of course, in the company of those who have professed their own conversions—certainly much easier than the alien godless environment of the public schools back home.

Aside from the perennial, elusive quest for summer romance, we are at camp, many of us, for the same reason that our parents want us there. We too want to claim the faith, not merely to win our parents' approval, but also because of a deep yearning for a religious experience that will meet our expectations and dispel our anxieties. We seek above all an experience that will yield the same spiritual fulfillment we see (or think we see) in our parents. That experience comes to some. Others grasp it for a time and then lose it, year after year. Still others find the standards too high and abandon the quest in frustration or despair.

For people of faith, of course, and for people who want to pass their faith to the next generation, there is no easy solution to this predicament. Abandoning children to their own devices violates everything evangelicals believe about nurture, and yet mapping their children's spiritual pilgrimages may, in the end, deprive them of the kind of forceful, dramatic conversion that shaped their parents' lives.

Will evangelicalism, then, inevitably suffer from a gradual enervation of religious ardor as the faith passes from one generation to the next? Sociologists like Max Weber, who talks about the routinization of religion, insist that the answer is yes. Fervent evangelical parents pray that the answer is no.

1987

CHAPTER 6

Georgia Charismatics

I N VALDOSTA, GEORGIA, a large billboard looms over North Valdosta Road, a winding, four-lane divided highway on the outskirts
of town. On a white background next to a bejeweled crown, tall,
bold letters spell out: CHURCH OF THE KING. Beneath that, a smaller
sign reads:

> **Sunday 10:30 AM & 7:00 PM Thursday 7:00 PM**
> **Stan J. White, Pastor**

The sign is tasteful and artistic, but it is also quite conspicuous, even
from a distance, part of the Mail Pouch Tobacco genre of American roadside advertising that grabs you by the lapels and demands your attention.

Less than a hundred feet away, in front of a parking lot and a gray
cinder-block warehouse, the same people responsible for the billboard have planted another, much smaller sign, perhaps three feet
wide and four feet high. You have to walk close to see the fine print
at the bottom, but it also reads CHURCH OF THE KING. Above that, a
familiar shield on a light blue and white background:

> **THE**
> **EPISCOPAL CHURCH**
> **WELCOMES YOU**

Therein lies a story.

THE NAME EMBLAZONED on the billboard belongs to a man in his late twenties with chiseled features and a slight frame. Stan White has dark hair and deep eyes that are brooding but not unfriendly. He carries a gentle and unprepossessing mien of seriousness about him; he's the fellow who asked too many questions in your high school algebra class. He comes to the office during the week dressed casually; on Good Friday, 1990, for instance, he wore a meticulously starched button-down shirt, designer denims, and boat shoes with white sweatsocks.

The prep-school attire, however, is misleading. Stan White has impeccable pentecostal credentials and boasts that he is a fourth-generation pentecostal preacher. "I'm very proud of my pentecostal heritage," he insists. White's great-great uncle, a Missionary Baptist preacher, had a pentecostal experience about 1908 and was promptly kicked out of the Missionary Baptist denomination. He then joined the Assemblies of God when it was organized at Hot Springs, Arkansas, in 1914. White's grandfather and grandmother were also ordained in the Assemblies of God, as was his father, James White, a native of Columbus, Georgia, who served churches in southern California and Florida before returning to Georgia twenty-five years ago to take over a struggling Assembly of God in Valdosta. James White, a handsome, white-haired gentleman known affectionately to his many devoted followers as "Brother Jimmy," guided Evangel Assembly of God from a handful of people in 1968 into one of Valdosta's largest congregations, with two weekly television broadcasts, a fifteen-hundred-seat auditorium, and approximately three million dollars in assets.

In the early 1980s, Stan White, after two years at Valdosta State College and a job in data processing at an oil company in Houston, felt a call to the ministry. He joined the pastoral staff of his father's church as minister of music in 1982. In the ensuing years the elder White, edging toward retirement, asked his son to take on more and more of the pastoral duties at Evangel. About this time, in the mid-eighties, some extraordinary changes began to take place in Stan's life and, by extension, in the life of the congregation at Evangel Assembly of God.

"Evangel had always been a teaching church," White explained, and beginning in 1984 or thereabouts the church started to talk about what it meant to worship God. "I began to understand the importance of worship," he said, "as more than just preaching followed by an altar call." White still believed then, as he does now, in the "present reality of the Holy Spirit. That doesn't mean that we speak in tongues in our worship services. Rather, we believe in tongues as a personal devotional experience." The "present reality of the Holy Spirit" manifested itself at Evangel Assembly of God in lively and spontaneous services marked by outstretched arms, dancing, clapping, and shouting.

Despite the spirited worship, however, White sensed that something was missing from the services, and he grew increasingly uneasy with the altar calls week after week that seemed to be directed toward winning new converts rather than nurturing those already within the fold. White turned to church history. Growing up pentecostal, he explained, he had little understanding of anything that had happened before the Azusa Street pentecostal revivals in Los Angeles just after the turn of the century. While reading Irenaeus and other church fathers, White became convinced that the early church had been both liturgical and sacramental, and that seemed to suggest that pentecostalism, despite its insistence upon the gifts of the Spirit as described in the Book of Acts, hadn't fully appropriated the richness of worship in the early church.

In pentecostalism, White explained, the sacraments are called "ordinances," and Evangel Assembly of God in Valdosta observed the Lord's Supper once a month at most and sometimes as infrequently as once a year. "We didn't treat them with any respect or dignity," he said. In the midst of rethinking evangelical worship, White became seized with what he calls an "ecumenical spirit." He studied Roman

Catholicism as well as Anglicanism, Lutheranism, and other high-church traditions. A friend gave him a copy of the Episcopal *Book of Common Prayer*, which White began using in his private devotions. Most important, he attended a liturgical church and, much to his surprise, felt a spiritual quickening. "I experienced God there," White said, his voice still registering astonishment several years after the event. "That wasn't supposed to happen. It shocked me."

Gradually, and somewhat tentatively, White shared some of his thinking with his family and with his Assembly of God congregation. He began to teach about church history, the creeds, and the sacraments. "We started incorporating some of those elements into our worship," he said, including a weekly celebration of the Lord's Supper. By 1987 Evangel Assembly of God in Valdosta, Georgia, was very likely the only pentecostal church in the nation to open its services with a processional.

A large segment of the congregation greeted these changes with enthusiasm, others with curiosity, even bemusement. Still others weren't so sure. On Thursday, August 11, 1988, the deacons called an emergency board meeting to remove Stan White as pastor. His father, James, who was semiretired by then and who had built the church from virtually nothing, tendered his resignation as well.

"I thought at the time, 'Well, it's over,'" Stan White recalled. If he still sounded a trifle defensive about the incident, he seemed not at all bitter. "They said my theology was newfangled," he said. "They didn't realize that my theology was old."

AT TEN MINUTES OF SEVEN O'CLOCK on Good Friday, 1990, a half dozen automobiles and pickup trucks gathered in the parking lot of Church of the King, the warehouse on North Valdosta Road that once served as a boat showroom. A small group of people, ranging in age from mid-teens to mid-sixties, congregated outside the door. Each new arrival set off another round of greeting and hugging. Nearly everyone carried two books: a Bible and a red leather deluxe edition of the *Book of Common Prayer*. Whereas the Bibles were worn and well-thumbed, the prayer books quite obviously were new, the gilded edges barely disturbed. These were celebratory, commemorative editions, for in two days, on Easter Sunday evening, the people gathered here, together with about two hundred of their fellow congregants from Church of the King, would be confirmed in the Episcopal Church.

Although the conversation occasionally touched on other matters, it quickly veered back to the events coming on Sunday night. "We're so excited, we can hardly stand it," one woman remarked before breaking into giddy laughter. "This is all still pretty new to us," a man explained, "but I think we're ready."

Ready or not, they had not come this far on impulse alone. After Stan White's ouster from Evangel Assembly of God, a number of people from that congregation urged him to start his own church and to continue combining pentecostal worship with liturgical forms. White claims that beginning another church was the farthest thing from his mind; he had no intention of dividing Evangel Assembly of God even more than it already was. "We're not rebellious people," he insisted. "We're not fighting people." The entreaties mounted nevertheless, and after consulting with his family and with other members of his former congregation, he decided to relinquish his Assemblies of God credentials and to announce a meeting for those who might be interested in forming a new church. Two hundred fifty showed up for what became the first gathering of Church of the King. Starting a church from scratch, however, proved to be no easy task. "We didn't have so much as a paper clip," White said. The fledgling congregation met at two other locations—a furniture warehouse and the city auditorium—before moving to the warehouse on North Valdosta Road.

Intellectually, White kept moving as well. He maintains that he was scrupulous about not violating Assemblies of God theology while at Evangel, but the lack of denominational constraints at Church of the King afforded him considerable freedom to experiment. The clergy started wearing vestments, the congregation repeated several creeds, and Church of the King celebrated the Lord's Supper every Sunday.

As the congregation approached its first anniversary in August 1989, White observed forty days of fasting and prayer in order to seek guidance and direction for the church. It had been a good year, on balance, with strong and growing attendance, a number of outreach programs, and general satisfaction with the attempt to combine historic forms with charismatic fervor. Church of the King was also interracial, with African Americans accounting for about 30 percent of its membership. "One of our real missions," White said, "has been to break down the walls of prejudice."[1] White himself, however, was growing restless. "I wanted not merely to implement these historic creeds and practices, but also to identify with the historic church," he explained. "I suddenly had the sense that I was just bootlegging all this."

White initially resisted those sentiments, and the sentiment that followed was even more preposterous. "I felt my spirit drawn to the Episcopal Church, almost like a call," he said. "I'm not spooky spiritual or anything like that, but I felt drawn to the Episcopal Church." White demurred at first, sure that his family, his pastoral staff, and certainly his congregation wouldn't abide such a dramatic move. "I just didn't think they'd go for it," he said, "and even if they did, I was *sure* the Episcopalians wouldn't go for it."

Finally, after a protracted inner struggle, White said, "Okay, God, I'll make some inquiries." White remembered that he felt at the time a bit like Abraham preparing to sacrifice Isaac, his beloved son, because he was certain that everything he had worked for would crumble in ashes once he declared his intentions to seek affiliation with the Episcopal Church. White first floated the idea with an acquaintance, Jacoba Hurst, rector of St. Anne's Episcopal Church in Tifton, Georgia, who later told me he was so astonished by White's overture "that I thought he had been under some stress." Hurst and White talked for five hours the next day, at the conclusion of which Hurst telephoned Harry W. Shipps, Episcopal bishop of Georgia. "There was a long silence at the other end of the phone," Hurst recalled, but he succeeded in setting up a discreet meeting. The bishop was a trifle skeptical at first, but White's earnestness and sincerity persuaded him to accede.

White then had to confront his congregation. His voice timid and anxious, he asked permission to pursue affiliation with the Episcopal Church, careful to point out that it was a long process and that their efforts might be derailed at any one of several junctures. "The words were barely out of my mouth," White recounted, "before the entire congregation rose from its chairs in a standing ovation."

CHURCH OF THE KING is by no means the Episcopal Church's first encounter with the charismatic movement. In the fall of 1959 the Reverend Dennis J. Bennett, rector of St. Mark's Episcopal Church in Van Nuys, California, began to speak in tongues. "It was an entirely rational experience, without hysteria or frenzy," he explained later. "One expresses without understanding. But you know it's love and devotion toward God. The exact meaning seems to come later, when you have developed the gift."[2] Bennett, himself born and reared in London, shared this discovery with his pastoral staff at St. Mark's, and soon other members of the suburban, upper-middle-class parish also began speaking in tongues.

Other parishioners looked askance at this new phenomenon. For Episcopalians, known to some wags as "God's frozen chosen," this was new and alien territory. With the endorsement of the bishop of Los Angeles, the vestry of St. Mark's secured Father Bennett's resignation. "It's a good thing this is all cleared up," one older parishioner remarked. "We're Episcopalians, not a bunch of wildeyed hillbillies!"[3]

Bishop Francis Eric Bloy of Los Angeles assigned a new priest to Van Nuys and expressly forbade speaking in tongues under Episcopal auspices in his diocese. Bennett accepted a call to St. Luke's, a mission parish in Seattle. His ministry there, marked once again by emotive outpourings of the Holy Spirit, transformed a dying church into one of the largest, most vibrant parishes in the nation.

In the three decades since the outbreak of *glossolalia* in Van Nuys, the charismatic renewal movement has taken hold within the

Episcopal Church, although it has by no means met with universal approbation. Some of the most salubrious parishes in the nation— St. Luke's in Seattle, Church of the Redeemer in Houston, St. Paul's in Darien, Connecticut—count themselves part of the charismatic renewal. In Darien, two parishes vie for the allegiance of the town's Episcopalians: St. Luke's, a traditional, highbrow parish, what some Britons might revile as "Tories on their knees," and St. Paul's, the charismatic parish.

The charismatic movement has caught on in other liturgical traditions as well, most notably in the Roman Catholic Church. In the winter of 1967 four members of the Duquesne University faculty, all of them Roman Catholics, attended a Protestant charismatic prayer meeting in Pittsburgh. There they received "spiritual blessings." Soon, similar stirrings occurred among Roman Catholics on other campuses, and by June 1967 Catholic charismatics organized a conference at the University of Notre Dame. The conference has taken place annually since then, growing each year, a reflection of the vitality of the charismatic movement within American Catholicism.

There is a general pattern to the growth of the charismatic movement. A group of people within a liturgical or high-church tradition seeks some kind of spiritual presence, a sense of immediacy or even of emotional fulfillment, so they turn to pentecostal or charismatic forms. These spiritual expressions, nevertheless, are rooted within their liturgical traditions. What makes the goings-on in Valdosta so extraordinary is that, in the case of Church of the King, the pattern was reversed. Here, a group of charismatics sought to ground their evangelical and spiritual vitality within the historic church.

That is not to say that individual evangelicals have not been drawn to liturgical traditions. Indeed, in recent years a large number of evangelicals have become enamored of high-church liturgy, especially that of the Episcopalians. The "evangelicals on the Canterbury trail" phenomenon has been well documented.[4] The Episcopal Church has attracted many young, educated evangelicals, in part because of the popularity of C. S. Lewis, an Anglican churchman, and also because it appeals to their sense of history, tradition, and aesthetics. Other evangelicals have gravitated to the sacramentalism of the liturgical church. Martin Luther's assault on the Roman Catholic doctrine of transubstantiation—that the bread and wine *actually become* Christ's body and blood in the course of the mass, even though they retain the outward appearance of bread and wine—prompted a rethinking of the sacraments and opened the door for other reformulations of sacramental theology. Although Luther (and Lutherans, his spiritual heirs) maintained a "high" view of the Lord's Supper, the theology of other Reformers reduced the bread and wine to mere symbols of the body and blood of Christ. Indeed, most American evangelicals have adopted Ulrich Zwingli's memorialist view of Holy Communion—the Lord's Supper merely *reminds* us of the death of Christ—rather than Luther's understanding that the communicant actually partakes of the grace of God.

A more exalted view of the sacraments also signals a subtle shift in theology. Traditionally, American evangelicals have defined conversion as an instantaneous, datable experience of grace akin to St. Paul's conversion on the road to Damascus and consonant with evangelicals' generally dualistic view of the world—good *versus* evil, righteousness *versus* unrighteousness. A fuller sacramental theology implies that God *continually* imparts grace to the believer in ways we cannot fully comprehend. The Christian life, in this view, is less a radical redirection than a spiritual pilgrimage.

The aesthetic deprivation so characteristic of evangelical worship should not be dismissed, either, as a factor in evangelicals' attraction to liturgical traditions. Many evangelicals, having grown weary of the relentless quest for novelty and innovation in evangelical worship, have opted instead for the ancient traditions of creed and liturgy that often come packaged with the strains of Bach, Mozart, and Haydn.

Most evangelicals, however, generally look askance at Episcopalians because—well, because Episcopalians have frequently looked askance at them. The United States has no established religion in the sense of a state church, but no denomination in America is more identified with the establishment—those who control wealth and power—than the Episcopalians.[5] Of the nation's forty-one presidents, twelve have been Episcopalians; twenty out of one hundred United States senators—one-fifth—identify themselves as Episcopalians, a representation far greater than their proportion in the American population. For much of this century, on the other hand, evangelicals have felt themselves cut off from the corridors of wealth and power and influence. They feel awkward with the formalism and ceremony of high-church liturgy. "I'm always uncomfortable in an Episcopal church," a Methodist told me once. "I feel like I'm at a fancy dinner party, and I'm never sure which fork to use."

Despite the growth of the charismatic movement, then, and the gravitation of some evangelicals to liturgical traditions, Church of the King, an entire charismatic congregation seeking affiliation with the Episcopal Church, remains something of an anomaly. This is not a congregation consisting overwhelmingly of educated, professional, upwardly mobile evangelicals. South Central Georgia has much to recommend it, with pine trees alternating with grassy fields and peach trees in neat, carefully calibrated rows. This is Baptist country (I tried to tally the number of Baptist churches between Albany and Valdosta, but I quickly lost count). Many of the restaurants in Valdosta will take a dollar off the price of your Sunday dinner if you can produce a bulletin as proof that you attended church that morning. Despite its undeniable charms, however, Valdosta, Georgia, hardly strikes a casual observer as the crossroads of culture, and that makes Church of the King's pilgrimage from pentecostalism to the Episcopal Church all the more extraordinary.

"I envision a church that is fully charismatic, fully evangelical, but also fully liturgical and sacramental," Stan White told me. "We want to see all those elements alive and working simultaneously."

CAROLYN DINKINS, an affable, attractive woman in her late thirties, sets a bountiful table at her lakefront home outside of Valdosta. She absented herself early from the Sunday morning service on Easter to complete preparations for the noon meal. Robert, her husband, stayed longer in order to socialize after the service and also, it seemed, to augment the guest list. Carolyn Dinkins took it in stride, and when it was time to sit down to macaroni and cheese, string beans, squash, creamed corn, roast venison, country stuffed sausages, apple cobbler, and buttermilk biscuits with Georgia cane syrup, more than a dozen people had gathered, a congenial mixture of visitors and old friends. Ed and Jane Black had driven down from the Atlanta area to witness the day's events. Gordon and Blake Weisser, retirees from Houston, put Valdosta on their itinerary when they read about Church of the King in an Episcopal newsletter.

For the Dinkinses, Ken and Rachel Reeves fall into the category of old friends. The Reeveses lived in Valdosta until recently; now they manage a trailer park in Dade City, Florida, but they hope to move back to Georgia soon. Patricia and Bennett Thagard are farmers outside of Valdosta. Bennett, a rugged, burly man, possesses a ready smile and a bone-crushing handshake, both of which have assumed the status of legend among the congregants at Church of the King. "When people found out a few years ago that Bennett Thagard had become a Christian," Ann White, Stan's mother, had told me on Friday evening, "they just couldn't believe it. 'Bennett Thagard?' they said. But let me tell you, the Lord just got a-hold of him!"

The Sunday table was abuzz with the historical significance of the confirmations that would take place that evening. The Prayers of the People at Church of the King that morning had included the petition that God would "do his thing tonight." Before dinner at the Dinkins home, the guests had gathered in the spacious kitchen and held hands in a large circle while Robert Dinkins prayed. He had acknowledged before God "the momentous occasion" ahead and asked that "the Holy Spirit will be there in all its power tonight." The excitement was building, even among the visitors. "When Gordon and I went to Canterbury," Blake Weisser, the voluble guest from Houston, said, "I felt like a pilgrim. Today I feel like a pilgrim in Valdosta." Robert Dinkins recounted his own pilgrimage. "I started attending Evangel Assembly of God in 1961," he said. "I used to be a segregationist till God turned me around." Dinkins recalled his initial misgivings about Stan White and his movement toward the high church. "He made me so mad sometimes," he said, shaking his head, but the more Dinkins studied the Bible for himself, the more persuaded he became that White was on to something. "The Lord began to lead the congregation into uncharted areas as far as the pentecostal movement is concerned."

Ken Reeves recalled his dismay when he learned that the deacons at Evangel Assembly of God had dismissed White. He and Dinkins tried to fight it at first. "We made it clear to the deacons that they weren't speaking for us," Reeves said. Several days later, however, a sense of peace descended upon Dinkins as he was driving home. "The Lord told me, 'I have done this thing. I have confused the deacons' minds.' By the time I got home," Dinkins said, "I had peace about it."

When I asked those gathered around the table what their emotions might be at their confirmation that evening, Carolyn Dinkins responded first. "It's a blessing that we're about to receive," she said. "We anticipate that something supernatural will happen to us." Rachel Reeves said, "I believe a divine impartation is going to take place tonight." Robert Dinkins went even further. "We really anticipate that the power will be so great that the priests won't be able to stand because of the presence of the Holy Spirit."

As part of the congregation's preparation for confirmation, the bishop had imposed a sacramental fast from mid-January, when he accepted them into the Episcopal Church as baptized members, until their confirmation on Easter Sunday evening. When I asked if there was a sense that they felt hungry for the bread and wine of Holy Communion, everyone around the table nodded. Carolyn Dinkins dredged up her best southern accent: "We are *ready* for the sacrament, honey!"

THE INTERIOR OF CHURCH OF THE KING, the former boat showroom, has been tastefully decorated in cool colors. The steel beams supporting the roof are white, with long rows of fluorescent lights suspended from them. The cinder-block walls sport a fresh coat of paint the color of eggshells tinted ever so slightly with a lavender hue. The carpet is plush and purple, and the congregation sits on comfortable chairs upholstered in a gray tweed fabric.

The decor may be cool, but the service is anything but cold. At six-forty-five the music started, loud and lively and celebratory. The congregation rose spontaneously to its feet:

> He's alive again.
> The stone's been rolled away.
> He's alive again.
> He's no longer where He lay.
> He's alive again,
> I can hear the angels say,
> "Let all the world rejoice, He's alive."[6]

Gregg Kennard, the church's minister of music, directed the fifty-voice choir and the orchestra—three trumpets, a violin, a flute, two clarinets, an electric bass guitar, and a percussion section, including timpani—from behind the keyboard of a synthesizer.

By the time the orchestra segued into the next song, "Celebrate Jesus, Celebrate!" some hands were clapping, while others flailed the air. "Let's bless the Lord," Kennard shouted into his microphone. The congregation obliged with arms beating the air in ecstasy. Each song dissolved seamlessly into the next; the congregation appeared to know—through intuition or practice, I couldn't be sure which—how to respond to each one. When the tempo picked up for "Sing unto the Lord a New Song," the congregation quickened its pace and began dancing, a kind of quick, rhythmic hopping from one foot to the other, with arms swinging up and back in a bouncy military swagger. Midway through "Sing unto the Lord a New Song," Church of the King looked more like Tuesday night aerobics class than Easter Sunday in an Episcopal parish.

Outside the sanctuary, crucifer, acolytes, dancers, thurifer, clergy, and bishops fell into line during "How Magnificent is Your Name,

O Lord," a loud and stately march. The acolytes in their new red cassocks looked a bit unsteady, their eyes shifting furtively as they processed around the back of the auditorium and up the center aisle, leaving the pungent, sweet smell of incense in their wake. The visiting clergy, Episcopal priests from all over the diocese and from other dioceses as well, numbered two dozen. They processed just behind the pastoral staff of Church of the King and sat in a special section to the right of the altar. Four bishops wearing miters and dressed in their liturgical finery brought up the rear, followed by Bishop Shipps, a tall, bearded man walking with his crozier, the symbol of his office.

There had been an almost palpable air of excitement in the auditorium since five o'clock that afternoon. The processional itself symbolized the extraordinary character of the evening's events—the venerable pageantry juxtaposed with loud and lively celebration—even as the music swelled toward a crescendo. With the cross and the banners in their stands, the clergy at their chairs, the dancers in repose, and the bishops at their stations, the singing finally reached a climax, whereupon the congregation, bishops and clergy included, broke into sustained and spontaneous applause.

Stan White, wearing a white surplice over a black cassock, stepped to the podium and savored the moment before leading the congregation in another song of praise. One of the bishops and several of the visiting clergy had their arms outstretched, the traditional pentecostal posture of praise to God and openness to the Holy Spirit. Only at the reading of the Psalm, well into the service, did the congregation sit down. "Happy are they who have not walked in the counsel of the wicked," the congregation said in unison, "nor lingered in the way of sinners, nor sat in the seats of the scornful."

My eyes wandered to the contingent of clergy seated in the section adjacent to me. When Jacoba Hurst brought Stan White, this erstwhile Assemblies of God pastor, before the commission on ministry for the Diocese of Georgia, Hurst feared that he had ushered White into the seat of the scornful. "Some of these guys are rather hostile, dour clerics who don't suffer fools gladly," Hurst told me. "They were reserved and cautious at first," he said, but then something extraordinary happened. "There was the presence of God in that room," Hurst said. "I couldn't speak. It was like some kind of revival." The committee interrogated White at some length and then asked him to withdraw so they could deliberate. Hurst noticed to his surprise that several members of the committee, these "hostile, dour clerics," were weeping. "I had a tremendous sense of destiny," he said about White's candidacy for ordination. "We felt that he was there by appointment from God. I really feel that he's been sent to the Episcopal Church."

John Howe, the bishop of Orlando, seemed to agree. When he strode to the podium to deliver the homily, he asked, "Are we having fun yet?" Judging by the congregation's enthusiastic response, the answer was Yes. "This is a very exciting evening," he said. "This is something, I think, of historic proportions." Howe's sermon referred both to the archbishop of Canterbury, the spiritual head of the worldwide Anglican communion, and Charles Parham, a pentecostal preacher from Topeka, Kansas, generally regarded as the progenitor of pentecostalism in America. Quoting a nineteenth-century Anglican churchman, Howe compared the Episcopal Church to a great carved marble fireplace and the spiritual ardor of nineteenth-century Methodists and twentieth-century pentecostals to a fire. The fire, Howe declared, belongs in the fireplace! "We welcome this congregation of charismatic Christians into our church," Howe said, whereupon the bishops, the priests, and the congregation responded with an ovation. "Let the fire loose in the fireplace," he bellowed in conclusion. "Amen!"

After yet another song, this one punctuated with rhythmic clapping, White stepped to the podium and echoed the refrain. Presenting his congregation as candidates for confirmation in the Episcopal Church, White addressed Bishop Shipps and said, "It's our desire to put the fire in the fireplace."

THE FIVE BISHOPS in all their high-church splendor spread out in front of the altar. Then the members of Church of the King, numbering well over two hundred, formed a single queue in the center aisle, each one waiting for the next available bishop. Each bishop dabbed oil on the candidate's forehead, laid his hands on the candidate, and recited the formula for confirmation from the *Book of Common Prayer:* "Strengthen, O Lord, your servant Rachel [or James or Nancy] with your Holy Spirit; empower her for your service; and sustain her all the days of her life. Amen." Each bishop, veteran of thousands of confirmations over the years, had his own style; the bishop nearest to me concluded each recitation with a smile and a light, playful slap on the cheek.

Many received their confirmations with outstretched arms. Not a few eyes were filled with tears, including those in the ranks of the clergy. The choir sang the Doxology in the background:

> Praise God, from whom all blessings flow.
> Praise him, all creatures here below.
> Praise him above, ye heavenly hosts.
> Praise Father, Son, and Holy Ghost.

Bennett and Patricia Thagard came forward, as did Ken and Rachel Reeves. Rachel's eyes were full when she turned away from the bishop; she sobbed after she returned to her seat. Robert Dinkins, the former segregationist, walked up the center aisle with Carolyn. As the queue began to thin out, Stan White announced, "If we've missed you, come on down.

After the congregation exchanged the peace, White stepped to the podium and introduced Bishop Shipps to a standing ovation. "I'm really not used to that kind of welcome," the bishop remarked, genuinely embarrassed. Then, recovering quickly: "I hope the clergy on my left will take note of it." Shipps said that the evening was "a very, very happy occasion for me," and added that it was "an Easter day that I will remember more clearly than any other in my life."

When White took the podium again, he ruminated a bit. He said that Church of the King sought "orthodox, creedal Christianity married and blended with the fire and vigor of the pentecostal experience." He recounted his own pentecostal roots: his great-great-uncle and his grandfather, both pentecostal preachers. His grandmother was also an Assemblies of God minister. White asked her to stand, one of the newest confirmands in the Episcopal Church. White then introduced his father, "Brother Jimmy," and his mother, Ann, also new Episcopalians.

Before the celebration of the Eucharist, Bishop Shipps consecrated the altar, a simple table of white marble that had been the object of considerable interest to members of the Friday evening prayer group. ("That's not at all what I expected, someone had remarked at the time.) During the Sunday morning service, Stan White had explained that the altar would be consecrated after the confirmations and before the celebration of the Eucharist that evening. "That doesn't mean you can't touch it or anything like that," he said. "It means only that the altar should be treated with reverence and respect." During that same service, at the conclusion of his extemporaneous homily, White had given an altar call, the script of which came straight from a Billy Graham crusade. He asked for all heads bowed and every eye closed. "You don't want to leave this place this morning," he implored, "without knowing that everything is right between you and God." White acknowledged each hand with a simple "yes" and then, as the synthesizer played softly in the background, offered a formula prayer for those seeking salvation. "Dear Jesus, I ask you to forgive me today," White intoned. "Cleanse me...wash me in your blood...make me righteous in your eyes."

With the consecration Sunday evening, Church of the King had a real altar, rather than the spiritualized altar most evangelicals refer to when they talk about "altar calls" or "laying all on the altar." "Sanctify this Table dedicated to you," the bishop prayed. "Let it be to us a sign of the heavenly Altar where your saints and angels praise you forever. Accept here the continual recalling of the sacrifice of your Son."

When it came time to receive Holy Communion—"the memorial of our redemption," in the words of the *Book of Common Prayer*—the celebrant held up the bread and the wine from the newly consecrated altar and announced "the gifts of God for the people of God." He invited the congregation to "take them in remembrance that Christ died for you, and feed on him in your heart by faith, with thanksgiving." The congregation queued up once more to receive the sacrament. A few genuflected, some dipped the wafer into the cup, a way of receiving known as intinction. Many turned away with tears in their eyes.

BY THE END OF THE RECESSIONAL (a reprise of "How Magnificent Is Your Name"), it was nine-thirty. The memorable service of "Confirmation, Consecration of an Altar, and a Celebration of the Holy Eucharist" had lasted more than two and a half hours. Euphoria had gradually given way to exhaustion. The congregation heaved a kind of collective sigh, and the reception afterward in the rear portion of the warehouse provided occasion to exchange congratulations and to evaluate the day's events. "If that don't move you, you got to be dead," one parishioner said breathlessly to another. "That's all I got to say."

Visitors were equally impressed. The Reverend Robert South had driven over six hundred miles from Belhaven, North Carolina, to witness the event. "This was so exciting, I had to come down," he said. "This is history in the making." Is this the wave of the future in the Episcopal Church? "I hope we don't stifle these people. I hope we'll adopt a lot of these things. This is what we should be doing." The Reverend Nan Peete, a black woman from the Diocese of Atlanta, also cited the event as "historic" and noted with satisfaction that Church of the King was "a truly integrated congregation." Peete's mother, who described herself as a high-church Episcopalian from Chicago, said, "It was just so different. It was wonderful, energizing, exciting!"

Bobby Ingram, another visitor, commended Stan White for his foresight. Ingram, headed for seminary in the fall, described himself as part of the "carnage" from a charismatic community in the Washington, D.C., area. There, he said, the leaders of the community became intoxicated with their own charisma and the power it afforded them. Ingram admired Stan White because he elected to "connect with some wisdom" by affiliating with a tradition that would hold him accountable lest he get carried away.

I asked the Reverend W. Birt Sams, a retired priest in the diocese, if he ever thought he would see anything like this evening. "Never, never," he said emphatically. "We have quite a lot of charismatic influence in this diocese," he added, "but this outdoes everything and anything we've ever had."

Many other Episcopalians concurred. Louise Shipps, the bishop's wife, said she was "overwhelmed" by the service. "We are really rejoicing in this," she said. "We are going to learn so much. We are being offered so much by these people." Brother Albert, an Episcopal monk dressed in a tunic and sandals, said simply, "This was quite an experience."

"I loved it," John King, an Episcopal layman from Waycross, Georgia, declared. "I think in about five years this church will be one of the largest in the diocese. It has an emotional appeal that a lot of the mainline churches don't have." Between bites of cookies, King tried to illustrate his point. "I defy you to either hum or whistle a song from the Episcopal hymanal," he said. The music at Church of the King, on the other hand, was lively and rhythmic. "People like that," he said.

Bishop Harry Shipps agreed. "I don't think this would go over big in Massachusetts," he acknowledged, but in the South, with its predominant evangelical ethos, Episcopalians are more attuned to evangelical sympathies. Judging from the overwhelmingly positive response he's had from other bishops, Shipps predicted broad acceptance of Church of the King within Episcopal circles. "Everybody," he said, "is just so excited about this." Although he anticipated that the "problem will be with liberals," he cited what he called the "remarkable unanimity" within the diocese. "I hope this is not an isolated phenomenon," he said. "I believe it's going to happen elsewhere. I'm convinced that the church catholic is going to include both Roman Catholics and pentecostals—and they're going to be a happy family."

Indeed, the Roman Catholics of Valdosta, at least, had weighed in with a large floral bouquet of "prayerful congratulations" to Church of the King. "If anyone had told me years ago that St. John's Catholic Church would be sending us flowers," Stan White remarked in the morning service, "I never would have believed them." The pentecostals in town were less forthcoming. When I asked James White, Stan's father, how his erstwhile colleagues in the Assemblies of God would react to the day's events, he shook his head. "I don't know if the Assemblies of God will pay any attention," he said sadly, "but they would probably dismiss it as a lapse into dead orthodoxy." Ann White was characteristically more direct. "I don't think they understand it at all," she said.

THE DIN OF THE FELLOWSHIP HALL began slowly to abate. The congregation, many of them newly rooted within historic Christianity, emerged from the sanctuary of Church of the King into the bracing air of a spring night in Georgia.

Throughout the evening Stan White wore a proud, fixed smile, the expression of a father having just announced the birth of his first child. His congregation's pilgrimage from the pentecostalism of Evangel Assembly of God to the charismatic fervor of Church of the King, rooted in the sacramentalism of the historic church, may have been long and gradual, but it had also been joyous, and it had culminated in sweet and unabashed celebration. No one, least of all Stan White, had second thoughts about the journey. "I see God's hand now," White said. "I'm almost thankful that the deacons released me. I can look back and see the providence of God."

1990

CHAPTER 7

Bible School

MULTNOMAH SCHOOL OF THE BIBLE sits on a tiny, seventeen-acre campus in a blue-collar residential neighborhood of Portland, Oregon. There is nothing even remotely distinguished about the campus. Whoever designed the buildings believed with a vengeance in the superiority of function over form and, accordingly, created an architectural paean to painted bricks and flat, warehouse-style roofs.

In all fairness, however, Multnomah officials cannot bear complete responsibility for the architectural atrocities on their campus; some of the buildings were already in place when the Bible school took possession from the Oregon State School for the Blind in 1952. The Bible-camp look at Multnomah nevertheless typifies an attitude toward culture and the arts that has been all too common among evangelicals in the twentieth century. They regarded aesthetics as a frivolity, an unspeakable luxury at a time when money could be better spent on missions or tracts or Sunday school curricula. When you add premillennialism to that mix, the doctrine that Jesus may return at any moment, you have further disincentive for investment in the arts. Why bother with worldly embellishments when this world is about to perish?

The students who enroll at Multnomah, however, care little about architectural niceties. They come to study the Bible. "I think that we do Bible better than most places," Ronald Frost, who teaches in the youth ministry program, declared. "That's the genius of the

Bible school." The school's motto, repeated endlessly in promotional materials, reads: "If it's Bible you want, then you want Multnomah." The school stipulates that 52 credits out of a total of 96 required for an associate degree or 128 for a bachelor's degree fall in the area of biblical literature and theology. Every student majors in Bible at Multnomah, and each may choose to specialize in one of the following fields: Christian education, music, missions, journalism, pastoral youth ministry, biblical languages, or women's ministries. The curriculum emphasizes basic biblical literacy, but it also offers an interpretive template through which to view the Bible. When I asked Duane Hallof, an upperclassman who also works part-time in the school's development department, to characterize Multnomah's theology, he replied, "Very conservative, but not limiting God. It's definitely not a charismatic school. They don't encourage the controversial gifts." Biblical inerrancy, he said, was "very high" on Multnomah's list of theological priorities, as was dispensationalism, the nineteenth-century doctrine of biblical interpretation that insisted that all of human history could be divided into ages or dispensations. When I asked Hallof whether *fundamentalist* applied to Multnomah, he became skittish. "It depends on what you mean by fundamentalist," he said warily.

Multnomah's theological pedigree, like that of many other Bible institutes in North America, is very much tied to that of Dallas Theological Seminary, which accounts for the strong emphasis on both biblical inerrancy and dispensationalism. Out of thirty-three full-time faculty at Multnomah, sixteen hold at least one degree from Dallas. John G. Mitchell, the school's founder, was a member of the first graduating class at Dallas Seminary, and he sought to bring its brand of evangelical theology to the Pacific Northwest when he mobilized a group of Portland-area ministers and businessmen behind his idea for a Bible school in 1936.

Accordingly, then, the curriculum includes courses in English Bible and theology as well as missions, evangelism, and spiritual life. B.A. students must learn New Testament Greek. Professors are eager both to demonstrate the internal harmony of the Scriptures and to advance particular interpretations. In a course on the Pentateuch, for example, the first five books of the Hebrew Bible, Professor Dale Wheeler devoted most of his fifty-minute class period to a demonstration that an apparent numerical discrepancy between Genesis and the Acts of the Apostles was really no contradiction whatsoever. "Does that blow the doctrine of inerrancy and inspiration?" he asked rhetorically after setting out the problem. "No, not at all." In the Acts passage, he said, Stephen was quoting from the Septuagint, which had the number wrong. "You will find places where writers quote sources that are inaccurate," Wheeler conceded, "but if it had been important to the point the Spirit would have made sure that Stephen did not quote an inaccurate number."

In a course entitled Ecclesiology and Eschatology, John Lawrence tried to impress upon his charges the importance of understanding eschatology, the doctrine of the end times. "Don't say prophecy is of no value," he said. "If it was of no value God wouldn't have given us so much of it." Lawrence was only beginning to warm to his point. "Don't let me hear from any of you that prophecy is not important," he said, his voice rising in earnestness. "I'm reacting to a generation that has said prophecy is not important, that only *now* is important. That's poppycock!" It was crucial for the believer to locate himself in God's plans for the end times, Lawrence said, and he went on to argue quite forcefully for a literal interpretation of the apocalyptic passages in the Bible. Allegorizing those passages was a "dangerous principle," he said. "If the literal meaning makes sense, seek no other sense, lest it become nonsense."

I asked him after class if he thought his approach to biblical interpretation was indebted in any way to the philosophy of Scottish Common Sense Realism so popular among nineteenth-century evangelicals, the notion that Scripture could be interpreted in the plainest possible way and uncluttered with cultural bias. Lawrence replied No. His model of "literal interpretation," he insisted, goes back to the New Testament, and, after he thought about it further,

he decided that the Antioch School had introduced this hermeneutic to the Christian church.

Multnomah School of the Bible represents a dying breed. Its
founding in 1936 was part of a much larger effort on the part of evangelicals in the middle decades of the twentieth century to establish
or shore up their institutions of learning against what they regarded
as the threat of "modernism" in the broader culture.

In the years after the Scopes trial of 1925, which convinced fundamentalists that American culture had turned against them, evangelicals withdrew from institutions they believed had been tainted by
liberal or "modernist" ideas. Evangelicals established their own institutions as alternatives. Indeed, evangelical schools, associations,
and agencies flourished in this period as evangelicals channeled
prodigious amounts of money and energy into this effort. Because
the modernists generally prevailed in the fundamentalist-modernist
controversies that convulsed American Protestantism—that is, liberals managed to retain control of denominational machinery and
assets—dissident, separatist fundamentalists had to start anew, constructing their alternative organizations from the ground up.

Bible institutes, which originally built upon the revival successes
of Dwight L. Moody and others late in the nineteenth century, appealed to twentieth-century evangelicals for several reasons. First,
they provided islands of refuge from the critical scholarship that
called into question traditional notions of biblical authorship and
cast doubts upon the reliability of the Scriptures. Bible institutes
also offered an alternative environment for the education of evangelical children apart from the corrupting influences of secular colleges
and universities, many of which had only recently "gone liberal" and
forsaken their conservative religious heritages. With their sons and
daughters at a Bible school, moreover, evangelical parents could
rest assured that their children would have plenty of help navigat-
ing clear of the intellectual shoals of liberalism and the seductive
currents of "worldly" behavior. An elaborate system of parietal rules,
all of them vigilantly enforced both by school officials and by peers,

governed the behavior of students and kept them isolated from the blandishments of the broader culture.

The isolation at a Bible school can become even more general than that. "There was always a provincial feel to Multnomah," an alumnus, now an editor for an evangelical publishing house, told me. Although he graduated in 1970, at the height of the social turmoil over the Vietnam War, he could recall no reverberations whatsoever on the campus. "It was as if the protests weren't happening at all," he said. "We were so absorbed in our little world."

With the proliferation of such institutions across the North American landscape, from Florida to Alaska, from Texas to Alberta, the Bible-school movement constitutes an intriguing chapter in the history of twentieth-century evangelicalism. Bible schools were an important component of the evangelical subculture, this network of institutions—churches, denominations, Bible camps, colleges, seminaries, publishing houses, mission societies—that evangelicals built in earnest after 1925. The subculture made possible a wholesale retreat from the larger culture. Evangelicals could socialize almost entirely among friends at their churches, send contributions to trustworthy evangelical agencies and missions, purchase reading materials from Christian bookstores, and send their children to Bible camps in the summers, to a Bible institute for higher education, and, perhaps, to an evangelical seminary for further professional training and a career in "full-time Christian service." This sense of envelopment within the cocoon of the evangelical subculture held strong appeal for evangelicals who believed that the larger culture was inherently both corrupted and corrupting.

In the last several decades, however, and especially since the mid-1970s, as evangelicals began to emerge, albeit tentatively, from their self-imposed exile, this suspicion of "the world" has dissipated considerably. The antipathy toward the broader culture so characteristic of evangelicals in the twenties and thirties has gradually given way to ambivalence. Even as many evangelicals retain the old rhetoric of opposition to the world, they are eager to appropriate many of that world's standards of success. This explains, for instance, the proliferation of prosperity theology in evangelical circles, the doctrine that God eagerly bestows the accouterments of middle-class materialism—automobiles, houses, furs, jewelry—upon the faithful. This ambivalence also impels many evangelical pastors to seek advanced degrees, both for the satisfaction of being addressed as "doctor" and also to brandish a title that, they believe, confers status within the larger culture. Whereas once evangelicals intentionally spurned higher education as a species of arrogance and compromise with the world, so many now openly court such approval that we are rapidly approaching the point where evangelicalism can claim more "doctors" than it can people.

Bible institutes have also fallen prey to these broader cultural forces within evangelicalism. With the attenuation of dualistic attitudes—us *versus* the world, righteousness *versus* unrighteousness—the image of the Bible institute as a kind of fortress against the assaults of intellectual liberalism no longer resonates as it once did. Many Bible institutes, accordingly, have undertaken their own quests for respectability. The patterns, in fact, are remarkably consistent. With an eye toward accreditation so that it can offer a bachelor's degree instead of merely a diploma, the school will shore up its offerings in the sciences and the liberal arts. This has the inevitable effect of de-emphasizing classes in the Bible, which had been at the core of its curriculum. At some point in the process the parietal rules ease a bit, and the name changes from "Bible school" or "Bible institute" to "Bible college," then simply to "college," and sometimes, with the introduction of advanced degrees, to "university." There are numerous examples of this phenomenon, but none illustrates the process more completely than Biola in southern California. The name Biola originally was an acronym for Bible Institute of Los Angeles, but the school changed its name to Biola College in 1949 and in 1981 adopted the moniker Biola University. School officials are now so intent on putting aside the institution's Bible-school connotations that they insist that *Biola* is no longer an acronym but a proper name.

To be sure, there are still many Bible institutes in North America that cling to their heritage as separatist schools. Prairie Bible Institute comes to mind, as does Taccoa Falls Bible College, Alaska Bible College, and many others. Moody Bible Institute in Chicago is probably the best known and the most prominent of the Bible schools, but for every Bible institute that remains, there are two or three that have evolved into liberal arts colleges or even universities.

What accounts for the difference? Why have some institutions contented themselves with their status as Bible schools while others have sought to redefine themselves? Surely the pressures of alumni and constituency play a role. Some see the introduction of a liberal arts curriculum as the catalyst for transition from Bible school to Christian college, a kind of slippery slope that leads ineluctably to an emphasis on so-called secular learning at the expense of the Bible.

My own bias, however, is that geographical and cultural location may be as big a factor as any. The schools situated in rural areas— Prairie Bible Institute in Alberta, for example, or Montana Wilderness School of the Bible—have maintained their insularity, drawing on the Jeffersonian ideal of the virtuous farmer as opposed to the less virtuous urban dweller. Likewise, the schools in cities seem to derive their very identity from the juxtaposition of good and evil, righteousness and unrighteousness. Ever since the late nineteenth century, when non-Protestant immigrants flooded American cities, evangelicals have looked at the city with a mixture of repugnance and missionary zeal. Urban schools like Moody, for instance, with its civil defense architecture and its maze of underground tunnels, even look like fortresses. These schools often trade quite self-consciously on their location, sending their students out into city streets on evangelistic forays and playing up their importance as an evangelical beacon in a hostile and godless environment.

Something happens, however, when a Bible school relocates to the suburbs, as many have done in the past several decades. Suddenly, the environment looks less threatening than it did in the city. The dualistic rhetoric softens, almost imperceptibly at first. The fortress mentality gives way to an accommodation to the surrounding culture, or at least an uneasy peace. It strikes me as no coincidence, for example, that Trinity Seminary and Bible College in Chicago became Trinity College and Trinity Evangelical Divinity School about the time the school took possession of its new campus at Deerfield, in the affluent northern suburbs, or that Detroit Bible College dropped "Bible" when it moved to Farmington Hills and changed its name to William Tyndale College. People familiar with Philadelphia College of the Bible claim that it has lost some of its separatist edge since relocating to the suburbs north of Philadelphia.

MULTNOMAH, HOWEVER, remains anchored in Portland and holds fast to its identity as a Bible school. Despite the presence of courses such as Chalk Drawing, Christian Camping, and Overhead Transparency Workshop, the curriculum at Multnomah is fairly demanding, if for no other reason than the sheer number of Bible courses required for graduation.

I found a strong whiff of apologetics both in the conversations and in the classrooms at Multnomah. That is to say that the tenor of theological discourse alternated somewhere between defensiveness and defiance. When, for instance, students or faculty talked about biblical inerrancy (a recurrent topic on campus), they were prepared without notice to recite all the arguments in favor of the doctrine and to rehearse the dangers of holding a contrary view. There was always, moreover, a tone of urgency about the discussion, a sense that the fate of the entire world hung in the balance.

The assumption underlying these discussions seems to be that the way to prevail on this or any other theological issue is to fashion a superior argument, to marshal all the evidence for your side in the battle against the forces of darkness, be they liberalism or modernism or secular humanism. The students' task, then, is to master the arguments, to be able to defend biblical inerrancy against those who might suggest that the Bible may indeed contain factual or scientific errors or, worse, that it is merely a record of the writers' experiences or understandings about God. Similarly, a basic course on theology would include the sundry arguments supporting the existence of God—teleological, cosmological, and so forth.

The premise behind this pedagogy is that he who crafts the better argument wins. If only we can fashion an airtight case for evangelical Christianity, the people at Multnomah seem to say, then the forces of darkness will crumble at our feet. The exercise of faith, which is, after all, the essence of religion, has been eclipsed by the quest for logical certitude.

I am struck by the poignancy of this enterprise, and by its futility. The evangelicals at Multnomah are, in many ways, still fighting the battles their religious forebears fought—and lost—a century ago. Evangelicalism lost credibility in the broader culture when it came under attack from nineteenth-century intellectuals for failing to measure up to scientific and Enlightenment standards of evidence and verifiability. At the time, many evangelicals dismissed those charges as irrelevant to faith; those who sallied forth to defend evangelical theology on logical or rational grounds found themselves over-matched, unconversant with the ideology and presuppositions of their adversaries.

Evangelical theologians ever since, still smarting from Enlightenment assaults, determined never to be beaten again, and so they have spent much of the past century boning up on their logic and shoring up their arguments. The only problem is that the intellectual ground has shifted. Most intellectuals have put those nineteenth-century debates behind them. Textual scholars of the Bible simply acknowledge the internal inconsistencies in Scripture; sociologists explain religion as a social construct; psychologists dismiss it as a quest for a father figure. Whereas at one time religion explained the vagaries of the natural world—thunderstorms, earthquakes, the vast reaches of space—science has now assumed that task.

In many respects, then, the theological discourse taking place among fundamentalists, and at places like Multnomah School of the

Bible, is an anachronism. They are busy waging battles that no one else cares to fight—and the ultimate irony is that, lacking a common enemy who will engage them, they have turned their intellectual guns on one another, engaging in bitter internecine quarrels about theological minutiae that no one outside of the subculture deems important.

Even within the subculture, many evangelicals have grown weary of this kind of light-heavyweight theological sparring. Increasingly, religion over the last century has devoted itself to issues of personal well-being. For most, religion in the waning decades of the twentieth century is a matter of experience or sensation, rather than empirically verifiable truth. Many evangelicals, especially pentecostals, have begun to recognize the importance of religious experience, even bodily expression, in worship. The genius of American pentecostalism over the last several decades, and the reason for its phenomenal growth, is that pentecostals have for the most part refused to be drawn into sterile, rationalistic arguments in defense of evangelical Christianity. Pentecostals understand that the essence of religion lies not in mere intellectual assent, but in religious experience.

FOR THE MOST PART the faculty members at Multnomah remain implacably opposed to pentecostalism, in part, I suspect, because religious enthusiasm, almost by definition, defies rational categories. Although Multnomah strongly encourages the cultivation of personal piety, that spirituality is measured and controlled, characterized by serenity rather than flights of ecstasy. The curriculum revolves around apologetics, the task of defending evangelical Christianity against its many detractors, and the faculty has an obvious interest in keeping it that way. But this intellectual fare is, quite frankly, rather boring by the standards of adolescent tastes.

What is it that draws students to Multnomah? Every answer I received to that question might have been lifted from the school's public-relations materials. "It's an excellent school," John Salters, who wants to go into mission aviation, said. "The teaching is excellent."

Brian Stubbs, who transferred from Moody Bible Institute, agreed. "I think all the professors here are right on," he said enthusiastically. Gwen Durland, a first-year student from Tucson, Arizona, said she had gravitated to Multnomah because she was thinking about missions. "Basically, I asked God where He wanted me to go, and also my pastor said Multnomah was an excellent school." Blaine Butcher, a senior, said that he "wanted to learn about the Bible and youth ministry and discipleship." He pronounced himself satisfied with Multnomah. "You get the dynamic of the truth set down in the class with the parallel of love to work that truth into the fabric of your life," Duane Hallof said. "It's a neat dynamic. I'm a completely different person than I was three years ago."

Indeed, the school's new public-relations slogan reads: "Multnomah deals in life change. Don't settle for less." Hallof credits the school with helping him to work through a troubled home life. "Multnomah is a general hospital for the church," he said, "and each individual receives intensive care." Several alumni I spoke with expressed appreciation for the spiritual direction they had received at Multnomah, although they conceded that they had since reformulated their theologies. Blaine Butcher, a senior, claims that Multnomah shaped his notions about vocation. "Before I came to Multnomah I was a Christian and all," he said, "but I didn't realize that I could have an impact in whatever field of work I chose. Multnomah has shown me how our Christian walk can affect every part of our lives, the way we view the world."

Rhetoric about "the world" frequently creeps into conversations at Multnomah, as when Gwen Durland described her "life change" at the school. "One thing I've been noticing lately," she said, "is that before coming to Multnomah I was really conditioned to worldly things, but being away from it and studying the Bible has shown me how conditioned a Christian can become when you're living in the world daily and you don't have your focus straight on God. It's also increased my desire to go into missions, either here or overseas, just seeing how bad the world is. I want to do my part. The world seems so hopeless and desperate."

Perhaps this comment hints at the appeal of Multnomah that underlies the public-relations copy. Without presuming to gainsay the sincerity of the sentiments I heard—that Multnomah offers straightforward instruction in the Bible, that it provides a warm and nurturing environment for Christian growth—I wonder if part of its attraction doesn't lie in its perpetuation of the old dualistic categories so characteristic of fundamentalism earlier in this century. For adolescents reared on the rhetoric of separatism from and suspicion toward the world, there is a reassuring familiarity to the environment at a place like Multnomah. "We draw in a number of students who have separatist tendencies," according to Frost, a graduate of Multnomah and Trinity Evangelical Divinity School. Identifying yourself as part of the righteous remnant in the midst of a society in moral decay, moreover, allows you to claim the moral high ground. "A lot of schools are really liberal, but Multnomah has held to traditional values," Durland told me. "Some schools say they're Christian, but they don't expect their students to live up to moral standards."

WITH ITS UNABASHEDLY CONSERVATIVE THEOLOGY and social values, an institution such as Multnomah tends to embrace change about as eagerly as a salmon seeks encounters with a hungry bear. The students I spoke with seemed entirely innocent of the cultural forces buffeting Multnomah, but faculty and administrators were keenly aware that the school faced some difficult choices in the coming years. "We're just about the last Bible school around, at least in the traditional sense of a three-year program," Garry Friesen, Multnomah's academic dean, said, his voice betraying a mixture of pride and apprehension. Even Moody, which most people at Multnomah regard as the school's closest kin, has recently moved in the direction of offering full-fledged baccalaureate degrees. "That leaves us pretty much alone out there," Friesen said, "with the exception of some of the smaller schools."

Multnomah's president, Joseph Aldrich, is an alumnus of both Multnomah and Dallas Theological Seminary. From the perspective of the president's office for the past thirteen years, Aldrich has witnessed important changes in evangelicalism, and he understands better than most the predicament of institutions like Multnomah. "Survival is a real issue in the Bible school movement," he said flatly. Thirty years ago a diploma from a Bible institute was sufficient for placement on a church or missions staff, he said, but no longer. "Our students simply cannot compete for jobs with other candidates who have bachelor's or Master of Divinity degrees. Increasingly, the rural community is the only one that a die-hard Bible college graduate can service."

In addition, changes in American culture have left their mark on places like Multnomah. In Ronald Reagan's America, evangelical adolescents were caught up like everyone else in the frenzied, headlong quest for affluence, and the road to riches seemed to lead through colleges, universities, and business schools rather than through a Bible institute. "Like it or not," Aldrich said, enumerating the difficulties facing schools like Multnomah, "divorce has hit evangelicalism." As a consequence, he said, the percentage of female students at Multnomah has dropped in recent years as evangelical fathers counsel their daughters to seek an education to prepare them for a career, in the unfortunate event that they might someday find themselves divorced and in need of work. More and more households are two-career families; wives are working. Increasingly, a place like Multnomah has to fight social and demographic trends in the larger culture. "We don't want to be culturally driven," Aldrich said, "but we have to be culturally aware."

Cultural awareness at Multnomah so far has not extended to gender roles (which may be another reason why female enrollment at Multnomah has declined). Although I heard none of the openly sexist rhetoric that I encountered at Dallas Theological Seminary, it was clear that women at Multnomah are little more than ciphers. Most of the female undergraduates specialize in women's ministries, with such courses as Personal Development, Biblical Perspective on Women, and Preparation for Marriage, which, according to the catalog, examines the components of "the distinctive Christian home; mating stages; the meaning of a Christian marriage; an analysis of the specific role of each member." Another course bears the title Christian Leader's Wife: "Preparation for the woman to serve with her husband in Christian ministries; her personal life, relationship in the home, management of the home, church involvement and hospitality."

I saw a poignant demonstration of those notions one evening during my visit, when Multnomah's academic dean and his room-mate, also a member of the faculty, invited me to their apartment for pizza and *Monday Night Football*. We were joined by a pastor and his wife who are serving an Evangelical Free Church in south-ern Oregon and, later in the evening, by a recent alumna of Mult-nomah. Half an hour or so into a very pleasant and animated con-versation (which, by the way, had nothing to do with football), I realized that something was wrong. The women were utterly silent. Indeed, after very brief, perfunctory introductions, they had nothing whatever to say. The men at the table made no attempt to include them in the discussion or to solicit their views—they even avoided making eye contact—and my own desultory attempts to draw the women into the conversation were met with embarrassed, even pained expressions. On more than one occasion one of the men would answer for them. What was even more remarkable about the exchange (or lack thereof) was that no one seemed to find it unu-sual and, as nearly as I could tell, it did not represent any deliberate attempt on the part of the men to snub the women. Everyone at the table simply shared the same set of assumptions about the place of women in polite conversation. In its attitude toward women, then, Multnomah has refused to assimilate to the larger culture, prefer-ring to cling to what they insist are Paul's injunctions about gender roles but which derive more directly from the nineteenth-century cult of domesticity. The school remains, in this respect, decidedly countercultural.

Simply swimming against the cultural currents, however, is a good bit different from staking out a positive identity. That leaves

Multnomah School of the Bible searching for a niche. The commercial success of Multnomah Press, which publishes books by faculty and other evanglical leaders such as Chuck Swindoll, most of them addressing some dimension of the Christian life, has burnished the school's image among evangelicals, but that notoriety alone will not ensure the school's survival. "We may be managing decline at the undergraduate level," Aldrich said candidly. "We may have to tune our model a bit, perhaps by cutting back from fifty-two hours of Bible." Aldrich and others at Multnomah, however, have reservations about moving toward a liberal-arts curriculum, what Aldrich called the "first-round temptation" for Bible institutes. "It will be a real challenge for the current and subsequent leadership of Multnomah to resist moving from the heart to the head in what we do," Aldrich said. "I resist moving toward an environment where the academic reigns."

Students concur. "They don't want the liberal arts because that will dilute the emphasis on the Bible," Duane Hallof said. "History will repeat itself," he added, citing the examples of Harvard, Stanford, Yale, and Princeton, all of which, he claimed, began with evangelical principles but were seduced into liberalism.

The school has added a Graduate School of Ministry to offer professional degrees, including the Master of Divinity, a three-year program with an emphasis on internships. Even Aldrich, however, seems to have reservations about shifting the locus of pastoral training from the undergraduate to the graduate level. "The seminary movement is not congenial to pietism in the same way that a Bible school is," he said. "That's a real loss."

Multnomah officials also recognize that theirs is a regional school. Out of a total student registration of 761, considerably more than half, 454 students, come from Washington and Oregon. California accounts for another 132 students. Such reliance on the region, however, implies a precarious dependency on what Aldrich calls "the spiritual wasteland of the United States." Several people during my visit cited statistics indicating that the rate of church attendance in

Washington and Oregon was the lowest in the nation. Only 3 percent of the population in metropolitan Portland attends church.

Believing that the school's future is tied inextricably to the spiritual welfare of the Pacific Northwest, Multnomah, in cooperation with the Navigators, an evangelical organization that emphasizes memorization of the Bible, has initiated an evangelistic campaign called Mission Portland that in many ways represents a return to the principles, the ideals, and even the triumphalism that animated the Bible school movement. "Mission Portland is a pilot project to see what it will take to conquer an entire city for God," said Greg Hicks, a Multnomah graduate and communications coordinator for the enterprise, "looking at all facets of ministry required to accomplish the great commission in an urban context." Mission Portland has determined that there are 108 different ethnic groups in the metropolitan area, and its organizers claim to be devising evangelistic strategies for reaching all of them.

Only a year into what is shaping up as a ten-year project, it's much too early to guess how successful Mission Portland might be and what effect it might have on Multnomah's enrollments in the coming years. The effort, however, has drawn early praise for its interdenominational focus and for its ability to bridge the chasm between charismatics and non-charismatics. Some evangelicals in the region even dare to use the term "revival." Whatever the outcome, however, it is clear that Mission Portland will have a salutary effect on Multnomah School of the Bible, if only because it revives the old dualistic rhetoric that was so characteristic of fundamentalism earlier in the century. It also emphasizes the place of evangelism and renewal that largely defined Multnomah in its early years, thereby reiterating the school's importance as a beacon to a sinful world. "We're trying to develop a formula that can be adapted to other urban contexts," Hicks said. "We want to reach as completely as possible the 1.5 million people in our Jerusalem."

IF THERE ARE 108 DIFFERENT ETHNIC GROUPS in Portland, however, no more than a dozen or so are represented at Multnomah.

With the exception of a few Native Americans, the racial, social, and ethnic composition of the student body is decidedly monochromic and homogeneous, a generalization that also applies to the faculty. One professor referred to one of his colleagues as "our avant garde figure" because "he goes to jazz festivals and things like that."

That raises an important question: What do Multnomah students do for fun on Saturday night? With strict injunctions against drinking, gambling, R-rated movies, dancing, and kissing, Multnomah has effectively narrowed the range of activities generally available to college students. How do Multnomah students compensate? I set out on an intrepid quest to answer that query, armed only with the knowledge that there was an interscholastic women's volleyball game scheduled for seven o'clock in the gymnasium. Not wishing to sit through the entire contest, I arrived at seven-forty-five but found that the game was over—forty-five minutes is barely long enough to break a sweat!—and only about a dozen students were left in the gymnasium. One was reading *The Cross of Christ* by John R. W. Stott. Perhaps, I thought, I would have better luck in the Student Center, an A-frame structure adjacent to the gymnasium, but I found only three people inside, all of them studying intently and no one wishing to be interrupted. Next stop: the lounges in the dormitories, but they too were deserted.

The Student Commons building, near the Prayer Chapel, houses the dining facilities, meeting rooms, and a coffee shop called Solid Rock Café. The café was empty, save for two attendants behind the counter. I placed an order, hoping desperately to strike up a conversation. "What do Multnomah students do for fun on Saturday night?" I asked cheerily. Both of them turned toward me with incomprehending stares, as though I had just demanded to know the square root of 1,379. I heard Johnny Cash's smoky voice rising over the café's sound system. One of the attendants managed to stammer that "a lot of students go home," and he seemed singularly unimpressed with my observation that most of the room lights in the dormitories appeared to be on. I lingered a few minutes longer, but it was clear that, for reasons I couldn't discern, the conversation had terminated.

On my way out of the building I spied a couple of students in one of the meeting rooms. They had just plucked two pumpkins from the autumn display in the lobby and had sat down to carve them into jack-o-lanterns. Chastened by my encounter with the garrulous attendants in Solid Rock Café, I decided to proceed slowly. "Do you mind if I ask you a couple of questions?" They looked at one another furtively and then decided with their eyes that it would be okay. Although they gave their names, I had the strong impression that they wished to remain anonymous. "What do Multnomah students do for fun on Saturday night?" I asked again. Once more their eyes met uneasily and the woman responded with the obvious: "Right now we're carving pumpkins."

That was the only stab at humor on the part of a student that I can remember in the entire week I spent at Multnomah School of the Bible. All of the students I encountered seemed to be inordinately serious, and I recall an observation by a Portland-area evangelical who, upon learning about my assignment, commented that she regarded Multnomah as a dreary place. "Whenever I'm on campus," she said, "I have this overwhelming urge to run up to the students and check their pulse." An alumnus later told me that he could remember "plenty of boring Friday and Saturday evenings" at Multnomah, and I wondered if that wasn't one of the real causes for decline in the Bible school movement—its inability to respond adequately to adolescent tastes or to construct a sufficiently compelling alternative to the "worldly" entertainments so widely available in the larger culture.

In the bowels of the Student Commons on a Saturday night, I had apparently failed to respond sufficiently to the hilarity of the comment about carving pumpkins, and when the man discerned that my question about student activities was serious and not frivolous, he quickly searched for answers. "We play Rook in the café," he said. I started to protest that I had just come from the empty café but, not wanting to be contrary, I pulled up short. The man read my mind, however. "That usually doesn't get started until ten o'clock," he said. They began scooping the insides of the pumpkins onto a sheaf of newspapers covering the table. A lot of students go to malls or to parks, he added, or to the local nickel arcade to play video games. On Friday nights one of the professors opens his home to students, who "drop by to discuss life and how it relates to the Bible." The woman nodded vigorously in agreement. "I don't know if you'd call this fun," the man said, "but a lot of students go and witness downtown on Friday and Saturday nights—talk to drunkards and stuff." Both of my informants had finished scooping out the entrails of the pumpkins. "Some students have musical interests," he said, and I remembered that I had noticed someone playing the piano earlier in the evening. "You find imaginative things to do," the woman said, "and it's really fun." Until the practice was recently forbidden by school officials, students would take a block of ice in the winter and ride it down a steep hill.

I allowed that, by the standards of most colleges, what they had described for me sounded pretty tame. "There's wilder stuff that goes on," the man said, a trifle defensively. Some students, he said, dress up like punk rockers and go to downtown Portland. "They fit right in," the woman added with a touch of sarcasm. "Play board games!" the man said suddenly, looking hopefully in my direction. "That's pretty popular. Card games. Board games." When I left, they were plucking pumpkin seeds out of the sinewy orange mounds on the newspaper.

I elected to pass on the Rook game; I couldn't bear the thought of more excitement and levity that evening. I jumped into my rental car and headed back to an empty hotel room.

1990

CHAPTER 8

Campaign Journal

SATURDAY, FEBRUARY 6, 1988 In the Masonic Lodge in downtown Des Moines, Iowa, I approached a young man who appeared to be in charge of the gathering. "Can you tell me where I might find Sarah Leslie?" I asked. "Oh, you're one of Sarah's people, too," he said, pointing to an attractive woman in her midthirties. "So am I."

Sarah Leslie and about one hundred other Republican Party activists had gathered for a G.O.P. precinct caucus training session in order to prepare for the Iowa caucuses coming up in two days. For Leslie, however, an evangelical who understands the political process better than many politicians, the session was just a refresher course; in fact, she had many other things on the agenda today, so she slipped out early.

Next stop: a live radio interview in Norwalk, Iowa, on KWKY, a thousand-watt station that features evangelical Christian programming. With the caucuses only two days away, most of the real organizing is completed; it's a matter now of seeing that "her people," most of them evangelicals who are newly active in the political process, go to the caucuses and make their voices heard. "We've actually been working on the 1988 caucuses for about five years now," she told me. "Now we want to make sure that our people get out on Monday night and express their views."

The radio provides an effective vehicle for doing just that. Sarah Leslie is president of the Iowa Right to Life Committee, an antiabortion organization, and Donald Thompson, host of the radio program, played one of Leslie's radio commercials encouraging voters to attend the caucuses. "Remember," the spot concluded, "if you don't attend, if you don't participate, you're giving up more than a vote. You're giving up an opportunity to change the pro-abortion, anti-family agenda at work in our country today. Don't miss this chance to represent life on February eighth."

A battery of other commercials followed, all of them urging listeners to attend the caucuses, then another of Leslie's radio spots. "First, we had abortion, and they said that was all they wanted." The voice was Sarah Leslie's. "Twenty million babies ago. Then we had infanticide, killing handicapped newborn babies. Now we have euthanasia, killing the elderly and sick. Will you be their next victim?" The commercial concluded: "Vote for life at your precinct caucus on February eighth. If you care, you'll be there." Yet another commercial implored listeners to "vote for Jack Kemp, the pro-family candidate who can win the presidency."

Two days before the Iowa precinct caucuses, it was clear that a real fight had developed for the evangelical vote. All the Republican candidates have courted this constituency, but the two who claimed the most support were Kemp, a Republican congressman from up-state New York, and Pat Robertson, the former head of the Christian Broadcasting Network who resigned his Southern Baptist ordination just prior to announcing his candidacy. Both had campaigned feverishly in Iowa, although the consensus was that Robertson had the superior organization. Indeed, Robertson promised to surprise the pundits with his showing on Monday night, and he claimed that he would bring in thousands of conservative evangelicals, many of whom had never participated in caucuses before. Kemp, on the other hand, who bills himself as the true ideological heir of Ronald Reagan, had sought to shore up his base among conservatives of all stripes, including evangelicals, by emphasizing his opposition to abortion.

Although Sarah Leslie, as president of a federal political action committee, feels she can take no public stand in support of one

candidate or another, she privately favors Kemp in large part because she feels he has a better shot at the nomination. On the radio
program, however, she said only that there are five pro-life candidates running for president; no Democrat in the race passes muster,
but all the Republicans, except for Alexander Haig, whom Leslie
regarded as "soft" on the issue, are considered acceptable to the pro-
life activists. Part of the reason why the Iowa Right to Life Committee has endorsed no candidate, Leslie explained, is that "we want to
stay united on our issue."

Thompson, the host of the radio program, announced that Leslie
would take questions from listeners. One query regarding the term
"reproductive freedom" came in during a commercial break. When
Thompson asked Leslie if she wanted to tackle that one, she replied,
"Oh yeah, I've got some good ammo on that." Back on the air, Leslie
explained that "reproductive freedom" simply means abortion-on-
demand, that it was just a code term that the pro-abortion lobby
uses to camouflage its agenda.

Another question came from a woman who said she was a registered Democrat but had Republican views. Did she have to attend
a Democratic caucus? "No," Leslie said. "The Republican caucus
may want her to somehow identify herself as a Republican. She may
go to a Republican caucus, but she may have to re-register if the
caucus asks her to do so." Leslie has heard that question a thousand
times by now, coming from Democrats who are disgruntled with the
failure of the Democratic Party to oppose abortion.

Thompson asked Leslie why Christians, evangelicals, should
attend the caucuses Monday night. Leslie explained that the eyes of
the nation will be on Iowa Monday, and this presents an opportunity
for the evangelical voice to be heard around the country. "Look at it
this way," she explained. "You're standing on a stage, and the spotlight's on you. And we're Christians. If we as Christians don't speak
out, nobody else is going to do it."

Thompson, who would be attending a caucus for the first time on
Monday, chimed in. "If you believe that these children should not

be aborted, then get out and do something about it. It may make the difference."

"That's right," Leslie added. "You might be that one vote at the precinct caucus that might turn it into a pro-life caucus."

After the radio program and on the way to lunch, Leslie explained her background and how she became involved in the fight against abortion. Sarah Leslie grew up in Plainfield, Illinois, a small town southwest of Chicago. Her parents were quite active in the civil rights movement, she said, so it was not much of a jump for her to become involved in the pro-life movement, which she regards as a logical extension of civil rights.

"I had a good friend when I was in high school. She had a boyfriend, and they started messing around sexually. Pretty soon she thought she was pregnant, but she was too scared to tell anyone or talk about it, and by the time she was four or five months along and she was starting to show, she figured she had no choice but to tell her folks. So she did, and they took her to some small-town doctor, and he told them about an abortion clinic in New York. So they flew her out to this abortion clinic. She had no idea at that time what an abortion was; all she knew was that it would take away her pregnancy. When she came back, she had a horror story to tell me. And she told it and told it and told it. She would call me every day for six months and cry and cry. The story was that she had to go through induced labor—horrible pain—and she was all alone. When she had finished giving birth to a dead baby, she saw dead babies in buckets all over the clinic. And this was legal in New York. The whole place was filthy and dirty. There were bugs crawling, there were mice. It was awful. But the most horrible aspect to her was that she killed her baby and that she'd had no choice in the matter. She just couldn't get over the whole experience.

"When I think about that ordeal," Leslie said, "I realize that my friend's experience had an impact on me, too. It affected my life a lot more than I realized at the time."

There were several more stops along the way to the presidency of the Iowa Right to Life Committee. An interest in Eastern mysticism led Leslie into the drug culture around 1970. She recalls hallucinations, experimentation with heroin, speed, alcohol. She remembers the death of a friend from an overdose. "Four months after I had gotten involved in the drug scene, I had lost my boyfriend. I made a conscious decision one day—it was September of 1970—that I did not care anymore about anything." Leslie seriously contemplated suicide and credits "the power of the Lord" with sparing her life.

Leslie left high school early on a junior-admission program at Drake University in Des Moines. "I had some friends in high school who were involved in the Jesus freak movement, and I had sat down with one girl and asked her to tell me what she believed. When I got to Drake I was still searching, so I went to some Inter-Varsity meetings and became friends with some of the people there. I did some speed one night that really knocked me out, and the next evening as I was waiting for my friends I encountered a girl with red hair who was holding a Bible in her arms. She looked at me and said, 'Do you know Jesus?' Right then and there, I accepted the Lord. It was November 12, 1971. I didn't do anything. The Lord came to me. That's when I became a Christian.

"This girl talked to me for awhile and then said that she would bring some friends by because I needed to be discipled. The people she brought to the door the next day were from Berkeley, California. They'd been through that whole scene, and they'd become Christians. They were Jesus freaks. They discipled me for the next six months, and I couldn't have done it without them. I never have seen or heard from them since then. All I can say is that they knew exactly how to disciple someone who'd been through what I'd been through. They just knew all the right Bible verses and how Satan was going to tempt me."

Leslie had organized a luncheon at the Crystal Tree, a posh restaurant near the airport in Des Moines. As the guests assembled, Senator Paul Simon of Illinois, a candidate for the Democratic nomination, walked over to the table and shook hands all around. Except for a visitor from New York, however, Simon's effort was wasted; everyone else at the table considered him an unacceptable candidate because of his pro-choice position, despite the fact that he is a devout Lutheran and the son and brother of Lutheran ministers. It was an awkward moment. When Simon asked who or what the group represented, there was some dissembling. Leslie finally answered, "Oh, this is just sort of an ad hoc group." The senator seemed satisfied, if a bit confused, and walked away.

The purpose of the luncheon was to rally the faithful. Those in attendance included Leslie; her husband, Lynn, an assistant director of personnel for the City of Des Moines; Donald Thompson, the radio host and a filmmaker;* the Reverend Craig Nelson, a recent graduate of Grace Theological Seminary in Indiana and now pastor of the Easton Baptist Church in Des Moines; and Mary Ann Gilbert from Indianola, Iowa, who handed me a business card identifying her as field representative for a Webster City-based organization called Iowans for Israel. Two members of the party arrived late: Congressman Chris Smith from New Jersey, who was in Iowa for the weekend to campaign for Jack Kemp, and Gaius Ives, the man from the Kemp campaign responsible for chauffeuring Smith to various engagements. Although he had known the congressman only a few hours, it appeared Ives was already a dedicated sycophant.

Smith, formerly the executive director of the New Jersey Right to Life organization, won election to Congress in 1980. At lunch, he emphasized his anti-abortion credentials and repeated other conservative nostrums such as support for the contras in Central America and the necessity to remain vigilant against the Soviets. But he was also eager to push Kemp. Many of his sentences began, "Jack and I served together on a committee that..."or, "Jack and I both feel that...."

Most of the people there already were in the Kemp camp, so Smith was preaching to the choir. The conversation around the table soon turned to expectations for Monday night. "Totally new

---

*This is the same Donald Thompson whose profile appears in Chapter 3.

groups of people are coming out to the caucuses for the first time," Sarah Leslie announced. Someone else reported that various evangelical churches were calling their congregations and telling them to go to the caucuses. The excitement already was building, and the consensus around the table was that there would be a large body of evangelicals at the caucuses this year who had never attended before.

The Iowa Right to Life Committee occupies a small suite of basement-level offices in northwest Des Moines. On the wall opposite the front door is a painting of Jesus kneeling in pain with an aborted fetus in His right hand. On another wall a poster reads: THE BABY WAS GONE...TAMMY HAD AN ABORTION AT 16. Elsewhere, a photograph of a fetus carries the inscription, "Speak out for the silenced minority," and a copy of a proclamation by the governor of Iowa declares January 22, 1986, as "Respect Life Day" across the state.

Two days before the caucuses, there was an air of dishevelment in the empty offices, the desks and tables filled with dog-eared telephone directories and empty soda bottles. The state maps taped to the walls showing congressional and legistative districts and the county maps showing precincts were marked and worn. On the floor in front of Leslie's desk lay a crib mattress and a child's pillow, and a large box of toys sat in one of the back offices.

Leslie volunteers her time for the Iowa Right to Life Committee, and so her children, Colin, Kate, and Meggie, often spend their afternoons in the office. Leslie has a woman come into her home three days a week to care for the children, but the fifty dollars every week is taking a toll on the family budget, and as soon as the caucuses are past, she said, she and Lynn will have to sit down and make some tough decisions. She spoke about the possibility of selling one of their cars or even their home, a modest, two-story frame house in West Des Moines, in order to make ends meet. Still, she harbors no regrets. "Most of us have such a conscience about our issue that if we've got available funds we'll sink them all into the cause, and we'll sacrifice if we have to. Sometimes you feel like a martyr, but most of the time you just figure that's the cost of doing something you believe in." She paused. "I think there's also a sense of urgency to the movement. Among those of us who are actively working, something is broken in our hearts. Every day I am painfully aware that four thousand babies are being murdered—every single day."

The Leslie children are robust and active. They romped freely amid the congenial chaos of the family household in the Valley Junction area of West Des Moines. "We've got three kids in a two-bedroom house," Leslie had told me as we approached the front door. Meggie, the youngest, was born in August 1986, but shortly thereafter, Leslie, a nursing mother, carted young Meggie along the campaign trail, working for the re-elections of Governor Terry Branstad and Senator Roger Jepsen (Branstad was successful; Jepsen lost to Tom Harkin, a Democrat). Meggie and her siblings competed with a flurry of phone calls for the attention of their mother, but about four o'clock in the afternoon, Leslie disappeared upstairs and, in what seemed like record time, made three beds, administered three baths, and folded a pile of laundry.

Leslie alternates between housewife and political activist with practiced ease. The night before, as she was preparing two dishes for a church potluck dinner, she received word that the Iowa Senate was considering legislation to establish a mandatory curriculum on contraception and family planning for the public schools. She excused herself early from the dinner, went to the office and ran off several hundred copies of a "legislative alert" that she then took back to the potluck dinner. There, the pastor and other members of the First Assembly of God helped her stuff envelopes so that her network of activists around the state would be poised to lobby against the legislation when it came up again the following week. "In this business," she said, "you see the power of being a Christian. The enemy would just come in like a flood if we didn't stand there."

SUNDAY, FEBRUARY 7, 1988   St. John's Lutheran Church, at the corner of Sixth Avenue and Keosauqua, is one of the venerable congregations in downtown Des Moines. On the Sunday before the Iowa caucuses, the Reverend Dr. Jerry Schmalenberger wanted to encourage his congregation to attend the caucuses. "Christ instructs us to take part in the government in which we live," he said. "I believe if we mainline, reasonable Christians don't take part in current politics, there will be those highly organized and much more fervent who will. They will represent Christianity in a way that is almost foreign to us and certainly will be an embarrassment to many. It will be a bitter pill for our brand of Christianity in the future."[1]

Schmalenberger clearly had his eyes on the evangelicals when he warned that "single-issue voters are the most dangerous." "Fundamentalists frighten me," he confessed, although he acknowledged them as "our brothers and sisters in Christ." The pastor assured his congregation that he would attend his neighborhood caucus. "If I go to a Democratic caucus, I'll do my best to insist that the caucus be honest about promising all sorts of giveaways with no tax increase and still reduce the national debt," he said. "If I go to a Republican caucus, I'll try my best to let others at the caucus know you can be a Christian and a 'Bible believer' without being a far–right-wing believe-as-I-do-or-you're-going-to-hell-for-sure person."

"We are also Bible-believing Christians," Schmalenberger insisted. "But the Holy Spirit speaks a different message to us from the same inspired word of God. It says we are to be peacemakers and learn to love our enemies and turn the other cheek and go the second mile." Schmalenberger stopped short of endorsing any political candidate or party, but he said he wanted a president who "will stand up for my human rights to dissent," for the rights of women, including "complete reproductive rights over their own bodies."

Such liberal notions do not sit well with most evangelicals, especially amid the highly charged political atmosphere in Iowa this weekend. When Schmalenberger's sermon came up in my conversations with Sarah Leslie, she laughed derisively and dismissed it with a wave of her hand. Across town on this Sunday morning, a much larger congregation heard a different message.

The First Federated Church in northwest Des Moines is any-thing but old and venerable. It is one of the new breed of evangelical churches that looks more like a concert auditorium or a sporting arena than a church. First Federated features television floodlights, roving cameramen, canned music, applause, blow-dried preachers, and a sound system that will knock your necktie askew. Politics was there, too. The pastor, the Reverend Tom Allen, introduced Pat Robertson's daughter and son-in-law, Senator Robert and Elizabeth Dole, and Senator Charles Grassley, one of Dole's principal support-ers in Iowa. "We need to be in prayer for the caucuses tomorrow night," Allen said, and his own pastoral prayer echoed the same themes that many of the Republican candidates had been sounding out on the stump. We need in this country to choose "righteousness over unrighteousness" and "that which is moral over that which is immoral," he said.[2]

Sunday evening services the day before the caucuses gave the candidates another chance to ply the religious vote. At six o'clock, the Reverend Paul Bawden of the Westchester Evangelical Free Church introduced Congressman Jack Kemp to his congregation and asked Kemp for a "brief word of encouragement." Kemp, who had a well-earned reputation for being anything but brief, stepped to the pulpit, introduced his wife, Joanne, and asked, "How can you be a Christian and *not* be involved in the political process?" He said there were three "great issues" in this political campaign: "the de-fense of Western Judeo-Christian values," the defense of "family and family values," and "the defense of the free-enterprise system." Kemp spoke of James Madison's "dear, dear Christian mother" and asserted that the U.S. Constitution was "inspired by the inspired word of the Bible." After about twenty minutes, Kemp urged the congregation to participate in the caucuses the next night and then walked down the aisle, pumping hands the whole way, just like any other candidate might work a union hall. At the narthex, the press entourage rejoined him, and they all drove off into the night toward another evangelical Sunday evening service.[3]

MONDAY, FEBRUARY 8, 1988   Caucus day. An inch or two of snow blanketed the state during the night, a reminder that Iowa lives according to the rhythms of nature, not the vagaries of the political process.

Maxine Sieleman and I agreed to trade interviews this morning in Norwalk. Sieleman, a gray-haired mother of five and now a grandmother, hosts the "Breakfast at KWKY" program each weekday morning, a show heard by nearly one hundred thousand people around the state. After the program, it was my turn to ask questions.

Sieleman, a member of First Federated Church in Des Moines, said that she had been involved in party politics for only a couple of years, but in that brief time she had been elected to the county and then the state central committee of the Republican Party. Yet 1988 would be her first presidential precinct caucus.

Abortion, she said, was the main issue that brought her into the political process. "I was concerned as both a parent and a grandparent with what was happening in our country. I was ashamed that I had not been a voice when the Supreme Court legalized abortion fifteen years earlier." Sieleman's range of political interests has since broadened. "I have a real concern for defense spending," she said. "It bothers me to think that we can trust the Soviets now. I heard it said that a number of years ago Daniel Ortega of Nicaragua came to this country with his military uniform, his slicked-back hair, and his professional glasses, and he was a communist. He comes now to our country with his designer clothes, his long hairstyle, and his designer glasses, but do we realize he's still a communist? I think there are some values being lost because we're not willing to back a country in trouble, whereas but for the grace of God that country could be us.

"When the last shot is fired, I want to be there, knowing that I did everything that I could do to make a difference. I really do believe that our freedoms are being taken from us one by one. I do not have the right to pray in school, and yet my children are being taught witchcraft in school. I don't have the freedom to express my views as a Bible-believing Christian in the schools, yet at the same time humanists can instruct my children. Here in Iowa, in fact, one parent was insulted because there was a prayer given at a baccalaureate service. There are no more baccalaureate services in Iowa because of this one parent. Now I as a parent wish to have my freedoms respected and maintained, and yet this individual, I feel, has infringed upon my rights as a citizen. Where is the balance in all this? There are times when I would love to find another Plymouth Rock and get in my boat and look for that free country where everyone would be free again and be respected as a human being and given the dignity that each human being is entitled to."

Sieleman insisted that it is not so much because she is an evangelical that she became interested in politics. "I'm a grandmother and I'm a mother and I'm a woman, and I've had enough. It's time now to pick up my skillet and my rolling pin and charge. It's time to say, 'I'm a homemaker, and I'm proud of it, and I carry that title with dignity.'"

Who's the enemy? "Satan. We're living in Satan's territory. This is spiritual warfare that takes many forms. It invades television. The media, the way the media has taken control of this country. Abortion. When the history of our age will be written, the books will ask, 'Where were the real Americans when they were slaughtering millions of babies—innocent babies?' The most dangerous place to be these days is inside a mother's womb. Where were the Americans when they allowed the minds of their children, the next generation of leaders, to be polluted by the filth that was coming through the television set? We are a blind, selfish generation."

In addition to her other activities, Sieleman serves as head of the Iowa chapter of Concerned Women for America, a conservative, evangelical, Washington-based lobby organization that claims over five hundred thousand members across the country. "I think women are the key to turning this nation around. I firmly believe that this is why Satan went to Eve, not Adam. I think the influence that women have on society Satan knew back in the Garden of Eden. He knew that if he could convince Eve, she could convince Adam. And so, therefore, if Satan can deceive women about the role God created them for, then the women will be able to confuse and influence men. I firmly believe the role of a woman today is to nurture our next generation. She has the power within her hands to either make or break a nation. A good woman can make a bad man good, but a bad woman can make a good man bad. A woman has tremendous influence upon her husband and her children. That frightens me, in a way, because I think women today have been confused about their roles as women. The secret to a woman's role, I believe, is authority and being submissive. And I feel that just as God asked the woman to bear children because He knew that she wouldn't want to put up with a pregnant man for nine months or He knew that a man could not tolerate the pain of having a child, God also asked her to be submissive, which is one of the hardest things that a woman is asked to do. But therein comes real peace. As we submit to God and become all we can be under God's authority, we find fulfillment. There's no limit to what women can do today."

Can they change the country? "Women *will* change the country. Women are the real key for turning this country around. When women can find their value in their relationship with Jesus Christ and see themselves as God made them, this frees them to go about doing whatever it is that God puts in their lives. I firmly believe that God has always worked through women. I think He's looking for women today to work through."

This idealization of femininity and domesticity is a relatively new phenomenon in Christian history, dating only to the nineteenth century. Historically, Christian theology has viewed women as temptresses, the descendants of Eve. In the nineteenth century, however, as men began to seek their livelihoods outside of the home and the farm, women, with the increased leisure time available to them because of the growing commercial economy that freed them from making soap and clothes and butchering meat, began to view the home as their particular domain. A passel of Victorian magazines advertised consumer goods through the mail and offered advice about decorating. Whereas the seventeenth-century Puritan father had as-sumed responsibility for the spiritual well-being of his family, Prot-estant women in the nineteenth century came to take responsibility both for the home and for the religious nurture of their families. The clergy lionized the piety of women and held them up as models of true godliness. Even Alexis de Tocqueville observed that in America, "women are the protectors of morals."[4]

The ideal of feminine spirituality and domesticity still has a powerful hold on the evangelical subculture, as I had discovered at Dallas Seminary. "Much like a thermostat, a woman determines the emotional climate in her home," a female student at Dallas had written in the seminary's magazine. "No other part of the world will be more affected by her influence than the place she lives, loves, and nurtures every day."[5] Men, who traffic daily with the world, are seen as vulnerable to worldly enticements, whereas a godly wife and mother will resist such blandishments. The feminist movement of the past quarter-century has bypassed most evangelical women pre-cisely because it threatens these Victorian myths. Phyllis Schlafly, who led the successful fight against ratification of the proposed equal rights amendment to the Constitution, remains enormously popular in evangelical circles, despite the fact that she is Roman Catholic.

There is another dimension to the mythology that has energized evangelical political involvement over the past decade. In addition to the domestic ideal and the myth of feminine spiritual superiority, many evangelicals also subscribe to the political myth about Amer-ica's "Christian" origins that Kemp alluded to on Sunday evening when he referred to James Madison's "dear, dear Christian mother" and to the belief that the Constitution was inspired by the inspired Word of God. Evangelicals have been eager in recent years to recast American history according to the shibboleths of the political right. These new histories have asserted (in the face of contrary evidence) that America was settled almost exclusively for religious reasons, and this revisionism has also given rise to rather comic attempts to transform people like Thomas Jefferson, Thomas Paine, James Madison, and Abraham Lincoln into something like fundamentalists.[6]

But these mythologies, both domestic and political, serve a useful purpose for activist evangelicals because they conjure images of a halcyon past when evangelical Protestant values prevailed in American culture, when a woman tended her domain in the household and thereby ensured the spiritual welfare of her family. The mythologies, no matter how far removed from reality, energize political involvement by serving as constant reminders of how decent and righteous America *used* to be and how far we have yet to go in order to reclaim those ideals.

Beyond the mythology, however, there is a symbolism that represents the displacement evangelicals feel in a pluralistic world that they believe has turned against them and their values. What symbolizes their alienation and vulnerability better than anything else is a fetus.[7] "The most dangerous place to be these days," Maxine Sieleman had said, "is inside a mother's womb." There is nothing more pure and innocent than a fetus. Indeed, the fetus serves as a marvelous symbol, not only for its Freudian or psychoanalytical connotations of crawling back into the womb to escape the buffetings of the world, but also because it represents evangelicals' own sense of beleaguerment and helplessness. Despite their political successes in the past decade, contemporary fundamentalists, like their predecessors in the 1920s, still see American culture as alien and their own survival as precarious. They must exercise extraordinary vigilance lest the forces of evil and darkness, usually identified as "secular humanism," overtake them.

I don't mean to trivialize the issue. Many evangelicals (and others) have put forward persuasive and even eloquent arguments against abortion; I find some of those arguments compelling, and most of them sincere. But it strikes me, at first glance, as an odd issue to serve as a rallying point for evangelical political activism. There is nothing in the Bible that *explicitly* condemns abortion, and the pro-life position does not appear to arise out of any abstract devotion to the sanctity of human life. Many pro-life evangelicals, for instance, also favor capital punishment, and the majority of evangelicals have seldom shied away from the exercise of military force.* I wonder, then, if evangelicals have reacted so vociferously to the abortion issue because they identify with the vulnerability of the fetus, its susceptibility to larger, alien forces outside the womb. Abortion, moreover, blatantly violates their two-pronged mythology. First, it contradicts the political myth of America as a Christian nation because it provides them with irrefutable evidence of the political process run amok; the Supreme Court, after all, sanctioned abortion in the first place, and venal, ungodly politicians have refused to override that travesty. Second, abortion violates the domestic Victorian myth of feminine spirituality: If women guarded their purity and contented themselves with their God-given roles as mothers and housewives, they would not seek abortions in the first place.

For people like Sarah Leslie, Maxine Sieleman, and countless other evangelicals, then, there may be a sense of urgency to their political activism that transcends mere advocacy. They, like the fetus, are engaged in a struggle for survival in what they view as an alien and threatening culture, and God is surely on their side in fending off the slaughter of the innocents.

Maxine Sieleman believes that one of the foot-soldiers in this crusade against evil in central Iowa is DeAnne Sikes, from nearby Indianola. When I talked with her on the phone several weeks earlier to arrange an interview, Sikes, a full-time homemaker and mother of three, spoke about the importance of "lobbying from the kitchen table" in those few quiet moments during the day when the dishes are done, beds made, and the children are either napping or in school. Until recently, she told me in her living room in Indianola, she had never written a letter to a senator or a congressman, never lobbied for anything. Now, she said, "they know me by name. I now

---

*In this respect, the "pro-life" moniker, which the activists prefer to "anti-abortion," is something of a misnomer.

realize I have a right to walk into that office and let them know how I feel. A couple of years ago I would *never* have done that. I would have been so intimidated."

No more. Through her involvement in Concerned Women for America, Sikes has learned to channel her indignation into the political process, arguing for continued aid to the contras of Central America, for a strong defense, against sex education in public schools, and against abortion. "I'm furious about abortion," she said, her voice rising. "Nothing makes me angrier than to think about people murdering human beings, especially these late-term fetuses. I know now that my vote is going to make a difference. Senators and legislators *do* listen. They have to listen when there's hundreds of thousands of us saying 'This has to stop.'"

The Iowa chapter of Concerned Women for America is still fairly new, but both Maxine Sieleman and DeAnne Sikes pointed to one victory that they considered significant. "When we got back from the national convention in Washington," Sikes said, "we were all fired up and full of patriotism. We met in a public library in Des Moines, and we wanted to open the meeting with the Pledge of Allegiance, but there were no American flags anywhere in the library. We made some phone calls and got the American Legion to take it on as a project and supply all the public libraries with American flags. We've gotten so lackadaisical in America that children in many schools don't even say the Pledge of Allegiance. In Nevada, Iowa, they leave out 'under God' and just say 'one nation, indivisible, with liberty and justice for all.' We just can't let that happen."

I asked Sikes, a Robertson supporter, what was at stake in the Iowa caucuses that evening. "I think tonight, for the first time ever, America is going to see grassroots, evangelical, fundamentalist people crawl out from where we've been hiding in our pews and saying, 'This is how I feel; I'm supporting a candidate who stands for traditional values.' I am tired of the trend in this country of a few very liberal Americans controlling what happens." Sikes singled out the American Civil Liberties Union and People for the American

Way as examples of pernicious liberal influences that she hopes to counteract by her involvement. "This is all totally new to me," she acknowledged. "I think most of the evangelicals, the church folks who will attend the caucuses this evening, have never been to a caucus before."

Back in Des Moines at the offices of the Iowa Right to Life Committee, Sarah Leslie was surprisingly calm and unruffled (even she seemed a bit surprised at this) at mid-afternoon on caucus day. She had fielded more calls asking for candidates' positions on abortion, and she had again coached others on what to expect at their precinct caucuses. "I guess we've done all we can do," she said, locking the office door. "We've got prayer chains going right now all across the state." She still expected a big turnout from her people.

At the first precinct in West Des Moines, both the Republicans and the Democrats met at the West Des Moines Community Center, albeit on opposite sides of a partition. Sarah Leslie was responsible for convening the Republican caucus at seven o'clock, and by the time I arrived at six forty-five, it was clear that the Robertson people were present in large numbers. "There's already a Robertson move to oust me as chairman," Leslie informed me as soon as I walked into the room. That movement never developed, but the Robertson people dominated the caucus at will. After checking the credentials of everyone in the room, Leslie called the caucus to order and then distributed tiny sheets of paper listing the names of the Republican candidates. When the straw poll was tallied, Pat Robertson received thirty-eight votes, nearly fifty percent of the eighty-one Republicans in attendance. Robert Dole was next with seventeen, George Bush had twelve, Kemp eight, Pete du Pont four, and one expressed no preference.

If Leslie, a Kemp supporter, was a bit stunned by the results, she betrayed no hint of it but rather continued with the business of the caucus. She opened the floor for nominations to the county convention, and each nominee then came to the front of the room and declared which candidate he or she favored and why. The

Robertson people predominated. "He best represents what is good for the family," one Robertson candidate for delegate said. "I support Pat Robertson based on his Christian beliefs," said another. An eighteen-year-old girl affirmed her support for Robertson and added, "I think it's really neat that teenagers can get involved in the political process."

Virtually all of the Robertson candidates for delegate conceded that this was the first precinct caucus they had ever attended. That clearly engendered resentment from the party regulars, some of whom allowed their frustration to boil over with angry warnings that Robertson was unelectable and that the presence of his supporters represented an unwelcome intrusion. "I'm a sixth-generation Republican," one man shouted, "and what I've seen here tonight is disgusting. This man will never be elected president, and if you insist on pushing him on the Republican Party, that's the quickest way to make sure that the people next door elect *their* man as president," he said, pointing to the partition.

Such appeals were largely unavailing. Of the four delegates elected from the precinct to the county convention, two were for Robertson, one for Kemp, and one (Sarah Leslie, a Kemp partisan) nominally uncommitted.

The crowd had dwindled considerably by the time the caucus got around to passing resolutions for the party platform. What followed was a kind of free-for-all, a conservative wish list. Proposals in favor of a balanced-budget amendment to the Constitution, a line-item veto for the president, mandatory retirement for Supreme Court justices, and the abolition of the Electoral College all passed by acclamation. "Hold the line on taxes," one man shouted; the caucus agreed. The issue of education aroused the most interest and the most passion. The caucus resolved to abolish the Department of Education, to allow a moment of silence for prayer in public schools, to mandate the daily recitation of the Pledge of Allegiance, and to support the voucher system, which would effectively provide public support for private, parochial, and religious schools by giving each child a voucher for use at any school of the parents' choice. When the discussion turned to school-based clinics, Leslie finally had her moment. The sentiment of the caucus was to oppose school clinics which, conservatives contend, exist primarily to provide contraceptives and abortion referrals. Leslie, as chair of the caucus, gently directed the group's attention to a sheet of resolutions that the Iowa Right to Life Committee had prepared for this purpose. The caucus unanimously concurred with the printed resolution opposing school-based clinics and thereby declared itself, by Sarah Leslie's definition, a "pro-life caucus."

For the national media, whose trucks and equipment blanketed downtown Des Moines, the real story of the evening was Pat Robertson. Robertson's "secret army," as it had become known in recent weeks, turned out in impressive numbers, giving the former television evangelist twenty-five percent of the Republican vote, a second-place showing behind Robert Dole's thirty-seven percent but well ahead of George Bush's nineteen percent. Jack Kemp won the allegiance of only eleven percent of Iowa's Republican voters.

At Robertson's headquarters at the International Trade Center in Des Moines, the crowd was abuzz with excitement. The candidate himself appeared several times, smiled benignly at the cheering supporters above him in the mezzanine, and then rode off in his limousine. "It's almost, like we say, you've got to give God the credit," Robertson declared in an interview.[8]

A young woman standing next to me in the crowd had driven all the way from East Lansing, Michigan, to be part of the victory celebration. When I asked if she was surprised by Robertson's strong second-place showing, she hesitated, smiled, and said, "I was hoping he'd come in first." On the other side of me, two local campaign workers festooned with Robertson buttons clearly were relishing their candidate's success as they watched the networks' coverage on a bank of television sets. "This is big news. This is big news," one of them said, almost breathless with excitement. "Satan has controlled politics for too long." His friend agreed. "I guess everybody knows now that Christians are serious."

SATURDAY, FEBRUARY 13, 1988   Cherry Marsh of West Lebanon, New Hampshire, has never met Sarah Leslie, DeAnne Sikes, or Maxine Sieleman, but she was grateful indeed for their efforts to propel the issues that are important to her to the forefront of the political debate in Iowa. As a leader of Concerned Women for America in New Hampshire, Marsh is also disturbed about legalized abortion and what she considers the lack of moral leadership in America.

Her candidate is Pat Robertson. Indeed, hers is a Pat Robertson family, with a bumper sticker that reads WOMEN FOR ROBERTSON '88 on their yellow Chevrolet sedan. Cherry's husband, Keith, is one of the pastors of the Dartmouth Area Christian Fellowship, a pentecostal congregation in Hanover, New Hampshire. Even Hannah, their five-year-old daughter, has caught the campaign spirit. She refers affectionately to "Pat" in the same way that other children might express their attachment to a teddy bear or a pet turtle. "When Pat becomes president, he won't say that, will he, Mommy?" Hannah said after her mother repeated one of the slogans of the pro-choice movement.

During the car ride between Hanover and Concord, about an hour away, I had the opportunity to ask Keith and Cherry Marsh, both political novices, about their involvement in Robertson's campaign. They remembered well their first encounter with Robertson at a pastors' luncheon in Concord, the state capital. "We really were impressed," Cherry said. At that time, Keith added, Robertson hadn't yet announced his candidacy but was traveling around the country soliciting advice about whether or not he should run for president. "The consensus of the meeting," Keith said, "was, 'God bless you, Pat; we don't think you can win, but you can raise some issues in the course of the campaign.'"

Both Keith and Cherry Marsh have since changed their minds about Robertson's chances. After his strong showing in Iowa, the Marshes became convinced that Robertson will eventually become the Republican nominee for president in 1988. Keith predicted a second-place finish in New Hampshire's primary on Tuesday, but added, "I think he could win." Indeed, both Keith and Cherry exuded an air of expectation, even giddiness, about their candidate's chances. Robertson, they pointed out, is well-organized in the South, where the so-called Super Tuesday primaries would take place in less than a month. "That's what's so fun working on this campaign," Keith said. "You know you're not alone." Cherry agreed. "We women volunteer in the evening, bring coffee to the campaign office, pray together, and get on the phones," she said. "We feel that we're making an impact. We're raising the standard of righteousness in this state. It takes time, it takes work to leave our cozy, warm homes. But it's been fun. We're all rookies, really."

Rookies. Yes, that was the word. At the Robertson celebration in downtown Des Moines the previous Monday, I had been struck by the demeanor of the crowd. They seemed uncomfortable, a bit out of place with all the flummery that accompanies a political campaign. Many seemed to wear their campaign buttons and the styrofoam "straw" hats uneasily, as though they weren't quite sure about the protocol of politics, like a high school junior at the prom uncertain about which lapel to pin his boutonniere on, his eyes darting furtively to search for clues from others in the room. The celebration at Robertson headquarters, though loud and jubilant, lacked the raucous abandon and the unabashed silliness of most political rallies. Many of those in attendance looked uncomfortable, as though they would rather be home in front of the television or in church at Wednesday night prayer meeting.

Indeed, according to polls, about three-fifths of Pat Robertson's supporters in Iowa had participated in the caucuses for the first time. The same pattern seemed to obtain in New Hampshire, where evangelicals like Keith and Cherry Marsh, with no previous engagement in politics, were becoming involved in the political process. "History will remember Pat Robertson because he's showing us Christians that we're a lot bigger than we thought we were," Keith said. "This campaign is knitting a lot of people together."

A few minutes after we arrived at the New Hampshire Highway Hotel in Concord, a huge Robertson motorcade, stretching two miles in length and numbering about two hundred vehicles, pulled into the parking lot. Cars, pickup trucks, even some motor homes all wore large, royal-blue Robertson signs. Robertson supporters emerged shivering from the cold into the lobby of the sprawling, two-story, white frame hotel. Campaign organizers had arranged for a buffet dinner upstairs at the hotel. The Marshes opted for Burger King down the street; I decided to mingle with the Robertson people. On the way to dinner, Madeline Flagg, who described herself as a born-again Christian from Nashua, New Hampshire, said that this was her first political campaign and that she had joined up with Robertson because "he understands the issues that affect us as a family. He believes in a strong defense. We don't feel we can trust the Soviets." Robertson's showing in Iowa, she said, indicated that he represents "the true conservative voters, not just born-again Christians."

I heard similar sentiments at the dinner table, many of them mixed with the kind of starchy conservativism for which New Hampshire is famous. When I asked Frank Anderson why he had settled on Robertson in 1988, he said the decision hadn't been that difficult. He quickly ruled out Bush, Dole, and Haig because of their ties to the Trilateral Commission and the Council on Foreign Relations. Jack Kemp, he said, was "too much of a statist." Beverlie Tuttle of Danbury, a born-again Christian for ten years and a member of Concerned Women for America, is a veteran of political battles. She and her husband publish a newspaper called *The Truth*, the cover of which carried a picture of a wooden horse with a sign that read: "The I.N.F. Treaty is a TROJAN HORSE." Tuttle believes that Ronald Reagan sold out to the communists by signing the treaty limiting nuclear warheads in Europe, and she cloaked her opposition to the treaty in biblical terms. "The Bible tells us not to be unequally yoked with unbelievers," she said. "Signing a treaty with atheists is being unequally yoked."[9]

For the past two weekends I'd been lunching and dining with conservatives, be they Jack Kemp's people or Pat Robertson's, and

I'd grown a bit weary of the steady diet of paranoia and conspiracy theories. I heard endless accounts of Soviet perfidy, the conspiracy of liberals in Washington, the abject failure of public schools to educate children (this argument is especially curious in Iowa, which for years has enjoyed the highest literacy rate in the nation). Pat Robertson and, to some extent, Jack Kemp apparently have tapped into this discontent. Some of the printed banners Robertson's campaign distributed read: NO AID TO COMMUNISTS, RESTORE FAMILY VALUES, AMERICA FIRST IN DEFENSE, and IMPROVE OUR SCHOOLS.

Back downstairs in the New Hampshire Highway Hotel, a large crowd gathered in the ballroom for an evening rally featuring the candidate himself. Reporters and photographers milled about the room talking to Robertson loyalists and snapping pictures of entire families dressed in Robertson tee-shirts. At about seven o'clock, an energetic young woman dressed in white sweatpants and a white Robertson sweatshirt grabbed the microphone and shouted, "Let's get our blood flowing. Pat Robertson's going to be the next president of the United States!"

After the first of three renditions of "This Land Is Your Land," the woman shouted, "Amen! Hallelujah! Righteousness exalts this nation!" She then taught the audience a campaign song, the words of which were distributed on "Americans for Robertson" letterheads. Sung (loosely) to the tune of "Row, Row, Row Your Boat," the words read:

> We're Pat's grass roots!
> Watch us grow!
> Taller, Taller, Taller, Taller!
> Smotherin' out the foe!

Everyone in the ballroom then rose spontaneously to the strains of "God Bless America," followed immediately by "America the Beautiful" and "My Country 'Tis of Thee." When it came time for "The Battle Hymn of the Republic," the crowd was getting warmed up. They clapped and stomped on the wooden floor, all the while singing "Mine eyes have seen the glory of the coming of the Lord."

When I sat down next to Keith and Cherry Marsh, near the stage, the crowd was in the midst of a chant: "We want Pat! We want Pat!" Cherry looked a bit sheepish. "This is the place where we cut loose," she said almost apologetically. "This is where we have fun." By seven forty-five the ballroom was filled, and a uniformed Army sergeant came to the microphone to lead the audience in the Pledge of Allegiance. When the recitation came around to "one nation under God," several people around me shouted "under God" in a defiant tone. During the singing of "The Star-Spangled Banner," the audience waved their styrofoam hats from side to side in unison.

The enthusiasm of the audience rarely waned, even during a succession of musical selections and speeches from lesser-light politicians eager to bask in Pat Robertson's spotlight. The master of ceremonies introduced one of the singers as "a young lady, the mother of five, and a perfect example of what this country stands for." Kelly Griswold walked onstage and sang "Ready for the Times to Get Better," which, she said, "is what's going to happen when Pat becomes president." Next to me, Juanita Cashulines, a Robertson volunteer from Hudson, New Hampshire, nodded in agreement. "The Lord's on our side," she said.

Meldrim Thompson, governor of New Hampshire from 1973 to 1979, is chairman of Pat Robertson's campaign in New Hampshire. When it came time to introduce Thompson, one of the junior politicians waxed rhapsodic, describing the former governor, who once proposed equipping the New Hampshire National Guard with nuclear weapons, as the "patriarch of conservatives in New Hampshire" and "one of the most wisest, most respected men in American politics." Thompson, a short, ruddy-faced man, acknowledged the cheers from the audience and then introduced Robertson. At that moment, the rally's enthusiasm reached a crescendo. "We want Pat! We want Pat!" The crowd's awkwardness and tentativeness, so evident earlier in the evening, gave way to boundless enthusiasm and adulation. Cameras flashed. Placards swayed. Keith and Cherry Marsh cheered and waved their hats high in the air. "Look at all them press people," one woman said, pointing to the phalanx of photographers and cameramen. "A month ago there were only three or four of them."

"When I look at all your faces and see your enthusiasm," Robertson began, "I believe we're going to see victory on Tuesday." The audience agreed. "I am *not* a politician," he continued, sounding a theme that plays well in New Hampshire. "As president of the United States, I am free to serve God as I see fit and to serve all the people of the United States." Several people shouted "Amen!" during Robertson's speech, especially as he proclaimed his support for individual initiative, freedom from communism, strong families, and "the preservation of life for the unborn." One voice said, "God bless you, Pat."

Robertson plunged into the audience to shake hands, to "press the flesh," as Lyndon Johnson used to say. Keith and Cherry Marsh passed up the chance to pump the candidate's hand, preferring to avoid the crush of people around Robertson. "I've shaken his hand before," Keith explained. Outside in the parking lot, however, a friend of the Marshes, a woman in her fifties and a member of Keith's congregation, ran up to the car. "He knows us. He knows us," she exclaimed breathlessly. "He said, 'God's going to work a wonder. I just know it.'"

SUNDAY, FEBRUARY 14, 1988 The Dartmouth Area Christian Fellowship meets in the Nugget Theater in downtown Hanover. The worship is pentecostal, an informal mix of guitars, singing, flailing arms, and spontaneous shouting from the congregation: "Thank you, Jesus!" "You're the king of all the earth!" Toward the front of the theater, one member of the congregation seems to be coaching a newcomer on the various techniques for waving his arms in the air. He then places his hand on the newcomer's head and unleashes a lengthy prayer that lasts through several songs. Some of the exhortations from the audience take the first-person voice of God: "I have given you spiritual gifts. You are a gifted people....You don't know when, but my Son is returning."

After an hour or so, the meeting adjourned for a brief intermission. Cherry Marsh introduced me to Rob and Margaret Drye from Plainfield, members of the congregation and Robertson supporters who are also active in the pro-life movement. The Dryes quickly volunteered that they were schooling their children at home and that their defiance of state regulations had involved them in all sorts of legal tangles. "We're not going to send our kids into the snake pit of the public schools," Rob said disdainfully. "The whole curriculum is designed to turn children against their parents." I asked if they weren't worried about their children's socialization in that they were separated from their peers. "Yes, we worry about socialization," Margaret said. "That's why our children are *not* in public schools."

At the front of the theater, Keith Marsh stepped behind a lectern and said, "Okay, saints, let's sit down now." He then invited members of the congregation to offer testimonies about what God had done in their lives. Two days away from the primary, politics was on the mind of some. "I just want to tell everyone who's concerned about the political scene in this country that Jesus Christ is the answer," one young man said. "We really need to pray for God's will to be done." Another man exhorted the congregation to "go out and vote on Tuesday. Ask God to bring forth who He wants to bring forth in this country."

An air of triumphalism tinged some of the declarations. "We know who the winning side is," someone said. "It's us." When one man casually let it drop that "I'll be voting for Pat Robertson on Tuesday," Keith Marsh hurried to the podium. "We don't endorse political candidates as a church," he pointed out. "Amen?"

For many evangelicals in America, the realm of politics is still alien terrain, and the propriety of various political activities is disputed. In the fifties, sixties, and seventies, many evangelical seminaries explicitly instructed their students not to express themselves politically in any way lest they compromise the effectiveness of their ministries. Evangelicals on the whole viewed politics with suspicion as a "worldly" domain unworthy of their participation beyond mere voting. It was not always so. In the nineteenth century, evangelicals shaped the nation's social and political agenda with their concern for such issues as abolitionism, prison reform, temperance, and sabbatarianism. Lyman Beecher mounted a moral crusade to outlaw dueling, and various missionary and benevolent societies worked for the amelioration of society.[10] Such activity coincided with their postmillennialist theological views.

By the turn of the twentieth century, however, teeming, squalid cities and rapacious industrialists hardly looked liked fixtures of a millennial kingdom. Premillennialism, with its expectation of a sudden, cataclysmic judgment of sinful society, better suited the temper of evangelicals at the turn of the century. By the time of the Scopes Trial in 1925, they were convinced that American culture was hopelessly damned, so they turned inward, awaiting their rapture into heaven.

Such attitudes did not lend themselves to political activism, and for half a century—from the Scopes Trial in 1925 until Jimmy Carter's campaign for the presidency, beginning in 1975—evangelicals largely steered clear of politics. By the late 1970s, ironically, many evangelicals, led by Jerry Falwell, Baptist minister and founder of Moral Majority, turned against Carter and saw in Ronald Reagan the kind of crusader who could arrest the moral decline in America by reinstituting prayer in schools, outlawing abortion, and stemming the tide of communism. Reagan's lack of success on those fronts only increased the determination of evangelicals to advance their agenda, and in 1988 they began looking for a new champion.

Still, there are anomalies in this moral crusade being waged in the precincts of Iowa and the purlieus of New Hampshire. The mood of triumphalism that surrounds Pat Robertson's campaign is curious in that most of Robertson's evangelical followers still claim to be premillennialists—that is, they expect the imminent return of Christ and the judgment of a sinful world—but they are acting increasingly like postmillennialists who have taken it upon themselves to usher in Christ's millennial kingdom. Indeed, there are many evangelicals whose premillennial scruples still will not allow them to participate in politics. In the course of our conversations, Keith Marsh recounted an argument that Robertson faced at the pastors' luncheon in Concord as he was deciding whether to run for president. "Wait a minute," one of the ministers said. "The next event on the eschatological clock is the return of Christ. Things in society should get *worse* rather than better. If Christians worked to turn our nation around, that would be a humanistic effort and delay Christ's return." In the euphoria of the 1988 presidential campaign, however, many evangelicals have brushed aside such naysayers, even though they may not admit to a shift in theology or even be aware of any contradiction between their premillennial convictions and their postmillennial activities.

Keith and Cherry Marsh are not bothered by such contradictions. At their home in West Lebanon, over a Sunday dinner of Yankee pot roast, carrots, homemade rolls, and mashed potatoes, I asked the Marshes and their friends, Dan and Barbara Gornell, to assess their first foray into politics. Barbara Gornell, a schoolteacher for many years, linked the evangelical surge into politics with the emergence of the Christian-school movement. "The curriculum in those schools emphasizes government through God, and this whole generation is coming up with biblical principles for government," she said. These principles are then picked up by the parents. "As you educate the children," she said, "you educate the parents."

Dan Gornell, who recently retired after a career in the Air Force, said he thoroughly enjoyed his volunteer work for Robertson's campaign. His daily duties include driving around in his pickup truck every morning and replacing all the Robertson lawn signs that had been torn down or vandalized the night before. In the past, he said, "there was a mindset that Christians shouldn't get involved in politics. But look at the Bible." He pointed to the examples of Moses and Gideon as political figures, and he placed Robertson in the same tradition as the leaders of ancient Israel.

"Pat Robertson has come along to champion our cause," Barbara Gornell said. "We're as amazed about it as everyone else, but we've got to make a stand here. The conviction of knowing you're doing something right keeps you going. Our ranks are thickening, and people are getting excited. This campaign has relieved a frustration in my life. I really *can* do something to change the system."

What would happen, I asked, if Robertson's campaign fizzled or if he were denied a place on the Republican ticket by a political deal of one kind or another. All agreed that they would be disappointed but that they would still work for the Republican nominee in November. Cherry Marsh conceded, however, that "I don't think we would work as hard for anyone else."

"It's a victory that Pat is even running," Keith Marsh said. "He has emboldened us not to be ashamed of our faith and beliefs. We're in it for the long haul," he added. "We'll be back in four years." Cherry agreed. "We're not going to give up," she said.

1988

CHAPTER 9

Mississippi Missions

O N JANUARY 15, 1987, the day I arrived in Jackson, the Mississippi legislature voted to set aside the third Monday in January as a state holiday in honor of Martin Luther King, Jr. The holiday, the legislature decided, would also commemorate the Confederate general Robert E. Lee. In Mississippi, apparently, when one hand giveth, the other taketh away.

Much of Mississippi still enjoys (yes, enjoys) a reputation as one of the last bastions of the Old South, a holdout against desegregation, civil rights, and change. Mississippi waited until 1986 to set up kindergartens in public schools, the same year it made schooling mandatory for the first time; children in Mississippi now have to remain in school until age ten. Not until 1975 did the state require that justices of the peace have at least a high school education.

Over the past century, however, Mississippi's most stubborn resistance to change has centered in race relations. Here in the state that provided the Confederacy with its only president, many whites still refer to the Civil War as the War Between the States, a moniker that insists that the South was an independent, sovereign nation. Ross Barnett, segregationist governor of Mississippi from 1960 to 1964, used to tell his white constituents, "The Negro is different because God made him different to punish him."[1]

If God ever flagged in His "punishment" of blacks, there were always plenty of whites in Mississippi ready to assume the responsibility. In 1964 three civil rights workers were slain and buried secretly in an earthen dam near Philadelphia, in Neshoba County. The year before, Medgar Evers, head of the National Association for the Advancement of Colored People in Mississippi, was murdered at his home in Jackson. In September 1962 President John F. Kennedy called in Army troops to quell the rioting in Oxford occasioned by the registration of James Meredith at the University of Mississippi. When a reporter asked if he didn't find it a lonely life as the only black on an all-white campus, Meredith replied evenly, "I've been living a lonely life a long time."[2]

In 1947 another young black man, also very much alone, stood at the train station in Jackson, Mississippi, with a lunch, a second-grade education, one change of clothes, three dollars, and a ticket to California. Even at sixteen, John Perkins would write later, "a guy has a lot to remember. And a lot to forget."[3]

As Perkins headed west, he recalled his childhood. Born to bootlegging sharecroppers outside New Hebron, in the Piney Woods section of central Mississippi, his mother had died of pellagra, a painful disease caused by protein deficiency, when Perkins was only seven months old. His father, seeking work, left about the same time. But what most seared his memory was a Saturday afternoon in New Hebron during the long, hot summer of 1946. His older brother Clyde, recently returned from Germany with combat ribbons, a Purple Heart, and an honorable discharge, stood in the alleyway queue for the "colored" entrance to Carolyn's Theater. A deputy marshal walked by, barked, "You niggers quiet down," and then, for reasons never clear, brandished his club. After sustaining one blow, Clyde Perkins grabbed the weapon and scuffled with the lawman, who then stepped back, pulled his gun, and pumped two shots into the black man's stomach.

Clyde Perkins died several hours later.

In California, half a world away from New Hebron, John Perkins traded his twenty-dollar-a-month Mississippi wages for ninety-eight cents an hour at the Union Pacific Foundry in South Gate. Far away from the blatant, overt racism, of Mississippi, Perkins encountered a world of possibilities and opportunities. He worked as a union organizer, served a tour of duty in Korea, got married, and held a succession of jobs that placed him on the road to middle-class respectability. He also undertook a spiritual quest that began with the Jehovah's Witnesses, continued with Christian Science and the Father Divine Peace Mission, and settled finally at evangelical Christianity.

Soon after Perkins "said yes to Jesus Christ," he became convinced that God wanted him back in Mississippi, the very place he had left "for good" in 1947.[4] When John and Vera Mae Perkins and five children clambered out of their '56 Chevy on June 9, 1960, they found a state that had changed little since that young man had left thirteen years earlier. The racial hatred he had encountered as a boy still festered. Blacks remained trapped in a cycle of poverty, despair, and oppression.

Yet Perkins's faith, he maintains, allowed him to face these conditions with energy and determination rather than resignation and despair. He insists that he did not return to Mississippi with any strong ideological convictions or strategies, that he was influenced only tangentially by Mohandas Gandhi, Martin Luther King, or the economic philosophies of the Nation of Islam.[5] Instead, while working at a job picking cotton, he began simply to foster a sense of community and eventually to organize various religious and social programs in Mendenhall that soon became known as Voice of Calvary Ministries.[6] He started vacation Bible schools in the summertime, taught classes in Bible at public schools, and purchased a large tent for religious meetings that featured Bible study as well as preaching. Perkins settled in and quickly expanded his activities, despite harassment from local whites.[7]

THERE ARE STILL TWO SIDES of the railroad tracks in Mendenhall, Mississippi. To the east, on a gentle rise overlooking the rest of the town, sits the white section, an area of well-manicured lawns and freshly painted houses on a grid of carefully calibrated streets.

Turning east at Mendenhall's only stoplight on Old Highway 49, you enter a wide Main Street flanked by meticulously clean stores. The street leads up the hill to the Simpson County courthouse, an imposing nineteenth-century structure crowned by a golden dome.

The "quarters" (the old slave quarters) lie in a flood plain on the other side of the tracks. Here the streets (some of them paved) meander randomly. Soft-drink vending machines sit on cluttered porches, delapidated automobiles rust in patches of weeds in otherwise barren front yards. There is plenty of squalor and neglect and bleakness here in the quarters. Yet amid evidence of decay and indifference, other signs, however tentative, indicate hope.

One of first problems that Perkins addressed after he settled in Mendenhall was housing. Most of the buildings in the quarters were owned by white landlords on the other side of the tracks who extorted a good deal of rent each week, but who provided little or nothing in the way of basic maintenance. When black tenants attempted to improve their living environment by making repairs or painting walls, landlords often succeeded in evicting them for "tampering" with the building. After the evictions and with no further investment of time or capital, the landlord would simply let the building again, this time at an increased rent that reflected the improvements made by the evicted tenant. Such a system understandably bred cynicism among residents of the quarters and quashed any incentive to improve their living conditions. Perkins believed that the answer lay in a fundamental recasting of landlord-tenant relations. With help from outside contributions and a loan from the Farmers Home Administration (FHA), a co-op housing group built five low-cost duplex apartments that still provide safe, sturdy housing in the quarters.

For Perkins, this sort of social activism was perfectly compatible with his understanding of evangelical Christianity, which he saw as addressing the *physical* needs of the poor as well as their spiritual needs. He had returned from California convinced that the emphasis on emotion and ecstasy so characteristic of black religion had served to inhibit real progress—intellectual and social—among rural blacks. "I saw very quickly after I returned to Mississippi that my gospel and their gospel were not relevant to the needs of the people," he recalled. "I had to combat the emotional, simplistic gospel that black folks had already accepted. It provided an emotional outlet for them, but little else."[8]

Perkins, of course, was not the first to draw such conclusions. The famous essay "Faith of Our Fathers" by W. E. B. DuBois identified three elements of slave religion, "the Preacher, the Music, and the Frenzy," and added that the latter "was the one more devoutly believed in than all the rest."[9] Daniel Alexander Payne, nineteenth-century bishop in the African Methodist Episcopal Church, believed that the real difference between master and slave lay in knowledge. Payne spent most of his ecclesiastical career urging the formation of colleges, seminaries, and curricula for the development of black leaders. During a tour of the Reconstruction South, William Wells Brown, sometimes called America's first black man of letters, visited "one of the most refined congregations in Nashville," where he encountered all manner of religious frenzy. Believing that such demonstrations were a scourge to black social, religious, and political advancement, Brown advocated an educated ministry but allowed that, "It will be difficult to erase from the mind of the negro of the South, the prevailing idea that outward demonstrations, such as, shouting, the loud 'amen,' and the most boisterous noise in prayer, are not necessary adjuncts to piety."[10]

As a result of Perkins's efforts, black religious piety in Mendenhall now encompasses worldly concerns as well as otherworldly. Under the auspices of Mendenhall Ministries (originally, Voice of Calvary Ministries), black evangelicals in the quarters operate a thrift store, which offers low-cost food, clothing, furniture, appliances, gardening supplies, and other necessities for poor residents. The Summer Enrichment Program employs high school and college students to tutor grammar school children in study skills. A savings plan requires young people to put half their earnings into savings, both as a way to learn discipline and to provide funds for college.

Outside of town a farm, purchased in 1980, provides food, a modest income for the organization, and training in agricultural techniques for local farmers.

In 1976 two Northern blacks, Dennis Adams, a physician, and his wife, Judi, an educator, came to Mendenhall. Although the government reneged on its promise to forgive eighty percent of his medical school debts if he practiced in a low-income clinic, Dr. Adams decided to stay, even though he earned as director of the Mendenhall Cooperative Health Center only a fraction of what he might make in another setting or in private practice.

Judi Adams, a striking, well-spoken woman who now assists in the administration of these various programs, initially invested her energies in the Genesis One School, a two-story cinder-block building that houses cheery, well-appointed classrooms. The school, organized by the community to provide a quality education for blacks and other poor people in the region who found such opportunities denied them in Mendenhall schools, now boasts that its graduates outshine their public school counterparts. This education, moreover, complete with remedial tutoring, school supplies, and two meals a day, commands only $650 a year in tuition—a sum, nevertheless, beyond the means of many parents in the area, who exchange volunteer work for a reduction in tuition.

Down the street from the school, the R. A. Buckley Christian Youth Center provides vocational training and recreation in the form of a gymnasium and, according to Judi Adams, "the best-equipped weightroom in the county." The Community Law Office, situated nearby in a small steel building, provides free or low-cost legal services to the poor of Simpson County. An assortment of pamphlets in the lobby offers general advice on the legal tangles routinely faced by the poor: threats of eviction, what to do if arrested, how to file for bankruptcy, how to avoid foreclosure. The staff includes a full-time attorney, several paralegal assistants, and interns from such institutions as Stanford, Duke, and Harvard law schools. In addition to its advocacy for individuals, the Community Law Office has filed class-action desegregation suits and has recently developed a three-session People's Law School to apprise the poor of their basic legal rights.

There is a sense of hard-won permanence in all this bustle in the quarters, a tribute to determination in the face of discouraging odds. From its inception, the work in Mendenhall has met with suspicion, if not outright hostility. Any organization that enlists the cooperation of blacks and whites is viewed askance in Mississippi—it is a "civil rights outfit" that threatens traditional notions of order. Life is seldom easy in the quarters, on the wrong side of the tracks, down the hill from the courthouse that sits atop the slope of Main Street in Mendenhall.

JOHN PERKINS KNOWS WHAT IT MEANS to live in the shadow of the Simpson County courthouse, knows about the unsubtlety of Mississippi justice. While spending a night in the county jail after protesting the beating of a young black by the police, Perkins conceived the idea of an economic boycott of Mendenhall businesses. Because the economic and political interests in Mendenhall were so entwined, he reasoned, such a boycott by blacks would be the best means to call attention to their systematic repression, the persistent denial of economic opportunity, harassment by law-enforcement officials, and the continued segregation of schools.

In the ensuing months, beginning the week before Christmas 1969, the blacks of Simpson County stayed away from the stores on Main Street and organized their own cooperative. Each Saturday, armed with a parade permit, they gathered at Voice of Calvary, the ministry's headquarters, and snaked their way through the quarters, across the tracks and Highway 49, up Main Street to the courthouse, chanting "Do right, white man, do right."

Under constant surveillance by the Mississippi Highway Patrol, Perkins and other participants recognized that such an assault on Southern norms would not go unavenged. Law-enforcement officials finally pounced on Saturday, February 7, 1970. After tailing two vans of students who were returning to Tougaloo College after participating in the weekly march, a Mississippi patrolman signaled one of the vans to pull over just beyond the Simpson County line in Rankin County. Soon one of the students telephoned Perkins to say that they were in the Rankin County jail in Brandon. When Perkins and two others arrived to set bail, they were met outside the courthouse by a dozen highway patrolmen who searched them, arrested them, and began beating them even before they reached the building. Sheriff Jonathan Edwards came over to Perkins and announced, "This is the smart nigger, and this is a new ballgame. You're not in Simpson County now; you are in Brandon."[11]

Then the beatings began in earnest. One of the students later testified that the sheriff assailed Perkins so vigorously that his "shirt tail came out." After a time, five deputies and twice that number of highway patrolmen took over. Thrown to the floor, Perkins tried to shield himself by rolling up into a ball, but "they just kept on beating and stomping me, kicking me in the head, in the ribs, in the groin." One officer jammed a fork up Perkins's nose and then crammed it down his throat before beating him to the ground again.[12]

Others, including some of the students, sustained injuries in jail that night, but Perkins remembers that while lapsing in and out of consciousness he resolved to face the issue of racism in Mississippi with a new strategy. Looking into the eyes of his attackers, into eyes contorted by hatred, he recalled later, "I saw what hate had done to those people." The white man "was a victim of his own racism," and the only way he could acquire a sense of worth was to subjugate the black man. "When I saw that, I just couldn't hate back."[13]

Although at the time some of the students feared otherwise, Perkins survived that night in the Rankin County jail, but he received no satisfaction at the hands of Mississippi justice: The criminal charges against him (for "contributing to the delinquency of a minor" by allegedly encouraging one of the students to remain in jail rather than leave, as the sheriff wanted) and his civil suit against the state of Mississippi ended in compromise settlements. Perkins insists that

his ordeal in Brandon and in Mississippi courtrooms did not em-
bitter him; instead he resolved "to take a gospel of love to whites
filled with hate." Whereas so much of his energies in Mendenhall
had centered on blacks and providing means for their spiritual and
physical well-being, he looked now toward "a ministry of reconciliation" that would transcend racial boundaries.[14]

In a period of physical and emotional convalescence following
the beatings in Brandon, Perkins began to sketch out a new strategy
molded around the three Rs: *relocation* into a needy community,
"turning statistics into neighbors"; *reconciliation* across racial, social,
cultural, and economic barriers; *redistribution* of resources equitably,
not through welfare or handouts, but by training the poor in vocational and management skills.[15] But if Perkins was prepared to take
on the issue of racism and reconciliation, he was not ready to return
to Mendenhall. On the advice of his doctor, he moved to Jackson.

As in Mendenhall, forty miles to the southeast, the range of programs begun by Perkins in the state capital is impressive. Anchored
in West Jackson, Voice of Calvary Ministries lies at the interstices
of three neighborhoods, just a few blocks from the Jackson State
University campus. Perkins recognized the importance of establishing an evangelical presence and seeking some kind of stability
in these transitional neighborhoods, an objective that continues to
the present.

Don Howie, director of study programs for the organization, informed me that each of the three neighborhoods requires a different
strategy to keep it from degenerating. In West Jackson itself, once
an all-white neighborhood and now biracial, Voice of Calvary wants
to see the balance and character of the area maintained, to stem the
"white flight" that has convulsed other neighborhoods. The Lynch
Street community, historically black, is probably the poorest area of
the city. Here, during my visit, not a block from one of Jackson's main
arteries, roosters behind ramshackle houses heralded the morning.
This community lost much of its stability when the court-mandated

desegregation of other areas, particularly the suburbs, made it possible for black professionals to live elsewhere. "Here we perform
a kind of triage," Howie said. "We're trying first to develop some
young black leaders in the community, but it's difficult to identify
them. Eventually, we hope to do more in the way of reclamation:
buy run-down houses, renovate, and rent them." Georgetown, the
third neighborhood, is also in transition—poor, but not so squalid as
Lynch Street. As we toured these streets, Howie, formerly the pastor
of a white, suburban church, pointed to one house after another that
the organization had purchased, renovated, and then rented. They
have even managed to sell some of the dwellings after fixing them
up. "Ownership is the ideal situation," he said, "both for the individual family and for the neighborhood."[16]

Other programs in Jackson resemble those in Mendenhall. The
Voice of Calvary Family Health Center offers low-cost health care.
Harambee Youth Ministries tutors young people of the community
in the Bible and in classroom skills. Thriftco, a cooperative that
began on the front porch of the organization's Fellowship House,
now has two outlets in Jackson and over two thousand members.
The International Study Center, run by Voice of Calvary, trains
people to launch out with initiatives similar to Voice of Calvary's,
both in the United States and in places like Haiti and South Africa.
The John M. Perkins Christian Community Development Institute
draws college students and summer interns who combine classroom
study with some form of on-the-job experience.

While I was in Mississippi, a group of eight students from Messiah College, an evangelical college in Pennsylvania, were participating in the study program. In exchange for four hours of credit
during the college's winter term, these students, all of them middle-
class whites, sat through a week of lectures on racism, the history
of blacks in America, and various evangelical strategies for helping
the poor. Lecturers spoke about such notions as individual, institutional, and corporate racism, the systematic exclusion of blacks from
economic opportunities. The students were told that convenience

stores—Circle K, Seven-Eleven—prey on the poor by locating in ghettos; their high prices for groceries (generally unavailable elsewhere) take money out of the community, and the marketing of ready-to-eat foods, candies, and soft drinks discourages proper nutrition. Students also learned that forty-four percent of blacks in Mississippi live below the poverty level, fifty-five percent of Mississippi blacks aged sixteen or over are unemployed, less than fifteen percent have graduated from high school, three-fourths of black rural homes in Mississippi lack plumbing facilities, and sixty-nine percent of the state's prison population is black.[17]

The students from Messiah also reviewed the biblical warrants for seeking justice, the jeremiads of the Hebrew prophets and the teachings of Jesus. During the second and third weeks, the students would assist in some program or project—the thrift store, the youth program, renovation of housing—but at the conclusion of the first week, they were invited to consider the ways in which America's polarized racial situation and inequitable economic conditions had affected their own attitudes and their perceptions of blacks. They were asked to understand the sense of hopelessness and the simmering rage in black ghettos.

Most of the students acknowledged that they hadn't considered these issues prior to their arrival in Mississippi. Several admitted that they had signed up for the course because it allowed them to evade the language requirement at Messiah (apparently, a "cross-cultural experience" satisfies the requirement). As Lemuel Tucker, president of Voice of Calvary, told me later, one of the purposes of bringing such students to Jackson was to "shake them up" a bit, help them to understand the racial situation in America from the other side of the fence. "I want to unsettle them, get them to rethink some of their assumptions, and then motivate them to work toward reconciliation," he said.

The force of this message lies not in rhetoric but in example. Voice of Calvary Fellowship in Jackson evolved hand in hand with Voice of Calvary Ministries, the umbrella organization for the various programs Perkins established. The Fellowship, an evangelical church, addressed the desire on the part of Perkins and many staff members for Christian worship that would be both evangelical and interracial. "Eleven A.M. Sunday morning," people around Voice of Calvary often say, "is America's most segregated hour." And nowhere more so than in Jackson. The Calvary Baptist Church, just blocks away from Voice of Calvary offices, is a huge, imposing structure that, with fences around its playground and high brick walls, resembles a fortress more than a church. Caught amid changing neighborhoods, Calvary Baptist, a white church, finds itself surrounded by a predominantly black population, and yet, I was told, any black who tried to enter on Sunday morning would be turned away. Voice of Calvary Fellowship, on the other hand, takes pride in its multiracial character. "We've learn to enjoy, to celebrate our differences," Don Howie explained. "One of the things we've noticed is that black and white music is so different. We sing the same songs, but we sing them differently." He smiled. "Sometimes before we sing a particular hymn or chorus, the leader will say, 'We're going to sing this 'the white way' or 'the black way,'" signaling a different tempo or cadence.

IN THE YEARS SINCE HE RETURNED to Mississippi in 1960, John Perkins has met with a kind of vindication. On February 7, 1980, ten years to the day after his beating in the Rankin County jail, the governor of Mississippi honored Perkins as the state's outstanding religious leader of the year. The organizations in Jackson and Mendenhall are healthy and growing and have spawned satellite projects in places like Perkins's native New Hebron. Volunteers come from all over the nation.

But if Perkins, now organizing a similar ministry in southern California, looked for monuments to his persistence, he doubtless would see beyond the buildings and programs and real estate in Jackson or Mendenhall. From the beginning, Perkins recognized the importance of developing leaders within the black community, and in so doing he perpetuated a long tradition.[18] Historically, the church has functioned as the primary agency for social change among blacks, in part because, since the days of slavery, it was the only social institution controlled by blacks. For more than two centuries black religion has provided the breeding ground for black leaders: Richard Allen, founder of the African Methodist Episcopal Church; Denmark Vesey, leader of a slave conspiracy in Charleston; Nat Turner, a preacher and visionary who led a slave insurrection in Southampton County, Virginia; black women such as Jarena Lee, Zilpha Elaw, and Sojourner Truth; and, in the twentieth century, Benjamin Hooks, Adam Clayton Powell, Malcolm X, and Martin Luther King, Jr., among many others. Even today, many black politicians are ordained and maintain close ties with the congregations that nurtured them.

"I think people development is the most important concept in the Christian faith," Perkins told me. "I feel very good about the black leaders that have emerged in Mendenhall and Jackson. Things will go on in Mendenhall for fifty years. Things will go on in Jackson for fifty years. (After fifty years, anything can go wrong.) I judge everything by community development, when indigenous people rise up to assume leadership roles."[19]

Dolphus Weary, now president of the Mendenhall organization, and Artis Fletcher, pastor of Mendenhall Bible Church, are both products of Perkins's efforts there. So is Melvin Anderson. Over the objections of his grandmother, who feared she might lose her job as a domestic in Mendenhall if her white employers learned that her grandson was involved with Perkins's group, Anderson kept stealing away to Voice of Calvary functions. He now heads People's Development, the non-profit housing ministry in Jackson, taking charge of the various renovation projects, looking out for real-estate properties, supervising volunteer workers. "Someone," he told me earnestly at lunch one day, "has to do this. It *has* to be done, otherwise these neighborhoods will be lost, fall into decay."

The Reverend Joseph Parker, affiliated with Voice of Calvary for much of the past decade, must also be numbered among Perkins's protégés. An ordained minister in the African Methodist Episcopal

Church, he recently accepted a call to the Greater Bethel A.M.E. Church in Mound Bayou, northwest of Jackson in the Mississippi Delta region. This historically black town of three thousand lies amid the worst poverty in the United States, in a region with the highest infant mortality rate in the nation. The last of four cotton gins in town closed a couple of years ago. The median per capita income, Parker told me, ranges between $3,000 and $4,000 a year.

I asked Parker to point to his successes over the past year in Mound Bayou. Usually if you lob a question like that in the general direction of an evangelical minister, you have to brace yourself for a flurry of statistics about conversions, the missionary budget, augmentations to church membership rolls, or the dramatic increase in Sunday morning attendance. He might also regale you with the latest plans for a building program. When I asked Parker about his work, however, he replied, "Well, we have a new business coming into town." He paused. "We may also have a dry-cleaning plant soon."[20]

Parker allowed that most white evangelicals would find such an appraisal bewildering. For them, Christianity cares little about social concerns or matters of justice. Mired in middle-class respectability, they cannot see that being black and poor in America breeds a resentment against the entrenched interests of white Christians, who purvey only a pale reflection of the gospel, what Perkins calls a "Jesus Saves—keep smiling" evangelism.[21] The whole gospel, according to folks affiliated with Voice of Calvary, demands working toward justice and basic economic opportunity for the disadvantaged.

It is a mark of the cultural chasm between white and black evangelicalism that these ideas are viewed askance by most white evangelicals, whose worship tends to be relatively controlled and "respectable," and whose politics gravitate toward conservative Republicanism. Black religion itself, with its emotion and frenzy, often strikes white evangelicals as alien and suspicious. Moreover, words like "justice" and "economic opportunity," when applied to the poor, smack of liberalism and imply a threat to the social and economic order that, on the whole, has treated whites kindly. Such rhetoric also sounds vaguely like the Social Gospel practiced by Protestant liberals at the turn of the century, which sought the redemption of sinful social institutions—predatory monopolies, unscrupulous landlords, unbridled capitalism—that kept the urban poor enslaved in poverty. Evangelicals overwhelmingly opposed the Social Gospel, preferring instead to emphasize the need for individual conversions rather than the overhaul of society. John Perkins is certainly no radical, but he and the people associated with the organizations he founded have sought to educate fellow Christians about the plight of the poor and to enlist their help in ameliorating the conditions that perpetuate black poverty.

How do white evangelicals respond to such overtures? I put the question to Dolphus Weary, head of the Mendenhall organization, and later to Lemuel Tucker, president of Voice of Calvary in Jackson. Weary contended that most evangelicals have yet to develop a strategy for dealing with the poor. But it's an issue, he said, that must be addressed if they mean to take seriously the precepts of Christianity. Tucker believes that evangelicals "are unprepared for justice. They've placed too much stock in some of the arcane issues of theology and defending their notions of orthodoxy and not enough emphasis on the basic issues of human dignity and justice."

Perkins himself sees progress, evidence that evangelicals are taking more seriously the social demands of the gospel. "I think programs like Voice of Calvary and Mendenhall Ministries offer real models of evangelism and social responsibility," he said. I asked him if he had encountered resistance from fellow evangelicals to his socially grounded Christianity. "In the early days, yes," he said, "but there's been an evolution. Now we're seen as something of an example, as pioneers. Once evangelicals found issues that they could be active on—issues like abortion and pornography—they began exerting more influence in the social arena. But they have not been very active on issues that affect the poor. The very fact that they began to be active on social issues, however, meant that they could no longer fault people like us for being involved in social action. Once the Moral Majority was organized, social action became acceptable among evangelicals." Still, Perkins, who serves on the boards of various evangelical organizations, cannot get evangelicals interested in sanctions against South Africa, which is seen, again, as a "liberal" cause. He believes that prosperity theology—the God-will-make-you-rich-and-happy notions propagated by such televangelists as Robert Schuller, Kenneth Copeland, and Jim and Tammy Bakker—has blinded many evangelicals to the needs of the poor. "This prosperity stuff is deadly," he said.[22]

IN SMALL MEASURES, PERHAPS, the message was seeping through. The students from Messiah College still weren't sure what the letters NAACP stood for, but after a week of lectures and a visit to Joseph Parker's church in Mound Bayou, some of them began to wonder whether, in some subconscious way, they too had been affected by racism and even now harbored certain assumptions or prejudices about blacks. "What's hit me the hardest," one woman volunteered, "is the notion that we might be prejudiced in certain ways and not even realize it. It's something we absorb from the broader culture, from television and commercials and Saturday morning cartoons. It's not something we decide. It's very subtle." Most still weren't convinced they were racist in any palpable way, but at least they were asking the question. Some acknowledged that they had felt uncomfortable in Parker's all-black church, that it was easier for them at the church dinner following the morning service to sit together rather than disperse throughout the fellowship hall. That experience, they said, taught them what it felt like to be a minority. One woman said that *Roots*, which they had seen on videotape that week, "made me feel extremely guilty—that we white people are scum for enslaving blacks."

Did others feel any personal responsiblity for the plight of blacks in this country? No, most still did not. But one man said, "Yes, I think we are responsible in that we are born into the system. If we're not vigorously attacking the system and trying to change it, we're a part of it, because we are white and benefiting from it." Another student added: "We hadn't really noticed the injustices before, but now that we see them we bear a responsibility. By failing to challenge the system, we become part of it, and we're culpable."

1987

CHAPTER 10

Bible Bazaar

I'VE OFTEN WONDERED what it would be like to bring back the fathers of western culture's most formative inventions to see how their devices have evolved over the generations. Would Alexander Graham Bell recognize credit-card telephones in our airports? In his wildest dreams, could Thomas Edison have imagined the fidelity of a compact disc? Could Guglielmo Marconi have envisioned facsimile machines, instant replay, or diamond-vision scoreboards? Even Henry Ford, I suspect, would be astonished at how thoroughly his invention has shaped American culture: drive-in banks, hardware stores, and funeral homes, a sprawling network of roadways, the alacrity with which we turn forests and fields into parking lots.

If Johann Gutenberg, inventor of movable type and publisher of the first Gutenberg Bible in 1456, were around today, I'd want to walk him through the exhibition hall of the Christian Booksellers Association annual convention. There he would find a bewildering array of Bibles: the *Living Bible*, the *Catholic Living Bible*, the *Christian Life Bible*, the *People's Parallel Bible*, the *New English Bible*, the *Revised English Bible*, the *Simple English Bible*, the *Daily Walk Bible*, the *Picture Bible*, the *Thompson Chain-Reference Bible* (fifth edition), *La Santa Biblia*, the *New American Standard Bible*, the *Disciple's Study Bible*, the *New International Version Personal Reference Bible,* *Dake's Annotated Reference Bible*, the *Discovery Bible*, the *Rainbow Study Bible*, the *International Children's Bible*, the *Open Bible*, the *Good News Bible*, the *Prophecy Bible*—to name only a few. He would also find Bibles available on cassette tapes (in several versions and at least twelve languages) and on computer diskettes (again, in several versions).

Gutenberg's invention made possible this proliferation of Bibles, but the Protestant Reformers—Martin Luther, John Calvin, Ulrich Zwingli, William Tyndale, Miles Coverdale, Thomas Cranmer—first seized on this invention and insisted that Bibles be made available to the masses. Vernacular translations appeared all over northern Europe and England in the sixteenth century. People began to read the Scriptures for themselves and no longer through the interpretive template of the Roman Catholic Church, which for centuries had relied on the Vulgate, Jerome's Latin translation of the Bible. *Sola scriptura*, reliance on the Scriptures only, became a hallmark of the Protestant Reformation. Just as Luther insisted that Christians had direct access to God through Jesus Christ and not through the mediation of priests, so too believers, Luther said, could interpret the Bible for themselves, absent the prejudices of Catholic theology.

The *Scofield Reference Bible* and the *Ryrie Study Bible* in their various guises—King James Version, New American Standard Version, New International Version—therefore require some explanation. The idea that the Bible should be viewed through a specific interpretive lens would have been foreign to the generation of Reformers who followed Gutenberg and who used his invention to propagate the Scriptures, shorn of Roman Catholic glosses, in the vernacular of the people. In truth, however, despite all the evangelical rhetoric about *sola scriptura* in the twentieth century, most evangelicals don't trust themselves to interpret the Bible, so they turn to others—local pastors, mendicant preachers and lecturers, authors of thousands of books, commentaries, and reference tools—for interpretive schemes.

American evangelicals, nevertheless, have an almost mystical attachment to the Bible.[1] I recall being told in Sunday school that a Bible should never be placed on the floor; to do so was a sacrilege akin to allowing the American flag to touch the ground. Evangelicals use the term "Word of God" synonomously with "Bible" or "Scripture," a reflection of the conviction that the Bible contains God's revelation to humanity. In 1978 George Gallup found that forty-two percent of Americans believed that "the Bible is the Word of God and is not mistaken in its statements and teachings"; thirty percent professed to read the Bible at least once a week, of whom twelve percent claimed to read the Bible daily.[2] Evangelical preachers liberally pepper their sermons with biblical proof-texts in order to substantiate their arguments. Evangelical theologians take great pains to demonstrate that their doctrines are *biblical* or *scriptural*, even if the exegesis sometimes is a bit tortured. The internecine warfare waged in evangelical circles over the doctrine of biblical inerrancy in recent years reflects the seriousness with which evangelicals view the Bible, asserting that the Bible was utterly flawless in the original autographs (which, of course, are no longer available). These high-pitched battles have become so intense that detractors have accused evangelicals of bibliolatry: elevating the Bible to the status of an idol that is itself worshiped.

Evangelicals heatedly dispute that charge, but in fact they ascribe extraordinary powers to the Scriptures. I suspect that even the most impatient Sunday morning channel-jumper has caught a glimpse of some televangelist thrusting a Bible high into the air, shaking it for dramatic effect, and extolling "the power of God's Holy Word" or waxing rhapsodic about "the precious Word of God." In a way, of course, such veneration is not surprising. The more extreme iconoclastic Protestants stripped the sacraments of all but symbolic meaning, so that today in most evangelical circles, baptism does not confer God's grace; it merely announces a believer's decision to follow Christ. Holy Communion, generally observed no more than once a month in evangelical churches, merely symbolizes the broken body and shed blood of Christ; nothing supernatural occurs, as with the Roman Catholic doctrine of transubstantiation, which holds that the elements *actually become* the body and blood of Christ, even though they retain the outward appearance of bread and wine. In a theology thus denuded of mystery, many evangelicals have vested the Bible with supernatural power. "God's Word will not return unto Him void," evangelicals often say, paraphrasing a passage from Isaiah.[3] And so American evangelicals have spent a great deal of time, money, and energy to propagate the Scriptures here in America and around the world. John Eliot, Puritan missionary to the Indians, translated the Bible into "the Indian language" (Algonquin) in 1661. The formation of the American Bible Society in New York City on May 8, 1816, knit together more than thirty separate Bible societies, all of them dedicated to propagating the Scriptures among various constituencies, regions of the country, or foreign nations; in 1979 alone, the American Bible Society distributed nearly 110 million Bibles (or portions thereof) just in the United States.[4] The Gideons, an organization of lay evangelicals with headquarters in Nashville, Tennessee, supply Bibles to hospitals, military personnel, and hotel rooms with the confidence that the mere reading of the Bible can transform sinners into saints. The Bible, the Gideons say in the introductory pages to their New Testament, "should fill the memory, rule the heart, and guide the feet." "Read it slowly, frequently, and prayerfully," they counsel. "It is a mine of wealth, a paradise of glory, and a river of pleasure. It is given you in life, will be opened at the judgment, and be remembered forever. It involves the highest responsibility, will reward the greatest labor, and will condemn all who trifle with its sacred contents."

If Bible salesmen conjure images of Depression-era shysters rumbling across the Kansas plains in model T Fords, that notion is hopelessly out of date. Bibles are big business. Nothing illustrates that better than the huge exhibition hall of the Christian Booksellers Association convention, a cavernous room full of elaborate, brightly lit displays, some of them reaching high into the air to attract maximum attention. The CBA convention functions as a trade show for more than five thousand Christian bookstores across the country; it is, in fact, one of the largest trade shows in the nation, with more than 350 exhibitors consuming 275,000 square feet of space.[5] Here publishers display their wares and make their pitches to retail store owners and buyers. I saw several sales representatives in polyester suits and bad toupees at the CBA convention who looked as though they'd be just as comfortable kicking tires on a used-car lot as thumping Bibles in an air-conditioned exhibition hall, but on the whole, if this convention is any indication, the Bible business is slick, glitzy, professional, and fiercely competitive, with salesmen— and a few women—to match. Publishers compete vigorously with one another for market share, retail shelf space, and what they call clerk involvement to sell their products. Here at the convention, they offered various incentives to buyers: favorable credit terms, deferred billing, free shipping. Wm. B. Eerdmans Publishing Co. of Grand Rapids, Michigan, gave a Droste chocolate bar to anyone placing an order. Moody Press, a division of Moody Bible Institute in Chicago, offered a Cross pen.

Bibles are big business. Word Inc. of Waco, Texas, which publishes books for the evangelical market, was purchased by ABC several years back. After fending off a number of hostile takeover attempts, Zondervan Publishing House of Grand Rapids, Michigan, which holds the coveted rights to the New International Version of the Bible, had agreed to a friendly takeover by Harper & Row, owned by publishing magnate Rupert Murdoch, just a week prior to the 1988 CBA convention.[6]

Bibles are big business—especially in America among evangelical households, most of which are more likely to stock a dozen Bibles than only one or a couple. How big a business? Figures are hard to come by because such firms as Zondervan and Thomas Nelson Publishers of Nashville remain tight-lipped about their Bible sales. In the course of the convention, I heard estimates ranging from $60 million to $200 million a year in the United States alone. No one can say for certain how many kinds of Bibles are available, but one distributor estimated that her company stocked over three thousand different translations and editions.

Bibles are big business.

But how do you keep selling Bibles in an already flooded matket? Mike Colacuori, who describes himself as an "official peddler" for Omni Sales in Indiana, Illinois, and Michigan, compared the demand for Bibles to the demand for new cars. People buy Bibles because the old ones wear out, because of the availability of new versions, or maybe because a reader is getting older and wants larger type, he said. "Sometimes people buy Bibles on a whim, for no good reason. Then you have the first-time buyers: new Christians and kids who grew up in the church."

Paul Shepherd and Ida Fitz know the Bible business as well as anyone. Ida Fitz's father-in-law started distributing Bibles to Christian bookstores twenty years ago. Today Riverside Book & Bible House, a family-owned business in Iowa Falls, Iowa, takes in $35 million a year, out of which, they estimate, Bibles account for more than $25 million, making them the largest Bible wholesaler in the world. "When I started in this business with Thomas Nelson thirteen years ago," Shepherd, now an executive at Riverside, said, "we carried only three colors: black, brown, and red." Now consumers choose from a variety of bindings. A few years back, he said, the hottest color was brown. "Now you can't give a brown leather Bible away." This season's big sellers? Taupe, gray, and mauve.

In order to sell more and more Bibles, publishers have devised all sorts of angles: new translations, new typefaces, new colors, new bindings. Thomas Nelson recently unveiled a leather-bound Bible with a snap enclosure and a shoulder strap affixed to the spine; it looks like an elegant handbag. Several years back one publisher purchased the rights to about a dozen syrupy cartoon-like illustrations and interleaved them into one of its translations to market it as the *Precious Moments Bible*. Another publisher produced a Bible that helps the reader peruse both Old and New Testaments in a single year. The large-print Bible, Shepherd said, has been one of the strongest sellers over the past decade, a reflection of an aging population of Bible readers. "It used to be that the last quarter of the year was our best season," Ida Fitz said, "but now the demand remains high the year round." People buy Bibles for births, confirmations, weddings, graduations, Easter, Christmas—even for returning to school. Florists buy small Bibles to stick into flower arrangements. "Our office windows overlook the warehouse back in Iowa Falls," Fitz said, "and I don't think there's a day that goes by when we don't look at one another as we see Bibles loaded into box after box and ask, 'Where are all those Bibles going?'"

Despite the inroads of large corporations into the Bible business, many people selling Bibles and Christian literature do so, at least in part, out of a sense of mission. "I've chosen to sell Bibles because it directly promotes the gospel," Mike Colaquori told me. "I wanted to be in this industry." Ida Fitz and Paul Shepherd take evident satisfaction in their work, not only because it provides them a good living—it surely does that—but also, they say, because it "gets the message out." Many of the retailers that a distributor like Riverside deals with every day share similar sentiments. In the 1970s, on the heels of the Jesus movement, many of the people who opened Bible bookstores were long on faith and short on finances, with a surfeit of naïveté and very little know-how. Ida Fitz recalls receiving credit applications back from prospective customers with "The Lord will provide" scrawled across the top of the applications.

The entire industry has become a good bit more sophisticated since then—and a good bit more profitable. Christian bookstores do about $2 billion a year in retail sales, a figure that has doubled since 1980 and is expected to reach $3.6 billion by 1990.[7] The Christian Booksellers Association, with offices in Colorado Springs, Colorado, discourages people from entering the business unless they can come up with at least $20,000 in capital. The CBA also publishes *Bookstore Journal* every month, a trade magazine burgeoning with four-color advertisements, and advises bookstore owners on such issues as inventory control, payroll, and retirement plans. At the annual convention, retailers can attend seminars with titles like "Wrapping Up a Sale," "Cost-Effective Advertising for Small Businesses," and "How to Capture a Piece of the Video Market."

AT SOME POINT (no one is sure exactly when) someone figured out that the patrons of a Christian bookstore will buy more than Bibles. In most such bookstores, Bibles now account for only about ten to twenty percent of sales. In mall stores, the percentage may be as low as five to six percent. The remainder of the receipts come from books, musical recordings, greeting cards, and other accouterments, all of which were abundantly in evidence in the CBA exhibition hall. A sampling of book titles offers a glimpse into the world of evangelical publishing:

> *How to Listen to God*
> *You Are Somebody: You're Worth More than You Think*
> *What It Means to Be Real*
> *How to Know You're Saved*
> *How to Be the Happy Wife of an Unsaved Husband*
> *The Sacredness of Sex*
> *Dark Secrets of the New Age*
> *Share the New Life with a Jew*
> *The Church Triumphant at the End of the Age*
> *Santa and the Christ Child*
> *How to Be a Good Dad*
> *Maximized Manhood: A Guide to Family Survival*
> *How to Keep Your Kids on Your Team*
> *Keeping Your Teen in Touch with God*
> *Conquering the Fear of Death*
> *The Joy of Feeling Good*
> *How to Be a Christian and Still Enjoy Life*

At the booth of Moody Press of Chicago, a large queue formed to receive free promotional copies of a new book entitled *Mormonism, Mama & Me*, signed by an older woman dressed in a gingham "granny" costume with matching bonnet.

At hourly intervals during the convention, a succession of authors and musicians stationed themselves at five different "Personality Booths" throughout the exhibition hall. There they distributed and autographed copies of their latest books or recordings. Every subculture has its own heroes and stars, a phenomenon evident by the long lines that formed at the "Personality Booths" when someone well known to evangelicals appeared. These "names"—Chuck Swindoll, Mike Warnke, John MacArthur, Florence Littauer, a singer named Carman, a pianist named Dino—are virtually unknown outside the evangelical subculture, but here at the convention they attracted throngs of groupies, young and old.

The groupies especially throng around recording artists, and there are plenty to choose from. So-called Christian music ranges from the punk-rock sounds of Youth Choir, Undercover, and Altar Boys to the heavy metal of Stryper, Saint, Messiah Prophet Man, Barren Cross, Resurrection Band, and Bloodgood. Carman, from what I was able to gather from descriptions of his music, is the evangelical counterpart to Julio Iglesias. Dino's style reminds many of Liberace. Some Christian artists, notably Amy Grant and Sandi Patti, occasionally produce hits that cross over to the secular charts. This "Christian" music—records, cassettes, compact discs, sheet music, orchestral backup tapes—accounts for a growing proportion—nearly twenty percent—of retail sales in Christian bookstores.[8]

The range of goods available at these bookstores, however, extends well beyond Bibles, books, and recordings. If you're serious about studying the Bible, you'll want a highlighter, a marker used to underline important or meaningful passages. If you use your Bible a lot, sooner or later you'll want to pick up a Bible tote of one kind or another. The BAC & Associates booth at the CBA convention offers a variety, ranging in price from $8.95 to $25.95: Deluxe Unlined Covers available in six designs (various doves, crosses, and fish), Premium Lined Covers, Deluxe Unlined Covers with Pockets, Petite Pastels, Tropical Treats (in colors like salmon and powder blue), Fabric Frillies (quilted fabric with lace edges), and top-of-the-line Trifold Bible Covers (leather-like vinyl with a locking clasp and an attache-style handle on the spine). Mountain Meadow Designs, doing business out of Utah, offers several styles in a canvas-like fabric. Bear Mountain Industries of Independence,

Missouri, a couple of booths away, is one of many vendors who specialize in quilted Bible totes with embroidery on the outside and lace on the edges, but these totes, according to one saleswoman, are double-faced with several inside pockets for notebooks and pens. The quilted totes from Com for Things in Holyoke, Colorado, feature lace, buttons, flowers, and ribbons in various designs. Horizon Publishers of Bountiful, Utah, offers both quilted and vinyl Bible totes, but they also carry smaller sizes for pocket New Testaments.

Several vendors at the CBA convention were selling Sunday school curriculum materials and church supplies such as candles, light fixtures, song books, vestments, and choir robes. Evangelicalism's involvement with the temperance movement in the nineteenth and early twentieth centuries led to the substitution of grape juice for wine in Holy Communion and to the abandonment of the common cup or chalice for small, individual-sized glasses barely larger than a thimble. Some years back, suppliers began providing disposable plastic communion cups. New Covenant Communion Supply out of Fort Worth, Texas, for instance, advertises "High-Quality Communion Cups That Never Crack, Stick, or Leak!"

Evangelicals have also tapped into the home video market. Videocassettes run the gamut from lectures and biblical expositions by such preachers as Billy Graham, Kenneth Hagin, and R. C. Sproul to a series of "Bear Hugs" animations and dramatized Bible stories for children to videos of feature-length films such as Donald Thompson's apocalyptic series, *A Thief in the Night, A Distant Thunder, Image of the Beast*, and *Prodigal Planet*. A salesman representing Maranatha Campus Ministries International in Gainesville, Florida, was promoting a ninety-minute videocassette entitled "Rock and Roll Search for God," an exposé of the "demonic aspect of rock and roll music," geared to college students. "After seeing this thing," the representative told me, "they either run toward Jesus and accept Him as their savior or they run back to their old sinful lifestyles."

Calendars and greeting cards also sell very well in the evangelical market. A woman from VALdyme Inc. in Roseville, California, was at the CBA promoting a desktop calendar called Vision Planner, which "helps today's Christian Family prioritize their lives for a satisfying balance between physical and spiritual priorities." Some of the features include pages for prayer concerns and "space each day to record an inspirational thought, reminder, or lesson; keeping Christian faith in daily practice."[9] Many evangelicals would much rather purchase "Christian" greeting cards than "secular" ones. "Things that we value in the body of Christ are often cheapened by such things as greeting cards," said Mike Colacuori, the Bible salesman from the Midwest. "I've seen a lot of cards that might not actually be dirty, yet the punch line is something that undermines traditional Christian values. If a Christian goes into business to sell greeting cards, he's performing a legitimate service." Evangelical customers apparently agree, for there has been a proliferation of "Christian" greeting cards (and greeting-card companies) in recent years.

Many companies manufacture pictures, posters, and wall-hangings of various kinds. Good Things Co. of Norman, Oklahoma, offers two posters (framed or unframed), one of them showing the books of the Bible and the other charting the genealogy from Adam and Eve to Jesus. Jeremiah Junction of Manchester, Connecticut, sells counted cross-stitch patterns in various "inspirational" designs. Max Greiner, Jr., a loquacious young artist from Kerrville, Texas, sells variations on his "Christian Butterfly" design, a butterfly with wings in stained glass and a body shaped like a fish, symbolizing Christ (the first letters of "Jesus Christ, Son of God, Savior" spell *ichthus*—the Greek word for fish). "This is the first original symbol in two thousand years of Christian history," Greiner told me. "In October of 1986 I was desperately trying to conceive of a unique jewelry design to give to my wife on her birthday. After two weeks without an idea, I finally said to God, 'I give up; I need a good idea quick, please!' Instantly after this prayer, the image of the upside-down *ichthus* with butterfly wings appeared in my mind's eye. This one simple idea is probably the most profound and timeless design that has ever come to me. It's ironic that I cannot accept the credit, which must go to God."[10]

Some of the items for sale at the convention are seasonal. JESUS IS THE ♥ OF CHRISTMAS and JESUS IS THE REASON FOR THE SEASON festooned a whole panoply of Christmas goods—cards, gift wrap, posters, figurines, coffee mugs. A number of companies have introduced entire lines of books, videotapes, and trinkets aimed at children; some have devised Sesame Street-like characters—Gerbert and Andy Ant—to promote their wares. Several vendors sell key chains, combs, and bumper stickers: JESUS IS MY ROCK AND MY NAME IS ON THE ROLL, WARNING: IN CASE OF RAPTURE THIS CAR WILL BE UNMANNED, and GET RIGHT OR GET LEFT, a reference to the impending rapture and the apocalypse. Some peddled sponges with various sentiments emblazoned on them: TRUST IN THE LORD, GOD CLEANS ME FROM THE INSIDE OUT, KEEP AFLOAT WITH GOD.

So-called Christian tee-shirts were everywhere. A company named Images in the Son, based in Orange Park, Florida, boasted that they have sold three billion shirts. One style showed two flamingos, one of which had its head in a bucket, along with the warning, YOU CAN'T HIDE FROM GOD! Kingdom Shirt Ministries of Edmond, Oklahoma, specializes in shirts that replicate well-known logotypes and advertising slogans with slight variations: JESUS—THE RIGHT CHOICE (AT&T), OVER 80 MILLION SAVED (McDonald's), JESUS CHRIST—HE'S THE REAL THING (Coke), JESUS—THE CHOICE OF THE LAST GENERATION (Pepsi), FOR ALL YOU DO, HIS BLOOD'S FOR YOU (Budweiser).

Tee-shirts are not the only apparel available. I didn't see them at the CBA convention, but someone told me about "Witness Panty Hose," which featured a fish design interwoven into the nylon and a Bible verse around the ankles. Christian World Inc. of Oklahoma City had perhaps the most lavish display at the convention, with French provincial furniture, plush purple carpeting deep enough to pitch you off balance, and fashionably dressed salespeople dripping in gold jewelry and hair-styling mousse. "Our products will always be unique and only the finest quality because we feel that as a Christian company, God expects us to do only the finest," Mark A. Stevens, president of the company, writes in Christian World's elaborate promotional materials. "I know that with your effort we can help to spread our Father's message to the greatest number of people possible." Christian World sells wedding accessories, table and bed linens, stick-up magnets, and "inspirational drinking glasses and mugs."

For $5.99, the World Bible Society sells a cassette called "Heavenly Touch—Spiritually Inspired Phone Messages for Your Phone Answering Device." Someone else offered a cardboard sun shield for the front window of parked cars. The outside reads JESUS IS LORD, and the reverse side says NEED HELP! PLEASE CALL POLICE. Sonshine Graphics of Corona, California, recently introduced "an exciting new product," a package of home security yard signs, home window decals, and car window decals, all in the shape of a shield with the rather intimidating legend: PROTECTED BY SHED-BLOOD SECURITY UNLTD. "Now believers can proclaim their belief in God's protecting hand in a very tangible and visible way," the ad copy reads. "shed-blood security unltd. offers the consumer the advantage of both discouraging would-be prowlers and an opportunity to witness to neighbors about their security in Christ."[11]

There is a strong conservative political bias permeating the Christian Booksellers Association. The 1988 convention took place during the same week that the Democrats were holding their national convention in Atlanta. The morning after Jesse Jackson's speech at the Democratic gathering, one exhibitor remarked that the Democrats needed a linguist to sort out Jackson's "'dis and 'dat." At one of the flag-bedecked booths at the CBA convention, men in red neckties, white shirts, and blue suits were hawking something called the American Prayer Action Calendar, which, for $6.95, suggests a different prayer concern—pornography, abortion, homosexuality—for every day of the year. "Our idea is to have Christians all across the country praying for the same issues every day," Harry E. Gibbons, author of the calendar, said. Several weeks hence, the readers would be asked to pray for the Republican national convention in New Orleans; this week, however, they were to pray for the Christian

Booksellers Association convention. Harvest House Publishers of Eugene, Oregon, were enthusiastic about a new book entitled *George Bush: Man of Integrity*. Another title available to bookstore buyers at the CBA was *A Fighting Chance: The Moral Use of Nuclear Weapons*, which had received lavish praise from several prominent conservatives. Robert Faid, who describes himself as a nuclear engineer and who holds a master's degree in theology from Coatesville Bible College, was at the convention pushing his new book, *Gorbachev! Has the Real Antichrist Come?*, which argues that Mikhail Gorbachev is the Antichrist predicted in the Bible. "Gorbachev meets fourteen of the sixteen prophetic identity clues in the Scriptures," Faid told me confidently. When you assign numbers to the letters in Gorbachev's name, using the Cyrillic alphabet, he said, it comes out to 666, the mark of the beast. Then there is the matter of the birthmark on the Soviet leader's forehead. "When I look at the top of Gorbachev's head, I see a red dragon and over the right eye, there's a tail that hangs, representing stars," Faid said. This, he believes, resembles the description of Satan in the book of Revelation. "If Gorbachev is truly the Antichrist," Faid concludes, "Satan branded him in his mother's womb."[12] Moreover, Faid said that he had computed the odds against Gorbachev's being the Antichrist; they work out to 710 quadrillion to one (specifically, 710, 609, 175, 188, 282, 100 to 1).

A NUMBER OF PEOPLE I SPOKE WITH expressed uneasiness about all the kitsch everywhere in evidence in the exhibition hall and the materialism implicit in its popularity. "It's almost a misnomer to call this the Christian Booksellers Association," Ida Fitz of Riverside Book & Bible House told me. "So much of the business transacted here is in gifts or what some people call 'holy hardware'; comparatively little has to do with books." So far, Riverside has stayed out of the gift business, although Fitz allowed that her company has already contemplated expansion into that area. "There's more markup in gifts," she said. "That's why bookstores like to move that merchandise."

Other long-term observers sense a real tragedy in the commercialism and the carnival atmosphere at the CBA. Jon Pott, editor-in-chief of Wm. B. Eerdmans in Grand Rapids, sees a trend away from quality literature and an increased traffic in self-help books and various trinkets. "This may be the last time I stay for the whole convention," he said quietly as he surveyed the exhibition floor. "I find it utterly demoralizing." When I asked Luci Shaw, a poet and head of Harold Shaw Publishers in Wheaton, Illinois, for her impressions of the Christian Booksellers Association, she looked down and shook her head. "Yesterday afternoon I got so fed up with the whole thing that I went home to my hotel and cried for two hours." She cited the quest for fame and fortune on the part of both authors and publishers. Within the world of evangelical publishing, she said, "authors become celebrities very fast, and money and power are so corrosive." Shaw, herself a product of the evangelical subculture, is clearly disillusioned. She is now an Episcopalian and has considered distancing her publishing house from the evangelical market. "But I can't do that," she said in a tone of resignation. "I have to make a living."

If Johann Gutenberg managed to make it this far on our tour of the CBA exhibition, I'd want to make one last stop, at the elaborate booth of Tyndale House Publishers, Wheaton, Illinois, publishers of the enormously profitable *Living Bible*, which has sold over thirty-five million copies since its release in 1970. Gutenberg might faintly recognize the fellow in ersatz Elizabethan costume standing atop a carpeted soapbox hawking Tyndale House's newest product, the *Life Application Bible*, which retails for $34.95 in cloth binding or $49.95 in bonded leather. This chap purported to be William Tyndale himself, the sixteenth-century translator of the Bible. During "Tyndale's" soliloquy, the publisher's sales representatives distributed small parchment-like folders to the gathering of onlookers. At the conclusion of his pitch, "Tyndale" instructed the crowd to break the seal and look inside for an illustration of the *Life Application Bible*, which provides not only the Scripture passages themselves, but also a "Life Application Note" to enlarge upon the message of the Scriptures. At the top of the parchment was a passage from the *Living Bible*:

> For neither you nor anyone else can serve two masters. You will hate one and show loyalty to the other, or else the other way around—you will be enthusiastic about one and despise the other. You cannot serve both God and money.[13]

The "Life Application Note" followed:

> Money has the power to take God's place in your life. It can become your master. How can you tell if you are a slave to money? (1) Do you worry about it frequently? (2) Do you give up doing what you should do or would like to do in order to make more money? (3) Do you spend a great deal of time caring for your possessions? (4) Is it hard for you to give money away? (5) Are you in debt?
>
> Money is a hard master and a deceptive one. Money promises power and control, but it often cannot deliver. Great fortunes can be made—and lost—overnight, and no amount of money can provide health, happiness, or eternal life. How much better to let God be your master. His servants have peace of mind and security both now and forever.

The sales representatives milling around the booth seemed pleased with the response. Tyndale had another winner.

Bibles are big business.

1988

CHAPTER 11

Episcopal Indians

According to Dakota legend, a young Indian woman and her child refused to accompany her tribe as they fled south before the advance of white soldiers. When some of her people later returned to the camp to find her, they discovered that she and the child on her back had turned to stone. That stone, called Standing Rock, has been held in reverence by the Sioux for generations, and today it rests on a pedestal in Fort Yates, North Dakota, overlooking, in the words of a nearby plaque, "the waters and the empire once held by the mighty Sioux Nation."

When Jesus commanded His disciples to preach the gospel "to the ends of the earth,"[1] He might have had in mind places like Fort Yates, North Dakota. Fort Yates may not be the end of the earth, but, as the old saw goes, you can see it from here. I was here to see what evangelical impulses persist within the Episcopal Church, a denomination not generally associated with evangelicalism, and also to assess the extent to which Christian missions engage in a kind of cultural imperialism, an insistence that converts adopt the missionaries' culture along with their religion. In the nineteenth century, mainline denominations—Congregationalists, Baptists, Methodists, Presbyterians, Roman Catholics—organized missions among the Indians, but most of them have since lost interest in the enterprise, even though they maintain a residual presence on reservations throughout the West. Here at Fort Yates in the Standing Rock Indian Reservation, a handful of Episcopalians are struggling to retain a foothold and to temper some of the cultural imperialism that has characterized Christian mission efforts in the past.

THE WATERS OF THE MISSOURI RIVER no longer flow at Standing Rock's feet; the United States Army Corps of Engineers saw to that some years back when they built a dam at Pierre, South Dakota. The river running past Fort Yates and the Standing Rock Indian Reservation became Lake Oahe, a huge expanse of water that swallowed up much of the land along the Missouri, clogged adjoining wells with silt, and left the carcasses of countless trees pointing their dead, whitened branches above the water in a kind of eerie and desolate beauty.

Lake Oahe provides irrigation, flood control, and recreation, but the waters no longer flow, and that offends Father Innocent Good House, a Sioux Indian and rector of St. Luke's Episcopal Church in Fort Yates. "An Indian believes that the waters of a river should flow," he said. The damming of the Missouri, he believes, underscores a difference between Indian and Christian religions and their views of the world. Whereas Indians believe in fashioning their lives in harmony with nature, Christians too often have interpreted the biblical injunction to have dominion over the earth as license to alter the created order, to tamper with its rhythms and control its unpredictabilities.

But Good House, a quiet, taciturn man of sixty-eight, is more interested in the parallels between Christianity and Indian religions and in convincing his fellow Sioux of the compatibility of those traditions. Over the course of several days, he pointed out those parallels. Both religions have sacraments. Both are monotheistic—Indians believe in the Great Spirit, the creator, while the Judeo-Christian tradition honors Yahweh, the creator. The Indian naming ceremony, when an Indian child of about twelve years receives an ancestral name, resembles christening or confirmation or the Jewish bar mitzvah. The rite of purification resembles baptism. In the course of a vision quest, an Indian goes up to a hill for four days of prayer, seeking spiritual guidance, an exercise not unlike Jesus' wanderings in the wilderness for forty days. Good House finds affinities even in social patterns. The extended kinship ties among Indians is similar to the fellowship of believers or the communion of the saints that characterizes the Church. Just as the early Christians of the New Testament held goods in common and provided for one another's well-being, Indians for centuries have practiced a kind of welfare system that, informally and by common consent, provides for the sick, infirm, and elderly. The Church has looked to elders for spiritual guidance and counsel; Indians venerate their elders, because they are closer to death and, hence, closer to God, and because they have amassed wisdom in the course of a lifetime.

It would be easy, I suppose, to dismiss these sentiments as mere puffery, the kind of inclusive posturing that liberal Episcopalians have elevated to an art form in recent decades. Episcopalians have never been noted for theological rigidity, after all, much less for evangelistic fervor, although there are a number of charismatic Episcopal parishes in the United States. But Innocent Good House carries about him a sincerity and earnestness—even a quiet passion—about both his faith and his heritage. He can speak in one breath about the importance of bringing his fellow Sioux to Christ and in the next about the necessity of perpetuating Sioux religious traditions without any sense that the two might be mutually exclusive.

The affinities between Christianity and native religions, however, have not always been apparent to Christians working among the Sioux. "When the missionaries came onto the reservation," Good House said, "they made me a Christian, but they also destroyed my language and my culture." The task of making Christians of the Indians was made easier, ironically, by the parallels between the two belief systems, parallels obvious to many of the Indians, even if the missionaries chose to ignore them.

Spanish missionaries—the Jesuits and, later, the Franciscans—began proselytizing the natives of the New World early in the sixteenth century. Conversion of the Indians provided a major rationale for colonization during the seventeenth century, as English Puritans, Dutch Calvinists, and French Jesuits sought to transform "savages" into Christians. In almost all cases, contact with the missionaries spelled disaster for Indian cultures. Exposure to alien diseases and viruses often decimated native populations.[2] In other instances, missionaries effectively disarmed the Indians, leaving them vulnerable to the attacks of other Indians or unscrupulous whites. Almost invariably, missionaries chose to ignore the commonalities between Christianity and Indian religions and demanded that their converts abjure all participation in native rituals. "The greatest problem of the missionary," Father Fermin F. Lausuén, head of Spanish missions in California, wrote in 1801, "was how to transform a savage race such as these into a society that is human, Christian, civil, and industrious."[3] Missionaries would go to almost any ends to convert the Indians—whom they regarded as barbaric, heathen, and godless—and to make them docile and even "white."[4]

John Eliot's mission among the Indians of seventeenth-century New England provides a good example. Eliot, a Puritan, took great pains to learn the Algonquin language and, by all accounts, genuinely cared for the Indians and sincerely sought their conversion. He demanded, however, that his charges give up their hunting-and-gathering way of life and segregated them into fourteen "Praying Towns." There he taught them to grow crops, required that they cut their hair, and even schooled them in the vagaries of Ramist logic, a system of thought propounded by a European philosopher that would tax the intellectual faculties of any theologian. Although they had converted to Christianity, these Red Puritans remained segregated in Praying Towns and were never fully accepted by the larger Puritan community. When the Indian rebellion known as King Philip's War broke out in 1675, prompted by the steady encroachment of the Puritans onto Indian lands, Puritan magistrates (over Eliot's objections) drove the converted Indians out of their settlements and onto Deer Island in Boston Harbor, where, without adequate provisions, many of them perished in the bleak winter of 1675–1676.[5]

In the nineteenth century, the United States government, armed with superior weapons and the doctrine of manifest destiny, subjugated the Indians militarily and herded them onto reservations. The Homestead Act of 1862 encouraged white settlement in erstwhile Indian territories. Christian missionaries from the East then began their efforts in earnest, often cooperating with federal agencies. Christianity became not merely another, purportedly superior, religion, but also a means for domesticating the Indians and schooling them in the superior ways of white culture. During my stay in Fort Yates, one of Good House's parishioners showed me a button issued in the 1800s by the U.S. Indian Department that she had found nearby in what was once the Dakota Territory. The design depicts an Indian and a plow, with sun and rain overhead. The surrounding motto reads, "God Helps Them Who Help Themselves," that familiar Christian bromide often attributed, inaccurately, to the Bible.[6]

Protestant missionaries among the Indians proffered their own cultural biases. After translating the Old and New Testaments and various hymnbooks into Dakota, a Sioux dialect, the Reverend Stephen Return Riggs also translated *The Pilgrim's Progress*, that classic of English Puritan spirituality, for the edification of the Sioux. In 1890, Miss Mary Collins and Grindstone, a converted Sioux, broke up a Ghost Dance at Chief Sitting Bull's camp on the Grand River and lured the Indians away to a Christian worship service.

Indian culture and traditions suffered under these assaults. Several people over the course of my visit listed the effects of this dissolution: despair, poverty, unemployment, exogamous marriages, and the breakdown of kinship ties. Indeed, a sense of hopelessness seems almost palpable at Standing Rock Indian Reservation. The signs of poverty abound. The unemployment rate among those sixteen and older is seventy-nine percent.[7] In the absence of jobs and industry, federal assistance provides the major source of income, yet the Sioux feel stifled by government regulations that restrict their use of the land. A once-proud people has been reduced to aimlessness.

Boredom exacts a toll. Bingo has become quite popular here. "There's nothing wrong with bingo itself, I guess," Father Good House told me, "but when people sell everything they have to play bingo, then it's wrong. If you would go into even some of the nicer houses in town here, you would see barely a stick of furniture. They've sold it off to get money for bingo."

The second "B" that plagues the Sioux, especially the young, is booze. "It's a big, big problem here," Good House said, "the number one problem," an assessment shared by virtually everyone I talked with on the reservation. Young Sioux turn to alcohol and often to drugs out of a sense of despair and hopelessness, drinking themselves into stupors that all too frequently turn violent. "Alcohol and drugs are ruining our Indian people," two Sioux women agreed. Several people told me of family members who had died because of the effects of alcohol, resulting either in suicide, automobile accidents, or outright violence. The problem, according to Edna Good House, the rector's wife, is especially acute among veterans. "They leave the reservation and join the army," she said. "The army teaches them how to kill, and when they get back here, resume their drinking, and get into an argument, they pull out a gun and start shooting."

"Look in any Indian cemetery around here," Father Good House added. "You'll see the headstones of people who died in their twenties and thirties."

St. Paul's Episcopal Cemetery, in South Dakota, about thirty-five miles south of Fort Yates, lies on a hill overlooking the village of Little Eagle. The barren, treeless landscape offers no relief from the hot sun and temperatures well in excess of one hundred degrees. Sweet clover, a yellowish wildflower and the only vegetation in sight, covers the hillside and much of the cemetery. A low wire fence surrounds the burial ground; a simple, wooden plank high over the gate identifies the cemetery on one side and, on the other, reads: JESUS SAID, "I AM THE WAY, THE TRUTH, AND THE LIFE". White, weathered crosses, most of them askew, pitched alternately by blistering heat and deadening frost, mark the graves of those who lie beneath the parched, cracked earth:

ORLIE L. LITTLE DOG
1960–1981
KATHERINE KILLS CROW
1959–1975
JOHN CARRION, JR.
1953–1972
CORNELIUS BOBTAIL BEAR
1957–1984
WILLIAM BOBTAIL BEAR
1958–1985

Another graveyard on a nearby rise, the Elk Horn Hill Cemetery, tells a similar story about depredations of alcohol and the perils of youth on the reservation.

Observers have long puzzled over the peculiar Indian vulnerability to liquor. Some posit a physiological weakness that leaves them susceptible, while others blame a lack of discipline. Sociologists cite a familiar litany of conditions—unemployment, boredom, a sense of powerlessness—that leads to despair and then to the bottle. Father Good House, while not dismissing these factors, believes that rampant alcoholism among the Indians arises from a fundamental confusion about who they are, a confusion born of cultural disintegration and this tension between the traditions of Indian culture and the demands of white civilization. "To me, drinking and violence are caused by culture shock," he said, "the result of an uncertain identity."

Good House wants to see the Sioux recover their heritage and traditions, and this weekend, beneath a relentless July sun, the Sioux of Standing Rock are trying to do just that. The Little Eagle powwow began Thursday evening with a gathering of spiritual leaders—ministers and medicine men—and will continue through Sunday. This annual event, observed in towns and villages throughout the reservation on various weekends during the summer, is a kind of extended family reunion, a time to celebrate Sioux traditions, renew acquaintances, and dine on such fare as cornbread, Indian tacos, and barbecued buffalo.

The centerpiece of the festivities this year is the dedication of a memorial to the 260 men and women of the Little Antelope district (the immediate area) who served in the United States armed forces. Throughout the afternooon of speeches and ceremonies, the residents of Little Eagle, who raised over $5,000 to erect the monument, regarded it with evident pride. Interspersed with speeches by local veterans, officers of the South Dakota American Legion, and a representative from Senator Tom Daschle's office, the Sioux conducted various dedicatory rites of their own, including a peace-pipe ceremony and a naming ceremony, performed by Joe Flying Bye.[8] "We seek the power to live upon this earth in a good way," one Sioux said, explaining the significance of the peace pipe. And then he reiterated, almost plaintively: "We still want to live upon this earth. We still want to live in a good way."

That evening, the powwow shifted to an arena outside of town for ceremonial dancing. On this dusty parcel of land covered with a fragile veneer of weeds sits a small, circular grandstand, rather rickety with age. Inside, Indians in a variety of ceremonial garb dance about the arena to the beat of drums and the chant of "singers" whose songs sound (at least to my ears) more like a high-pitched, cacophonous whine than music. The entire scene, though rich in history and tradition, also contains its share of incongruities. The singers—paunchy men seated on lawn chairs and hunched over a bass drum that looks as though it was purloined from a high school band—project into a microphone that amplifies the sound across the arena through large, gray speakers. A warren of concession stands, selling hot dogs, ice cream bars, and Coca-Cola, rings the grandstand. Beyond that, Indians visiting the powwow from greater distances have pitched canvas tents or parked camping trailers and motor homes.

Inside the arena, the dancing continues to the music of successive groups of singers, representing various towns on the reservation. The dancers, most of them young, prance around the arena in steps that range from nimble and elegant to plodding and heavy-footed. By about nine o'clock, the gaits have slowed somewhat, and no one minds when the announcer calls for an intermission, during which Vernon Iron Cloud, a Congregationalist minister from Cannon Ball, conducts a naming ceremony for a young Sioux girl. Indian rites such as this provide the occasion for elaborate gift-giving. After the young girl receives her Indian name, her family carries armloads of gifts into the arena, most of them hand-made star quilts, for distribution to friends and relatives. The patriarch of the family then takes the microphone to offer an elaborate apology that he cannot give more gifts. If we had a little more money, he says, we might be able to do more. As it is, the distribution of three to four dozen quilts takes more than half an hour.

Such gift-giving in itself represents an affirmation of Indian traditions. It cements kinship ties and celebrates interdependence. "No Indian keeps a star quilt that she has made," Edna Good House explained. "She always gives it to someone else. It's the Indian way."

There's no such thing as a rich Indian, several people told me. "A true Indian does not accumulate worldly goods," Father Good House said. "Very seldom will an Indian have an estate go to probate. He simply leaves nothing behind."

After the naming ceremony and the distribution of gifts, the dancing resumes and continues into the early morning hours. A powwow, Father Good House believes, is an important exercise in the conservation of Indian ways, and for Little Eagle, this year's powwow comes at a propitious time. In recent weeks, three young people of the village have died in alcohol-related violence. Some are so desperate for alcohol that they have taken to separating the alcohol out of Lysol, a cleaning disinfectant. (Good House recently conducted the funeral of a young man in Fort Yates who tried to do this, apparently while already intoxicated. He separated it incompletely and died when the chemicals burned his mouth, esophagus, and stomach.) In Little Eagle, Good House told me, "the social problems are escalating—they're killing each other and drinking—because we don't have a stable economy. When there's no work, the social problems escalate. Too often, the Church's efforts have amounted to a band-aid ministry; the problems are getting bigger, and the Church's ministries are getting smaller." Moreover, the economic conditions and the struggle for economic survival, he said, have cut into the attractiveness of the Church.

VIRTUALLY EVERYONE AGREES that the Sioux have evinced a greater interest in their traditions in recent years. The occupation of Wounded Knee, South Dakota, in 1973 dramatized some of the Indians' grievances against the federal government in particular and white civilization in general. Since then, more and more Indians, many of them young people, have tried to regain touch with Indian culture.[9] Many have embarked on vision quests. Courses in reservation schools teach Indian history. Boys take an interest in Indian rites and ceremonies. Girls are learning to quilt, make earrings, and bead with a loom. I spoke with several women who regret having failed to learn to "speak Indian" from their grandmothers, who had spoken nothing else. Alice Jewett, a middle-aged women and mother of three, can make a star quilt in three days. "I want to learn to make moccasins," she said, adding, however, with a note of sadness, that Indian traditions are "slowly fading out." She counsels her children to learn Sioux and to "marry their own kind." But they don't, she said in a tone of resignation.

Father Good House had warned me that I would encounter a spectrum of opinions regarding the compatibility of Sioux traditions and Christianity. He has noticed in recent years a waning of interest in the Church among the youth in proportion to the resurgence of interest in native traditions. "The search for roots," he said, "is often painful and slow, yet it's important." I met several strict traditionalists who adhere only to Indian religious rites and who reject

Christian traditions altogether. Two women, one from White Horse and the other from Wakpala, South Dakota, saw no contradiction between Indian religions and Christianity. These women, both of them Episcopalians, participated enthusiastically in the Little Eagle powwow. They acknowledged, however, that most churches are not so tolerant. The pentecostals, they said, call Indian traditions "devil worship," the "devil's doings," and accuse participants of "dancing for themselves." "They run down the peace pipe," Alice Jewett said. The Catholics, after decades of resistance, are starting to blend traditions, but the Mormons and Jehovah's Witnesses, relative newcomers to the reservation, denounce the practitioners of Indian ceremonies as "sinners." The Mormons came into Wakpala, Beverly Howard said, and "messed up a lot of church members"; the Witnesses, she added, "mix us up." Both women agreed that the Mormons, the Jehovah's Witnesses, and even pentecostal groups prey on the confusion Indians feel about the legitimacy of their traditions.

JUST A FEW BLOCKS FROM THE POWWOW, one of Little Eagle's streets dissolves rather unceremoniously into a gravel parking lot surrounded on three sides by mobile homes. Straight ahead, one trailer sits behind piles of scrap lumber. To the right, a second white trailer sports a makeshift wooden entryway shaped like an A. On the left, looking slightly more dignified, a larger mobile home serves as the present church building for the Little Eagle Holiness Church. I caught up with the Reverend John Bush, pastor of this church, late on Saturday evening. The sounds of the powwow across town drifted by, and yet this dusty parking lot bustled with activity. Bush himself, a somewhat rakish looking fellow in denims, western shirt, and a straw cowboy hat, appeared to be working with several others on some kind of construction or clean-up project, and it quickly became clear that he had little interest in the goings-on across town.

The next afternoon I sat down with Bush, his wife, DeVonna, and three of their friends who were visiting from Green Grass, South Dakota. John and DeVonna Bush, both Ogallala Sioux Indians from the Pine Ridge Indian Reservation in South Dakota, became Christians under the ministry of Wesleyan Methodist missionaries. They decided to become missionaries themselves, attended Northwest Indian Bible School in Albertson, Montana, and came to Little Eagle to begin a holiness church in 1981.

I asked Bush how many of his congregation had participated in the powwow that weekend. "Probably all of them," he said, a bit uneasily. When I asked if he objected to their participation, Bush became evasive. "God has to deal with each person individually," he said. "People will continue to do things until God shows them differently. Each person has to have his heart open to God."[10]

How did he feel about the compatibility of Indian traditions and Christianity? "You can't mix Indian religion and Christianity," Bush said. "A long time ago Indian religions were all right—before Christianity; after that, there was a new way, through Christ. Now there's a better life, a better way." Marie Fiddler, one of the friends from Green Grass, said that her ancestors had engaged in Indian religious rituals before the missionaries came, but "once the church came, they put those Indian traditional practices aside. At that time there was no Bible. That's why them people lived that way."

DeVonna Bush recalled an encounter with Indian traditionalists when she was a teenager. "They look down on you if you're a Christian and accuse you of following a white man's religion. I was called a traitor by a medicine man." For a time she tried to reconcile Christianity with her people's traditions. "It took me a while to realize it was wrong to mix the two," she said. Her husband reiterated that a true Christian "can't mix the Bible and traditions," which he characterized as heathen and pagan.

When I rehearsed for them the parallels between Christianity and Indian religions that Father Good House had pointed out to me, they were singularly unimpressed. Episcopalians on the reservation, I said, see nothing evil or sinful about incorporating native rituals into their worship services, that in fact those native rituals represent an affirmation for Indians of who they are. Yes, they are Christians, but they are more than that. They have an ethnic identity as Indians as well.

"When the medicine men pray," Marie Fiddler responded after a pause, "they pray to someone between earth and heaven and not to God." But wouldn't they insist they were praying to the Great Spirit, which might simply be another name for God? "We have to have a standard, and the Bible provides that standard," Bush said. "When the Bible came in, it showed them that Jesus was the only sacrifice. After that, the peace pipe didn't have any place in worship. We're not here to change the way they live. We're here to tell them that there is a better way through Jesus."

Several times in our conversation, Bush cited the Sioux Sun Dance ceremony as an example of the paganism inherent in Indian religions. A Sioux who wants to perform the Sun Dance ritual will seek out someone who has performed the ritual himself. The candidate then undergoes an extended period of instruction and preparation, lasting up to a year. The dance itself, held during the moon of the ripening chokecherries, lasts several days, during which time the candidate dances for long intervals and neither eats nor drinks. A circular arbor of poles covered with leafy boughs surrounds the dance site, and a sacred lodge, where the candidate receives his final instructions, is constructed slightly to the east. A forked cottonwood tree, located in the center of the dance arbor, serves as the Sun Dance pole.

At dawn on the final day, mentor and candidate greet the sun and pray for strength. A peace pipe is passed to all assembled for the ceremony, amid the smell of burning sweet grass, a purifying incense. After further ritual preparations and dances, the candidate's skin is pierced just below the shoulder and a skewer inserted like a hatpin. A rawhide thong then attaches the skewer to the top of the cottonwood Sun Dance pole. Once secured, the Sun Dance proper begins, amid the songs and encouragements of fellow tribesmen. The candidate dances slowly at first, gazing constantly at the sun, and then the tempo gradually quickens as the dancer, borne along by hunger, thirst, pain, and fatigue, receives his vision. The ceremony concludes only when the candidate's gyrations succeed in tearing the skewer free from his flesh.[11]

Bush dismisses all this as paganism and quite unworthy of anyone who considers himself a Christian. Father Good House, who has never witnessed a Sun Dance, confesses to some discomfiture about the ceremony, but he believes that the intimations of sacrifice for the good of the community and even the self-inflicted torture recall Christ's sufferings and crucifixion.

THE 1982 HYMNAL OF THE EPISCOPAL CHURCH contains a hymn adapted from a Dakota Indian chant:

> Many and great, O God, are thy works,
> maker of earth and sky;
> thy hands have set the heavens with stars;
> thy fingers spread the mountains and plains.
> Lo, at thy word the waters were formed;
> deep seas obey thy voice.[12]

The congregation at St. Luke's in Fort Yates didn't sing that hymn the morning of my visit, but there were other reminders of the compatibility of Christianity and Indian traditions. A God's eye hangs above the lectern; an Indian ceremonial staff hangs over the board that announces the morning hymns; an Indian star quilt behind the altar reminds parishioners of the God whose realm extends to the four corners of the earth.

Innocent Good House's homily noted that a misguided search for meaning sometimes leads to cults, sometimes to alcoholism. "We need a commitment to God," he said, "to stand against the plagues of alcohol and drugs." Railing against a faith that makes no demands of the faithful, he said that Christians of our day have reduced the cost of discipleship to rummage-sale prices. He emphasized to his parishioners the importance of personal devotions and evangelizing their friends for Christ.

The Prayers of the People that morning included petitions for the sick, the imprisoned, and those troubled with alcohol. Father Good House uses every opportunity at his disposal to warn against the evils of liquor. When an Indian lives beyond age fifty-nine, he told me several days earlier, he is regarded as an elder in the Sioux kinship system and is accorded certain privileges, including the right to be heard. Whenever Good House conducts the funeral service for a young victim of alcohol, he counsels the survivors to avoid a similar fate. "Of course I preach on the resurrection," he said, "but I also emphasize that we who remain are the ones who have to do something about this problem." A poster in the narthex of St. Luke's depicts two Indian women with tears running down their faces, against the background of a liquor bottle. "Alcohol is not only harmful to your health," the legend reads, "but to the ones you love too!"

Father Good House sees some signs of hope, however tentative, among his people. For many years, he was the only Indian rector on the reservation, until Father Harold Eagle Bull took the parish at Cannon Ball, twenty miles north of Fort Yates. He cited various programs, funded by the Diocese of North Dakota, aimed at young people. "These people are beginning to learn something about God the creator," he said. Some of the younger Sioux, Good House believes, are also beginning to attach a stigma to drunkenness. Many Indians are trying to recover their traditions, and still others, though far fewer in number, have responded to his vision of a faith broad and inclusive enough to embrace their hereditary culture.

But the obstacles persist. Only about two dozen parishioners had shown up for the Sunday service. The original mainline denominations that evangelized the Indians have largely lost interest in Indian missions, giving way to groups like Jehovah's Witnesses, Bush's holiness church, and the well-financed Mormons, who condemn native religions and lure many of the best students off the reservation to be educated in Mormon schools. As the proliferation of these churches on the reservation suggests, the hard-nosed refusal to countenance Indian traditions is clearly more successful than Good House's belabored attempts to reconcile Christianity with native rituals. Some of that success doubtless derives both from a lingering sense of the inferiority of Indian culture and from an unambiguous call to renounce all native traditions.

Father Good House's efforts at reconciliation also suffer from the lack of institutional support. The Episcopalians have virtually abandoned mission work among the Indians in favor of more contemporary concerns such as the ordination of women, gay rights, and liberation theology that, ironically enough, advocates the struggle of the poor in Latin America against oppressive social institutions. That irony deepens if Innocent Good House is correct in his assertion that Christian missionaries, including Episcopalians, contributed to the cultural disintegration that lies at the heart of the social problems now confronting the Sioux.

The cultural imperialism of nineteenth-century missions and the destruction of native culture have indeed left indelible scars. Father Good House's evangelistic efforts on the reservation have met with some deep-seated resentment toward Christianity. "I don't think many of the Sioux have forgiven the Church for what it has done to us," he said quietly. "I think that some sort of public reconciliation should be one of the priorities of evangelism among the Indians." Edna Good House, a member of the board of trustees of Standing Rock College in Fort Yates, told of divisions that have afflicted the community in recent years, bitter disagreements that led to the establishment of a second high school in the town. "The community is divided," she said, "because we don't hear the gospel." She also said that when her husband retires in two years there will be no one to take over the church in Fort Yates. "That person would have to be in seminary now," she said, "but he would have to pay his own way. The people here have no money."

As I prepared to leave Fort Yates, Edna Good House, in the best Indian tradition, insisted on lading me with gifts: two quilted pillows and an Indian star quilt. "An Indian never says 'goodbye,'" she said, "only 'see you later.' We have no word for 'goodbye.'"

"The Sioux language has no curse words, either," Father Good House added. "It's a beautiful, beautiful language," he said wistfully.

Since the waters of Lake Oahe rose two decades ago, only a single road, a narrow isthmus, connects Fort Yates with the rest of Standing Rock Indian Reservation. On the way out of town I passed the original gravesite of Sitting Bull, General Custer's nemesis at Little Big Horn, who died in the 1890s while defending the Sioux Ghost Dance. At Highway 1806 I turned right and headed north along the once-flowing waters of the Missouri.

1987

CHAPTER 12

Camp Meeting

FOR SOME MONTHS I had been looking for a Southern camp meeting to get a flavor of old-time religion. There are plenty to choose from in America today, from Alabama to Oregon, Florida to California; one directory, published by Asbury College in Kentucky, listed 114 camp meetings for 1987, but even this list was by no means exhaustive.[1] Then one day a brochure arrived in the mail. "Enjoy a Southern Vacation in a Spiritual Atmosphere," it said, sounding more like an invitation to a cruise than a revival. The theme of this year's conference was "Free Indeed," which could mean almost anything from a kind of right-wing, patriotic freedom to freedom from sin—or a combination of the two. Camp Freedom advertised itself as "wholesomely interdenominational," but I had little else to go on before my arrival in St. Petersburg, Florida.

The rising bell at Camp Freedom chimes at six-thirty. When I pulled into the campground shortly thereafter, it was still dark. By seven o'clock the faithful had gathered in the chapel (known here as a tabernacle) for Morning Prayer. Brother Bedsaul Agee, a large, portly man with a booming voice, took charge of the meeting and introduced Brother Homer Rissinger, frail and infirm, to deliver the morning meditation. Rissinger's Bible shook noticeably as he spoke about his concern for the "falling away from holiness principles" among the people of God.

Holiness. A large sign over the platform behind Rissinger read HO-LINESS UNTO THE LORD. The people who run Camp Freedom come out of the holiness tradition, a movement emanating from John Wesley's conviction that the biblical injunction "Be ye perfect" should be taken literally and that complete freedom from sin was possible in this life.[2] Wesley's belief in "entire sanctification" became popular in the nineteenth century, especially in Methodist circles. The holiness movement emphasized the centrality of sanctification or the "second blessing" of the Holy Spirit, which followed the experience of conversion. The second blessing eradicated "inbred sin," perfected the will, and thereby rendered the believer free from sin. By the close of the nineteenth century, however, the Methodist hierarchy had grown chary about the enthusiasm and emotion that attended holiness gatherings, so many of the people drawn to holiness beliefs broke away from Methodism (and other denominations) to form holiness churches, such as the Church of the Nazarene and the Pilgrim Holiness Church. Other denominations also retain strong ties to the holiness movement, including the Wesleyan Church, the Bible Methodists, the Brethren in Christ, the Salvation Army, and the Church of God (Anderson, Indiana), among others. Those in the holiness tradition emphasize the gifts of the Spirit, including divine healing, and their worship tends to be lively and enthusiastic.

Brother Rissinger, I am certain, was once a lively and enthusiastic preacher, and even now there are flashes of his former fire when he inveighs against the holiness people who dare to attend church only on Sunday mornings and not on Sunday evenings and during the week. "Time is getting short," he warned, "there is not much time anymore." As evangelical preachers are wont to do, Rissinger talked about his own religious experiences. "The Lord sanctified me in 1945," he said. "The feeling was wonderful. I've never had the same feeling since." He compared the Christian life to a pond and said that if there is no overflow to the pond, it becomes stagnant and covered with scum. "I truly don't like to see all that scum on top," he said. "We need to get rid of the scum. The world is looking to us for spiritual refreshment. That life of yours should be continually flowing. Let your life overflow."

When Rissinger sat down, Bedsaul Agee took charge once again and thanked "the dear brother" for his meditation. He then invited the congregation forward for prayer, whereupon everyone gathered near the platform, knelt, and began praying aloud—simultaneously. The effect was a cacophonous murmur accented by an excited emphasis from time to time that punctuated the din. "Amen!" "Oh, Father!" "Praise the Lord!" "Burn within our hearts and stir us, Lord!" "Praise Jesus!" "Hallelujah!" "Father, we want a blessing. We want to feel it. Give it to us, God. *Glo-ry* to Jesus!"

The overall effect was a long, plaintive wail. At various moments, a head rose and a handkerchief wiped a tear before the head bowed again to resume praying. "Burn within our hearts and stir us, Lord!" "Amen!" "Praise Jesus!" "Heal the sick." "Help us Lord, in a special way to get the victory done!" "Heal the sick." "Oh, Jesus, Jesus!" "Help us, Lord!" "We love thy truth. We love this book!" one man said, raising his Bible. "Fill us today!" "May our souls be blessed. May we be comforted." "Amen!"

After about fifteen minutes, the collective murmur rose to a crescendo, full of noise and excitation, like a long-distance runner expending a final burst of energy in a chug toward the finish line. The praying continued for another ten minutes, but one by one members of the congregation rose from their knees, adjusted eyeglasses, and waited in silence for the eight o'clock breakfast bell.

The gathering was all white and quite elderly—I didn't see anyone who looked under fifty—but I was still puzzled about the group's denominational ties. Nearly all of the women wore white bonnets on their heads, the sort of covering that most of us associate with the Amish. A few of the men had long beards. Some of them wore suits and neckties, others wore suits and dress shirts buttoned to the neck, but no ties.

At the close of the prayer meeting, a man who introduced himself as Larry Strouse came up to me and said, "I don't believe I've seen you here before. Are you a Christian?" By now, toward the end of my travels, I should have been prepared for the question, because I had faced it so often. It was, I had decided long ago, just another way of asking, "Who are you? Can I trust you?" As we stood in line at the dining hall, Strouse began to address some of my questions about Camp Freedom.

Most of the people there came from the Great Lakes region: Pennsylvania, Michigan, Indiana, Ohio, Minnesota, Ontario. Many were Wesleyan Methodists or Brethren in Christ. A lot of the folks at Camp Freedom, Strouse told me, had grown up as Mennonites or Amish but had abandoned those churches after their experience of sanctification. Strouse, dressed in a sportcoat and tie, leaned toward me and lowered his voice. "There's no salvation in them there customs and traditions," he said. "Most of them Amish people aren't even saved." Many of those who had been born again, like the ones at Camp Freedom, maintained their traditional dress, even though they had been excommunicated by their fellow Mennonites and Amish.

At breakfast, I sat across the table from Jacob and Ada Sollenberger, beekeepers from Franklin County, Pennsylvania. With only the slightest prompting, they told me their life stories. Both grew up in the Old Order River Brethren, a religious group begun in the eighteenth century by Jacob Engle and so named because most of his followers lived along the Susquehanna River in Pennsylvania and because of their insistence on baptism by trine (threefold) immersion in a flowing river. Ada Sollenberger, a warm, lovely women of seventy-five, and Jacob, her bearded husband, seventy-one years old and a bit quieter than his wife but no less genial, were dressed as though they had just stepped off the set of *Witness*, Hollywood's 1985 motion picture about the Amish. "The Bible teaches modesty and simplicity," Mrs. Sollenberger explained. "Romans 8 tells us to present our bodies as a living sacrifice to the Lord, and First Corinthians instructs the women to keep their heads covered."

Despite her upbringing, Ada Sollenberger said, "I didn't start to serve the Lord until I was twenty-six years old. I had a real experience with God," she said. "Before that I dressed quite fashionable. I could show you pictures." A couple of years after her conversion, she met Jacob at a River Brethren love feast in Jacob's parents' home. They were married after a short courtship; forty-seven years later they clearly remain devoted to one another and openly affectionate. "God did not get me a husband until I got my life turned around," Ada said, placing her arm around Jacob's shoulders.

Even though they were both born-again Christians when they married, their second blessings didn't come until later. "When the Lord took our second child," Ada said, "I was just broken. But then the Lord touched me and I was filled with the Holy Spirit. This was in 1944." Shortly thereafter, she continued, "Jacob had his big experience with the Lord."

"I had church pride," Jacob interjected, meaning a kind of religious arrogance. "But then I was filled with the Holy Ghost."

"It happened at home in bed," Mrs. Sollenberger added, without a trace of guile or irony. "The Lord filled him up with glory. We knew we had found something wonderful."

Because the River Brethren did not believe in the second blessing, the Sollenbergers gravitated toward the Brethren in Christ in 1951; "putting on the uniform" of plain-style dress was a conscious decision that accompanied their joining the Brethren in Christ. The Brethren had a dress code in those days, although they have since abandoned it. The Sollenbergers have retained the old rigor and even seemed, at various times in our conversations, a bit defensive about it. "When you see a policemen or a soldier or a nurse in uniform," Ada said, "you know who that person is and what they stand for. The same should be true with Christians. The Bible says, 'Come out from among them and be ye separate.'" While it is true, Jacob added, that "'man looks on the outward appearances and God looks on the heart,' the outward appearance is the only basis that other people have for judging what's *in* the heart."[3]

Although all holiness people certainly do not insist on plain-style dress, moral strictures and behavioral taboos are common, even though they have eased somewhat in recent years. Dancing, card-playing, alcohol, motion pictures, and "worldly" music are all viewed askance in holiness circles. They are entertainments of the devil that lure the unwitting into sin, debauchery, and prurience. Women must never cut their hair because it is given as a covering, a conviction that accounted for all the buns and "doorknobs" I saw at Camp Freedom.[4] Holiness scruples forbid the wearing of cosmetics or jewelry. Dress should be modest at all times, as I was quickly reminded after I slipped away for a run during my first day at Camp Freedom. When I returned, an elder of the camp hurriedly pulled me aside, put his hand on my shoulder, and gently but quite emphatically informed me that the camp "has a rule about not wearing shorts on the campground."

THE TRADITION OF CAMP MEETINGS in America reaches back to the late eighteenth century, and they became a fixture of religious life in the South during the Second Great Awakening of the early nineteenth century. The Second Awakening, a widespread revival that convulsed three theaters of the new nation—New England, western New York, and the Cumberland Valley—tamed some of the rowdiness of frontier life. Indeed, there was plenty to tame, especially in the South. One in three brides was pregnant, according to some estimates. Alcohol consumption was prodigious and (literally) staggering, due in part to the cheap and plentiful supply of grain. Inebriation led to abuse of wives and children, neglect of the fields, and outright violence. Americans of the early republic drank on the average of five gallons of ninety-proof alcohol a year, more than triple today's consumption. Children and even infants were given liquor, and drinking began with breakfast and continued before, during, and after meals. Water was thought to have no nutritional value; indeed, according to some wags, it was good only for navigation. Even Benjamin Franklin opined that if God had intended man to drink water, He would not have given him an elbow capable of raising a wine glass.[5]

Camp meetings of the early nineteenth century brought religion to the frontiers and changed some of those habits. Word circulated among the frontier settlers about the time and location of a camp meeting, and entire families loaded into wagons and gathered at the appointed place for preaching and revival—as well as for some surreptitious drinking and carousing. The camp meeting functioned as a huge social occasion, bringing together people from widely dispersed settlements in a large region, but it also schooled them in enthusiastic, evangelical religion. In perhaps the most famous camp meeting of the Second Great Awakening, approximately twenty-five thousand settlers gathered at Cane Ridge in Kentucky in August 1801. Many souls were saved at gatherings like Cane Ridge—although cynics have argued that even more were conceived—and these revivals were marked by what contemporaries called spiritual "exercises." The barking exercise, for example, was quite common; people who came under the influence of the Holy Spirit barked uncontrollably. Others were afflicted with the "jerks," when their bodies contorted involuntarily. Others danced or laughed or fell to the ground under the influence of the Spirit, and some accounts tell of heads rotating 360 degrees.

The camp meeting became a fixture of American religion in the nineteenth century; by mid-century, in fact, various manuals appeared with instructions about how to conduct a successful camp-meeting revival.[6] It was important to locate the meeting near a creek or river so that water would be available. Those attending the meeting camped around the edges of a clearing, where the meetings took place. The days were highly structured, beginning each morning with family prayer at five o'clock and concluding late at night with the evening service, where most of the conversions took place. In between, the day was filled with several prayer meetings, a morning and an afternoon service, and a time during which the laity could seek spiritual guidance from the many clergy in attendance.[7]

Camp meetings were not confined to the South. Amid the urbanization of the latter part of the nineteenth century, places like Ocean Grove, New Jersey, and Oak Bluffs, Massachusetts, provided physical and spiritual renewal for the weary industrial worker. The camp meeting itself became institutionalized; permanent campsites with wooden pavilions replaced the open fields.[8] Camp meetings endure in the twentieth century, although the substance varies greatly. The Indian River Camp Meeting in South Carolina is really a huge, extended family reunion, an event so large and important that politicians, even senators, regularly drop by. There is no longer much religious fervor to such gatherings, at least by the standards of Camp Freedom and other holiness camp meetings tucked away in the hills of West Virginia or the backcountry of North Carolina or hard by the Gulf of Mexico in Florida.

Camp Freedom itself is rather inauspicious. It lies on a modest acreage across Fifty-fourth Avenue from the Sons of Italy lodge. The permanent sign for the campground reads:

> **CAMP**
> **FREEDOM**
> **6980—54TH AVE. N.**
> **YOU ARE WELCOME!**
> **DELIVERANCE FROM SIN**
> **IN CHRIST**

A special sign announced the camp meeting, lasting twelve days, from late January into early February: COME—BE BLESSED BY OLD TIME GOSPEL PREACHING AND SINGING.

Palm trees and citrus trees line the edges of the property. There are a few permanent cinder-block buildings on the campground, including the dining hall, various offices, and motel rooms. Most of the area, however, is set aside for camper trailers. By almost any standard, the accommodations are modest. The grounds themselves are rather unremarkable and certainly not secluded. Traffic roars by only one hundred yards away from the tabernacle, a white, very plain, cinder-block building which is clearly the centerpiece of the campground. The tabernacle seats two or three hundred people on

homemade wooden benches that only recently have been upholstered. The ceiling is low, supported by pine rafters. Two parallel
strings of fluorescent bulbs provide the lighting. A huge platform
dominates the front of the auditorium, flanked on the left by a ten-
by-fifteen-foot room with a sign on the door that reads "Men's Prayer
Room." The "Ladies' Prayer Room" is on the right. Between them,
running in front of the platform, is a two-foot-high wooden altar rail
that sits on a patch of carpeting placed there for the comfort of those
who come to kneel at the altar.[9]

BECAUSE HOLINESS GROUPS BELIEVE in the gifts of the Holy Spirit,
divine healing is often a part of their gatherings, although, unlike
pentecostals, they generally frown on speaking in tongues. I heard
a good deal of shouting and ecstatic utterances during my visit to
Camp Freedom, but nothing that could be confused with speaking
in tongues. The directors of the camp meeting scheduled only one
service of healing but decided to offer it early in the revival so that
the sick and infirm might be able to enjoy what one preacher called
"the fullness of healing" for the remainder of the camp meeting.

At the beginning of the Friday afternoon healing service, called
"Christ's Miracle Moments" in the brochure, Brother John Rosenberry, one of the many clergymen at the camp, stepped to the pulpit
and announced, "I feel healing in this atmosphere this afternoon."
Bedsaul Agee gave the sermon. "Our God is able to meet our needs,"
he said. "I had a hand with three withered fingers, and the flesh was
restored on those in two days, and the doctor said he never saw anything like it in all his days. Of course he didn't. It was a supernatural
miracle of God!" Agee promised healing and even "deliverance from
evil spirits" to the faithful. He then invited them to come forward
to the altar rail for healing. "How about you this afternoon," he said,
"do you think God has a miracle for you?"

Simon Lehman, director of the camp meeting, then came to the
pulpit to expand the offer to those who were not present at the service. Two ushers passed out white paper cocktail napkins to people

in the congregation who wanted to request prayer for "a beloved friend or relative." Lehman instructed them to write the name and the affliction of the absent loved one on the napkin. The ushers collected the napkins, and Lehman then invited members of the congregation who sought healing to walk forward to be anointed with oil, in the manner prescribed in James 5. "There's room at the cross for you," Lehman said. "Jesus loves you. He wants to touch you."

I had noticed an air of expectation throughout the campground that morning in anticipation of the healing service. "I said to Jacob this morning," Ada Sollenberger told me, "that I really didn't need healing today, unless the Lord wanted to help me with my weight. The Lord has blessed us with six children, and I've never gotten my weight back down to where I wanted." Ada Sollenberger did not walk forward, but Jacob did, along with many others in the congregation. They were met at the front by the clergy, in teams of two, who knelt beside each individual, quizzed him or her about the affliction, and, placing their hands on his or her shoulders, prayed for healing. The tabernacle reverberated with plaintive moanings and shouts of deliverance mixed with stern admonitions to "rebuke the power of evil" and "heal this affliction in the power of Jesus' name." After each prayer, the clergy pulled out small vials of oil from their coat pockets and dabbed a tiny bit of oil on the forehead of each supplicant. When the clergy finished with those who had come forward for healing, they divided up the stack of cocktail napkins and essentially repeated the same process, touching the oil to the napkins.

Despite its obvious peculiarities, the entire service was conducted with decorum and dignity, not the frenzied, carnival atmosphere that I'd witnessed at the Capstone Cathedral in Phoenix. After the prayers, Lehman asked the clergy to spread the cocktail napkins across the length of the altar rail; he then instructed the members of the congregation who had requested healing for others to pick up the napkins and send them to the afflicted loved ones. He asked, finally, for testimonies of healing from the congregation. None was forthcoming, so Lehman hedged. "Now there may be some who don't *feel* healed yet," he said. "Don't go by feeling. Go by the Word of God. Go by faith that you are healed in the name of Jesus."

JUST AS THERE WAS NO SHORTAGE of services at Camp Freedom (three a day, in addition to the sundry prayer meetings), so too there were plenty of preachers—about a dozen, including those who dropped by for guest appearances. Most of them were quite skilled. Their stentorian voices alternated between shouts and whispers. Their fists pounded the pulpit. They offered graphic descriptions of the perils of worldliness and sin. And they kept the attention of their audiences, who responded with "amens" and tears and wailing and shouted affirmations.

One visitor, Brother Paul Martin, president of Penn View Bible Institute, a small holiness school in Pennsylvania, echoed the general suspicion of worldliness and of learning that is fairly common in holiness circles. "We get so wrapped up in psychology and general psych and other psychs that we're all psyched up," he said derisively. Martin bragged that Penn View was a "conservative holiness Bible school, a Bible institute with a camp-meeting atmosphere," and that "the students who leave us know they're saved and that they're sanctified before they go out and face the world. There's a world out there that's dying and going to hell," Martin said. "We need to reach them. We need to be bold for Jesus Christ."

Indeed, one of the recurrent themes in the preaching at Camp Freedom was the need to eschew "worldliness" and separate from the world. "Wouldn't it be wonderful if our grandchildren, our great-grandchildren, if it could be said of them, 'They are totally separated, they don't have the diseases of the rest of the world'?" Bedsaul Agee intoned. "We are strangers and pilgrims here. We are not a part of this society. We belong to the heavenly throng, and we ought to act like it while we're here. We ought to live like it and enjoy the blessings thereof."

"In the world but not *of* the world" is a favorite aphorism among holiness people (and evangelicals generally). It helps if you can

identify those who are worldly, those who stand outside the ken of righteousness, not only for the ostensible purpose of bringing them into the fold, but also because it vindicates your own standing as someone special in God's eyes. After one of the services, Philip Compton from South Carolina, eighty-two years old and a regular at Camp Freedom, cornered me. "Do you love Jesus?" he asked. "I love Jesus. You know why I love Jesus? I love Jesus because He first loved me." Compton, a bald man with a weathered face, walked around the campground with a handful of books. I had noticed him huddled at various times with other people, thumping the books like a used-car salesman kicking tires. He pulled out a paperback he had written and published himself entitled *Give the Family Something Better*. "I'm against pornography and abortion," he announced. "And *abortion* is the right word for it. You know why?" He looked at me earnestly. "Because you oughtta shun abor-shun."

At the conclusion of another service, the preacher in charge of the meeting invited responses or testimonies from the congregation. An older, white-haired woman near the front rose to her feet and unleashed a long harangue about worldliness and her anxieties about the younger generation. "Oh, my Lord," she wailed, her voice rising and falling for dramatic effect, "my concern is have I prayed enough. This morning at ten minutes to three, I wondered why I was awakened, so I began to pray, and I asked God to take care of the one that needed it the most because I don't always know why I am awakened. But I'm so glad. If the Lord has to give me pain in my arm to get me awakened early in the morning and talk to Him, I'll take the pain." Her voice became shrill and insistent. "I have been burdened for our young people. Friday and Saturday nights I pray more than ever for some mother's child out on the streets and nobody to pray for them. My heart is burdened for our young people. I'd just love to take them all in."

At the Saturday afternoon service, the people of Camp Freedom got a look at some exemplary young people from Hobe Sound Bible College, a holiness school across the state. The men were dressed in ties, white shirts, and three-piece suits. The women wore plain, very modest dresses and no makeup or jewelry, except for wrist-watches. In keeping with holiness scruples, the women had very long hair wrapped into buns either on top or in back of their heads.[10]

But if the students from Hobe Sound represented all that was virtuous and lovely in the eyes of those at Camp Freedom, there were always reminders of the perils of worldliness. That night, as the congregation gathered for the evening service, the man seated next to me, who had taken an interest in my research, pointed to an attractive, blonde woman in her mid-thirties. She was dressed fashionably, her shoulder-length hair pulled back in a pony tail. She wore makeup and gold jewelry, a string of pearls and high heels. She would have attracted attention almost anywhere, but against the very bland pastiche of Camp Freedom, she drew the eyes of the congregation like steel shavings to a magnet. "See that girl there," my informant said. "She was brought up strict, but she reversed." This woman, the daughter of one of the preachers at the conference, was a pharmacist back in New Jersey. She was also divorced and had, in the words of the man next to me, "fallen away from the Lord." There was a lesson in all this, of course. "That's what happens when you go the way of the world."

The service in the tabernacle that evening opened with a lively song whose chorus went:

> He brought me out of the miry clay.
> He set my feet on the rock to stay.
> He puts a song in my heart today,
> A song of praise. Hallelujah!

Such rejoicing is all the more powerful when juxtaposed with a reminder of the depredations of the world, the miry clay of sin. Brother John Rosenberry obliged. "Our hearts go out to the world in which we live," he prayed. "The world of teenagers, of kids out on the street who need Jesus. They're suffering terrible things in New York and San Francisco and Calcutta. We need to bring Jesus to the world."

There is a kind of protocol that governs behavior at holiness or pentecostal gatherings. In some churches, worshipers lift both arms high into the air, palms up, to indicate that they are affected by the Holy Spirit, or, more precisely, to indicate a broken, obedient will, receptive to the Holy Spirit. At Camp Freedom, protocol dictates a brief, discreet wave of one arm. When some element of a prayer or a song or a sermon strikes a chord, members of the congregation simply lift a hand and wave it quickly, in the manner of a second-grader trying to catch the eye of her teacher. The congregation also responds with amens and shouting, especially in the presence of a skilled preacher.

Brother H. E. Schmul from Salem, Ohio, widely regarded as the best orator at the camp meeting, stepped to the pulpit. His theme tonight was repentance, or the lack of it. He bemoaned the fact that he saw little difference between Christians and "the world" and wondered if that similarity had something to do with the prevalence of "health or wealth or prosperity gospel," the notion, immensely popular in many evangelical circles, that God wants to make you rich. Too much of the preaching today, Schmul said, "does not disturb the sin" in people's lives, "their adultery or their immorality or their fornication or their cheating or their lying or whatever."

Schmul himself would not be guilty of such reticence. Sin, he said, "is a moral corruption that will result in final separation from God." Schmul became more and more impassioned as the audience shouted him on. "It's a madness. It's a madness that, 'regardless of the consequences I have to do it. I have to shoot it. I have to drink it. I have to smoke it. I have to have it. I have to have him. I have to have her.' It's a madness. People rush into this regardless of the consequences." He paused and lowered his voice. "One thing that is happening is good, even though it's bad. I'm talking about AIDS," he said. Schmul dismissed the various education programs directed against the spread of AIDS. "The real answer is a change in the hearts of men," he said. "God's way of all purity, of all chastity, is the way. God's plan is the *only* way! Amen." The AIDS epidemic,

Schmul suggested, was having a salutary effect. "Some people are backing up on this homosexual thing. Some of the gays that had to have sex the homosexual way are changing their minds after seeing their buddies drop off or fall over like flies. When they're sure that a person who has AIDS is going to go down the tubes and go out into eternity—they're really beginning to change their minds a little," he said with evident satisfaction.

Only the blood of Jesus Christ will cure sin, Schmul continued. "No man, no man, *no* man ever sins purely out of weakness but lets himself go in his weakness to do as he wills." Here Schmul touched on a matter of perennial controversy within Protestant circles: the extent to which an individual is responsible for his or her salvation. Citing the New Testament writings of St. Paul, Martin Luther and John Calvin had insisted that we all inherit Adam's sin and that only the grace of God, mediated through Jesus Christ, delivers us from the condemnation we so richly deserve. We can do *nothing*, they insisted, to earn our salvation; God, in His inscrutable wisdom and mercy, has chosen to rescue us from the squalor of our sinfulness, *regardless* of our merit.

In an age inebriated with self-determinism, Lutheran or Calvinist theology does not sit well. It seems narrow and fatalistic. But such naysaying misses the point. Luther had been profoundly troubled about the state of his soul. He couldn't escape a sense of his own unworthiness and his insouciance toward God. Was he saved or damned? Had he prayed enough? Had he received the Eucharist often enough? Had he sinned since his last confession? The slightest lapse, he believed, meant perdition.

Luther's confessor finally advised him to study Paul's letters to the Romans and the Galatians in the New Testament. There Luther "rediscovered the gospel" that liberated him from the works-righteousness of medieval Catholicism and from the burden of earning his salvation. We are saved by grace through faith in Jesus Christ, Luther concluded, not by dint of our own efforts, which fail pitifully before a holy and righteous God. Good works, then, are not a condition of salvation; rather, they follow in the life of the believer as a natural response to grace.

In many Protestant circles, however, Luther's breakthrough, which John Calvin codified and systematized in the *Institutes of the Christian Religion*, has been compromised by a theological strain generally known as Arminianism, named for Jacobus Arminius, a Dutch theologian of the early seventeenth century, who restored human agency to the doctrine of salvation. Anyone can choose to follow Christ; by the same token, anyone can lose his or her salvation by falling back into sin. There is no such thing as "eternal security." While this theological recidivism obfuscated the Reformation's insistence that the grace of God alone provided deliverance from sin, Arminian theology (also known as Wesleyanism, for John Wesley) caught on in America. Its emphasis on human agency worked well in the revival meetings on the frontier. Preachers sought to persuade and cajole sinners into the kingdom—salvation, after all, was simply a matter of choosing God over Satan, good over evil—and the self-determination implicit in Arminian or Wesleyan theology appealed to Americans of the new nation who had recently taken control of their political destiny.

Arminianism long ago eclipsed Calvinism in American Protestantism. Camp-meeting evangelists and Methodist circuit riders carried it to the frontiers, and it persists to the present among holiness people, who believe that their salvation hinges on their probity and their ability to eschew evil. For Brother Schmul, then, conscious or deliberate sin is not, as Calvinists insist, a consequence of our fallen nature; it is a matter of our volition and specific transgressions of sundry moral codes, and the responsibility to resist temptation lies with the individual. Moral lapses are deadly. "I don't believe there are Christian men who are going to be taken up in the rapture from the arms of a harlot," Schmul preached. "I don't believe they're going to put a hole in the ceiling of these various dives and saloons around the country where the saints can move out of those places when Jesus comes. I don't believe that. The Bible doesn't teach that.

There's no grounds for it in the Word of God." The congregation responded with hearty amens. Even those who carry grudges in their hearts, Schmul said, "are going to the same hell along with the harlots and the prostitutes and the drunkards and the swearers and the ne'er-do-wells."

True repentance, Schmul said, meant leaving the old sinful life behind. "There is no cheap grace," he concluded. "There is no cheap salvation. Saving faith is impossible without repentance and obedience and renunciation."

WHAT WAS ALL THIS RHETORIC about "worldliness" that pervaded the preaching at Camp Freedom? Unlike Calvinism, which holds that the elect of God attain salvation regardless of merit and cannot resist God's grace, the Wesleyan tradition views salvation as a matter of volition—we must *choose* to forsake our sinfulness and follow Christ. "We don't go to heaven to become saints," Edsel Trauten, one of the preachers at Camp Freedom, said. "We become saints to go to heaven." We must prove ourselves worthy of salvation on earth before we can hope to receive a reward in heaven. Brother Schmul said that a believer's identification with Christ "will lead you against the world, against the flesh, against the devil; it will lead you to opposition; it will lead you to persecution; it will lead you to fiery trials; it will lead you to a place of contradiction with the world." He then warned of the consequences of equivocation. "If you are seeking an accommodation with the world," he said, "then, friends, you are fooling yourself, and you are toying with your eternal destiny. We are not citizens of this world; we are citizens of another country." Life on earth, then, is a constant struggle to root out sinfulness and show oneself worthy of salvation; sanctification, or the "second blessing" of the Holy Spirit, cleanses sin, but there is no "eternal security" in the Wesleyan tradition. Just as we come to God of our own volition, so too we can lose our salvation by lapsing into sin.

Indeed, sin cannot be taken lightly in Wesleyan theology. "My friend," one of the preachers shouted, "if you're really converted, you're going out of the sin business, you say goodbye to the world." The repeated, insistent warnings against the depredations of the world, then, are more than mere rhetorical flourishes. The destiny of one's very soul is at stake. The moral and behavioral strictures shield the believer from sin and temptation and keep him or her on the narrow road to heaven. "We know you're all trying to get to heaven," Brother Lehman told one of the gatherings. "Some of you aren't ready yet, but we'll try to get you ready."

All of this issues in an underlying, though largely unspoken, anxiety. The people at Camp Freedom sing the old Protestant hymn, "Blessed assurance, Jesus is mine / Oh, what a foretaste of glory divine!" but I encountered precious little assurance beneath the fragile veneer of confidence.

One afternoon, I struck up a conversation with "Roger," a youthful-looking gentleman in his late sixties.[11] Roger lives and works in Indiana most of the year, but he arranges his vacation time so he can be in St. Petersburg for the camp meeting every winter. He asked if I had toured the campground, and in the course of our walk he related the story of his life. "The Lord sure helped me," he began. "He saved me from a life of sin when I was seventeen. I lied and cheated; I would steal. But you can't find joy in serving the devil. You can find pleasure, but it's only for a season. Jesus is the only one that satisfies. He is the *only* one."

After his conversion, Roger felt obligated to make restitution for all of his youthful misdeeds. "I went back to five-and-dimes and grocery stores and so many places to apologize to storekeepers for the things I'd stolen. I'd do work for them to make it up. I even went back to schoolteachers to apologize for cheating on tests and assignments. I'd been to twelve different schools in twelve years, so that took some time and effort, but I did it." Roger credited his mother with being a godly influence in his life. "I surely had a wonderful mother," he said. "My mother never had a haircut in her life, never wore jewelry or cosmetics. I'm sure glad the Lord saved me from a life of sin."

By this time, I had heard countless conversion narratives at Camp Freedom, and nothing in Roger's account struck me as unusual. After a pause, however, he continued. "I want to tell you something else. May I?" he asked. "When I was growing up, I was always kind of a sissy. I found myself attracted to boys rather than girls." He hesitated. "I'm a homosexual." He spat out the words in disgust. Roger had some sexual encounters with older men when he was a teenager, but after his conversion at age seventeen he promptly broke off all such relationships. Coping with his sexual urges thereafter without giving in to temptation, he said, was hell. In addition, he faced suspicion and ridicule from his peers. During World War II, he recalled, "people constantly would ask me why I wasn't in Europe fighting for my country."

"I remained celibate for thirty-seven years," he continued, "but then I felt myself falling into temptation." His voice became intense, almost fierce. "I was lean in my soul at that time, and I would pray, 'Lord, help me get my mind on you.'" Despite those prayers, however, Roger lapsed into sin, a year-long relationship with a younger man. "It still haunts me," he recalled. "It's a blot on my life. I finally came to the point where I said, 'Lord, it's either you or the world.'"

As Roger continued his story, he struck me suddenly as a tragic figure, a man haunted by what he considered a wanton transgression deep in his past. I tried to imagine the self-hatred he felt, the sense of vileness that shadowed him constantly. Indeed, there was a sadness to many of the people I had met at Camp Freedom. Even as they spoke of the sweetness of Jesus and their deliverance from sin decades earlier, I detected an underlying uneasiness, an uncertainty about the fate of their souls. The need to keep a strict moral accounting for one's life reminded me of Martin Luther's anxieties about whether or not he had sinned since his last confession, thereby imperiling his immortal soul. The insistent proclamations and the triumphal hymns about deliverance from sin at Camp Freedom sounded tinny to me, an exercise in self-persuasion. The seductive darkness of the "world" for most of us—and even, I suspect, for more than a few at Camp Freedom—lies not in the taverns and bordellos and movie theaters but much closer to home, in the recesses of the heart. It's easier, though, and a good deal more comforting, to insist that the enemy is outside rather than inside. You need to shore up your defenses and patrol the ramparts to keep the adversary at bay.

For Roger, however, the enemy had penetrated the fortress, and even these many years later he couldn't be certain about the effects of that contamination. His intensity had abated now, and he spoke in measured tones. He alternated between expressing his own deep sorrow and repeating the bromides of sermons he had heard for half a century. "To know the Lord is life eternal, but to know the world is nothing," he said. "My biggest regret is that I cannot say that I've been faithful to my Lord for a full fifty years; instead, I fell back into sin thirty-seven years after I had given my heart to God."

He paused, dabbed the corners of his eyes with a handkerchief, then looked away into the distance. "Sin is not worth it," he said, "because that one little sin may keep you out of heaven."

1988

CHAPTER 13

City Crusade

O F ALL THE SPLENDORS OF NEW YORK CITY, none rivals a Sunday afternoon in Central Park. Bikers and joggers, intent on their revolutions, glide by on the winding, six-mile roadway that encircles the park. Horse-drawn carriages clatter past, straining to evoke the halcyon days of a bygone era. Young children and their parents queue up at the carousel or gawk at the polar bears in the Central Park Zoo. Americans of Italian descent play bocce ball on the bowling green; Americans of all descents play softball on dusty fields below the Sheep Meadow. Just outside Tavern on the Green, the city's main preserve for tourists, a line of salubrious roller-bladers waits to demonstrate its skill at weaving through an obstacle course of aluminum beer cans. At the Strawberry Fields off Seventy-second Street, visitors pause at the monument to John Lennon, who weaved his dreams at the Dakota, just across Central Park West. Throughout the park aspiring musicians and performers of various sorts try to draw crowds and attract donations.

On a September afternoon in 1991, the final day of summer, another performer came to Central Park seeking to draw a crowd and attract donations. Unlike the guitarist at the foot of the mall, however, this performer had the advantage of name recognition and ambitious advance work. For weeks, New York subways and newspapers had carried advertisements with a rather jarring headline: YOU'RE BORN. YOU SUFFER. YOU DIE. FORTUNATELY, THERE'S A LOOPHOLE. The loophole, of course, wasn't specified, but the ad beckoned New York to attend "An afternoon in Central Park with Billy Graham," where, presumably, the loophole would be disclosed.

THE CROWD STARTED GATHERING at ten o'clock, even though the rally wasn't scheduled to begin until four in the afternoon. Many brought picnics and blankets to ensure a place near the rostrum. By two-thirty steady streams of people were spilling onto the Great Lawn like rivers into a reservoir. Legions of police officers directed the flow.

The music began well before four o'clock. Sandi Patty, whose metier is Christian pop, prefaced her song by saying, "It's wonderful to be in a place that is so full of darkness to be so full of light today." That theme permeated the entire event. Graham's ads in the subways had enumerated the woes of the city: a half million heroin addicts, sixty thousand homeless, an annual murder rate in excess of two thousand. "It's easy to feel a sense of despair," the copy read.

Graham himself elaborated on that theme. In the first of two appearances before the crowd, he declared that "New York City was a place in desperate spiritual need." Sixty percent of New York's adults are single, he said. "To be without God in New York is to be terribly lonely."

American evangelicals have long viewed cities as habitations of evil, prurience, and unbridled sensuality. After the Civil War, northern cities grew exponentially. From 1860 to 1890 the populations of New York, Philadelphia, and Baltimore doubled; Kansas City and Detroit grew fourfold, Chicago tenfold; Omaha and Minneapolis were fifty times larger in 1890 than they were in 1860. Some of the migrants were blacks from the South, whose presence exacerbated racial tensions and labor unrest. Most of the newcomers came from across the Atlantic, so that by the final decades of the nineteenth century American cities were teeming with non-Protestant immigrants, most of whom did not share evangelical scruples about temperance. In a memorable passage from *How the Other Half Lives*, published in 1890, Jacob Riis tried to calculate the ratio of churches to taverns in New York City south of Fourteenth Street. He counted 111 Protestant churches and

4,065 saloons. "Where God builds a church the devil builds next door a saloon, is an old saying that has lost its point in New York," he wrote. "Either the devil was on the ground first, or he has been doing a good deal more in the way of building." Riis also found that the taverns commanded considerably more loyalty than did the churches. "I am afraid, too," he wrote, "that the congregations are larger by a good deal; certainly the attendance is steadier and the contributions more liberal the week round, Sunday included."[1]

American cities around the turn of the century were indeed dreadful places; the brutality of life could be overwhelming, especially to the working classes who toiled twelve-hour days and seven-day weeks. Wives and children worked in sweat shops, and families lived in squalid tenements that were infested with disease, drunkenness, and prostitution. The infant mortality rate sometimes reached twenty percent.

Evangelicals did not ignore urban problems altogether. Charles H. Parkhurst, pastor of the Madison Square Presbyterian Church in New York, preached a sermon on Valentine's Day of 1892 excoriating the corruptions all around him. The police and the Tammany Hall politicians, he charged, looked the other way and allowed brothels, opium lairs, and gambling parlors to flourish. Parkhurst characterized the leaders of Tammany Hall, the Democratic political machine that ran Manhattan, as "a lying, perjured, rum-soaked and libidinous lot." He unleashed his homiletical assault against "the official and administrative criminality that is filthifying our entire municipal life, making New York a very hotbed of knavery, debauchery and bestiality."[2] After Parkhurst confessed before a grand jury that he had no evidence to substantiate his charges, he went undercover into the subterranean world of bordellos, gambling emporiums, and drug dens, compiling the affidavits and police badge numbers that would eventually topple the Tammany Hall machine.

Other evangelicals sought to check the spread of sin in more conventional ways. Organizations such as the Salvation Army and the Young Men's Christian Association addressed social needs by providing shelter, meals, and recreation. (In 1891 the YMCA secretary from Springfield, Massachusetts, devised an indoor game with a round ball and peach baskets—basketball—in an effort to keep urban youths occupied during the winter months.) The Salvation Army built rescue homes for prostitutes, organized slum brigades to fight disease and filth in the tenements, and even established farm colonies in Ohio, Colorado, and California to relocate miserable urban dwellers to more bucolic environments.

For the most part, however, evangelicals found the problems of the cities intractable and far too daunting. They preferred the safety of rural areas and small towns where both social and political conservativism were more to their liking. Dispensational premillennialism, moreover, with its insistence that Jesus would return at any moment, provided a convenient alibi. The world was getting worse and worse, evangelicals believed, and there was precious little they could do about it outside of making an effort to save individual souls. Whereas more liberal Protestants adopted what became known as the Social Gospel, an attempt to convert sinful social institutions as well as sinful individuals, evangelicals for the most part channeled their efforts into mass evangelism, like the crusades of Dwight Lyman Moody and Billy Sunday, the former second baseman for the Chicago White Stockings who taunted and cajoled his auditors to "hit the sawdust trail" and give their lives to Jesus.

BILLY GRAHAM LACKS THE FLAMBOYANCE of Billy Sunday, but he stands within the same tradition. Tradition holds that the night Sunday died—November 6, 1935—William Franklin Graham, Jr. hit the sawdust trail himself in an itinerant evangelist's tabernacle in Charlotte, North Carolina. The gangly teenager was unaware of the coincidence, but over the course of a remarkable career Graham has appropriated many of the same techniques as his evangelistic predecessor, including the tenacious courting of civic and religious leaders, meticulous planning, and prodigious advance work. In the months preceding the New York crusade, evangelicals from New Jersey to

Long Island had been preparing for the rally in Central Park. Graham himself had visited New York several weeks earlier to call on the media, politicians, and religious leaders—the Roman Catholic archbishop, Jewish rabbis, the head of the National Council of Churches—all in an effort to charm (and disarm) potential critics and engender enthusiasm for the event.

This was not Graham's first crusade in New York. In 1957 he filled Madison Square Garden for ninety-seven days with an uncompromising evangelical jeremiad against the perils and depredations of urban life. In his opening sermon the young evangelist read the biblical lesson of Sodom and Gomorrah but substituted "New York" for the names of those notoriously wicked cities. Graham's 1957 visit to New York City was important in other ways. He enlisted the cooperation of liberal Protestants in that crusade, and many fundamentalists have never forgiven Graham this betrayal. Incredibly, they regard him as a flaming liberal.

GRAHAM'S SERMON ON THE GREAT LAWN in Central Park, beneath a crystalline sky, could not have been more traditional by the standards of American evangelicalism. As he approached the podium a second time, the crowd hushed. Fathers hoisted small children onto their shoulders so they could catch a glimpse of the famous preacher, the man who, according to his surrogates, has communicated with more people than anyone else in history. Someone waved a sign that read: CALLING NEW YORK BACK TO GOD.

On this September afternoon I had come to Central Park not so much as a historian or a journalist but as a pilgrim. Mired in a rather difficult passage in my life, I felt confused and lonely and abandoned. I sought some comfort and assurance in what evangelicals call "old-time religion." Perhaps the evangelist could show the way. Perhaps I could find solace in the familiar pieties of my childhood.

Graham took as his text John 3:16, those "twenty-five wonderful words," according to Graham, that provide a succinct summary of the New Testament. "God loves you," the evangelist repeated three times, and then he proceeded with an outline of evangelical theology. Adam chose evil over good, he said, and all of humanity suffers from the consequences of that choice. Humanity has a disease called sin, and we all fall short of the glory of God. Fortunately, Graham preached, there was a way out: "God became a man, and that man was the Lord Jesus Christ." The audience applauded. Reconciliation with God now was possible, Graham concluded, through repentance of your sins and by placing your faith in Jesus.

Graham's formula for "getting right with God" is almost as familiar as John 3:16. Because most evangelicals hold a rather narrow view of the sacraments—baptism and Holy Communion function merely as symbols of an individual's relationship with God and a reminder of Jesus' crucifixion—evangelicals rely instead on a formulaic prayer to express repentance and acknowledge Jesus as savior. The genius of this prayer lies in its simplicity. It need not be repeated verbatim, but some variant of it, evangelicals believe, spells the difference between heaven and hell.

The sun in Central Park began to slink toward the horizon. Graham had not been at the top of his form today, and he seemed to know it. The breeze tousled his hair. The crowd was growing restless, and he struggled to hold their attention for a few more moments while he closed the sale. Repeat this prayer after me, he said: "O God, I am a sinner." Scattered voices on the Great Lawn murmured in response. "I'm sorry for my sin. I turn from my sin. I receive Christ as savior. I confess him as Lord. From this moment on I want to follow him and serve him in the fellowship of His church. Amen."

Typically, at this point in most of Graham's crusades the choir behind him would sing "Just As I Am," while the redoubtable evangelist beckoned the multitude to walk toward him and receive Jesus.

> Just as I am, without one plea,
> But that Thy blood was shed for me,
> And that Thou biddest me come to Thee,
> O Lamb of God, I come, I come.

The arms of Cliff Barrows, Graham's song leader, would beat the air, and the preacher repeated his plea. "Your buses will wait," he assured the wavering. "Come and receive Jesus into your heart."

> Just as I am, and waiting not
> To rid my soul of one dark blot.
> To Thee whose blood can cleanse each spot,
> O Lamb of God, I come, I come.[3]

And come they did. Hundreds and thousands and hundreds of thousands over the years streamed toward the evangelist, many with tears streaming down their faces. They were anxious or scared or lonely, and they came forward to offer their sad, broken lives to Jesus. Graham understood that, and he received them gently. His counselors, specially trained volunteers from local churches, met each seeker, read from the Bible, prayed, and offered assurances of God's forgiveness before sending the new convert back into the night.

But on this afternoon in Central Park there was no invitation to walk toward the rostrum and no singing of "Just As I Am." Counselors, armed with packets of literature, were stationed strategically across the Great Lawn and available for consultation. Graham concluded with, "God bless you, and God bless New York," and took his seat. Near me a woman leaned toward her husband as they walked toward Central Park West. "He really has a soothing voice," she observed, nodding in the direction of the gray-haired evangelist.

DESPITE THE BEST EFFORTS of the Graham advance team, an event such as this is certain to attract its share of zealots, kooks, and rabid fundamentalists (the distinctions aren't always clear). Representatives of an organization called Inspiration Books East, Inc., out of Jemison, Alabama, distributed an eighty-page booklet railing against ecumenism generally and the Roman Catholic Church in particular.

The most colorful demonstration came from a group of middle-aged Koreans who wore red smocks over their suits. The front of the smock read JESUS LOVES in white block letters, and the back announced:

RAPTURE
IN OCT. 28, 1992
JESUS IS COMING
IN THE AIR

One especially fervent disciple kept shouting "Alleluia, Alleluia!" as he pushed pamphlets into the hands of passers-by. Occasionally his excitement got the better of him. He would yell "On October twenty-eighth," spread his arms wide in a kind of frenzied desperation, and then jump into the air, arms and legs flying. "Alleluia!" Another man in a red smock held a megaphone: "Prepare for the coming days... Rapture!...Rapture!...Rapture!...October twenty-eight at ten A.M."

The pamphlet itself, published by an organization called Mission for the Coming Days, which claims to have offices in New York, Los Angeles, and Seoul, Korea, met with curiosity from some, but more often with derision. "How can you say that when it's against the Bible?" one man shouted at a pamphleteer. Several yelled "No man knows," a reference to Matthew 24:36, where Jesus says that no one knows when the Son of Man will return to earth. One woman, Janice Mitchell of Brooklyn, grabbed her Bible, turned to this passage in Matthew, and approached the man with the megaphone. "No man knows," she repeated, pointing to the page.

"Holy Spirit give the date," the megaphone replied, "I don't want to argue." He resumed his pitch. "Rapture! Rapture! Rapture!... Human history will end in 1999!" (Apparently their calculations accounted for a seven-year tribulation after the rapture in 1992.)

A half dozen police officers watched the scene with growing bemusement. Evangelicals, eager to dissociate themselves from what they clearly viewed as a fringe group, tried to refute the claims. "I'll call you on October twenty-ninth," one man said, "and if you answer the phone, can I call you a false prophet?" Eddie Rojas, Richard Rojas, and John Davis, teenagers from an evangelical church in Brooklyn, spied me perusing the pamphlet. "Throw it away," they implored. "That's a lie from the devil." Jesus was indeed coming again, they said, but they didn't know when. They tried to gather as many pamphlets as they could, tear them up, and deposit them in a nearby trash can.

Another evangelical confronted the man with the megaphone. "When it doesn't line up with the Word of God," he said in exasperation, "it's of the devil himself. The blood of many, many souls will rest on your shoulders." Clearly disappointed that he was unable to exact some form of repentance, he turned to the crowd that had gathered around him, and his mood turned to resignation. "Don't argue, folks," he said, "just pray for them." Then, walking away, he pointed to the October 28, 1992, date on the cover of the pamphlet. "I just wish it was ninety-one," he said. "Ninety-two is too far away."

Once the crowd had dissipated, I approached the man with the megaphone. How did he know that Jesus was returning on October 28, 1992? I asked. "The Holy Spirit give the date," he repeated. Gave it to whom? To him? "No," he said, "to two thousand Koreans all around the world." I wanted to know when this prophecy had come— had it come simultaneously to these two thousand people?—but he was growing impatient with my queries. "Can't speak English," he said petulantly. I observed that he had been speaking fluent English a moment ago, but he turned away. An elderly Korean woman stepped forward. "Fast for thirty days," she said, stabbing earnestly at my chest with her finger, "and then the vision come."

ON MY WAY OUT OF THE PARK I asked Officer Efrain Roman if the police had encountered any problems with the crowd. "No, none at all," he replied. "I wish they were all like this."

By the time I reached Central Park West the sun had nearly disappeared beyond the Hudson. The chill of autumn lurked in the shadows. I headed west on Eighty-fourth Street and turned north on Columbus Avenue, walking quickly past what remained of the tony cafés that heralded the gentrification of the Upper West Side in the 1980s. I stopped in one of them to make a phone call, but no one answered.

That afternoon Graham had told me about my sinfulness, a condition I share with all of humanity, but I knew that only too well. What I needed at this juncture of my life, I think, was affirmation, not condemnation, but evangelicals, feeling battered themselves by the larger culture for most of the twentieth century, have not been especially good at affirmation. Indeed, over the course of my travels throughout the evangelical subculture I had been surprised at how quickly various preachers had been able to resurrect feelings of guilt and inadequacy in me, demons that I'd spent the better part of a decade trying to exorcise.

I continued north on Columbus, past Spanish grocery stores and abandoned crack houses. At 110th Street a panhandler outside a pizza shop rattled his coins in a paper cup, pleading for more. As I crossed the street and headed up the incline toward Morningside Heights, Harlem lay to my right. A Black Muslim spread his tiny carpet in the direction of Mecca and prepared to pray. Across the street and directly behind the Cathedral of St. John the Divine, an imperious Gothic structure still under construction, another African American washed his car in water pirated from a fire hydrant. A bit farther on an urban scavenger was trying to strip one more part from the carcass of an abandoned automobile. At the Grotto Church of Notre Dame, two homeless men asked for whatever change I could spare.

A full moon hung above Harlem in the early evening. Tiny eddies threw leaves against park benches. I crossed Morningside Drive, sat down on the front steps of my apartment building, and contemplated once more my afternoon in Central Park with Billy Graham. Leaving the familiar comforts of the evangelical cocoon for the uncertainties of the broader culture had been difficult for me, even painful. There were times when I longed for the old certainties, when I sought refuge in evangelicalism's lack of ambiguity.

At the same time, I knew better. The real drama of life lies not in clinging to the bulwark of moral absolutes but in using a moral compass to navigate along the shoals of secularism. That course, however, is fraught with perils and ambiguities. For someone nurtured in the bosom of evangelicalism but now finding himself in unfamiliar currents, the voyage is sometimes treacherous and often lonely.

For me, Billy Graham's simple pieties fell short of the mark. The evangelical subculture, which prizes conformity above all else, will never again recognize me as its own, except for the prodigal that I suppose I am. But while most evangelical prodigals, in my experience, have discarded their faith altogether, I was trying to sift through the cultural baggage of American evangelicalism to see if there was anything of value for me at its core. I wanted to believe that there is: the juxtaposition of the doctrine of depravity with a radical understanding of God's ineluctable grace. The emphasis on one at the expense of the other defines the difference between evangelical and liberal in contemporary Protestantism. Liberals tout God's grace and forgiveness without taking adequate account of depravity. Graham and other evangelicals know all about depravity—and they can unleash a barrage of statistics and anecdotes to demonstrate the reach of human sinfulness—but they understand correspondingly little about grace. How else do you explain the imposition of behavioral strictures on themselves and their children to protect them from the temptations and perils of the world outside of the subculture? It may not be a popular position, but I'm inclined to embrace both depravity and grace simultaneously, in part because I have seen powerful evidence of both in my own life.

Had Billy Graham in any way advanced my understanding of this conundrum that lay at the root of the human condition, that defined my own condition, suspended somewhere between depravity and grace, between sin and forgiveness? No, I'm afraid not, but I may have been asking too much. The familiar pieties no longer resonated with me as they once did, although I remembered that something had caught in my throat when George Beverly Shea belted out "How Great Thou Art" in his tremulous baritone.

My response, of course, had more to do with emotions than intellect. The ponderous strains of "Then sings my soul, my savior, God, to thee" evoked something in me—childhood innocence, perhaps, or a hankering for simpler days. When I considered evangelicalism through the soft-focus lens of sentiment and nostalgia, I found it quite attractive. When subjected to the harsher glare of rational scrutiny, however, the patina began to fade.

But no one can fully separate emotions and intellect. We are all of us complicated beings, no less complex than New York City itself— as dazzling as a Sunday afternoon in Central Park or an evening stroll along Fifth Avenue, as nefarious as a crack house, as wretched and pathetic as the homeless men who sleep on park benches across the street from my bedroom window. Perhaps it was the stale, old dualistic rhetoric itself, from which evangelicals have derived such comfort for most of the twentieth century, that I no longer found compelling. The human condition will not yield to simple dichotomies: good or evil, saved or damned, rational or emotional. Why was it, for instance, that I found myself even now, seated on the front stoop, harboring an irrational resentment against Graham for failing to conclude his Central Park rally with "Just As I Am"?

The September sky had turned to indigo, and the moon over Harlem ascended toward the heavens. I stood and went inside, climbed the stairs, and returned to a fourth-floor apartment, just as I was.

1991

CHAPTER 14

Oregon Jeremiad

O REGON'S HIGHWAY 66 meanders west out of Ashland, hugging the sides of mountains on its way toward Klamath Falls. At Greensprings Summit, elevation forty-five hundred feet, the road levels off a bit, then begins a gentle descent and winds past Tubb Springs, a small roadside state park. The late afternoon sunshine coming through the pines dapples the macadam road. A logging truck rolls by, heading the other direction toward the sawmill down in the valley.

Just past a fire ranger station and beyond the twenty-two mile marker, a small green sign announces LINCOLN. Several shingled buildings come into view, behind them a few cows and chickens and horses, a mill pond, an abandoned sawmill of corrugated steel, and a bark burner, rusted and listing slightly, looking like an inebriated, oversized tipi. A sign in front of one of the roadside structures reads: THE OREGON EXTENSION OF TRINITY COLLEGE. To the left, on a gentle rise opposite the larger buildings, five houses and five cabins nestle among tall pines. Wood-smoke curls out of the chimneys in early November, the fragrance mixing pleasantly with the scent of pines in the thin mountain air.

The whole panorama, framed by larger mountains in the distance, is arresting. Surely even John Henry, a hard-nosed businessman of the 1920s, must have thought so. Henry constructed this logging camp, but, in a fit of pique at Franklin Roosevelt's New Deal, decided to close up shop in the 1930s. The property then devolved upon a succession of owners, and by the 1960s and early 1970s, having withstood various communitarian experiments, the buildings had fallen into disrepair.

Enter Douglas Frank and Thomas (Sam) Alvord. Frank and Alvord came upon Lincoln in 1974, near the conclusion of a western tour that had taken them through Montana and Idaho in search of land. They represented a small group of people from Illinois who wanted to establish an alternative education program for college students.

By the summer of 1975, Lincoln bustled with activity. Five faculty members, most of whom had been associated in some way with Trinity College, an evangelical liberal-arts school in Deerfield, Illinois, moved with their families into the houses on the property.[1] Teams of volunteers evicted the goats and squatters who had occupied the cabins. They carted away truckloads of garbage, patched the plumbing, installed kitchens, repaired fences, and painted the cabins. One of the large buildings became the library, which also serves as study area, lecture hall, and social meeting-place for the community. By Labor Day, twenty-two students took up residence in the cabins and prepared for four months of rigorous interdisciplinary study.

For Frank and Alvord, the Oregon Extension grew out of years of friendship and endless hours in front of campfires in the wilderness talking and dreaming about the future. In the 1960s they, together with Jim Titus, Frank's brother-in-law, directed Camp Sandy Hill for Boys in Maryland. After Frank became a professor of history at Trinity College, he, Alvord, and Titus formed Trek Inc., a not-for-profit organization that took small groups of teenagers (some of them wards of the court) for ten-day canoeing excursions into the Boundary Waters Wilderness of northern Minnesota.

The "Trek Curriculum," though not overtly evangelical or confessional, sought to teach values and instill a sense of responsibility in its young charges. "Think before you act," they were admonished. "Remember that every action has a consequence.[2] Those lessons, of course, took on a special urgency in the wilderness, days away from emergency help and suburban amenities, where an errant match or a food pack left at the side of a portage trail could spell catastrophe.

Back at Trinity College, Frank quickly became one of the most popular members of a young, energetic faculty who, under the protection of an indulgent dean, encouraged their students to think critically, to examine their faith and ask questions of themselves and their superiors. Frank's outward appearance doubtless contributed to his popularity and to the mystique that came to surround him. Here was a man of impeccable evangelical credentials—reared in a missionary household, a graduate of Wheaton College—who sported long hair, granny glasses, a beard, and dressed in denims and work shirts. But if his appearance excited the curiosity of young, impressionable fundamentalists, most of them from conservative homes, his classes got them thinking. An advocate of the Socratic method—education, he once told me, is the art of asking the right questions—Frank turned his quick wit and his restless intellect loose on several generations of students. In United States history, he started them questioning some cherished shibboleths about America's past and prompted them to consider some of the darker corners of American history: America's treatment of Indians and blacks, he suggested, belied its putative Christian origins; the consumer culture that so dominates American life, he pointed out, exacted a price from the less fortunate and the Third World. In a course on contemporary world affairs, students from conservative Republican households began questioning for the first time the morality of America's involvement in Vietnam.

After several failed attempts to find a church in the Deerfield area that maintained a critical distance from suburban, middle-class values, Frank, Alvord, and others organized a "house church," a group of evangelicals who met for worship in each other's homes. Here, amid a ferment of ideas and personalities, they began to concoct plans for a college semester in the wilderness, an enterprise that would combine their love for the outdoors with their appetite for ideas.

As it took shape in the autumn of 1975, the Oregon Extension, this community of scholars at Lincoln, offered a curriculum that invited students to examine twentieth-century ideas, values, and norms from an evangelical perspective. Each of the four month-long segments of the semester (Modern Visions of Society, Science and Technology in the Modern World, Modern Visions of Humanity, Religion and the Human Condition) opened with a week of introductory lectures, extensive common readings, and group discussions. Over the next two weeks, students chose topics germane to the particular segment and, under the direction of a faculty member, prepared papers or some other project that reflected their reading and thinking on those topics. At the end of the third week the community gathered to listen to various findings, an occasion for interaction and discussion. During the fourth week, students and faculty took off on some sort of outing—backpacking in Yosemite, climbing Mount Shasta, spending several days in San Francisco or on the Oregon coast—during which time, under informal circumstances, they continued to discuss ideas, to rehash what they'd read and what it meant.

The formal structure of the semester has changed little since the program began in 1975, although the content of the readings and the nature of the discussions have evolved somewhat. When I knew the program in its early years, the faculty evinced a suspicion of institutions generally, especially evangelical institutions, a vague uneasiness about the Church in general and evangelicalism in particular. This suspicion, in some degree a product of the iconoclastic tenor of the times, reflected a sense that evangelicalism had slipped its theological moorings—that it had lost its prophetic voice and thereby had rendered itself irrelevant to thinking Christians. The folks at Oregon wanted not so much to engage the evangelical subculture about its shortcomings as to harangue it or, perhaps worse, simply ignore it.

I caught up with Doug Frank in San Francisco in the fall of 1986, eleven years after the Oregon program began. For two days we walked the streets, visited bookstores in Palo Alto and Berkeley, and talked. I then traveled back to Oregon with Frank and his students to observe life at Lincoln.

EARLY IN OUR CONVERSATIONS, Frank recounted for me a chapel service he had attended during a recent visit to an evangelical college. The sermon that morning, delivered by the college's president, used the New Testament, in Frank's judgment, to "baptize" American consumerism and extol the virtues of prosperity theology, the notion that God is itching to fulfill the material desires of every Christian. The president, preaching on a text from the third chapter of Paul's epistle to the Philippians, implied that his recently acquired sports car was God's reward for his work and faithfulness. Because of his financial status, moreover, his wife could now indulge her taste for imported antiques. God never intended for us to be poor or deprived, he argued, echoing the bromide so popular in contemporary evangelicalism. God wants us to live full and happy lives.

The preacher ignored key portions of the text entirely. In verse 10, Paul writes that those who seek to know Christ must partake in the "fellowship of His sufferings," but the sermon mentioned nothing about suffering; instead, it seemed to promise the good life to anyone who wanted it. Nor did the preacher bother to mention the cross of Christ, which is at the center of the chapter and, indeed, the whole epistle. "It was a classic case," Frank said, "of distorting a passage to make it palatable to middle-class kids who want to go out into the corporate world and rise to the top for Jesus."

The issue of how evangelicals have misunderstood and, at times, deliberately misused the Bible has plagued Frank for years. Only after coming to terms with our inherent sinfulness, he argues, can we know the full embrace of God's love and forgiveness, the unspeakable gift of God's grace. But grace too often is neglected in evangelical circles, where there is a tendency to dwell on the law of judgment rather than the gospel of God's grace. "All I hear within the evangelical subculture these days is the law, one version of the law or another; they're all competing. They're all determined to make us feel guilty and give us burdens too heavy to bear." Frank sees the consequences of exalting law over gospel in the evangelical students who come to study with him in Oregon. "Our kids show it," he said, "and they hate it. Our students come to us with the burden of being a Christian on their backs. They're bent over with it." Some of them have dispensed with their faith completely. Others try hard to maintain the pious lifestyle they were told to live, but they feel burdened with it. "It's the law," Frank said. "Paul is right in his epistle to the Romans: The law kills. It's supposed to drive us to the grace of Christ, but evangelicals wield it as a weapon against one another and against their enemies, and it drives people away from Christ."

In Frank's opinion, this emphasis on the law and its exclusionary tendencies encourages evangelicals to draw lines and to make judgments about the spiritual condition of others, to impose a kind of dualism on the world. "We put ourselves on the good side of that line and figure out who's on the bad, so we can take our shots across the line and justify ourselves." Frank believes that the Bible teaches that only Christ can justify. "That's why the doctrine of justification in the Bible is so beautiful," he explained, "because God does it for us. When *we* do it, we always have enemies; you can't justify yourself without making an enemy."

The temptation to moralize, Frank contends, afflicts all of evangelicalism, both left and right. Right-wing fundamentalists such as Jerry Falwell, Pat Robertson, and Tim LaHaye have garnered media attention in recent years with their excoriations of sinfulness in American society, but there is also a less visible evangelical left wing, the best example of which is the Sojourners Community in Washington, D. C., publishers of *Sojourners* magazine. This group had its genesis at Trinity Evangelical Divinity School in Deerfield (which shares a campus with Trinity College). *Sojourners* consistently decries the arms race, American intervention in Central America, and espouses other generally liberal political views on the basis of an evangelical understanding of the gospel. While Frank finds himself in general sympathy with its political views, he sees the same moralistic tendencies in *Sojourners* that he sees in Falwell, a heavy weight of judgment that extends even to the magazine's graphics. "That's a consequence of their evangelical theology," he said. "It's not that we shouldn't say things are wrong, but moralism has to do with lines, with pointing fingers. It doesn't make an analysis of evil that's 360 degrees, that says 'we're all culpable, we're all encompassed within the same human determinisms.' And therefore, that type of moralism doesn't very often acknowledge its own complicity. Moralism assumes autonomous human beings who are free to make autonomous decisions about right and wrong, and even when it notices that people don't often do that, that people generally choose the wrong over the right, it still assumes that those decisions can be made. Therefore, there's a burdensome feel to moralistic analysis. It's the law. It's finger-pointing."

In refusing to acknowledge our own fallenness before God, Frank says, we fall prey to self-righteousness and pride and even hatred. "If you buy into a kind of logical, rationalistic, legalistic evanglicalism, you can't get past that. So I'm not sure you can really love, because you're constantly drawing lines, making judgments about others, and your love becomes condescension. It's conditional, and it's reaching down to the other, reaching across the line to the evil one. It's not embracing one who is within the same circle of sinfulness as you are. I think Paul, the apostle, draws a circle around all of us and says, 'we're *all* sinners.'"

What Frank calls rationalistic evangelicalism doesn't admit of that possibility. It draws rigid lines separating good from evil. One of the most persistent refrains in evangelical sermons is the contrast between Christianity and the world. "I'm to the point now when I know I'm in the presence of bad theology when I hear that line being drawn," Frank said. "I'm not in the presence of the gospel.

"What distinguishes a Christian from a non-Christian is confession, that we confess who we are, that we fall within that 360-degree circle of sinfulness. There's a certain freedom in that, in acknowledging our humanity, our sinfulness before God and recognizing that Christ alone restores us to a relationship with God. That ability to confess, to acknowledge my fallenness, it seems to me, is a wonderful gift. I cannot with any justification walk down Castro Street and think of myself as better than the gay couples who walk by arm in arm. I cannot do that. I'm one with them in some respects, and if I thought about it for about twenty seconds, I could think of some ways in which I am just like them."

Rationalistic evangelicalism lies at the root of these moralistic impulses. Rationalistic theology, which Frank traces to Enlightenment influences, strips the Bible of its dynamic character. "Evangelicals start with an inerrant Bible, which says that the Scriptures are without error in the original autographs—which, by the way, we don't have. *Inerrancy* is a rationalistic term; it doesn't talk about a living Word. Evangelicals, it seems, need a Bible that can be nicely categorized, outlined, systematically organized, doctrinally elaborated, and all that stuff, so they can have all their 'i's dotted and 't's crossed. It places some kind of guarantee on our theology. It's necessary somehow to give credibility to the fact that we have abstracted a theological system away from the Bible and then presented it as the truth. But that whole process kills the living truth somehow."

The evangelical fondness for proof-texts, seizing on a specific Bible verse to shore up every argument, follows from this rationalistic bent. "We have a verse for everything. That's part of the rationalism. We treat the Bible as a series of numbers having little or no relationship to one another. We take a number here and a number there and plug them into our little grid."

There is, as Frank points out, an irony in all this. Evangelicals were under attack by rationalists—by Darwinism and the canons of the Enlightenment—at the turn of the century. Rather than continuing to insist on the importance of faith, however, evangelicals bought into a rationalistic epistemology entirely. As a consequence, the evangelical subculture today is peppered with groups organized to prove the existence of God, to supply evidences for miracles, proofs for the resurrection, and even to propagate something called "scientific creationism," which seeks to vindicate the Genesis account of creation. "Rationalism is a tight logical system," Frank says. "You're either right or you're wrong. If your logic works out, then you're right. You win. And I think evangelical logic-choppers buy into that because it gives them a sense of certainty. It adds up. If the logic adds up to your conclusion, you need to brook no opposition. It's really a tool of violence.

"The Pharisees in the New Testament are a good example of that. They're the most moral people in the Bible, and yet they're the ones who kill Jesus. The Pharisees become almost the centerpiece of the New Testament as a paradigm of fallen humanity, and yet these are the most moral, most religious people in the first century. They even use their absolute morality against Jesus. They come to Jesus and say, 'Hmm, let's see now. By the terms of our absolute morality, you have just broken the Sabbath.' So we have human beings using absolute morality to do violence against God, even as they insist that God is the author of their morality. These are moral people. They're not bastards any more than we are. Absolute morality makes legalists. So in that context morality becomes a tool of violence. The gospel says we're all bastards, but God loves us anyway. The moralist says, 'Maybe you're a bastard, and I *used* to be one.' That's a betrayal of the gospel, the good news of our salvation through Christ. The Bible teaches that Jesus saves us in spite of ourselves."

CLEARLY, WHAT ANIMATES FRANK is what he calls "the life of the mind." He reads voraciously and widely, even obsessively—fiction, theology, sociology, psychology, economics, history—and he loves talking about ideas. A book is seldom out of reach. He is himself relentlessly rational, and so his criticism of evangelical "logic-choppers" sometimes cuts close to home. But he is not one-dimensional. He enjoys music and good food (we made more than one pilgrimage in San Francisco in search of the perfect sourdough bread). He seems to gather strength and sustenance from the wilderness, and occasionally he will take a break from study to split wood for the houses and cabins at Lincoln. He regularly leavens his conversations with a gentle humor, which he often turns on himself in a self-deprecating way that suggests that, however earnest he may appear at times, he prefers not to take himself too seriously.

Life at the Oregon Extension revolves around intellectual pursuits, and, in that way, Lincoln represents an extension of Frank's own eclectic interests. Although Frank, graying now as he approaches his mid-forties, seems uncomfortable about assuming leadership, the other faculty seem tacitly to acknowledge that much of the spirit, energy, and direction of the Oregon Extension comes from him. Not that everyone else is just a bit player; indeed, one of the striking characteristics of the place is its sense of collegiality, of shared purpose. The faculty as well as the entire college program tend to ignore the boundaries of traditional academic disciplines. During my visit, Sam Alvord, who holds several advanced degrees in English, lectured on Jacques Ellul, a French sociologist. Jim Titus, Lincoln's resident biologist, has recently shown an interest in Martin Luther and Reformation theology. John Linton, who joined the faculty in 1980, reads everything from astrophysics to Old Testament, the field in which he earned his doctorate.

The result is a kind of cauldron of ideas, regularly seasoned with new insights and constantly stirred and restirred in discussion, whether structured discussions in the classroom or informal conversations on a wilderness trail or over coffee at the Mountain View Inn down the road. Because the faculty and students read many of the same books, there is a common intellectual genealogy that shapes their thought. Frank first read and lectured on Jacques Ellul in the autumn of 1975, the year the Oregon Extension opened. "I had a sense that Ellul was on to something," Frank recalled. Ellul, a Christian, sees the modern believer as caught in a dialectic, torn between two commands: "do something" and "whatever you are doing means nothing." Ellul's reading of the Bible and his understanding of the human condition lead him to be suspicious of political change and human institutions generally, and that suspicion allows the Christian a certain detachment, an indifference to the success of his or her actions. Changes in the world, Ellul believes, are often cosmetic. The real lostness, boundness, captivity of the human condition has not changed; we've just changed the outward appearance of our masters. Humans are captive to a whole variety of determinisms—sociological, economic, biological. Paradoxically, according to Ellul, the beginning of freedom is the acknowledgement of our unfreedom, an awareness of the determinisms that bind us and circumscribe our lives. Real freedom is an experience that can occur only by the grace of God and in the presence of the revelation of God in Jesus Christ.

Ernest Becker, a cultural anthropologist, also has had a formative influence on the people at Lincoln. In *Escape from Evil*, Becker argues that all evil and misery in the world can be traced to man's fear of death and his attempts to make himself immortal. Man devises all sorts of constructs to convince himself that he will live forever, and he invests himself in heroic figures who define the enemy and then symbolically slay that enemy. People project their own puny selves onto the hero and feel as if they're full of power and righteousness. This allows them to avoid facing their own mortality. Evangelicals, Frank says, have consistently rendered their allegiance to such heroic figures, various charismatic, pugnacious leaders like Billy Sunday and Jimmy Swaggart who take on and conquer the enemy, and who in so doing vindicate the power and righteousness of their followers.

Other intellectual influences on Frank and the Oregon program include social critics such as Wendell Berry and Philip Slater, sociologists like Peter Berger and Max Weber. In recent years, they have been reading the theology of William Stringfellow, Vernard Eller, Martin Luther, Søren Kierkegaard, and Karl Barth.

That pantheon of theologians certainly places the people at Oregon outside the mainstream of evangelical thought, whose taste in theology frequently runs more toward Carl F. H. Henry, Chuck

Swindoll, and Robert Schuller. Indeed, it is difficult to escape the impression that the geographical isolation of Lincoln, for all its bucolic delights, has bred an intellectual isolation as well. Frank and his colleagues sometimes resemble prophetic curmudgeons, dressed in sackcloth and ashes and crying doom, primarily for one another's benefit. In the early years of the Oregon Extension, they regularly brought in outside lecturers, but that practice has waned. "We're finding fewer and fewer people who speak our language," Frank conceded, "who address the kinds of issues we care about."

Frank thinks the arrival in 1980 of John Linton, a Bible scholar, goaded the folks at Lincoln to return to the Bible with renewed seriousness and fresh understanding, absent the biases of their fundamentalist upbringings. "Linton has taught me to read all the ethical tables in the Bible—particularly the passages where Paul says do this, do that, don't do this, don't do that—the way Karl Barth read them," Frank said. "Barth believes that the imperative is always imbedded in the indicative. He points out that there's always a statement before and after those ethical tables that we don't actually do those things we're supposed to, and yet God forgives us. We are saved, now and forever, despite our shortcomings. Barth says that it's in the context of knowing the embrace of God that we can carry out these things. That gives a very different feel to the ethical tables from what I was taught growing up."

The evangelical weakness for moralizing, however, gives these ethical tables exaggerated importance. "There are relatively few of these tables," Frank notes. "It's just that we evangelicals have pulled them all out and memorized them and made our kids memorize them. We're drawn to them like a magnet." Frank sees this evangelical reliance on rigid, legalistic morality as a symptom of adolescence, and he has thought for some time about evangelicalism as a type of sustained adolescence. No stage of life is more prone to hero worship than adolescence. An adolescent is strongly influenced by group conformity and the expectations of other people; it's a stage in which self-consciousness is at its height. "I see the evangelicals' penchant for gazing inward to assess their own spirituality as a heightened form of self-consciousness," he said. "They're constantly comparing themselves to the standards of spiritual behavior they've established and asking 'How am I doing?' and 'Am I good enough?' and 'How do I appear to others?'" Spiritual appearances are very important to evangelicals, just as an adolescent spends a lot of time in front of the mirror.

Adolescence is also a period of rebellion, a search for individuality, identifying yourself in opposition to authority—feeling on the one hand that you have to submit to authority and on the other hand chafing under it and wishing you could be your own boss. "My instinct is that evangelicals don't love God very much, that they relate to God the way a child or an adolescent relates to an authority figure," Frank said. "So there's often a lot of fear in their motivation, and there's mistrust of who God is. And I think there's also a lot of anger, but it's all suppressed because, of course, you can't be angry with God any more than an adolescent is supposed to be angry with his parents."

THE LINCOLN CHRISTIAN CHURCH meets in the pine-paneled cookhouse early on Sunday mornings. People from both the Oregon Extension and the surrounding mountain community gather for worship just as the sun clears the surrounding mountain ridges and chases off the white, wispy clouds that shroud the tops of the pine trees. The morning chill lingers, however. Like everything else here, worship at the Lincoln Christian Church is casual, not all that far removed from the house-church days back in Deerfield; the people here have little patience with ritual or formality of any kind. Patsy Alvord plays the piano, and the congregation—students, faculty, mountain folk, and children, lots of children—sings with exuberance. Sam Alvord, wearing corduroy pants and a crew-neck sweater, rises to welcome the worshipers. Looking across the congregation of thirty or so seated before him, he acknowledges the return of some who have been away for several weeks and then welcomes a former student, an alumnus of the Oregon Extension from its early years. "You haven't changed much," Alvord tells him. "It's good to see you again." He then asks if there are announcements, prayer requests, or items of thanksgiving. Several ask prayer for family members or neighbors. Someone says, "I'd like to thank whoever it is who gets up early on Sunday mornings to start a fire in the stove so it's nice and warm for church." After a pause, Howard Claassen, a retired physicist from Wheaton College who has built a home there on the mountain, says quietly but with evident satisfaction, "I'll consider myself thanked."

In addition to his teaching responsibilities and other tasks around Lincoln, Alvord, known sometimes as Marryin' Sam for all the weddings he has performed for former students and community folk, has taken on the role of unofficial pastor of Lincoln Christian Church. There is a genial ease to the proceedings, an informality that extends from the welcome to the prayers to Alvord's brief homily, which concludes the meeting.

In some respects, as befits a community centered around learning, the Sunday Bible study that follows the worship service is more important than the service itself. After a twenty-minute break, John Linton shambles into the room. Linton is the picture of perpetual dishevelment, and he takes a lot of good-natured ribbing from his colleagues. Dressed in denims, hiking boots, a flannel shirt, and a pea-green army coat, he seems to have a steaming mug of coffee fused permanently to his right fist. He wears a brown woolen stocking hat pulled down over his longish, straight hair. ("I think he puts that hat on about the first of November," Frank commented, "and doesn't take it off again until sometime in April.") Linton, however, with the earnestness with which he approaches the Bible, has added a whole new dimension to the community at Lincoln. In Frank's words, "Linton's gotten us into the Bible." Linton himself, with characteristic understatement, says, "I have the fond hope that the Bible might mean something."

It's easy, Frank thinks, for evangelicals to dismiss the Bible, even though they give lip service to its importance and constantly argue its inerrancy. "It's so obvious to me now that when you take a book like the Bible, declare it inerrant, and extract everything from it and put it all into a nice, neat little system and tell your kids what they're supposed to believe, the book becomes dead. I remember when I was maybe thirty saying something like—I'm embarrassed to tell about it even now—saying something like, 'Well, what's so difficult to know about the Bible? It says we're supposed to love each other, so let's just get busy and do it!' That's a very pious way of saying 'This is just a book that has an idea in it that God wants us to understand and try to work out in our lives,' as if we were autonomous people who could just start doing that, as if we didn't have to hear on a daily basis who we are and who God is in contradistinction to ourselves.

"So what Linton does is he's brought the book alive for us. Through him, we're hearing the Word being spoken afresh. Sometimes he takes a passage of Scripture that we, growing up in evangelical households, have heard all of our lives and he'll put an inflection on a word and we'll see it in a whole new light. It's exciting stuff."

Linton pulls up a chair in the middle of the room and announces that this morning's study centers around Hebrews 6, a passage that has long bedeviled evangelicals because it seems to admit of the possibility that a believer might lose his or her salvation. After reading the chapter, Linton asks, "Did you hear anything as this chapter was read that you wanted to get into?" There follows a series of questions which Linton acknowledges with only a sentence or two, but he is merely collecting the thoughts and comments of the group, almost relishing their confusion.

Linton leans back in his chair. "Here's what I think is going on. The writer is talking about contrition or penance, not as a one-time occurrence, but that all of life should be an act of contrition. Here's how I would want to interpret this. When the Bible speaks of enlightenment, both here and in the first chapter of John, it makes it clear that the true light which enlightens every man is Jesus. He comes unto His own, and His own reject Him. That's a sad story, unbelievably sad. But as many as received Him, He gave to them the authority to be the children of God. You can't then invent all sorts of things in the Christian life to try to get enlightened. That's a key move, because we're forever trying to devise programs to get enlightened, to make us more spiritual, as though Jesus hadn't already enlightened us.

"The writer of Hebrews says that such enlightenment lies beyond our power. We don't have this freedom in ourselves; it is God's gift. And can we be certain that God has given it to us? Yes, of course; He's sworn once to Abraham and another time when he said, 'thou art a priest according to the order of Melchizedek forever.' The traditional, fundamentalist way of reading this passage engenders doubts about whether or not our salvation is secure, but that's not what the writer is saying at all."

As the discussion continues, Linton grows more and more animated; the caffeine apparently has kicked in. "Now if you're following this even roughly, you're probably wondering what this Melchizedek business has to do with this. What is it about Melchizedek and Jesus being a priest after the order of Melchizedek? What does it mean that Jesus is a priest forever, and how is that a rebuke to people who are trying to make a new foundation?"

"He's doing it for them," someone answers.

"He's doing it how often for them?"

"All the time."

"That's right. Somehow, Jesus is serving you as priest in a way that you can't get around. So don't start a new foundation based on your own righteousness or contrition. You've got a high priest in Jesus who lasts forever and ever and ever. You know who makes repentance for you? Jesus makes repentance for you. He repents. You think that you're repenting? Well, yeah, that's a good thing. You ought to do that. But don't confuse it with the repentance that's done by the priest, Jesus, who mediates between your sinfulness and God's holiness. Jesus is doing that forever!"

Linton's approach to the Bible has influenced everyone at Lincoln. "Linton has an almost mystical attachment to the Bible," Frank said. "There may be something to that."

THAT EVENING IN HIS LIVING ROOM, I remarked to Frank that I didn't think he would willingly have called himself an evangelical ten years ago. He said no, probably not—certainly not with any enthusiasm. Even now, he sometimes refers to evangelicals as "they" and at other times as "we," an ambivalence born, it seems, not so much of rebellion as of sadness at the ways evangelicals have misused the gospel. "But I've come to see that I *am* an evangelical," he insisted. "It's part of who I am, my history. At some psychological level, I'm thoroughly in the camp. There was a point ten years ago when I was trying to get free of the subculture. Now I feel like I'm almost being forced out of it, not by people but by a kind of despair."

Frank spoke in slow, measured phrases. A chilly autumn breeze swept in through the screen door. "I'm increasingly gripped by the tragedy of the subculture, by the harm it does to its people, especially its kids. It's becoming more and more clear to me that the subculture is based on lies and denials. It doesn't understand the gospel. What is this good news that we're supposed to be so excited about? Evangelicals don't have a clue, it seems to me. It's appearing to me more and more as a real tragedy. This group of people, and I among them for a long time, that felt as if it was the guarantor of orthodoxy in America and even the world, is blind. Its very gospel is secularized; it has bought into a rationalistic, secular epistemology. It's become more interested in morality than grace, and in that way it's just like any other subculture. Every subculture is interested in morality. We're no better than the Mormons; in fact, in terms of morality, we're not as good as the Mormons. The Mormons outdo us. If that's what the gospel is all about, then they're to be emulated. But they don't understand the gospel, either. We think we do.

"It just seems like a tragedy to me, all these people going through these motions and all these big churches, and all our kids seem like they're more and more lost. More and more of our students have little or no interest in God or hate God altogether. They think of Him as a being who gives them rules but doesn't love them."

But Frank's theology, let alone his temperament, will not allow him to succumb to despair. His newly recovered sense of identity as an evangelical has led to engagement with other evangelicals, an almost messianic effort to save evangelicalism from itself, even though he recognizes the danger of falling into the very moralistic trap he argues against. "I suspect that, so often, even the way I talk about a theology that doesn't draw lines resorts to line-drawing in spite of itself," he acknowledged, "by saying the way you read the Bible is wrong." Frank's book, *Less Than Conquerors: How Evangelicals Entered the Twentieth Century*, explores the ways in which evangelicals betrayed the gospel in the face of various cultural pressures around the turn of the century.[3] He argues that fundamentalists went wrong after the turn of the century when they became enslaved by a contrived, legalistic ethical system—a set of behavioral strictures and taboos—which effectively institutionalized their penchant for line-drawing. They also embraced dispensational premillennialism, which identified evangelicals themselves as the only moral people left in the world. Dispensationalism, as put forward by John Nelson Darby, C. I. Scofield, Dwight Moody, and others, was based on the premise that the world was getting worse and worse. Dispensationalists smugly insisted that they knew what others, whom they labeled non-Christians, did not—namely, a plan for the ages, as revealed in the recondite passages of Scripture, that identified evangelicals as the righteous remnant and, therefore, privy to God's secrets. Frank's book interleaves history with theology, sociology, and cultural analysis, an interdisciplinary approach that clearly reflects his intellectual tastes.

He has also lectured at various evangelical colleges around the country, and on August 23, 1986, he addressed the faculty of Wheaton College, the bastion of evangelicalism where he earned his bachelor's degree twenty-three years earlier. Frank spoke of the brokenness and pain that he has witnessed among so many adolescent evangelicals, a sense of alienation from a God who demands all sorts of moral and behavioral concessions from them—the God of their parents' making, who is more interested in exacting tribute than bestowing His grace. He noted that these students, products of a consumer culture that values appearance above all else, have become very adept at hiding the pain they feel behind well-scrubbed facades of happiness and piety and self-assurance.

I asked Frank to distill the argument of his next book, a work now in progress. "Evangelicals have lost sight of the good news of the gospel," he said, "the possibility that in Jesus we see God's suffering for all of us. He turns our sin and violence against Him to our good and declares His mercy—unlimited, free mercy—to all of us. We can now live in a kind of thankfulness and freedom, accepting that mercy.

"That's such good news to me. It just sounds like such good news to me. I can declare that good news. My job isn't to go out and say to someone, 'Unless you repent, you shall surely die, and I shall not,' or something like that, but rather, 'You and I are both really messed up, and God declares that He loves us both and continues to forgive us day by day and shows His mercy infinitely and eternally to us, regardless of our merit.'

"When have evangelicals ever taken seriously the statement of Jesus on the cross, 'Father, forgive them, for they don't know what they're doing'? We don't take that seriously. We say, 'Father, we'll forgive those who know what they are doing, who say that they're sinners and repent.' It's conditional. But Jesus says about even His killers, who are *not* repentant—they're not weeping and wailing and gnashing their teeth; they're probably jeering and cheering—but Jesus says, 'Forgive them, they don't know what they're doing.' That's very good news, that somehow, way over our heads, in ways we are not even free half the time to admit or understand or explain, Jesus is forgiving us. That's real good news to me. I don't think evangelicals understand that concept. Evangelicals so often are the bearers of bad news: 'Unless you repent, you shall surely die.' That's true, but that's not the whole story. And if you *do* repent, evangelicals insist, then you've got to get your whole life organized and start jumping through these hoops and being a good Christian. At any time, you could fall out of fellowship with God. You've got to show yourself to be better than the rest of the world so you can be a witness for Christ. That keeps us from doing what Jesus did, which is hang around with sinners and drunks. We don't do that.

"I want this next book to stop evangelicals dead in their tracks. I would love to do that." The crusty prophet has emerged again. He hesitated, laughed at his own pretensions, and then continued. "I would love to see the whole evangelical subculture in this country raising its hands in praise to God and saying, 'We are sorry bastards, but God is merciful.' Wouldn't that be wonderful? There'd be a revival! That would be so refreshing. 'We are sorry bastards. Lord, have mercy.'"

1986

CHAPTER 15

Prime Time

T HE FAMILY LIFE CENTER lies on the edge of Baton Rouge just down the road from the newly opened Mall of Louisiana. The parking lot for the shopping mall is burgeoning on a Sunday, while the acres of parking for the Family Life Center are nearly empty. Such a juxtaposition might occasion yet another commentary on spiritual apathy, misplaced priorities, and the false gods of consumerism, until one remembers that the preacher behind the pulpit at the Family Life Center on this Sunday—as well as most Sundays—is a man named Jimmy Swaggart.

To suggest that Swaggart is behind the pulpit, however, is somewhat misleading; he has never submitted easily to the constraints of pulpits—or, for that matter, to any other conventional boundaries. Instead, he bobs and weaves and shouts and cries and spins his own magic. "Preaching is like an orchestra," Swaggart told me. "You have to be loud one moment and quiet the next. You've got to keep the people's attention. You've got to keep the people's attention." Throughout a raucous and controversial career now in its fourth decade, Jimmy Swaggart has rarely had trouble keeping people's attention.

DESPITE THE DEARTH OF CONGREGANTS, my presence at Family Life Center was not entirely welcome. I had made the mistake of chatting with the women at the welcome booth and, in the process, disclosed naïvely that I was in town to write about Jimmy Swaggart Ministries ten years after his celebrated—and very public—downfall.

I had just settled into my seat in the sanctuary, already awash in klieg lights, when one of the ushers, dressed in a burgundy sport coat, sat down beside me. "I understand you're a reporter," he said. I allowed that that was close enough. "First of all," he barked, "no pictures in here." As I looked around, I understood why. The last time I had seen Swaggart on television, which was several years ago, it had occurred to me that all the camera angles had been rather narrow, suggesting that they were trying to cover up for the fact that the congregation was small. Indeed, the entire wraparound balcony of the octagonal building was closed, shrouded in darkness, and huge sections of the main floor had been cordoned off by dark, burgundy curtains, which matched the carpeting and the blazers worn by the ushers. "And the other thing," the usher announced brusquely, "I'm pretty sure Don and Jimmy don't want you here. In fact, I'll check with Donnie right now."

Within minutes, Donnie Swaggart, Jimmy's son, a stocky man with an athletic build, dressed nattily in a dark, double-breasted suit, came bounding from the backstage area, almost running toward me. "What are you doing here?" he demanded. When I explained that I was writing an article for *Christianity Today*, Donnie Swaggart's eyes flashed. "I don't like the press," he bellowed. "How come you didn't tell us you were coming?" I explained that I had called the office several times over the preceding weeks to inquire about dates and that I had made no attempt to hide my purpose for visiting. "Well, you didn't talk to me," he said, his tone softening slightly.

"Listen, I've seen characters like you before," he continued, resuming the bluster and wagging his finger in my direction, "and you know what? It's the so-called Christians who are the worst." Ten o'clock was fast approaching, and Donnie had to assume his place on the stage. "Just remember," he continued, "blood is thicker than water. Do whatever you want to me, just don't touch my parents or my kids. If you do, I'm coming after you, you understand?"

Although I found these threats more amusing than intimidating—should I expect a knock on the door some night and a couple of thugs with cigarettes dangling from their mouths: "Hey, buster, some preacher fella from Baton Rouge wants to have a little chat wid you"?—Donnie Swaggart clearly was paranoid about my presence. Throughout the service he kept stealing glances in my direction. A rather large usher whose name tag read "Bill Wilson" was assigned to follow me, tracking my serpentine movements after the service. Although I managed to lose him a couple of times, he caught up with me, breathing a bit heavily, and resumed his surveillance. When I approached Jimmy Swaggart, who had changed into a turtleneck and was greeting congregants near the stage, Wilson fidgeted nervously but kept his distance.

Swaggart himself couldn't have been more gracious. He is a kind man who, unlike some televangelists, is not afraid to meet your eyes. Lest there be any confusion or false pretenses, I informed him immediately of my purpose for visiting Baton Rouge and told him of my admiration for his preaching abilities. The prospect that the article might appear in *Christianity Today*, however, brought a change in his countenance, not so much anger or defiance, as it had with Donnie, but sadness. "I'm afraid I won't be able to help you," he said, shaking his head. "That magazine has said some pretty hurtful things about me." He shifted his eyes briefly toward the middle distance, then back at me. From the corner of my eye I could see my tail, Bill Wilson, shuffling nervously. "Listen," Swaggart said kindly, "I'm not always right about this, of course, but I'm pretty good at judging people, and I detect a good spirit about you. But I don't want anything to do with that magazine. In fact," he continued, suddenly laughing, "I don't even want anything *good* about me going into that magazine!" He grabbed my hand, shook it warmly, and drove home the point. "I'm sorry. If you were writing for the *Washington Post*," he said, "that might be a different matter."

As I turned away, back toward Bill Wilson, so we could resume our choreography around the Family Life Center, I too was sorry. Jimmy Swaggart is an enormously likable man, and I would have loved to chat for awhile about life and preaching and failure and grace and the many doctrines we held in common, including providence.

LITTLE DID I KNOW that an affirmation of providence would occur within the hour, but to convey the scale of this theological demonstration I must reveal a mundane personal detail: I rarely eat lunch—once or twice a month, at most, and only when a business or social occasion demands it. As I pulled out of the parking lot at the Family Life Center, however, and past the vast array of restaurants on Bluebonnet Avenue, I abruptly decided to pull into a large, well-advertised seafood restaurant. I wanted to look through Swaggart's autobiography, *To Cross a River*, which I had just purchased in the bookstore, and, relieved that Bill Wilson and the usher corps had not confiscated my notebook, I wanted to review my scribblings from the morning.

The hostess seated me at a table next to a fairly large group, headed by none other than a man wearing a gray turtleneck—Jimmy Swaggart. He noticed me almost immediately and, without a moment's hesitation, invited me to join them. I assured him that I had not followed him to the restaurant, but he was unconcerned and introduced me all around—his wife, Frances, his mother-in-law, and a missionary family from South Africa.

Swaggart was relaxed and expansive. Although he dropped out of high school, he is an exceedingly bright, literate, and articulate man. In the course of our conversation he talked about the preachers who had influenced him, A. N. Trotter and John R. Rice, a fundamentalist with whom Swaggart had formed an improbable friendship. "I've preached a lot of his sermons over the years," Swaggart said, citing one of his favorites in particular, whose theme was "all the devil's apples got worms." He said that he had developed "my own style," but he very much admired the oratorical abilities of Martin Luther King, Jr., E. V. Hill, and "some white guy with a bald head." When I ventured the name Tony Campolo, Swaggart recognized it immediately. "Yeah, that's him! That guy can preach," he said, slapping the table with evident appreciation.

Swaggart's autobiography cites a couple of other preachers as influential in his early years. J. M. Cason, a young evangelist, held revival meetings in Swaggart's hometown of Ferriday, Louisiana. He made an impression on Swaggart as "a highly emotional man who cried and preached at the same time."[1] Another young preacher, Cecil Janway, also played the piano. Swaggart remembers that he "brought life" from the church's ragged upright piano, "life which flowed throughout the church building."[2]

To this day, Swaggart opens his services at the keyboard, his right leg thumping up and down in time to the beat. As with many pentecostal services, the opening songs blend seamlessly one to the next. "There is power in the blood" segues into "Alleluia, fill us afresh today." As the music whips the congregation into a frenzy, Donnie Swaggart claps and hops in time to the beat and then grabs a microphone. "I'm here to serve notice on the devil today," he exclaims, "there's power in the blood. There's power in the blood of Jesus Christ." The congregation concurs with shouts and applause. "There's a new sheriff in town," Donnie announces. "The devil has been defeated!" He does a little dance as the music segues back into "Power in the Blood."

After still more music and an exhortation to "give the Lord a big hand," the crowd hushed as a woman in the front row spoke in tongues. Someone from the choir offered an immediate interpretation. Donnie once again grabbed the microphone. "I don't know if you can hear it. The Holy Ghost is saying, 'I'm about to enlarge your borders here at the Family Life Center. There's not going to be an empty seat in the house.'"

FOR TEN YEARS NOW, there has been a surfeit of empty seats in the Family Life Center, which has a capacity in excess of seven thousand. The last full house, in fact, gathered to witness the famous confession on February 21, 1988. "I do not plan in any way to whitewash my sin," Swaggart said in the wake of disclosures about having visited a motel room with a prostitute. "I do not call it a mistake, a mendacity. I call it sin." In a soliloquy that was baroque and eloquent at the same time, Swaggart apologized to his wife, his son, and his daughter-in-law. He apologized to the Assemblies of God, "which helped to bring the gospel to my little beleaguered town, when my family was lost without Jesus, this movement and fellowship that girdles the globe, that has been more instrumental in bringing this gospel through the stygian night of darkness to the far-flung hundreds of millions than maybe any effort in the annals of history." He apologized to the "godly" pastors of the Assemblies of God, to its evangelists, "who are heralds and criers of redemption," and to its missionaries "on the front lines of darkness, holding back the tides of hell."

Finally, Swaggart apologized to Jesus, "the one who has saved me and washed me and cleansed me." Swaggart's jaw quivered; rivulets of tears flowed down his cheeks. His eyes turned toward heaven. "I have sinned against you, my Lord, and I would ask that your precious blood would wash and cleanse every stain until it is in the seas of God's forgetfulness, never to be remembered against me anymore."

The performance was vintage Swaggart—complete with anguish and tears and self-flagellation—but if God forgot his transgression, few others did. For Swaggart's many critics, moreover, he had finally received his comeuppance. Swaggart had earlier criticized "prettyboy preachers," a thinly veiled reference to Jim Bakker, his fellow Assemblies of God minister and rival televangelist. Marvin Gorman, a pentecostal preacher from New Orleans, had also tangled with Swaggart, and Gorman was the one who produced evidence that Swaggart had entered a Louisiana motel room with a prostitute—not for a sexual liaison, it turns out, but to engage in some sort of voyeurism.

Believers shuddered at the toppling of yet another televangelist, and the media, already in a feeding frenzy in the wake of Bakker's tryst with Jessica Hahn, had a field day. Swaggart became the object of ridicule and derision. He had engaged in something that was portrayed not so much as immoral as it was tawdry. Some commentators made much of the fact that Hahn (after the requisite plastic surgery) appeared in *Playboy*, while the woman linked with

Swaggart appeared in *Penthouse*. Swaggart promised to submit to the discipline of the Assemblies of God, with whom he held ordination credentials. He offered what the denomination characterized as a "detailed confession," which demonstrated "true humility and repentance" on Swaggart's part. While the Louisiana District of the Assemblies of God imposed a three–month silence, which Swaggart accepted, the denomination extended the discipline to two full years. Swaggart, however, chose to abide by the Louisiana punishment. He resumed preaching on May 22, 1988, Pentecost Sunday, explaining that "Jesus paid the price" for his sins.

Swaggart may have had little choice. Put simply, the scale and the reach of his operations in Baton Rouge and around the world demanded a steady infusion of cash. Donnie was not yet ready to step in—he had neither the experience nor the charisma—and Jimmy recognized that he had to go back on the air in an effort to salvage the various components of his empire.

In retrospect, that decision was probably a miscalculation. "He has isolated himself from those who could have helped eventually restore his ministry with integrity," *Christianity Today* opined. "Swaggart was too impatient, too friendly with power, too short-sighted to see beyond his immediate desires and goals."[3] The general presbytery of the Assemblies of God defrocked Swaggart for violating the terms of their suspension; Swaggart had burned his bridges with his own denomination. His base constituency had already eroded, and Swaggart certainly did not help himself with his own recidivism. In 1991 he was stopped by police in Indio, California, while driving with a woman who claimed to be a prostitute. The result was predictable. More scorn, more ridicule, more empty seats.

THE COMPOUND THAT STRADDLES BLUEBONNET ROAD has a forlorn look to it. With the huge infusions of cash from his television program—Jimmy Swaggart Ministries pulled in $141.6 million in 1986, the last full year before the scandal—Swaggart had built an impressive empire: the massive Family Life Center, television production facilities, an administrative center for his world-wide operations, and Jimmy Swaggart Bible College across the street.[4] Most of the flagpoles, each of which once represented a foreign nation where Swaggart maintained a presence, are empty. The fountains are dry, the landscaping neglected and overgrown. At the Bible college, weeds and a chain-link fence surround the shell of what was to be a high-rise dormitory, its construction abruptly halted after the scandal. Only about forty-five students attend the school now, Swaggart told me wistfully, a campus built to accommodate hundreds more. The entire scene resembles a fly trapped in amber, frozen in time.

And yet, a decade after the scandal, Swaggart soldiers on. He leaves the piano, steps onto center stage, removes his glasses, and exclaims, "I don't know about you, but I'm happy this morning!" He initiates a reprise of "I've got the Holy Ghost down in my heart, just like the Bible says," and then, referring to a recent downturn in the financial markets, remarks: "If you get your joy out of Wall Street, well, you got quite a jolt a couple of weeks ago." He invites members of the congregation to come forward for healing. As the choir and the congregation sing "Holy, Holy, Holy, Lord God Almighty," Swaggart, his son, and several elders pray for each one. Swaggart laid his hands on one woman and prayed, "May the power of the Holy Spirit flow into her and give her what she needs." He took particular compassion on a man who was badly deformed. "Lord, touch my brother," he cried, with his hands on the man's forehead, "from the top of his head to the soles of his feet."

Divine healing has always been a central tenet of Swaggart's ministry. The death of his baby brother, Donnie, when Jimmy was only four made a deep impression on him. While preaching his first revival in Sterlington, Louisiana, Swaggart came down with pneumonia (the same illness that had felled his brother). Swaggart went to the hospital but left after a couple of days, still burning with fever. He fell into a deep depression. "Dark, gloomy thoughts roamed through my mind," Swaggart recalled. "It seemed as if every demon in hell had crawled out to battle with me."[5] He read a passage from the book of Joshua, with the admonition to be strong and of good courage. "God's healing power surged through my body," Swaggart said. "It was like fire in my veins."[6] He went on to impart his healing gift to others—as well as to the battered, blue Plymouth he used during the early years of his itinerancy.

THE QUICKEST ROUTE FROM BATON ROUGE to Ferriday, Louisiana, is U.S. 61, also known as the Great River Road. It winds north past refineries along the Mississippi River, past antebellum plantations that have been turned into museums, and past sharecroppers' cabins sitting next to their modern counterpart, that peculiarly American oxymoron, the mobile home. Baptist churches outnumber gas stations and restaurants and taverns and just about every other sort of establishment in the piney woods of Mississippi. At Natchez the road connects to U.S. 84 west across the kudzu banks of the Mississippi River and back into Louisiana to Ferriday, just up the road.

When I told Swaggart that I planned to visit Ferriday, he said, "Well, it's still there." The large sign on the edge of town, just past Martin's Auto Shop & Used Tires, reads:

> **FERRIDAY, LA**
>
> **VISIT OUR MUSEUM**
>
> **HOME OF:**
>
> **JERRY LEE LEWIS   HOWARD K. SMITH**
>
> **MICKEY GILLEY   PEEWEE WHITTAKER**
>
> **JIMMY SWAGGART   ANN BOYAR WARNER**

Ferriday is a town of convenience stores, cinder-block laundromats, and abandoned houses. Most of the shops along Louisiana Avenue were shuttered years ago, although the hardware store and the pawn shop remain open. Many of the houses in town, not just the mobile homes, sit atop piles of bricks or cinder blocks, testimony to the perils of life on a flood plain. Poverty abounds on both sides of the tracks, even though the tracks themselves were removed some years ago.

After driving around town for half an hour I still hadn't located the Assembly of God that had been organized in 1936 by pentecostal missionaries Mother Sumrall and her daughter Leonia. When I asked for help in a convenience store, one of the customers interjected, "Oh, I can help you. Jimmy's my cousin." Carolyn Magoun (who later clarified that she was actually Frances's cousin, not Jimmy's) directed me to the First Assembly of God at the end of Texas Avenue and threw in the directions to Jerry Lee Lewis's home, which has been made into a museum, and Mickey Gilley's place. The Swaggart house, she said, had been torn down a long time ago.

When I offered that Jimmy Swaggart has had a rough time in recent years, Magoun agreed. "Yes, he has," she said, shaking her head, "but people just forget that we're all human." She added that when Frances Swaggart grew tired of the media glare during her husband's troubles, she would often slip away into the relative anonymity of Ferriday and Wisner, her hometown, just up the road.

The tiny clapboard building at the end of Texas Avenue was sagging somewhat, but it sported a fresh coat of white paint. I pulled into the gravel parking lot where Swaggart's uncle, Elmo Lewis, Jerry Lee's father, had pulled in with his sleek, black Cadillac in the spring of 1958, interrupting a church picnic. Elmo Lewis had just returned from Memphis with the news that Sam Phillips, the producer of Sun Records who had discovered Elvis Presley, Johnny Cash, and Jerry Lee Lewis, had sent for Swaggart. Phillips had heard Swaggart sing and play the piano and found his keyboard style virtually indistinguishable from that of his cousin, Jerry Lee Lewis; he wanted to start a gospel line at Sun, with Swaggart as his first artist.

Swaggart was at that time, in his words, "a small time, wrong-side-of-the-tracks Pentecostal preacher" earning thirty dollars a week—on good weeks. He had a wife and a young son and the battered, blue Plymouth. He preached in a twenty-dollar Stein suit and a single pair of shoes, while his cousin, known nationally as "the wild man of rock-and-roll," was pulling in twenty thousand dollars a week.

Uncle Elmo had left the Cadillac running. The contracts were waiting in Memphis, and Swaggart had been scheduled into the recording studio the next morning. Swaggart paused, surveyed the church folk, and said no. "I can't do it," he said finally, and the black Cadillac pulled away.

Swaggart believes that God gave him his musical abilities. After the arrival of Cecil Janway, the young preacher-pianist, to the Assemblies of God church in Ferriday, Swaggart prayed for a miracle. "'Lord,' I said, 'I want you to give me the gift of playing the piano.'" Swaggart was so fervent that he even attached conditions to the request. "'If you give me this talent, I will never use it in the world,'" he promised, adding, "'If I ever go back on this promise, you can paralyze my fingers!'" The gift came that very evening, a gift that he tried to refine with lessons from the local band director, but Swaggart quit after four lessons, concluding that "playing by the book was a waste of time."[7]

PLAYING BY THE BOOK has never been Swaggart's forté. His preaching style is inimitable, and he is a consummate showman. (I often tell students that if they want fully to appreciate Swaggart's artistry, they should tune him in on television, turn off the sound, and watch his facial expressions and his gesticulations.) At eleven-thirty on Sunday morning, an hour and a half after the service began, Swaggart announced, "I'm not going to preach long, just enough to get through." He recited his text, Matthew 3:11, from memory and prayed that "as the bush burned before Moses, let this bush burn." He was already weeping, saying, "I know I'm nothing."

He recounted the baptism of John along the "reedy banks" of the River Jordan. Swaggart loosened his necktie. "I believe that Jordan rained with shouts that day," he said. "There's nothing like people getting saved." His voiced cracked. "Forgive my emotion," he said and then launched into a riff: "When people come to God the drunkard puts down his bottle and the drug addict his drugs!" He recounted that "Jesus came to my house" when Swaggart was five; his parents were converted. "When they got saved," Swaggart exclaimed, "the fighting ended." Behind Swaggart, in the pastors' gallery adjacent to the choir, Donnie Swaggart was sobbing convulsively. "I'm not going to push any more on this message this morning," Swaggart said, after a pause. "Here's what the Holy Ghost tells me to say to you right now," he continued, pacing the stage. "Come to Jesus."

And they came. Maybe not the hundreds, as in years past, but scores. They filed to the front steps, where boxes of tissues had been placed discreetly around the stage. Swaggart had invited them to come for salvation, for healing, for release from the bondage of sin or addiction.

As MEMBERS OF THE CONGREGATION streamed toward the octagonal stage in response to Swaggart's altar call, a fascinating tableau unfolded. Donnie Swaggart, having dabbed his tears, strode purposefully into the audience, picked out a good-looking young couple, guided them forward, and positioned them in front of one of the television cameras. He began praying fervently and animatedly. The camera's red light flicked on obligingly, while the couple, especially the man, looked rather bewildered. Midway through the prayer, moreover, Donnie signaled to one of his associates to bring someone else. He moved to another camera and repeated the performance.

Donnie Swaggart clearly is positioning himself for an even greater role in Jimmy Swaggart Ministries. He is the heir apparent, and when his father announced on Sunday morning that Donnie would preach that evening, the son let out a whoop, prompting his father to compare him to a race horse chomping at the bit.

When I arrived for the six o'clock service, my friend Bill Wilson was waiting for me in the lobby, still eyeing me suspiciously. Jimmy Swaggart again opened the service at the piano, while Donnie tried to imitate his father's style. "The devil does not own this town," he shouted. "He doesn't own this town. He doesn't own this state. He doesn't own this nation."

In show business terms, Donnie Swaggart was dying out there, so his father stepped from behind the piano and, smooth as butter, came to the rescue. After a few remarks about his early days as a preacher, he began spontaneously to sing "The Old Rugged Cross." A woman near the stage was slain in the Spirit, caught as she fell backward by a man in a burgundy blazer. "Let me tell you," Swaggart told the congregation, "you'll make it if you hold to that cross." The music shifted to "O, Happy Day" and then "Where Could I Go But to the Lord?" "The crippled man can still go to him," Swaggart declared. "The drunk can still go to him. The lost sinner can still go to him."

Donnie, wearing (honest to God) blue suede shoes—midnight blue loafers to match his shirt and his pocket square—again rose to the microphone and this time rose to the occasion. His father, seated behind him, was his biggest cheerleader, offering hearty "amens" and applause. Donnie, preaching from Numbers 13, proved that he is a competent, even better-than-average preacher, "reading" his audience in good pentecostal fashion, trying one theme after another until something clicks. That Sunday night, it was his recounting of a interracial revival he had preached recently in Orlando, Florida. "We don't need Farrakhan," he shouted. "We don't need Jesse. We need Jesus!" The congregation cheered. "Racism is destroying this nation," he continued, "but Jesus is the cure."

The soaring rhetoric was a digression, but it worked; he had the attention of the audience. Swaggart then settled back into his theme, that "we are well able" to possess the land. For the younger Swaggart that meant that the congregation, despite its setbacks in recent years, should move forward in faith. "The devil took his best shot, but we are well able to go up and possess the land," he said. "At times it doesn't seem like there's many of us, but there's more for us than there are against us." He talked about filling the cavernous Family Life Center once again, and he even talked about resuming construction on the high-rise dormitory across the street. "Doubt says the church is half empty," he declared, "but faith says the church is half full."

In the course of the service, I had noticed a thirty-something woman from afar. She had been one of the most enthusiastic participants in the service, arms outstretched, weaving back and forth with her eyes closed. Her name, I learned, was Vickie Whittenburg, and when I asked her why she attended Swaggart's church, she replied that it was "the Word, nothing but the Word." She professed not to be bothered by Swaggart's past transgressions. "It's the anointing, regardless of the sin in one's life," she explained. "It's a gift from God, and God doesn't take it back."

Ralph Walker, an usher, stopped by to join the conversation. "Nobody can preach like Jimmy Swaggart," he said. "I've never known anyone like him. I started listening to him on the radio. I was a heathen. I was just a rank heathen." Walker began attending the church when "it was bulging at the seams," he said, pointing to the empty balcony. "I had to stand at the back of the balcony."

Both Whittenburg and Walker consider themselves a remnant of the faithful. Whittenburg was drawn to Swaggart, in part, because of her passion for the underdog. "He's a fighter," she said. "I've never felt that I wanted anyone to make it as much as him, regardless of any error or failing on his part." Walker ventured that the downfall happened because Jimmy Swaggart Ministries was getting too big.

Lorraine Thomas had moved with her husband, a preacher (now deceased), to Baton Rouge from Arizona in September 1987, just months before the scandal unfolded. "God said, 'Go there and lift Jimmy up because he's going to go through a great trial,'" she recalled. All three said that they met with ridicule when they told others that they attended Swaggart's church. "Is he still preaching?" friends ask incredulously.

As the klieg lights dimmed and the conversation drew toward a close, Whittenburg asked, "Do you mind if we pray with you over this article?" A small crowd encircled me and joined hands. "Lord, we pray that you would send your Spirit upon this man as he writes this article," Walker intoned. "Help him to remember the things he should remember and forget the things he should forget."

IN THE DECADE SINCE THE TELEVANGELIST SCANDALS, many have forgotten the shame that was heaped upon evangelicalism in the 1980s, and evangelicalism itself, the most resilient and influential movement in American history, has, in fact, managed to survive, even prosper. I wonder, however, if the fixation on the financial shenanigans and the sexual escapades of the scandals has allowed evangelicals to dodge some thorny questions. Surely the transgressions of Bakker and Swaggart were not that much more egregious than Pat Robertson and his son pocketing an estimated $227 million from the sale of the Family Channel to Rupert Murdock, a property that Robertson developed from the tax-deductible contributions of the faithful. A focus on the peccadillos of Bakker and Swaggart deflects attention from theological issues surrounding televangelism. The obscene sums of money pouring into the televangelist's coffers is an invitation to abuse, and one can only speculate on how much of that revenue has been diverted from local congregations.

Evangelicalism, with its relative lack of creedal formulas and the absence of strong ecclesiastical structures, moreover, has always been susceptible to the cult of personality, a weakness only magnified by television. Evangelicals once harbored a healthy—though, at times, excessive—suspicion of worldliness, but they, too, have been infected by the culture of celebrity. While evangelicals have always been citational in the expression of their beliefs, the fixation on celebrity in the last couple of decades has produced an important shift. Evangelicals once referred directly to the Bible as the basis for their theology, but now, more often than not, the citation has been filtered through the conduit of the celebrity preacher: "As Dr. Swindoll says...," or, "Dr. Schuller says...," or, "Dr. Dobson believes that...."

Finally, while only the most obdurate Luddite would deny that the gospel can be proclaimed over the airwaves, evangelicalism's barren sacramentalism—most evangelicals hold to a memorialist view of the Lord's Supper, for instance—and its emphasis on the sermon has led some viewers to suppose that a Sunday morning in the easy chair might be the rough equivalent of an hour in the pew. Besides, those televangelists, with their high-tech graphics and their cuddly musicians, sure know how to put on a good show!

But no one, not even Swaggart, with his remarkable artistry, has found a way to sustain the community of faith over the airwaves. Worship surely must be something more than watching a preacher trying to project bonhomie and intimacy into a television camera. Shouldn't the Christian doctrine of the incarnation mean something? Jesus took on a fleshly form, after all; he didn't rent satellite time. The gospel itself was flesh and blood, not an image flickering across the television screen, the medium capable of such extraordinary deception. No, the gospel is tactile and visceral, incarnate, the very characteristics we celebrate in Holy Communion. Blessed are the present, Jesus seems to be saying throughout the New Testament. Blessed are the present, for they are here and not absent.

SWAGGART'S SERMONS AND HIS AUTOBIOGRAPHY are replete with references to the devil and to darkness. He speaks of being "anointed by the devil" as a young man, while playing the piano in a competition, and another time when the "darkened, oppressive forces of hell had been unleashed against me."[8] He wrestled with demons luring him to the movie theater and the temptation to follow his cousins, Lewis and Gilley, into the secular music business. But for every account of slipping into dark waters, Swaggart eventually claimed a victory. "Jerry Lee can go to Sun Records in Memphis, I'm on my way to heaven with a God who supplies all my needs according to His riches in glory by Christ Jesus," he declared after a bout of envy at his cousin's wealth. "I didn't know how to explain it, but I knew I had won a great victory over the powers of darkness."[9]

While preaching in Ohio on the camp-meeting circuit many years ago, Swaggart was awakened by a flash flood. The raging waters, he said, nearly swept him and his wife away, but God spared them. "The devil had tried to take our lives and I realized the struggles would become more intense as I moved forward with God," Swaggart recalled. "For years to come, I would dream about struggling against that current and almost drowning."[10]

For more than a decade, Jimmy Swaggart has been struggling against the current. But when he responds to his critics by saying that "as many scars as I have another one doesn't really matter," I suspect he's talking about something more than scorn and ridicule and declining revenues. When Swaggart refers to the "stygian night of darkness," the reference is internal as well.

Perhaps that's why Swaggart makes us uncomfortable. All of us wrestle with demons, whether we use that terminology or not. They may or may not be sexual, as with Swaggart, but from time to time we feel ourselves slipping into dark waters, and the undertow seems all too overwhelming. Swaggart, with his tears and his sweat and his tortured confession, seems all too human, and, let's face it, evangelicals prefer their heroes to be anodyne and in control, tidy and triumphant. Swaggart makes us uncomfortable by reminding us of ourselves, but instead of facing our faults, our fallenness, our humanity, it's easier to change the subject and dismiss Swaggart with ridicule. More's the pity, for it is only by gazing into the mirror of our own wretchedness that we begin to comprehend the magnificence of grace.

A decade ago, groping for an explanation for his transgression, Swaggart remarked, "Maybe Jimmy Swaggart has tried to live his entire life as though he was not human." We've known about Swaggart's humanity for a decade now, and when in the course of a sermon he segues into "Amazing grace, how sweet the sound that saved a wretch like me," some would dismiss that as contrived and disingenuous, just another part of his act.

I think he knows whereof he speaks.

1998

CHAPTER 16

Sound Check

O N A PLEASANT JULY EVENING IN WESTERN NEW YORK, two distinct groups of people filed into the open-air amphitheater just up the hill from Lake Chautauqua. The denizens of the Chautauqua Institution (which was founded in 1874 to train Sunday school teachers) were overwhelmingly white, elderly, upper middle class, and terminally addicted to learning and the arts. On most nights during the summer season, after a full day of lectures and symposia, Chautauqua offers a performance of some kind at the pavilion—ballet, Chautauqua's own symphony orchestra, or, as on this night, an outside musical group—and residents and visitors are accustomed to wandering in the direction of the pavilion after supper to locate friends and sample the cultural offerings.

The other constituency clearly had been looking forward to tonight's performance for some time, a band called Jars of Clay. A group of high school and college-age students congregated in the orchestra section and, in anticipation of the concert, executed a call-and-response cheer that has become commonplace at Christian music concerts:

> We love Jee-sus!
> How about you?

The other side answered:

> We love Jee-sus, too!
> How about you?

Some of the older folks, looking up from their books or newspapers, seemed a trifle befuddled by this uncharacteristic outburst of enthusiasm.

At a few minutes after eight, the orchestra section began a rhythmic clapping. This tee-shirt crowd appeared to be more clean-cut than many of their peers—"It's a real good concert to work," one of the security guards had told me, "people are pretty well-mannered"— they are more likely to sport dental braces than body piercings.* The warm up group, called Silage, hails from California. In a relatively short period of time they produced a lot of sweat and a lot of noise and, well, at least lived up to their name. Judging by the audience response, the high point of the set came when the lead singer doused the first few rows with a bottle of Poland Spring water, although whether it represented an evocation or a mockery of aspersion—or neither—I couldn't be sure.

Following a quick reconfiguration of the set, machines at either side blew artificial smoke across the stage. The orchestra section rose to its feet, and those in the outlying seats again looked up from their reading. The main event took the stage and opened with "Liquid," the first song on their debut, self-titled album, *Jars of Clay*. The music was loud, but there was a sweetness here lacking in the warm-up band.

> This is the one thing,
> The one thing that I know.

> Blood-stained brow,
> He wasn't broken for nothing.
> Arms nailed down,
> He didn't die for nothing.[1]

As the group moved on to "Tea and Sympathy," a cut from their second album, *Much Afraid*, the young people in the orchestra section

---

*Please note that this account is a conflation of two concerts—the first on July 17, 1998, at the Chautauqua Institution in Chautauqua, New York, and the second on November 6, 1998, at the DECC Auditorium in Duluth, Minnesota.

swayed back and forth in time to the music, arms upraised and interlocked.

The older folks in the upper reaches of the pavilion weren't so sure, offering only polite applause. A bearded man in his early fifties wadded cotton in his ears to stave off the decibels. An elderly woman left after the second song. "We've heard that nine different presidents have been on this stage," Dan Haseltine, the lead singer, said between songs. "I suppose if you put them all together they could probably rock."

BANTER IS NOT JARS OF CLAY'S STRONG SUIT. The band members are young, barely older than college age themselves. They have affected something of a grunge look—a couple of them seem to take pains to convey the impression that they have spent more time with a parole officer than a youth pastor—but, in fact, it appears that they would be just as comfortable in polo shirts or even neckties. The band members met as students at Greenville College, a Free Methodist, liberal-arts school in central Illinois, where they majored in a discipline called "Contemporary Christian Music." In the fall of 1993, Haseltine, Charlie Lowell, Stephen Mason, and Matt Bronleewe collaborated on an original song, "Fade to Grey," for a studio project in a recording class. They performed it at a campus hangout, Underground Café, and the response emboldened them to work on other musical compositions. When it came time to choose a name Lowell, the keyboardist, suggested Jars of Clay, from 2 Corinthians 4:7: "But we have this treasure in jars of clay to show that this all-surpassing power is from God and not from us."

During the spring semester of 1994, the group produced more songs and made a couple of appearances at music festivals. Someone noticed an advertisement for a talent contest; Jars of Clay submitted a demo and became one of ten finalists. On April 27, 1994, they performed in Nashville for the Gospel Music Association Spotlight Competition and won grand prize as the best new Christian band. By the time they returned to Greenville to complete the semester they were receiving phone calls on the pay phone in their dormitory with offers of contracts from record companies.

That summer they decided to make a run at a music career, although Bronleewe elected to continue school and get married. Lowell recruited a friend from high school, Matt Odmark, to take Bronleewe's place at guitar, and the group moved to Tennessee. During the fall and winter, they produced their debut album, which was released in May 1995 to critical acclaim. "Quite possibly the hottest new band of 1995," one reviewer exuded, "pure acoustic music with a rock twist." Another review cited their "creative excellence" and said that the opening track "blows the doors off the walls that still separate Christian rock from the greater world of music." Fans apparently agreed, sending the album to double-platinum status and a Grammy nomination for Rock/Gospel Album of the Year. "Flood," a song about the deluge of Noah's day, crossed over onto alternative and "mix" stations as well as MTV and VH-1. Overall, according to *CCM Magazine*, Jars of Clay had enjoyed "the most successful Christian music debut ever."[2]

Much Afraid, their second album, did even better than the first, winning the Grammy in 1997 for Pop/Contemporary Gospel Album of the Year and several other awards. According to Jennifer Bachman, a management agent for another Christian artist, "Jars of Clay has become a standard of comparison in contemporary Christian music." Critic Kent Zimmerman credits the group with "redefining the genre."[3]

Warren Pettit, an associate professor of music at Greenville College, has had ample opportunity to reflect on the success of Jars of Clay. As the faculty member most involved with the students majoring in contemporary Christian music, Pettit has been asked countless times if he anticipated that the "Jar boys," as they came to be called, would make it big. When I put the question to him, he shook his head and shrugged. "Of course not," he said. "They were just students freshman year like everybody else." Pettit began to take notice, however, when he accompanied the group to a performance at one of the side stages at Six Flags theme park. "I saw that a bunch of junior high girls were walking by. They stopped, sat down, and listened."

Pettit remembers clearly the day a student engineer burst into his office with a mix of "Fade to Grey." "What do you think?" the student asked excitedly after Pettit listened to the cut. "I don't know," he replied, "because I've never heard anything like this." The musicologist in him eventually waxed analytical. "If I had to deconstruct what they were doing," he said, "they were using what we call samples or loops—two- or four-bar drum or percussion sound bites repeated over and over—then on top of that was a folk acoustic guitar rock sensibility. But the way they had organized it," Pettit said admiringly, "there was just something different about it."

In order to understand the appeal, however, you have to mix in what Pettit calls the intangibles: the artists themselves, the music, the lyrics. "If you take the totality of all that," he said, "there was something quirky about it. I thought they were very brave and clever in assimilating what appeared to be very dissimilar elements." Pettit was particularly taken with the combination of a Gregorian chant with a rhythmic dance sample in "Liquid," but he also cited the whistling, the use of a child's voice, as well as a recorder and stringed instruments. "Jars of Clay rejected the mechanistic, techno, synthesizer pop of the late 1980s," Pettit said. "It wasn't part of their vocabulary."

The music industry was enchanted, and the "Jar boys" climbed aboard what Pettit called "an absolute ballistic missile" to stardom. For Jars of Clay the fast track to success was heady at times—concert appearances with Sting, *The Late Show with David Letterman*, several motion picture soundtracks, and a jealously protective management that insisted, for example, that band members were so busy that I couldn't conduct even a brief interview until the following year.

AN ALTOGETHER TOO BRIEF, UNSCIENTIFIC, and occasionally irreverent history of evangelical music in America might sound something like this: We begin with the *Bay Psalm Book*, published by the Puritans in 1640. The Puritans, of course, shunned ostentation the way that John Calvin avoided the Song of Solomon, and so they sang Psalms to simple meters. Isaac Watts introduced his *Psalter*, a paraphrase of the Psalms, to England in 1719; the American edition, printed by Benjamin Franklin, appeared a decade later. Evangelical music during the revival and camp-meeting era of the Second Great Awakening conveyed the simple doctrines of evangelical piety, and the rise of Methodism introduced the stirring, sometimes magisterial music of John Wesley and Charles Wesley into the evangelical hymnal.

The feminine ideal of piety in the nineteenth century, especially when combined with the temperance crusade, brought overtones of sexuality and sentimentality to evangelical music. Faithful, patient mothers waited for their wayward sons to return home and come to Jesus—"Tell Mother I'll be There"—and the intimacy was apparent in such songs as "Jesus, Lover of My Soul," "My Jesus, I Love Thee," and in the enduring popularity of "Rock of Ages, Cleft for Me." A resurgence of muscular Christianity at the turn of the twentieth century sounded the notes of militarism: "Lead On, O King Eternal," "Stand Up, Stand Up, for Jesus," "Onward, Christian Soldiers." During the carnage of the world wars it is not surprising that hymns about blood were popular in evangelical churches—"Nothing but the Blood of Jesus," "Are you Washed in the Blood?"—and evangelicalism sustained the notes of triumphalism—"Victory in Jesus," "'V' Is for Victory"—through the postwar, Cold War era.

The most dramatic changes in evangelical music since the colonial period began in the tumultuous decade of the 1960s. Throughout American history evangelicalism has demonstrated a remarkable knack for survival by tapping into the prevailing popular tastes, whatever they might be at any given time. Although it would be an understatement to say that evangelicals were slow to warm to rock 'n' roll, by the late 1960s some evangelical musicians recognized that the strains of "Make Me a Blessing" and "Bringing in the Sheaves" (which I used to think was my mother's laundry song: "bringing in the sheets") could no longer compete with "Hey, Jude," "Alice's Restaurant," and "I Can't Get No Satisfaction."

At least partially at the behest of the Southern Baptist Convention, Ralph Carmichael, an evangelical musician who had grown up enamored of the big bands, decided to try his hand at composing sacred music that would be more palatable to the younger generation. He sprouted mutton-chop whiskers, and although his pieces still favored the big, symphonic sound of violin strings rather than electric guitar strings, his compositions, which included "A Quiet Place" and "He's Everything to Me," quickly became popular with the under–thirty crowd. Soon many evangelical congregations were faced with the prospect of either supplementing or replacing the venerable old hymnals that had been around for what seemed like, well, generations.

The Jesus movement, just then aborning at Haight-Ashbury in San Francisco and on Huntington Beach in Orange County, carried Carmichael's revolution even further. Chuck Smith and Calvary Chapel, located in Costa Mesa, California, lured hundreds of hippies into the evangelical fold, and many of them, unfettered by the conventions of middle-class evangelicalism, unleashed a remarkable burst of musical creativity. The melodies of groups like Love Song, Danny Lee and the Children of Truth, and others that appeared on the Maranatha! label in the early 1970s were simple and unpretentious, utterly without guile and largely innocent of theological categories (with the possible exception of premillennialism). Larry Norman—whose rhetorical mantra was "Why should the devil have all the good music?"—added the harsher sounds of rock 'n' roll, and a flurry of other artists followed his lead, including John Fischer, Andraé Crouch, Chuck Gerard, Keith Green, and Randy Stonehill.

As Norman and his confrères entered the music scene, however, other, larger forces were at work in American evangelicalism. For the first time in nearly half a century (since the Scopes trial of 1925), evangelicals were beginning to venture, albeit tentatively, out of their cozy subculture into the larger world. Even this modest dangling of toes into the water was heady and invigorating; for someone who grew up singing in the junior choir, the possibility that long hair and rock 'n' roll might be justified for spreading the gospel was positively titillating. Besides, if Jerry Falwell, who in 1965 had declared that he "would find it impossible to stop preaching the pure saving gospel of Jesus Christ, and begin doing anything else," could create the political lobby Moral Majority in 1979, then clearly the rules of evangelical engagement with the larger culture were changing. Evangelicalism was still a subculture, but it was no longer a counterculture, as it had been during the middle decades of the twentieth century.

The 1980s will be mistaken by no one for a golden age of creativity—as his critics were fond of remarking, Ronald Reagan brought to Washington some of the greatest minds of the seventeenth century—and evangelical music fared little better. With few exceptions, it was derivative and predictable, reflecting a kind of "me, too" approach to secular music. Countless evangelical groups aspired to mimic the folk music of Peter, Paul & Mary or the popular ballads of Simon and Garfunkel. Amy Grant and Sandi Patty were the Belinda Carlisle and Barbra Streisand of evangelical music, and as long as heavy metal remained part of the secular music vernacular, several evangelical bands, like Petra, Stryper, Guardian, and Whiteheart, sought to baptize that, too.

The justification for all this was that these evangelical musicians were simply preaching the gospel in a new medium and that all you had to do was pay close attention to the lyrics. True enough, perhaps, but the lyrics tended to be facile, sometimes a mere reworking of pronouns so that the pining "I love you" songs of secular music became "He loves you." In the case of heavy metal (or, more recently, ska, a blend of punk and reggae) critics maintained that the "gospel message" was so buried beneath the beat and the pyrotechnics and the keening guitars that it would take J. Edgar Hoover and a score of minions several weeks to unearth it.

The musicians themselves tended to ignore their critics, especially the older generation of naysayers. Contemporary Christian music, as it came to be called, was nothing if not popular, with a market share that grew every year. Several artists, notably Amy Grant and Michael W. Smith, became "crossover" stars when their releases were ranked on both the Christian and the pop charts. Contemporary Christian music was a huge industry, not merely a niche market, bringing in an estimated three-quarters of a billion dollars annually by the mid–1990s. In the late 1980s and early 1990s, several labels were taken over by secular corporations that recognized the potential for profits. In 1998, according to *Billboard* magazine, the contemporary Christian music market share of the recording industry had exceeded that of jazz, classical, New Age, and soundtracks.[4]

"PRIDE IS ONE OF THOSE THINGS that tells us we can do anything on our own," Haseltine tells the Chautauqua audience. "This is a song that talks about breaking down pride and experiencing love":

> The marionette has your number
> Pulling your arms and legs till you can't stand on your own
> Dragging your conscience on the stage
> and your heart gets rearranged
> and you cannot tell your mentor from your Maker.[5]

Here, it seems, lies the classic evangelical dilemma of being *in* the world but not *of* the world, along with warnings about fleeting fame.

> Look at the crowds bleeding with laughter
> Over the way you entertain at beck and call
> They don't see behind the lights, or the painted background
> They just like to see you fall.[6]

Another song, "Worlds Apart," rehearses the importance of humility and warns of the blandishments of what evangelicals used to call "worldliness":

I am the only one to blame for this
Somehow it all ends up the same
Soaring on the wings of selfish pride
I flew too high and like Icarus, I collide
With a world I try so hard to leave behind
To rid myself of all but love
to give and die.[7]

A theological gloss here might point out that it is preeminently our attachment to this world that mires us in self-absorption. Jesus calls us to self-renunciation.

To turn away and not become
Another nail to pierce the skin of one who loves
more deeply than the oceans,
more abundant than the tears
Of a world embracing every heartache.

The refrain includes the phrases "take my world apart" and "broken on my knees."[8]

Lyrics like this may come at a propitious time for evangelicals. In the middle decades of the twentieth century the most damning epithet you could level at another evangelical was that she or he was "worldly." The stigma of "the world" began to dissipate in the 1980s, however, as evangelicals themselves became more worldly, intoxicated by political power and apparent cultural influence.

If these lyrics betray an awareness of the perils of fame and the enticements of the world, other Jars of Clay songs also suggest a surprising theological maturity. Haseltine, still in his twenties, is the principal lyricist for the group's compositions, although he routinely shares credit with other band members. The theology represented here is light years away from the cheap affirmation and the abject subjectivism of so much of the popular evangelical music since the 1960s, when the fare ran to "Jesus is just all right with me" and "Jesus made me higher than I've ever been before." This "pronoun trouble" has persisted into the nineties and crops up everywhere—"You got *me* believing that You would die for *me*," "You will never let *me* down," "Love *me* good"—and, sadly, much of this vapid, self-referential theology has leeched into the let's-just-praise-the-Lord "praise music" now so ubiquitous in evangelical worship. Phrases like "Sing Alleluia to the Lord," "Father, I adore you," "Jesus, you are Jesus," and "Shine, Jesus, shine" may evoke a reverential mood, but they carry little theological freight.

Just as Christian music has changed over the centuries, so too the theological sophistication evident in Haseltine's lyrics heralds a shift in popular evangelical music away from the rhapsodic, dreamy mantras of praise songs and the self-absorption of contemporary recording artists. As Douglas Frank has observed, even though "a naked human being hangs at the center of the Christian faith," evangelicals have devised all manner of theological conceits to divert attention from the dying Christ, and they do so, more often than not, by fixating on God the Father, All-Powerful and Triumphant. Haseltine's theology pushes deeper, forcing us to look beyond the saccharine Jesus of evangelical sentimentality—"Jesus Is the Sweetest Name I Know," "Precious Name, O How Sweet"—and gaze upon the naked, tortured body hanging on the cross. "The message of Christianity is a hard thing to want to spend time pondering," Haseltine says. "The fact that we are sinners, that apart from Christ we're nothing, those are things that are not easy to listen to, and yet Christian music tries to make whatever they do easy to hear. It's the good package mentality. When reality starts filtering into that, it tends to shake things up a bit because what people expect Christianity to be is not reality."[9]

The music of Jars of Clay invites us to consider again the Jesus on the cross. It dispenses with the triumphalism—the bravado and the posturing—that has infected evangelicalism for more than a century now: "We Shall Shine as Stars in the Morning," "We Are More than Conquerors." The Jesus portrayed here is not the conquering hero, nor is he the heartthrob of some fawning adolescents. He is the Man of Sorrows, acquainted with grief. Jesus carries to the cross the burdens of humanity, but therein lies the gospel, and the supreme paradox of faith is that only when we take full account of our sinfulness can we begin to understand the magnitude of grace: "Empty again / Sunken down so far... So I lay at Your feet / All my brokenness."[10]

"It's in despair that I find faith," Haseltine writes; time and again his words portray Jesus as the Suffering Servant.[11]

> Arms nailed down,
> are you telling me something?
> Eyes turned out,
> are you looking for someone ?[12]

Eyes are a recurrent image in Haseltine's lyrics. "Oh, it's not hard to know what you're thinking / When you look down on me now," he writes in "Fade to Grey."[13]

"We've all grown up in the church," Haseltine explains, with no hint of apology, and herein may lie a clue to their effectiveness. Haseltine, like other contemporary artists, is grounded in evangelical theology, but he is not afraid to frame the rudiments of Christianity for a larger audience and to do so without resorting to evangelical jargon. "They approached music from the heart as opposed to formulas," said Robert Beeson, the man who signed Jars of Clay to the Essential label, recalling what impressed him initially about the group. "They cut through the clutter in that there was nothing else like them."[14] Haseltine himself puts it slightly differently. "We're a band that likes to ask questions and get people to ask questions," he said, "and perhaps that will lead them to Jesus."

FOR THE CHRISTIAN MUSIC INDUSTRY, in late April all roads lead to Nashville, the annual convention of the Gospel Music Association, a gathering for recording companies, distributors, hordes of hyperactive publicists and press agents, and the artists themselves. My many months of persistence and dozens of phone calls had finally paid off. After I had furnished Jars of Clay's management with my life history, a theological statement, hat size, photo ID, and a complete set of fingerprints, they graciously consented to allow me to fly to Nashville for what they assured me was at least a fifty–fifty shot at a half-hour interview during Gospel Music Week.

I approached the meeting with some trepidation because in the intervening months I had become quite enamored of Jars of Clay, especially their lyrics, which seemed to represent almost a quantum leap beyond the pablum of most Christian music. What if the band members turned out to be vacuous, the intellectual equivalent of cheese whiz or Christian music's answer to Britney Spears and the Backstreet Boys? I thought it unlikely, but still I did not want to be disappointed. As the fresh-faced band members shambled aboard the Essential Records tour bus for our interview, they looked a bit bewildered, still more dazed than jaded by their success.

The band members hail from different theological backgrounds, ranging from Presbyterian and Episcopalian to the General Association of Regular Baptists, a denomination usually associated with a fairly starchy brand of fundamentalism. Despite the fact that they attended Greenville, a Free Methodist school in the Wesleyan tradition, their theology is decidedly Augustinian or Calvinist, consistently portraying Christ as the relentless pursuer:

> Someday she'll trust Him and learn how to see Him
> Someday He'll call her and she will come running
> and fall in His arms and the tears will fall down and she'll pray,
> "I want to fall in love with You."[15]

Calvin, along with Martin Luther (and both of them echoing Augustine and the apostle Paul), insisted that sinners could do nothing to earn forgiveness; salvation was the gift of God, available by grace, through faith. "I believe that I have nothing to do with my salvation," Matt Odmark declared without hesitation when I asked about the theology that informs the group.

Jars of Clay characterizes its musical style as "acoustically driven alternative pop." When asked to list musical influences, they cite the

Beatles, Toad the Wet Sprocket, Radiohead, the Jayhawks, Simon and Garfunkel, and James Taylor. I noted that they had listed no Christian artists; after an embarrassed silence Haseltine admitted, "I don't think we have many influences in Christian music." That may account for the appeal of Jars of Clay to an audience that transcends the evangelical subculture. By tapping into mainstream music, they have avoided the lyrical and stylistic inbreeding that afflicts some of the other contemporary Christian music groups.

How effectively has Jars of Clay pushed beyond the boundaries of the evangelical subculture? The performance at Chautauqua provides one example, and in 1996 Jars of Clay turned down invitations to play at both the Republican and the Democratic National Conventions. ("We don't want to be a political band," Haseltine explained.) A friend informed me of yet another venue that had opened to Jars of Clay. Their music, he said, was popular in gay clubs in New York City. Imagine, he said, "three thousand gay men dancing to 'Flood' and all of them with their shirts off."

I asked the band members to imagine that. "Good," Haseltine said finally, after the initial surprise had worn off, a surprise that seemed to be tinged with embarrassment. "That's the way it should be." Mason agreed. "I think we get excited at the thought of our music being played there," he said. "We couldn't reach them directly, but maybe our music can." Odmark saw the prospects for conversion. "If people dig the song and go out and buy the album and come to Jesus...." His voice trailed off to consider the possibilities.

Left unspoken—and unchallenged—was the assumption that the habitues of gay clubs stand in special need of conversion, but the popularity of Jars of Clay in markets beyond evangelicalism raises an issue that has bedeviled many Christian musicians. While "crossover" success remains an elusive goal for most Christian artists, those who have successfully crossed over onto the secular music charts have faced stiff scrutiny from other evangelicals. Amy Grant probably set off the criticism with her hit single "Baby, Baby," and the latest chapter of the controversy was unfolding during Gospel

Music Week. A group called Sixpence None the Richer had released a single, "Kiss Me," that had rocketed to the top of the secular charts. "Kiss Me" has roughly as much spiritual content as a steel-belted radial tire, but because the group had enjoyed initial success in the Christian market it begged the question of whether or not the song was "Christian" music. The Gospel Music Association has stepped in to adjudicate such matters, coming up with an unwieldy set of definitions that make the tax code read like a nursery rhyme, but the fact remains that any group that crosses over into the secular market faces a predictable din of criticism that it has "gone secular."

Although there is no evidence that Jars of Clay has soft-pedaled its theology to appeal to the secular market, they too have been criticized. "It can start to get to you when people ask over and over again, 'Are you going secular?'" Mason said wearily. "Well, what do you define as secular? Do we want to reach unchurched people? Of course. And we're not going to hide what we believe to do that. But the greater our reach becomes, the more suspect our faith and commitment in the eyes of some people. It's like 'either you're in or you're out.' There's got to be a third rail where music can just be music. And in the end there's really nothing we can do but be who we are."[16]

During their visit to Nashville, Jars of Clay was taking a brief hiatus from the recording sessions for their third album. "We don't know what it's going to be yet," one member confessed, although Haseltine expressed the cautious hope that the album would contain "lyrical moments that will set new benchmarks" for the group. Indeed, I had heard from several sources that the album's producer was pushing them hard, and they all agreed. In Jars of Clay's previous efforts, some of their best work has come in the studio, where a riff or an improvisation sparks a burst of creativity.

How does the creative process work for Jars of Clay? "Dan keeps a journal," Stephen Mason explained, referring to Haseltine. "Then we'll start a riff on a guitar, and it emerges from there." Haseltine is diffident and self-effacing, often averting his eyes as he gathers his thoughts. "I never know what I'm writing until a couple of years later," he said. "God is the one who's working, pushing the pen a bit." When I repeated to Haseltine what Brian Hartley, a professor at Greenville, had said to me about Haseltine, that he was "something of a mystic," Haseltine looked confused, clearly wanting me to define the term. I suggested that a mystic was someone with an almost intuitive grasp of God and spirituality; Haseltine, with characteristic modesty, demurred. "No, I wouldn't say that I have any grasp at all. I prove that every day."

I tried another tack, floating the names of John Donne and George Herbert or T. S. Eliot as possible sources of inspiration. Once again I had to explain the references. Haseltine shrugged and shook his head, suggesting that his real inspiration lay in the old hymns. "Hymns are the closest thing to poetry that I read," he said, somewhat apologetically. "I use them as a foundation for what I write." He looked away. "I think what gets us is the magnificence of God and how puny and wretched we are," he added. "Nothing does that like a good hymn."

Dusk has finally descended on Chautauqua. The group sings "Oh, sweet Jesus, you never let me go," while the audience again sways to the music, arms upraised. A woman in her early twenties, eyes closed, performs a kind of willowy dance. Stars have punched a million holes into the summer sky, and the concert is winding down. "When you look at the depravity of man and the brilliance of God and the gap in between, we decided to write a song about it," Hazeltine announces. "Being the creative bunch that we are, we called it 'Hymn.'" It open with just a few, spare notes on an acoustic guitar.

> Oh refuge of my hardened heart
> Oh fast pursuing lover come
> As angels dance 'round Your throne
> My life by captured fare You own
>
> Not silhouette of trodden faith
> Nor death shall not my steps be guide

I'll pirouette upon my grave
For in Your path I'll run and hide[17]

The crowd rises, arms outstretched, responding, perhaps uncon-
sciously, to the resurrection motif. The man with cotton in his ears
has long since left. "We like to close our concerts with 'Hymn,'"
Mason told me in Nashville, "because it takes the focus off of us."

Oh gaze of love so melt my pride
That I may in Your house but kneel
And in my brokenness to cry
Spring worship unto Thee

The lyrics evoke the poetry of Herbert or Donne or Rainer Maria
Rilke, more elegy than anthem.

When beauty breaks the spell of pain
The bludgeoned heart shall burst in vain
But not when love be 'pointed king
And truth shall Thee forever reign

Sweet Jesus carry me away
From cold of night, and dust of day
In ragged hour or salt worn eye
Be my desire, my well spring lye[18]

A slight chill blows off the lake, and it's time to head back into the
night. Only the benediction remains:

Oh gaze of love so melt my pride
That I may in Your house but kneel
And in my brokenness to cry
Spring worship unto Thee
Spring worship unto Thee
Spring worship unto Thee.[19]

Amen.

1998

CHAPTER 17

Kinkade Crusade

"MAKE YOURSELF AT HOME." The pleasant young woman pointed to a loveseat in a small room. "This is the best way to appreciate Thomas Kinkade's genius as an artist."

My wife and I had happened upon Collector's Corner Gallery on the village square in Pella, Iowa. Collector's Corner, it turned out, was a furniture store that also sold lithographs and paintings, many of them by Kinkade, a kind of neo-Impressionist artist who bills himself as the "Painter of Light." I had made some offhanded, dismissive comment to the effect that these lithographs were mass-produced for people who bought paintings that would coordinate with the colors of the living-room sofa.

Melissa Slings, whose business card read "Art Consultant," gently disagreed and proceeded to offer an impromptu mini-course that might have been called "Thomas Kinkade Appreciation 101."Anyone who deals in Kinkade's lithographs goes through a special training program to become a sales consultant, and she was prepared to, well, enlighten us.

Lesson one commenced in the tiny, carpeted cubicle with the loveseat. A large, framed lithograph of Kinkade's "Lamplight Bridge" hung directly in front of us. "Just sit back and relax," Slings, an earnest woman in her twenties, instructed, "and look at the painting." She reached for the dial of a rheostat, which controlled the track lighting in the small room. "Watch as the light dims," she said, "and you'll see the painting take on its own glow. It's like magic."

Yes, indeed. As the light waned, the canvas assumed a kind of luminosity. The street lamps glowed from atop their stanchions on the gentle arc of a stone bridge, and the cottage radiated a soft, buttery light from its mullioned windows. The effect was soothing and dreamlike, and in my reverie I had no difficulty imagining the residents of that cottage in denims, flannel shirts, and thick wool stockings stretched out in front of the fireplace, a favorite novel in one hand and a mug of steaming cider in the other, a yellow lab at their feet and a Brandenberg Concerto playing softly in the background.

Magic, indeed.

Slings went on to explain the elaborate coding that goes into every Kinkade painting. He includes a Bible reference and a fish (*ichthys*) with his signature, and he conceals the letter N at least once on every canvas in honor of his wife's name, Nanette. The names and images of his four daughters appear also, as does, occasionally, the visage of a friend.

WILLIAM THOMAS KINKADE was reared in a single-parent household in Placerville, California, a small town in the foothills of the Sierra Mountains. As early as age four, he showed artistic promise. His mother encouraged him. Young Thom Kinkade would disappear for hours with his sketchbook and return with drawings of the natural beauty all around him. "My whole life was absorbed with my art," Kinkade recalled many years later. "I was known by my schoolmates as the kid who could draw." By the time he was a teenager he was working with oils and as an apprentice to Glenn Wessells, a California Impressionist who'd had a major influence on the American art scene in the 1940s and 1950s.

Kinkade studied at the University of California, Berkeley, and at the prestigious Art Center College of Design in Pasadena, California, although he dropped out of both schools. In 1980, while a student, Kinkade, in his own words, "came to have a personal relationship with Christ." His mother had reared him in the Church of the Nazarene, but an adolescent rebellion turned him away from evangelicalism.

His involvement with Calvary Chapel in the early 1980s reconnected him to the faith of his childhood.[1]

Kinkade and a college friend spent a summer traveling around the country, sketching scenery and collaborating on *The Artist Guide to Sketching*, which became a best-selling instructional book. The success of the book led to a stint in film animation, during which Kinkade learned more about the effects of light. After the film's release, he decided to devote his professional efforts to creating and marketing his own art. About the same time, 1982, he married Nanette, his childhood sweetheart.

Kinkade published his first print for commercial distribution, "Main Street at Dusk—Placerville," an idyllic rendering of his hometown, in 1984. Five years later he and a friend, Ken Raasch, founded Lightpost Publishing, which went public as Media Arts Group in 1994. In 1995 he was named Artist of the Year by the National Association of Limited Edition Dealers, and for the ensuing three years Kinkade was designated Graphic Artist of the Year by the same organization. In 1999 he was voted into the *U.S. Art* Hall of Fame.

"My paintings are halfway between a memory and a daydream," Kinkade told me in his spacious studio in a coastal mountain setting in northern California. "I try to produce a re-creation of the past without the hard edges."

The studio, awash in sunlight, has a huge, vaulted ceiling and a massive stone fireplace. "I wanted a place that felt like Yosemite," he explained, "and I needed a big space because I'm working on some big paintings."

Kinkade himself is a large man, expansive and eager to talk about his work and his faith. "My whole ministry is an expression of Matthew 5:16," he says: "Let your light so shine before men, that they may see your good works, and glorify your Father which is in heaven." Kinkade calls himself the "Painter of Light" because of his Christian convictions. "Light is what we're attracted to," Kinkade said. "This world is very dark, but in heaven there is no darkness."

Kinkade, fresh from an early-afternoon jog and a shower, sits on the edge of the fireplace, hunched forward, sipping from a glass of sparkling water. "Paintings are the tools that can inspire the heart to greater faith," he says. "My paintings are messengers of God's love. Nature is simply the language which I speak."

Indeed, most of Kinkade's art, including the work in progress at the other end of the room, depicts the natural world. Some of his paintings are representations of specific places, but most are composites of various scenes, images from the artist's head. "The ideas come out of nowhere," he said, and some of the inspirations come from sketches he makes while sitting in church. Sometimes people will see a painting and tell him, "Yes, I've been there," and then provide the name of a mountain range. "I have to correct them," Kinkade said, "and admit that I made it up. I call them the Kinkade Mountains!"

With the practiced ease of an insurance agent listing his products, Kinkade ticks off the themes that animate his art: home, family, faith in God, the beauty of nature, celebration of romantic moments, a simpler way of living. "I love to create beautiful worlds where light dances and peace reigns," he says. "I like to portray a world without the fall."

With its plush, dark carpeting and incandescent lighting, the reception area for Kinkade's publishing house and warehouse looks like a living room in an upper-middle-class suburban home. "Lightpost Publishing," the receptionist chirps into the phone. "Thank you for sharing the light." Several of Kinkade's paintings line the wood-paneled walls, and a display case holds samples of some of Kinkade's licensed products: suncatchers, Bible totes, bookmarks, vases, a computer screensaver. Denise Sanders, Kinkade's assistant and my tour guide, ushers me into a conference room with still more Kinkade products: flower arrangements, a tea-pot, a collectible stein, a night light, note cards, a wastebasket/umbrella stand, a fountain, a lamp, Hallmark Christmas ornaments, a La-Z-Boy recliner upholstered with a fabric covered with

N's (for Nanette). "People love these pieces," Sanders says, "because they hit all the price points."

Indeed, there seems to be no limit to the licensing possibilities for Kinkade's work. Inserts in newspapers regularly advertise Kinkade commemorative plates and Thomas Kinkade's Lamplight Village: "Meticulously handcrafted and carefully hand-painted for exceptional realism." If a licensing arrangement with Taylor Woodrow Homes goes as planned, it may soon be possible to live in a full-scale Kinkade village. The company recently broke ground on an one-hundred-unit residential development in Vallejo, California, "entirely themed" from Kinkade's paintings, with lamp-posts, gardens, and gazebos. "We've designed the entire community as close as possible to the feeling and flavor of the paintings," Raffi Minasian, senior director of licensing and product design at Media Arts, told me. The houses, which will cost somewhere in the mid-$300,000 range, will be built in the English country garden style, with the interiors designed, Minasian said, "to promote family interactions" and decorated top to bottom with Kinkade paintings, furniture, and accent pieces.

Further back into the San Jose warehouse, which covers 100,000 square feet, past racks full of canvases in various stages of production, Sanders showed me how the Kinkade "magic" evolves. After the artist completes one of his paintings (at a rate of approximately one a month) it is rushed into production—or, rather, reproduction. Digital images of the original are turned into lithographs, which are then mounted onto canvases, thereby approximating the look and texture of the original painting. The next step is highlighting, another Kinkade innovation. Most of the pieces move into a roomful of easels where artists, seated side by side at a long table, apply dots and squiggles of particular colors to places on each canvas that Kinkade has specified, thereby rendering a three-dimensional feel to the canvases. A few of the pieces, however, those designated for higher prices, move into the studios of what the company calls "master highlighters," more highly skilled artists who have been specially trained by Kinkade himself. These "Renaissance Editions" fetch about $6,000 per copy. Canvases highlighted by Kinkade himself command anywhere from $30,000 to $60,000 each.

Farther back in the warehouse, other workers place the highlighted paintings into frames and tack on brass plates with the title of the painting and the artist's name. The Kinkade warehouse employs approximately four hundred workers, who produce and ship seven hundred to a thousand framed and highlighted pieces a day. Kinkade has imposed elaborate quality-control checks at every point in the process, from the arrival of the lithographs to shipping. In most cases, anything that falls short of the standards is destroyed, although the company occasionally offers an imperfect piece to employees at a reduced price.

Some of the reproductions go directly to consumers, especially those who are members of the Thomas Kinkade Collectors' Society, but most go to company-owned galleries or to any one of approximately two hundred "signature galleries" around the country. These "signature galleries" are specially licensed stores, most of them located in shopping malls, that sell only Kinkade merchandise.

The whole operation is slick and professional. Media Arts Group, Inc., which owns Lightpost Publishing, is traded publicly on the New York Stock Exchange. The company rang up more than $120 million in sales during the 2000 fiscal year. Kinkade's stake is something like 3.1 million shares, which has made him a very wealthy man.

"A FEW YEARS AGO I LOOKED AT MY SAVINGS ACCOUNT and at the various blessings God has given me," Kinkade told an interviewer in 1999, "and I realized that from a material point of view, there wouldn't be any more reason I would have to work." The artist, forty-one years old at the time, continued his thought. "At that point, you have to work out some other drive. And the drive is not material. The drive is not commercial success. The drive is utilizing whatever talent you have to bless others."

Having attained the commercial status of "America's most collected artist," Kinkade now feels able to think more broadly about what he wants to do with his success. "I want to use the paintings as tools to expand the kingdom of God," he said. Several years ago Kinkade entered into an arrangement with World Vision, an evangelical humanitarian organization, whereby if people sponsored a child for a year, they would receive a Kinkade print. "I grew up in poverty by this culture's standards," Kinkade explained, which is why he feels a special affinity with the work of World Vision. Kinkade calls the marketing scheme "leveraged giving," and World Vision has seen a dramatic increase in contributions. According to Marty Lonsdale, vice president for marketing at World Vision, Kinkade's "generous gift of a print has influenced many thousands of people to give to World Vision, and these donors have demonstrated a high degree of commitment to our ministry."[2]

Kinkade's other plans are more ambitious. "Art as a form of expression in Western society is dying," he said, taking another sip from his sparkling water. Kinkade pointed out that art programs are subject to budget cuts in schools around the country, even in artist colonies like Carmel-by-the-Sea, California, just a few miles down U.S. Route 1 from San Jose. Kinkade wants to design an art curriculum for the schools, one that avoids the depredations of Modernism and emphasizes the development of traditional skills. "Art is not an option," Kinkade insists. "I want to build the new iconography for the coming millennium."

The word *millennium* has particular meaning for Kinkade. One of his recent paintings is called "Sunrise: A Prayer of Hope for the Millennium of Light" to mark the turn of the twenty-first century. "I believe Jesus is coming again in this new millennium," he said matter-of-factly. "Our life is like a vapor."

Kinkade's sense of living in the last times lends an urgency to his agenda. "Art transcends cultural boundaries," he declared. "I want to blanket the world with the gospel through prints. This is a very thoroughgoing form of evangelism." He noted that ten million people have already brought Thomas Kinkade into their homes. "A painting is a *presence* in the house," he insists, and he believes that his paintings are "messages of God's love" that will be handed down through the generations. Kinkade pointed to one of his prints hanging in the studio. "Paintings are the tools that can inspire the heart to greater faith."

Kinkade's portrayals of sylvan cottages and cobblestone pathways and garden gazebos are much more, in the artist's judgment, than pretty pictures. They are, in fact, powerful weapons in the war against unbelief and, more particularly, against the corrosive effects of Modernism. "I see a campaign for culture shaping up around me," he declared. "Art is the hot button in the cultural battle at play right now."

Kinkade leaned forward, his voice rising in intensity. "The disintegration of the culture starts with the artist," he declared. "In a way, Modernism in painting is responsible for *South Park* and gangsta' rap. I'm on a crusade to turn the tide in the arts, to restore dignity to the arts and, by extension, to the culture."

Kinkade drew a deep breath and proceeded to outline his battle plan. The first step, already accomplished, was to devise and promote the first commercially successful artist in the culture: Kinkade himself. "We wanted to create the first mainstream superstar," he explained. Second, he built a highly successful corporation around him, with lucrative licensing arrangements and its own manufacturing plant that produces what he calls "semi-originals" for distribution throughout the world.

Now, using the financial resources that have accrued from steps one and two, Kinkade has embarked on the third phase of his campaign. He has established the Thomas Kinkade Foundation as a way to resist, in the artist's words, "the art culture that is so inbred." Kinkade characterizes the work of the foundation as "a form of sabotage," and he lapses into militaristic imagery: "I view it as a Trojan horse that we're sending into the enemy camp."

When the subject of modern art comes up, Kinkade becomes even more animated. He opens his riff with a quote from Pablo Picasso, who said, "I came to destroy beauty." "The whole Modernist lie is that art is about the artist," Kinkade says, which has led to contempt for the audience. It has also led, he believes, to what he calls the "fecal school" of art, or "bodily function" art, a reference to the work of Robert Mapplethorpe and to a controversial 1999 exhibition at the Brooklyn Museum, which featured a depiction of the Blessed Virgin smeared with elephant dung, the creation of British artist Chris Ofili. The travesty of Modernism, Kinkade believes, is that it has become an "inbred, closed culture." The result of Modernism's contempt for the audience, he insists, is that museums are dying.

At this point, Kinkade's plan becomes audacious. He claims that just as the Impressionists of the late nineteenth century reacted to the "dead art" of the preceding era, so too his own work brought light back into the art world late in the twentieth century. Now he aspires to encourage other artists. He wants to establish what he calls the Academy of Traditional Art, which would recognize traditional artists for their contributions to Western culture, perhaps with an Academy Awards-style presentation. He also wants to erect a series of alternative museums. "I don't want to clean up the outhouse," Kinkade declared, "to close the Whitney. I want to build a temple next door." He drew a contrast between the sterility of modern art galleries and museums and the comfortable ambience of Kinkade's galleries, with soft lighting, wood paneling, and deep-pile carpeting. "Walk into one of our galleries," Kinkade said, "and you're at home."

THE WHITNEY MUSEUM OF AMERICAN ART, located at Madison Avenue and Seventy-fifth Street in New York City, opens its doors without charge to the public on Friday evenings at six o'clock. Outside of the entrance and at several places in the lobby the museum has posted warning signs, black letters on an orange background:

PLEASE NOTE
Some of the art work in "Alice Neel" and "Barbara
Kruger" may not be appropriate for children.

The exhibit on the top floor offered a kind of retrospective of modern art, "Art in America from Hopper to Pollack," featuring pieces from the Whitney's own collection. The artists represented here range from Edward Hopper and Thomas Hart Benton to George Bellows, Jackson Pollock, Alexander Calder, and Georgia O'Keeffe. The retrospective leads from Urban Realism to Gestural Painting and Early Abstract Expressionism.

I was particularly struck by a small painting by Peter Blume, "Light of the World, 1932." The piece depicts several people gazing dumbfoundedly, even worshipfully, at a large, light-bulb-like contraption, which was clearly meant to represent the wonders of technology and Enlightenment rationalism. In the background stood a medieval church, its windows darkened and its doors closed, and a beleaguered, distressed-looking monk taking in the scene. Further in the background was a pastoral scene very much like one that Kinkade might paint, but the central characters had their backs turned against that tableau, the church and the technicolor sky, so enraptured were they by the marvels of modernity and technology.

An exhibition of the works of Alice Neel, a New York bohemian artist who lived in Greenwich Village and in Spanish Harlem, marked the centennial of the artist's birth. Neel's portraits of various friends, lovers, and acquaintances show a lot of frontal nudity (male and female). Her palette is dark and brooding, and some of the characters have an almost feral look to them. Taken together, the Neel exhibition, with its odd constellation of characters who moved in and out of Neel's orbit, might be seen as a chronicle of the breakdown of the nuclear family.

The Barbara Kruger exhibition is a calculated assault on the senses. Her signature is black-and-white photographic images overwritten with white block letters reversed out of red banners. Kruger's most famous image, designed for the 1989 March on Washington in support of women's rights and the pro-choice movement, is a photograph of a woman's face, the image half negative and half positive, overwritten with "Your body is a battleground." Other works in the exhibition lampoon intolerance, consumerism, and religious belief: "How dare you not be me?"; "I shop therefore I am"; "My god is better than your god. Wiser, more powerful, all-knowing, the only god." A photograph of a serpent-handler bears the caption "Believe like us," while the voice of a preacher rants in the background.

Kruger's work is unrelentingly cynical, violent in its own way. This is not so much art as assault, with more than a little hypocrisy thrown in: Kruger's screeds against consumerism have been silk-screened onto tee-shirts, which are available for purchase in the museum store.

In its own way, however, Kinkade's art is just as tendentious as Kruger's. Kinkade insists that there is goodness and beauty in the world, beauty that is worthy of celebration and replication. The created order, his work declares, has redemptive power. It can soothe and heal, as anyone who has climbed a mountain or paddled a canoe in the Boundary Waters Wilderness will attest. Kinkade's paintings bring a representation of creation into the living room, a representation relatively unfiltered by contemporary artistic conventions.

Kinkade's critics—and he does not lack for critics—fault him precisely for that, for flouting contemporary artistic conventions. "He doesn't look like an artist who's worth considering," Robert Rosenblum, a curator at the Guggenheim Museum, sniffed, "except in terms of supply and demand."[3] Other critics use adjectives like "cheesy" and "clumsy" and phrases like "slickly commercial kitsch." Jack Rutberg, an art dealer in Los Angeles, told the *Wall Street Journal* that Kinkade's paintings are "the pet rock of the art world."[4] Kenneth Baker, art critic for the *San Francisco Chronicle*, asks: "Do we want what we call 'art' to serve this social function of quelling our anxiety in an almost pharmaceutical fashion?"[5]

Kinkade remains unmoved by his critics, and he may have found an unwitting ally in Phillippe de Montebello, the redoubtable director of the Metropolitan Museum of Art in New York. In an op-ed article in the *New York Times*, de Montebello lamented that "so many people, serious and sensitive individuals, are so cowed by the art establishment or so frightened at being labeled philistines that they dare not speak out and express their dislike for works that they find either repulsive or unaesthetic or both."[6] Kinkade himself puts it differently. "High culture is paranoid about sentiment," he told the *Times*. "But human beings are intensely sentimental. And if art does not speak a language that's accessible to people, it relegates itself to obscurity."[7]

Kinkade's populist sentiments mirror that of evangelicalism more generally. One of the hallmarks of evangelicalism, especially in America, is its disdain for pretension and high culture, its ability to speak the language of popular culture, be it the colloquial hymns of the nineteenth century, the folksy cadences of Billy Graham, or the food courts of suburban megachurches. Evangelicals like Kinkade care little for the approbation of the cultural elite. "The critics may not endorse me," Kinkade says defiantly, "but I own the hearts of the people."[8]

FOR ANYONE FAMILIAR WITH KINKADE'S WORK—and given the reach and the marketing savvy of Media Arts Group, Inc., it would be difficult to imagine anyone who is not at least dimly aware of his work—it will come as no surprise that Norman Rockwell was a major and formative influence for Kinkade. "Whether you're looking at a snow-frosted scene of Christmas Eve churchgoers, a tiny thatched-roof cottage in England, or a rambling old mid-west farmhouse, you can sense that each Thomas Kinkade painting portrays some delightful, storybook, charming place he would love to share with his adoring daughters," Kinkade's promotional materials read. "The love, care, and beauty shines through each image he shares."

Just as Rockwell sought to depict the delights and the quirkiness of small-town life that he knew was dying in the age of mass communications, fast food, and interstate highways, so too Kinkade offers bucolic landscapes accessible only to the imagination. "A piece of art is a compact form of the universe," Kinkade says. "I try to make the world comfortable and understandable." There are surely differences between the two men. Rockwell depicts life before television sitcoms and before Ray Kroc decided that all Americans had an unalienable right to a Big Mac; Kinkade evokes a world before Eve and Adam developed a craving for apples. Rockwell was also the master of character, the small, telling detail or expression—comic or poignant or both—while Kinkade studiously avoids anything that might remotely resemble portraiture or caricature. When people appear in his paintings, which they rarely do, their visages are nearly always blank or nondescript, almost like an Amish doll. "That's so the viewers can imagine themselves into the scene," Denise Sanders, his assistant, told me, a bit defensively.

Despite their stylistic differences, both Kinkade and Rockwell provide glimpses into a world that is not *surreal* (as with some forms of modern art), but *unreal*. Kinkade's landscapes invite the viewer, in the artist's words, to "imagine a life where there is plenty of time, plenty of energy, plenty of opportunity for everything you feel is important—plus a little left over for some things you simply enjoy."

Kinkade's paintings provide shelter, a kind of enwombing. The space he portrays is female space, characterized by interiority. There is nothing angular in his paintings; the lines are soft and rounded and inviting. Kinkade's art is quintessentially evangelical in several ways, not only in its populism, its use of Bible verses, and in its commodification, but also in its introversion. Just as evangelicals emphasize an inward piety over outward forms—"invite Jesus into your heart"—the light in Kinkade's paintings has been tamed and domesticated and internalized.

The art of Thomas Kinkade offers an oasis, a retreat from the assaults of modern life, a vision of a more perfect world. Who among us wouldn't like to catch a glimpse of that world from time to time, to picture life before the fall? But we live and move and have our being in a fallen world, and it is our lot as humans to negotiate that world. Kinkade's paintings furnish little guidance for that enterprise (other than to remind us that goodness and beauty once prevailed on earth), but that may be too much to ask of any artist. Although the viewer can imagine herself in Kinkade's paintings—cross-legged in front of the campfire, meandering through luxuriant gardens, sitting down to a Victorian Christmas dinner, or cozying next to the fireplace—she still stands *outside* the frame. Despite the artist's evocative talents, Eden remains elusive—even, I suspect, in the Kinkade village now under construction in Vallejo, California.

2000

CHAPTER 18

Purpose Driven

E VANGELICAL MEGACHURCHES (generally defined as congregations of a couple thousand or more) have flourished across
North America over the past several decades. The landscape
of suburb after suburb has been altered by the construction of these
behemoth operations, characterized by sprawling campuses, acres
of parking lots, and architecture that ranges from the audaciously
awful to criminally negligent.[1] These megachurches became so
common that they descended into cliché. Aside from the undistin-
guished buildings, each features amoeba-like parking lots and elaborate traffic-control apparatuses, a huge array of special-interest small
groups known as "cells," large, box-like auditoriums with an arboretum
of plastic shrubbery that won't wilt beneath the klieg lights, huge
television monitors, a band of musicians called a "praise band" or "worship team," and a sound system capable of removing dental plaque. In
southern California, the megachurch pastors have added yet another
cliche, the Hawai'ian shirt: Chuck Smith at Calvary Chapel (Santa
Ana), John Wimber at Vineyard Christian Fellowship (Anaheim), Leo
Giovenetti at Mission Valley Christian Fellowship (San Diego), and
Rick Warren at Saddleback Church (Lake Forest).

In everything from food portions to automobiles and vacation
homes, Americans are impressed with quality, but we are utterly
dazzled by size. The Grand Canyon is undeniably beautiful and the
Mackinaw Bridge an engineering marvel, but what really astounds
us is the scale. Evangelicals recognized the importance of scale long

ago—the open-air preaching of George Whitefield in the eighteenth century at places like Society Hill in Philadelphia, where Benjamin Franklin estimated the crowd at ten thousand, the massive camp meetings of the antebellum period that attracted as many as twenty-five thousand, and the urban revivals of Billy Sunday and Billy Graham in the twentieth century. Graham's crusades were notable for their meticulous planning and precise execution, but the sight of a packed stadium and hundreds or even thousands coming to Jesus was overwhelming.

Sometime early in the twentieth century, evangelicals came to believe that their churches should be large as well. In the era of the so-called institutional church movement early in the century, Russell H. Conwell of the Baptist Temple in Philadelphia fashioned a kind of full-service church, with a community center and an adult-education program so extensive that it evolved into an entire university, Temple University. Calvary Chapel, the creature of the Jesus movement of the early 1970s, grew so quickly that it became one of the first congregations to be referred to as a "megachurch."[2] Probably the best known megachurch of the late twentieth century was Willow Creek Community Church in South Barrington, Illinois, in the northwest suburbs of Chicago.[3] Founded in 1975 on the basis of a door-to-door market research survey to learn why suburbanites stayed away from church, Willow Creek grew to an average weekly attendance of somewhere around seventeen thousand by the turn of the twenty-first century. It featured a myriad of programs, parking lots that extend to the horizon, and a shopping mall-style food court. Its formula for success was widely studied and imitated by evangelical pastors who aspired to build their own megachurches.

And many did. Megachurches have flourished within evangelicalism over the past several decades; some of the better-known congregations include Prestonwood Baptist Church in Plano, Texas; Vmeyard Christian Fellowship in Anaheim; Bellevue Baptist Church near Memphis, Tennessee; Hope Chapel in Hermosa Beach, California; Springs of Living Water Church in Winnipeg, Manitoba;

Southeast Christian Church in Louisville, Kentucky; Lakewood Church in Houston; Willingdon Church in Vancouver, British Columbia—to name only a sampling. Typically, these congregations feature a charismatic pastor and an array of small-group programs targeted to specific audiences—young couples, divorced women, parents of teenagers, siblings of those in prison, senior citizens, those struggling with their weight. Though sometimes derided by critics as "Cafeteria Christianity" or "Christianity Lite," the mega-churches have had enormous appeal, especially in the suburbs, where they blend into the surrounding culture. Willow Creek, out-side of Chicago, for instance, looks like a suburban corporate office park, complete with ducks swimming on an artificial pond. Employ-ees at Willow Creek refer to the pastoral staff as their "administra-tive team" and to the sum total of their programs as their "product."

The particulars of other megachurches may differ slightly—Bellevue Baptist outside of Memphis, for example, emphasizes a kind of hyperpatriotism cloaked in militaristic language, an approach that appeals to many southerners—but those who operate evangelical megachurches have their fingers firmly on the pulse of their targeted audiences.[4] Critics often object that the "suburban captivity" of the megachurches inevitably compromises the gospel, but evangelicals have demonstrated throughout American history—from Gilbert Ten-nent and Francis Asbury to Billy Graham and Rick Warren—that they know how to appeal to the masses better than anyone else. When Robert Schuller accepted what was essentially a missionary posting to southern California in 1955, for example, he figured out very quickly that Orange County was an automobile culture. He rented the Orange Drive-in Theater, distributed handbills inviting locals to "worship as you are…in the family car," and then perched himself atop the con-cession stand and preached to the headlights.

Indeed, the genius of evangelicalism throughout American his-tory is the almost uncanny ability of evangelicals to speak the idiom of the surrounding culture, whether it be the persuasive rhetoric of George Whitefield in the open fields of the eighteenth century, the frontier preaching of the circuit riders in the nineteenth century, or the dramatic, flamboyant sermons of Aimee Semple McPherson in the Echo Park neighborhood of Los Angeles, where she was conscious of competing with Hollywood across town. Evangelicals have proven themselves especially fluent in speaking the language of suburbia in the second half of the twentieth century. The founders of megachurches have brilliantly exploited three characteristics of American society: size, consumerism, and formula. No congregation in America better exemplifies all three than Saddleback Church in Lake Forest, California.

LIKE MEGACHURCHES ELSEWHERE, Saddleback offers multiple weekend services in an effort to accommodate the crowds: four-thirty and six-thirty on Saturday evening, nine and eleven o'clock Sunday morning, and four-thirty and six-thirty Sunday night.[5] The main service takes place in the commodious Worship Center; as the congregation gathers, dressed in everything from beach togs to sport coats, the screens above and flanking the stage announce various church events—"Homeschool Information Night," "Laugh Out Loud Comedy Night," "The Prayer Ministry Needs Your Help!" along with "Please silence your cellphones during the service"— much the way that movie theaters barrage their audiences with ads before the show. Although the posted starting time on this Saturday afternoon is four-thirty—and megachurches like Willow Creek in Illinois begin and end *precisely* on time—this is southern California, so nobody seems to mind that things get going a few minutes late. The service itself opens with "praise music" conducted by the worship team, an ensemble of musicians and singers led in this instance by a guitarist in his early thirties with a crown of peroxide spikes and a, well, unusual configuration of facial hair.

After several songs, some raucous and others meditative, one of the church's pastors, wearing jeans and an open-collar, short-sleeved shirt over a tee-shirt, walks to center stage. "If you're visiting with us," he says cheerily, "welcome to Saddleback." By the standards of megachurches everywhere, the worship service here is rather unre-markable—a few songs, a couple of announcements, a sermon, and then a closing song. About the only thing I found a trifle unusual was that congregants began trickling toward the exits at the conclusion of the sermon, and they flooded to the exits during the closing song; but that is unusual only by the standards of megachurches and not according to the standards of southern California, where fans start leaving Dodger Stadium at the seventh-inning stretch in an attempt to avoid the scourge of traffic.

What sets Saddleback apart from other megachurches is what goes on outside of the Worship Center. The church operates what it calls "venues" scattered across the campus. A group for singles, called Element, takes place in a large tent-like structure, with loud music, smoke machines, and an elaborate light show projected onto the white interior walls. The children's ministry, called All Stars, occupies two entire buildings, with age-appropriate programs from nursery through grammar school. The WildSide tent, "Church for Junior Highers," has foosball and air hockey tables in the rear; the stage looks like a comedy club or a *Saturday Night Live* set. High schoolers gather around large tables in their own tent. The Ohana venue, across from the Beach Café and adjacent to the junior and senior high tents, appeals to the area's Pacific Islander population with hula-style music and picnic tables beneath grass-covered cano-pies. The Terrace Café overlooks the entire operation; worshipers there can enjoy the service by way of video feed on large-screen televisions while sitting with friends at café tables, sipping coffee, and eating their morning pastry. While the kids have their own pro-grams, all of the adult venues follow a similar pattern. Opening music (of various styles) and announcements are calibrated to the particular audience, then when Rick Warren (or another pastor) starts preaching, the worshipers scattered around the campus switch their attention to the large video screen for the sermon.

This configuration for evangelical worship owes less to tradi-tional churchmanship than it does to nearby Disneyland. The

venues at Saddleback resemble the various theme-park locations—
Frontierland, Main Street U.S.A., the World of Tomorrow—at the
"Happiest Place on Earth," just miles away. The idea for remote,
decentralized worship arose from the exponential growth at Saddleback Church; necessity, as they say, is the mother of invention. "We
didn't start venues to have more hooks in the water," one pastor
conceded. "We did it because we needed more seats."

ON MARCH 30, 1980, RICK WARREN, a graduate of Southwestern
Baptist Theological Seminary and a former youth pastor in Los Angeles, convened sixty people at Laguna Hills High School for the initial meeting of what would become Saddleback Church. His sermon
that first Sunday was a testament to audacity as he related his aspirations for the new church. "It is the dream of a place where the hurt-
ing, the depressed, the frustrated, and the confused can find love,
acceptance, help, hope, forgiveness, guidance, and encouragement,"
he said. "It is the dream of welcoming twenty thousand members
into the fellowship of our church family—loving, learning, laughing,
and living in harmony together." He spoke of "sending out hundreds
of career missionaries and church workers all around the world," and
of building "a regional church for Southern Orange County—with
beautiful, yet simple, facilities." The congregation that morning must
have gasped at the preacher's ambition, but Warren, ever driven, was
relentless. "I stand before you today and state in confident assurance that these dreams will become reality," he concluded. "Why?
Because they are inspired by God!"

Twenty-five years later, that vision has been realized. Twenty-four
thousand people attend Saddleback's services on a typical weekend;
forty-five thousand showed up at Easter. The church counts twenty
thousand members, and unlike other Protestant congregations, where
someone could spend close to a lifetime trying to *remove* his name
from the membership rolls, Saddleback takes pains to ensure that
theirs are active, resident members. (The church has a separate
category for "occasional attendees," those who show up four times a

year, typically Christmas, Easter, Mother's Day, and one other; the tally for that list comes in at eighty-two thousand.) What makes those numbers even more impressive is that most, nearly four out of five, members at Saddleback were converted and baptized at Saddleback. "The dirty little secret at most megachurches," according to Warren, "is that most of their numbers come from transfer growth, not conversion growth." Saddleback Church reports fourteen thousand baptisms over the past eight years, over two thousand during 2004 alone. When it came time to plan for the twenty-fifth anniversary of Saddleback Church in April 2005, Warren and his fellow pastors booked Anaheim Stadium. No other facility was adequate.

Saddleback also belies the popular notion that evangelicalism appeals principally to those mired in lower socioeconomic classes. There may have been some truth to that among pentecostals early in the twentieth century, but evangelicalism is—and has been throughout American history—a middle-class phenomenon, and its real growth throughout the twentieth century has taken place in the suburbs. American suburbs certainly have their share of those struggling for economic survival, but others do quite well indeed. At Saddleback, for instance, after the tsunami hit Asia in December 2004, the congregation raised $1.5 million for humanitarian relief in a single offering. With little advance notice and minimal publicity, the congregation recently collected $52 million in pledges ($7 million in cash) for an expansion of its facilities. Saddleback, Warren declares, "is the most generous church in America."

IRONICALLY, WARREN HIMSELF, who grew up in a small town in northern California, professes to be uneasy with large congregations. "I don't really like big churches," he says. "People put up with size because they find something meaningful in the services." For someone who is uncomfortable with scale, Warren has adapted very well, but Saddleback—and evangelicalism generally—is all about adaptation and experimentation. "We've done more things that did not work than did," Warren says. "We're not afraid to fail."

Indeed, experimentation in evangelicalism, worship styles in particular, has given rise to something akin to a cult of novelty. Evangelicals, generally suspicious of tradition and largely untethered by creeds, liturgical rubrics, or ecclesiastical hierarchies, are not afraid to try new approaches. Nor are they reluctant to abandon something that doesn't work. Warren hails the "entrepreneurial spirit" at Saddleback, citing it as "the Bell Laboratories of evangelicalism." The church, he says, "is a body, not a business, an organism, not an organization." So, Saddleback, despite a staff in excess of 150, has no organizational chart and no clearly defined polity. "It's total chaos," Warren said with a laugh, "but it works."

If Warren takes a dismissive attitude toward church structure—"Every time you take a vote," he says, "you create division"—he is anything but cavalier about organizing his ideas. Aphorisms trip off his tongue. "It's not about creeds," for instance, "it's about deeds." Or: "I'm in the paradigm business, not the program business." He organizes his thoughts schematically, five points here and three points there, sometimes alliterative, at other times simply mnemonic. His "Catalytic Transformation Model," for instance, calls for evangelical congregations to Adopt the Purpose Driven paradigm, Become a healthy church, Contribute to other churches, and Deploy to the world. In making the point that he does not in any way identify with the machinations of the Religious Right, to take another example, Warren declared, "it's not my goal to save America; I'm asked to save Americans." Another time he allowed that "we don't need the unity of conformity; we need the unity of community." "Fulfilling your mission in life is not crossing the sea," he declared, "it's seeing the cross."

Warren's generic term for all this wisdom is "purpose driven," as in the "Purpose Driven Church," the "Purpose Driven Movement," and the "Purpose Driven Life." Tee-shirts worn by some on the Saddleback campus read, "Got Purpose?" Warren wrote *The Purpose Driven Church* as a way of communicating his ideas to other pastors interested in church growth, but his sequel, *The Purpose Driven Life*, launched Warren into the stratosphere of best-selling authors.

The Purpose Driven Life, which proposes to answer the question in the book's subtitle, "What on Earth Am I Here For?" has sold well over twenty million copies in hardback, making it, according to Warren, the best-selling hardcover book in American history.

Warren insists that his success and notoriety as a best-selling author hasn't changed him; he still drives the same four-year-old Ford he did before hitting the charts, and he now practices what he calls reverse tithing, giving away ninety percent of his income and living off ten percent. The royalties have allowed Warren to refund to the church every dime of salary the congregation paid him for the past twenty-five years, and he has now set his sights on goals far larger than expanding the facilities in Lake Forest, California. "I believe we're on the verge of a second Reformation," Warren told me on an outdoor patio adjacent to his modest office. "The message must never change, but the methods must change in every generation." In his characteristic schematic style, he noted four major trends reshaping religious life in the twenty-first century: the explosive growth of the church in the southern hemisphere, the increased irrelevance of denominations, the revitalization of local churches (at the expense of denominational structures), and the rise of global religious networks, made possible by advances in communications, especially the internet.

Warren is in many ways a modest and unassuming man, with a receding hairline, dressed in khakis, loafers (no socks), and the ubiquitous Hawai'ian shirt, but there is nothing modest about his ambitions. The second Reformation that he heralds will coalesce around five issues: the mobilization of Christians, the multiplication of churches, the eradication of global giants (disease and hunger), cooperation among congregations, which will lead, finally, to the evangelization of the world. "God gave the technology to allow the Reformation," Warren said, referring to Martin Luther and the Gutenberg press. Similarly, Warren believes that God gave the internet to the church, and Warren means to use it to expand the Purpose Driven Movement and to spread the faith by establishing a network of Purpose Driven churches, which already number somewhere between forty and fifty thousand congregations in the United States alone. "There is no nation big enough to solve the world's problems," Warren says, and this provides an opening for the global church.

How does he plan to accomplish this? Warren's approach combines technology with a New Testament model to create yet another of his trademark schemes. When Jesus sought to spread the gospel, Warren says, he dispatched his followers and instructed them to seek out the worthy person or the "man of peace" in each village. Under the terms of his P.E.A.C.E. plan, Warren wants to send emissaries to towns and villages throughout the world to identify leaders and implement his scheme: Plant churches, Equip leaders, Assist the poor, Care for the sick, and Educate the next generation. This, Warren believes, is what he calls the DNA for the second Reformation. "The Purpose Driven paradigm," he insists, "is the Intel chip of the twenty-first-century church."

Warren's goals? Ten million churches associated with the movement, one hundred million small groups, and one billion disciples. He calls it "exponential thinking," and it reflects once again the innovative nature of evangelicalism. Warren is not afraid to dream big or to "think outside the box," nor is he afraid to discard old or no-longer-effective ideas. "Everything manmade has a shelf life," he says. "It doesn't last. Even good organizations lose their effectiveness." Then he adds, with disarming candor: "Saddleback is not that great a model anymore."

THOUSANDS OF EVANGELICAL PASTORS, however, beg to differ. Every May, Saddleback hosts a conference for church leaders eager to learn the formula for success at Saddleback. The annual Ministry Conference draws pastors from all over North America, and even beyond. I noticed nametags from Greenville, Texas; Lewiston, Idaho; Fresno, California; Palm Coast, Florida; Virginia City, Nevada; Clovis, New Mexico; Brattleboro, Vermont; and Casper, Wyoming. Conferees also came from Nigeria, the Philippines, South Africa,

Hong Kong, and Venezuela. Helge Hollerud, a tall, white-haired Norwegian from the Evangelical Lutheran Free Church, was head of a delegation of eighty church leaders from Norway. "It works," he said of Warren's formula for church growth. Even dying parishes in the state church of Norway have come alive using ideas adapted from Saddleback. Carlos Herrara of Guatemala City, Guatemala, was one of nine church members visiting Saddleback "to learn the Purpose Driven purposes," he said. Herrara, seated on a patch of grass beneath a palm tree, paged through his notes and heaved a sigh. "We've got a lot to do when we get back."

For the better part of a week, close to four thousand church leaders attended seminars with titles like "Preaching for Life Change," "Congregation & Community Care," "Launching a Purpose Driven Church," "Leading Your Church through Change," and "Resourcing the Purpose Driven Church." The leader of the latter told his audience to "focus on growth, not maintenance," and he warned against using church resources for such staples of pastoral care as counseling. A professional counselor "is a drain on your resources," he said. "Pastoral care can be a debt." On the other hand, he added, "staff people who can attract a crowd are a good investment."

The "Purpose Driven Preaching" session featured one of the pastors on the staff at Saddleback, who urged his auditors to take risks. "It takes a lot of courage to be a good preacher," he said. "If you're afraid of the opinions of other people, you need to get out of the ministry." Other homiletical advice was more practical. The preacher allowed that he derived more of his sermon ideas from Dave Barry, syndicated humorist with the *Miami Herald*, than he did from stodgy biblical commentaries, and he told of another sermonic device commonly used at Saddleback, tag-team preaching, in which Warren or another pastor will begin the sermon and cover the first couple of points, then disappear backstage as another pastor does points three and four, and then reappear for the conclusion.

The pastors and session leaders took a lot of questions from conferees eager to master the Saddleback formula for church growth.

One of the visiting pastors wanted to know what kind of large-screen monitor Saddleback uses in its venues; the answer came with specific advice about where to position the monitor. "The quality of your sermons is important," one of the session leaders advised. The leaders at Saddleback had a great deal of wisdom to dispense regarding music and sound systems. "If there's not a consistent sound every week," one cautioned, "the venue will die." "The architecture of your music program needs to be open," another said.

What about children? "We don't allow children in the Worship Center," came the answer. Saddleback, in fact, siphons all children off to the children's programs and doesn't allow kids under five in any of the venues. "They'll destroy your service," the pastor warned. One conferee, eager to apply the Saddleback formula to his congregation in Vista, California, worried that his auditorium seated "only five hundred or so." What to do? Answer: create more venues.

ONE OF THE MANY BOOTHS ON THE CAMPUS of Saddleback Church invites congregants to sign up for baptism. An attractive, four-color brochure lays out Saddleback's views on baptism and answers questions about the rite. Though the church dropped the word "Baptist" from its name long ago, and Warren does nothing to advertise his affiliation, both he and the church are technically members of the Southern Baptist Convention. "We remain in the denomination more for their sakes than for ours," he told me. "Denominations are dying, even evangelical ones."

The trademark belief of Baptists everywhere is adult, or believer's, baptism as opposed to infant baptism. Whereas Roman Catholics hold that the sacrament of baptism washes away the taint of original sin, and therefore should be done in infancy, most evangelicals subscribe to a Baptist position (regardless of whether they identify themselves as Baptists or not) that baptism is, in the words of the Saddleback brochure, a "symbol of Christ's burial and resurrection" and a "symbol of your new life as a Christian." "Baptism does not make you a believer," the brochure reads, "it shows that you already are one! Baptism does not 'save' you, only your faith in Christ does that. Baptism is like a wedding ring—it's the outward symbol of the commitment you made in your heart."

When a believer signs up to be baptized at Saddleback, she is given postcards to send to friends and family, inviting them to the event. Baptisms themselves take place after every worship service in a small pool carved into the patio area adjacent to the Worship Center. One of the pastors, dressed in swimming trunks and a Saddleback polo shirt waded into the water after a Saturday-evening service. As the first candidate, an eight-year-old boy, approached him, the pastor, holding a wireless microphone, asked, "What does it mean to you—to be baptized?"

"I want to worship Jesus, and I want to follow him as my Lord and Savior," the boy replied.

"Brian, have you accepted Jesus Christ as your Lord and Savior?"

After an affirmative response, the pastor placed his arm around the boy's shoulders and dipped him backwards into the water. "Buried with Him in baptism," the pastor said, then, lifting Brian from the water, "and raised anew."

The audience hooted and applauded. Many stayed to witness other baptisms, while others headed toward the parking lots, past the Patio, the Terrace Café, the High School and the Ohana venues, and the newest temporary structure on the Saddleback campus, the singles' ministry, Element. The pastors at Saddleback, always looking toward the next horizon, are talking now about a new venue to appeal to the area's Vietnamese population. Another pastor, citing the popularity of a local country FM station, is pushing for a venue that would feature country music. "South Orange County is full of rednecks," he declared rather indelicately. "We're going to do our best to tap into it."

2005

CHAPTER 19

Latino Evangelicals

THE SCENE AT THE CHURCH OF THE REFORMATION in Washington, D.C., just a couple of blocks from the Capitol, was a mixture of resolve and celebration, equal parts political rally and family reunion. People milled about on the front steps of the Art Deco building, posing for photographs, greeting old friends, and making new acquaintances. Inside, the congregation was strikingly well dressed and multicultural, a mixture of Hispanics, African Americans, and Anglos. A few raised their hands and waved their arms to the music, a gesture of openness to the Holy Spirit.

The congregation sang, "The Lord Hears the Cry of the Poor," inspired by Psalm 34. "Let the lowly hear and be glad," the lyrics read, "the Lord listens to their pleas." The pleas on this day revolved around immigration reform. Jesus instructed his followers to care for "the least of these," and a poster outside the church quoted the words of Jesus in Matthew 25: "For I was hungry and you gave me something to eat, I was thirsty and you gave me something to drink, I was a stranger and you invited me in."

As this gathering in Washington attests, evangelicals of a growing diversity are taking those commands seriously. The Evangelical Immigration Table, the umbrella organization for the initiative, includes such affiliates as Liberty Counsel on the right and Sojourners, which tilts toward the left. On the side of a church van across the street from the church was painted LOVE MEMORIAL BAPTIST CHURCH, GOLDSBORO, NC.

Bill Hybels, who founded Willow Creek Community Church in the northwest suburbs of Chicago, addressed the congregation, as did Lee de Leon, pastor of Templo Calvario, an evangelical congregation in Santa Ana, California. They made the case for immigration reform, including a path to citizenship. Orlando Findlayter, senior pastor of New Hope Christian Fellowship in Brooklyn, prayed that God would touch the hearts of the Congress of the United States. "Take away their heart of stone and give them a heart of flesh," he intoned. Even Richard Land of the Southern Baptist Ethics and Religious Liberty Commission, one of the more reliable shills for far-right policies, threw his support behind immigration reform. For too long, Land said, our government has had two signs at the border: "No Trespassing" and "Help Wanted." This is a propitious moment, he added.

Gabriel Salguera, president of the National Latino Evangelical Coalition, delivered the call to action, alternating smoothly between Spanish and English. "The time has come," he said. "Nothing changes without courageous people demanding it." He led the congregation in one of the standards of the civil rights movement, "Ain't Gonna Let Nobody Turn Me Around," and issued a rallying cry: "We're going to be walking the halls of Congress, and they don't know what's coming."

NOTHING HAS ALTERED the face of evangelicalism more profoundly over the last several decades than the growth in the number of Hispanic evangelicals. Although the preponderance of the estimated fifty-two million Latinos and Latinas in America are Roman Catholic, evangelicalism is increasing its market share, especially among the younger generation. According to the Pew Forum on Religion and Public Life, more than two-thirds of Hispanics in the United States are Catholic; by 2030, however, that percentage could drop to half, with evangelicals poised to harvest many of those defections.

What's the attraction? The answer to that question is complex, and it begins with the immigrants themselves. With the surge of evangelicalism, especially pentecostalism, in Latin America, many immigrants are already Protestant when they arrive in the United States. Among the others, some associate Roman Catholicism with the grinding poverty of places they left. Why not start anew—religiously as well as economically? When we were filming the *Mine Eyes Have Seen the Glory* documentary among Hispanic evangelicals in the Coachella Valley of southern California, several members of the pentecostal congregation argued that evangelicalism, with its emphasis on the Bible alone and the priesthood of believers, conferred agency on immigrants; it encouraged them to take charge of their lives and to become upwardly mobile. In addition, the congregation itself provided a support network to help new members of the community secure jobs and housing.

There may also be another dynamic at play in the Hispanic movement from Catholicism to evangelicalism. With its ecstatic worship style and its emphasis on the gifts of the Holy Spirit, pentecostalism in particular may be more akin to the practices of Catholics in Latin America. In many places, Catholicism in North America is more staid, and Hispanics are gravitating to the livelier worship of evangelicals.

New Life Covenant Church, in the Humboldt Park neighborhood of Chicago, is nothing if not lively. No gathering of evangelicals these days is complete without a "worship band"—keyboard, drums, a couple of guitars, and several vocalists. At New Life, at least on this Sunday, all of the instrumentalists were male and the vocalists female. "God, you are glorious," they sang in the lilting rhythms of the genre known as "praise music." The audience here in the auditorium of Roberto Clemente High School is a mixture of Hispanics and African Americans. A few Anglos are present, but they are a distinct minority. Everyone is standing, some with arms in the air. As the music continues and the worshipers file in, the tempo speeds up and the decibels rise. Lyrics projected onto the screens bracketing the stage segue into the second song, "Jesus, We Shout Your Name." Indeed.[1]

After a couple of songs—and this too has become so characteristic of evangelical worship that it's formulaic—there follows an interval that I have come to call the Murmuring Moment. It works like this. At the conclusion of the second or third "praise song," one of the vocalists, eyes closed, head uplifted, one hand clutching the microphone and the other, palm flattened, extended to the ceiling, begins to intone a kind of breathy mantra: "Thank you, Jesus . . . can we just worship him?" The other performers, along with members of the audience, follow suit, arms upraised, swaying back and forth, murmuring. "Hallelujah!" "We love you, Jesus." The keyboard noodles quietly, reverently, in the background. "You were there, O God," the vocalist intones softly, and the audience replies with similar affirmations of the Almighty. This is the moment when, especially in pentecostal gatherings, some members of the congregation begin speaking in tongues.

The first time I encountered the Murmuring Moment, years ago, I thought it was quite beautiful. There are few things I find more haunting and moving than genuine, spontaneous *glossolalia*, or speaking in tongues. But the Murmuring Moment has become so predictable that it seems contrived to me, even coercive. It's as though the worship leaders are saying, "Now, folks, twenty minutes into the service, we're going to speak in tongues." Something that I had always understood as sacred and spontaneous is now programmed, routinized, almost compulsory.

After the Murmuring Moment at New Life Covenant Church, the musicians move into a variation on "Amazing Grace," which includes the phrase "my chains are gone, I've been set free" and concludes: "unending love, amazing grace." By the end of the song, Wilfredo De Jesús has jumped onto the stage and positioned himself behind a simple podium. He's wired with a headset microphone with a tiny arm that reaches in front of his mouth. "How many been set free?" he shouts. "Amen?"

His congregation is dressed casually, but De Jesús wears a tan suit, a white shirt, and a steel blue necktie. He has a friendly mien and the solid build of a running back. "Grace," he says, "is about paying it forward," which is his sermon title for this morning. A large, professionally produced banner to his side announces the topic of a sermon series that he is just now concluding.

> **GOD**
>
> **MEANT IT**
>
> **FOR GOOD**
>
> ----------
>
> **THE STORY OF JOSEPH**

De Jesús welcomes visitors, including those watching online. He then plays a video clip about the current sermon series, one with all the production values of a Hollywood trailer. "C'mon, give the Lord a praise offering," he says, and the congregation responds with applause. "We love God, but we're cool, too." De Jesús moves into the announcements, which include the Wednesday night Bible study but especially stress what the church calls HopeFest, billed as a "Back 2 School Outreach" to the community. Sponsored by the church, Pepsico, Joyce Meyer Ministries, and the Norwegian American Hospital, HopeFest supplies children with backpacks, clothes, and haircuts in advance of the opening of school in the fall. Physicians and nurses will provide vaccinations. The church expects to distribute five thousand backpacks, and De Jesús is appealing for volunteers.

He also appeals for funds. On the morning of my visit to New Life Covenant Church, the Sunday edition of the *Chicago Tribune* ran a photograph of the demolition of St. James Roman Catholic Church in the Bronzeville neighborhood on the south side. Despite the protests of parishioners and an appeal to both the Vatican and the notoriously dysfunctional Chicago City Council, the Archdiocese of Chicago ruled that the costs of renovating the limestone building were prohibitive. The archdiocese has promised to construct a smaller building in its place.

New Life Covenant Church has the opposite problem. Since Wilfredo and Elizabeth De Jesús assumed leadership in 2000, the congregation has grown from sixty-eight to over fourteen thousand, making it the largest in the entire Assemblies of God denomination. New Life Covenant conducts its Sunday services in several places: four services at Roberto Clemente High School, two services at the "Spanish Campus" on North Mozart Avenue, and a service at the "NorthWest Campus" on West Diversey. The model is similar to the one followed by Saddleback Church, Rick Warren's megachurch in Orange County, California, but with one important difference. Whereas Saddleback has many "venues," each with its own music and worship culture, all of which give way to the sermon piped in from the Worship Center, New Life has different preachers delivering more-or-less the same sermon in the different locations. At a staff meeting during the week, the pastors coordinate their outlines and talking points, but each preacher delivers his own sermon, some in Spanish and others in English. "I've come to the conclusion," De Jesús says, "that it's probably best that we open up more churches around the world than one big church where people would come to hear me."

Despite his success—or, more likely, because of it—De Jesús hankers for his own church building, one that will allow him to centralize his operations. "It's not about building a building," he told his congregation. "It's about expanding the kingdom." (If I had a dollar for every time I heard a preacher say it's not about the building, I could construct my own megachurch.) New Life Covenant Church, according to De Jesús, hopes to move into its new $9 million facility by the end of the year.

The offering takes place to the strains of another praise song, "Let the Glory of the Lord Rise among Us," and De Jesús reminds those watching the webcast that they can also give online. In the lobby of the building, the church has provided two ATM-like consoles (on wheels) that allow congregants to give with their debit cards.

De Jesús's sermon, "Pay It Forward," made the case that the followers of Jesus should repay evil with good. "The cost of reconciliation can be expensive," he warns. It's easier to hold grudges, "but if you live off that pain, you'll become bitter." De Jesús is a good and effective preacher. He paces around the stage and into the audience, and he's trying to ramp up the enthusiasm. "Ya' hear me?" he asks. "Can I get some help here?" The congregation obliges, in the call-and-response style of African-American worship, with *amens* and interjections like "C'mon now!"

"Don't pay evil with evil," De Jesús warns. "Pay evil with good." And, like any good evangelical preacher, De Jesús provides suggestions. "Be a courteous driver on Fullerton or Division Street." "Maybe you can go to Humboldt Park and just clean up the park." "Shop at local stores so that money can stay in your community."

THESE ARE HEADY DAYS for Wilfredo De Jesús. His praying hands appeared on the cover of the April 15, 2013, issue of *Time* magazine, and he was pictured inside and featured prominently in the cover story, titled "¡Evangélicos!" A couple of issues later, *Time* also included De Jesús on its annual list of "the 100 most influential people in the world."[2]

But his life has not been easy. De Jesús was reared by a single mother in Humboldt Park; his father was an alcoholic, and his mother broke the news of his father's defection when Wilfredo was eight years old. "As soon as she told me the painful news, I ran to the bar to beg my father to stay," De Jesús recalls. "Somehow, the tears and pleading of his little boy didn't make any difference to him. When I walked out that day, I had a sick, empty feeling."[3] Wilfredo had five older siblings. "Everything in life was against me: dysfunctional family, failed at third grade, couldn't read, had no father figure, surrounded by gangs and drugs," he said. "Yet God in his infinite wisdom chose my life." He became an evangelical in 1977. He was working that summer in a youth program for the city of Chicago and had been placed in an Assemblies of God church, assigned to maintenance work for a day camp. "I never left," he said. "The love of those young people melted my heart." The former Catholic "prayed to accept Jesus as my Savior, and my life changed forever."[4] De Jesús graduated from Roberto Clemente High School in 1982, the same venue where the church now conducts its Sunday services.

He studied for a year at North Central Bible College in Minneapolis before transferring to Trinity College in Deerfield, Illinois. After graduating with a major in communications, he earned a master's degree in Christian ministries from North Park Theological Seminary on Chicago's north side.[5]

In 2000 his father-in-law retired as pastor of two Assemblies of God churches in Chicago. The smaller congregation, consisting of only sixty-eight people, asked De Jesús and his wife to submit their names for consideration. Wilfredo De Jesús was already serving part-time as assistant pastor and also as executive assistant to the head of the Chicago Public School System. De Jesús purchased a farm outside of the city and made it into a refuge for recovering drug addicts and prostitutes. He purchased a liquor store in the neighborhood and converted it into a café. Although he continued Spanish-speaking services, he found that many of the sons and daughters of immigrants preferred to hear sermons in English.

These days, De Jesús, who is known to his congregation as "Pastor Choco" (for his skin color and for his childhood fondness for chocolate), devotes most of his energies to New Life as well as to causes both local and—like immigration—national. He is vice president for social justice for the National Hispanic Christian Leadership Conference, which represents thirty-eight thousand churches. But his heart remains in Chicago and more particularly Humboldt Park. His residence, which he shares with his wife and three children, is there too. "I could have built anywhere, in the suburbs or away from the city, away from the crime, but I am compelled, provoked by the Holy Spirit, to minister to 'the least of these,'" De Jesús told a reporter. "There is no doubt I have this connection with the poor and less fortunate."[6]

Concern for those Jesus called "the least of these" drives the agenda at New Life Covenant Church, which provides food and clothing pantries, job training, mobile soup kitchens, and ministry to those in prison. The church fights sex trafficking, gangs, and drug abuse. De Jesús sees immigration as a family issue; the existing policy of deportation sunders families rather than keeping them together. Immigration is also a humanitarian issue. One of the church's brochures quotes a passage from the New Testament book of Hebrews: "Don't forget to show hospitality to strangers, for some who have done this have entertained angels without realizing it."[7]

Between the second and third services, a man who identified himself as Victor and who described himself as one of the pastor's "armor-bearers," ushered me to a backstage room to meet De Jesús, who we found picking at a fruit salad. When I registered surprise that he had not mentioned to his congregation that the United States Senate had, just a few days earlier, approved an immigration bill, De Jesús brushed it aside, pointing out that the larger fight loomed in the Republican-controlled House of Representatives. "I'm no fool," he said. "I want to use my voice at the right time." But he reiterated his support for immigration reform. "It's breaking up families," he said of the existing system. "As Christians, we have an obligation to speak toward the systems that exist that are broken, that are causing the injustice."

De Jesús's vision extends beyond immigration. "The Hispanic evangelical is possibly the last line of defense for America," he said. "We're not afraid to say what we believe." On *Windy City Live*, a local Chicago television program, De Jesús had declared that many Hispanics were "moving from Catholicism to Christianity" and that over the last twenty years "we've been seeing an exodus from the Catholic church to the Christian church." Nevertheless, he sees massive political potential in an alliance between evangelical and Catholic Hispanics.[8] "Both groups fear God," he told me. "Both groups love family. Both groups love the institution of marriage." Another aide signaled that De Jesús needed to prepare for the next service. "Latinos are the hope for America," he said.

De Jesús himself keeps a close eye on the political arena. "I encourage every pastor, every Hispanic pastor, to get involved in the political realm," he said in an interview.[9] From 2007 until 2010, he was a member of the Chicago Zoning Board of Appeals. In 2009 an alderman who had accepted an appointment in the governor's office endorsed De Jesús to complete his term on the City Council, citing the pastor's commitment to social justice. Opposition from the gay community over De Jesús's denunciations of homosexuality, however, torpedoed that appointment. In 2010, when longtime mayor Richard M. Daley announced that he would not seek reelection, De Jesús decided to enter the race for mayor. Announcing his candidacy, De Jesús spoke about his roots in Humboldt Park, touted his fiscal responsibility in handling church matters, and asked rhetorically what qualified him for office. "I believe that God qualified me," he said. "Number two, I believe that the president of the United States qualified me when he appointed me as a surrogate to travel for him for fourteen months when he was running for president."

As it turned out, Barack Obama had another surrogate in the mayoral campaign: Rahm Emanuel, former White House chief of staff. De Jesús pulled out of the race a month before the Democratic primary.

GABRIEL SALGUERO, head of the National Latino Evangelical Coalition, had warned me that Hispanic evangelicals defy easy categorization. "When I identify myself as a Latino evangelical," he said, "they don't know what to do." Latino evangelicals, he claimed, supported George W. Bush in 2004 and Barack Obama in both 2008 and 2012. "We're swing voters," he said. "We're up for grabs, but we're a force to contend with." De Jesús puts it differently. "We don't represent the donkey or the elephant," he said. "We represent the lion," the Almighty, the Lion of Judah.[10]

Salguero, the son of a pentecostal minister, is pastor of Lamb's Church, a congregation in lower Manhattan affiliated with the Church of the Nazarene. He was born in New Jersey and educated at Rutgers, New Brunswick Theological Seminary, Princeton Theological Seminary, and Union Theological Seminary. Like De Jesús, Salguero's heritage is Puerto Rican. His church offers services in Spanish and in Mandarin, reflecting the demographics of the surrounding community.

"I don't think that it takes courage for me to take a stand on immigration," Salguero said, but he characterized the push for legislation as a "watershed moment" for evangelicals in general and for Latino evangelicals in particular. He expressed confidence that Congress would eventually do the right thing and pass immigration reform, including a path to citizenship for those here illegally. When asked what other issues loomed on the horizon, Salguero talked about the tragedy of "massive incarceration" in the United States and the scourge of poverty. He cited the vast "economic divide," which he attributed in part to "issues of education and educational opportunity."

Salguero worries that political and religious operatives, seeing the electoral potential in Latino evangelicalism, will court Hispanics for political gain. "We need thinking evangelicals," he said. "We don't want to become tools of any type of extremism." Salguero characterized Latino evangelicals as socially conservative and economically progressive, but he shies away from political labels. "Why can't I just be a follower of Jesus working for the common good?"

The rise of latino evangelicalism suggests that evangelical political activism may finally be coming of age. Evangelicals in the nineteenth and early twentieth centuries crowded toward the left of the political spectrum. They worked for the abolition of slavery, equal rights for women, and the establishment of public schools. Evangelicals opposed dueling as barbaric, marched in the vanguard of peace crusades, and advocated the rights of workers. Many prominent evangelicals, from Charles Grandison Finney to William Jennings Bryan, spoke out against the ravages of unbridled capitalism.

The aberration in evangelical political behavior emerged with the rise of the Religious Right in the late 1970s. In their quest for political influence, evangelical leaders like Jerry Falwell and Pat Robertson cast their lot with Ronald Reagan against Jimmy Carter, a fellow evangelical. Over the ensuing decades, the Religious Right marched in lockstep with the Republicans and became, in the process, the party's core constituency. Politically conservative evangelicals supported massive increases in military spending, for example, while opposing equal rights for women, positions utterly at odds with those of their evangelical precursors. Opposition to abortion and to same-sex marriages became their signature concerns.

Beginning with the 2008 election, however, a younger generation of evangelicals began to discern a much broader spectrum of "moral issues," including war, poverty, and the environment. The evangelical groundswell for immigration reform suggests a maturing of those concerns. More than three decades after the emergence of the Religious Right, many evangelicals are pushing for a realignment of evangelical politics, moving away from hard-right policies to reclaim the mantle of nineteenth-century evangelicalism, which, like traditional Catholic social teaching, invariably took the part of those on the margins of society, those Jesus called "the least of these."

The evangelical embrace of immigration reform represents a kind of redemptive symmetry. Just as a path to citizenship allows immigrants to emerge from the shadows and seek a better life, so too evangelical advocacy on their behalf allows evangelicalism to reclaim its noble legacy. "I think the Hispanic community can rise up and speak to bodies of organizations within our city, our nation and say, 'Wait a minute, we have convictions,'" De Jesús says. "When you talk about issues in our nation, who's fighting these issues?" Many of those fighting for the institutions of marriage and family, he insists, are Latino clergy. "I think the church should lock arms with our Hispanic brothers and sisters and live out the gospel."[11]

Gabriel Salguero takes a historical perspective. "I have no interest in refighting the culture wars," he said. "I don't think they should have been fought the first time around."

2013

Epilogue

M Y INTERLOCUTOR has been gazing out the window. He turns now, clears his throat, and regards me across the desk.

"You seemed to let that Frank character speak for you several chapters back," he says. I allow that, well, yes, perhaps I did. What I admire about Frank, I explain, is his ability to maintain a distance from all the ephemera of American evangelicalism without discarding his faith. It's my impression, moreover, that most people reared in the evangelical subculture either embrace it altogether or abandon it altogether. Either option strikes me as disingenuous, an easy way around a tradition that is at once rich in theological insights and mired in contradictions.

A prominent historian of American religion is fond of describing evangelicalism in America as a mosaic, a metaphor intended to convey a sense of its multiplicity, diversity, and complexity. While I sympathize with the sentiment behind such a description, American evangelicalism as mosaic is an image that I've never found compelling. It belies, I think, the folk appeal of evangelicalism, its grassroots character. For me, a mosaic conjures European patronage rather than American piety. If you study a mosaic from a distance, moreover, an overall design comes into focus.

Discerning any single pattern in American evangelicalism is difficult at best. Beyond general—but by no means unanimous—agreement on personal conversion, the importance of Scripture, and the expectation of an apocalypse, evangelicals contend with one another over the rigor of those beliefs and the appropriate expressions of piety. Splitting theological hairs over such recondite doctrines as premillennialism or the gifts of the Spirit or the exact mode of biblical inspiration has become something of a sport in evangelical circles, but one that is played with ferocious earnestness. The slightest deviation from the position that one or another group stakes out as "orthodox" provides the occasion for expulsion or schism.

Belief has always been important to evangelicals. "*Believe* on the Lord Jesus Christ, and thou shalt be saved," the Authorized Version admonishes.[1] Evangelicals regularly repeat that refrain, and, lacking hierarchial structures or liturgical rubrics, evangelicalism in America is held together in large measure by its insistence that followers subscribe to a set of doctrines, however variously they might be defined from one evangelical congregation to the next. That in itself, I think, sets evangelicalism somewhat apart from other religious traditions in America. Jews in America (as elsewhere) are bound by their common identity as a separate people. Roman Catholics acknowledge a common authority, even though of late they have not followed the dictates of that hierarchy. Methodists rely on a strong organizational structure; for many Lutherans, there is a kind of vestigial ethnicity that unites the various groups. Episcopalians historically have been latitudinarian in their theology, but what distinguishes them is their worship, their shared liturgy as prescribed in the *Book of Common Prayer*. The history of mainline Presbyterianism over the past century can be read as a retreat from confessionalism, so that what holds Presbyterians together is polity, the impulse to do everything "decently and in order." Denied ordinations and heresy trials among Presbyterians in recent decades have been challenged successfully on *procedural* grounds, not on the basis of whether or not the principal affirms the right doctrines.

These are generalizations, to be sure, but one of the reasons that belief is so important to evangelicals may be that they cannot claim any of these other "adhesives" as the basis for whatever cohesion exists among them. Evangelicals unite instead behind a charismatic leader, a common spiritual experience, or a set of doctrines—and, more than likely, some combination of the three. Convictions are essential to that mixture. We live in a skeptical, post-Enlightenment age where belief has become unfashionable; the liberal and ecumenical trends in Protestant theology, furthermore, have blurred doctrinal differences in the name of unity, toleration, and inclusiveness. But while many theologians and denominational leaders plunged headlong into the ecumenical current, a large number of their communicants stayed on the riverbank.[2] People need boundaries in their lives, a sense of limits, a feeling for what is appropriate and inappropriate, right and wrong, true and heretical.

Evangelicalism provides that. For a growing number of Americans, it offers an unambiguous morality in an age of moral and ethical uncertainty. It offers theological surety in a culture that is not yet ready to divest itself entirely of its belief in God. For many people in the waning decades of the twentieth century who recognize that science and technology has not been the promised savior of civilization, belief is more comfortable than unbelief, faith is preferable to doubt.

Despite the evangelicals' general insistence on belief, however, they cannot agree on any one configuration of doctrines. And so, paradoxically, their doctrinal precisionism has produced the incredibly diverse evangelical subculture in America: fundamentalists, pentecostals, charismatics, Wesleyans, Nazarenes, Assemblies of God, Church of God, Church of the Open Bible, fifty-some stripes of Baptists, not to mention independent, non-affiliated congregations that go by names like Evangelical Chapel or Community Bible Church. All of them fall (more or less willingly) under the rubric of evangelicalism.

Were I to designate a metaphor for this rather unwieldy evangelical subculture, I'd find the image of a patchwork quilt more satisfying than a mosaic. A quilt, especially one produced at a quilting bee, is folk art rather than fine art; it requires the work of many hands, each of which contributes its own "signature" to the project.

Its beauty, moreover, lies precisely in its variegated texture and even, sometimes, in the absence of an overall pattern. Unlike a mosaic, it is also quintessentially American.

Evangelicalism itself, I think, is quintessentially American. Religious disestablishment—the absence of a state church—gave rise in the United States to a kind of free market of religion. Various denominations and individual congregations compete with one another for popular followings, thereby lending an unmistakably populist cast to religion in America. Evangelicals have always fared well in this competition. Their preachers have mastered the art of oral discourse, especially persuasive rhetoric, in a nation of talkers, among a people who pick up a telephone rather than write a letter, who enjoy the static-borne banter of CB radios, who are addicted to talk of all kinds, including the prattle of commercials and talk shows on radio and television. Evangelical preaching and worship, casual and nonliturgical, comes across well in the open fields of the eighteenth century or over the airwaves of the twentieth.[3] Indeed, the informality of evangelical worship reflects the larger culture. We Americans prize informality, witness our impulse to address others, even fresh acquaintances, by their first names. Other countries mint coins or strike medals to commemorate important occasions; in America we silk-screen a few dozen tee-shirts: TANGLEWOOD 50, THE INDY 500, RAGBRAI XVI, HANDS ACROSS AMERICA, SUPERBOWL XXI.

America is also a media culture—more particularly, a television culture. Television is the great validator. Appearing on television (for whatever reason) makes you *someone;* without it, as any also-ran politician can attest, you are no one going nowhere. The televangelists understand that, I think. They understand Americans' fixation with celebrity, and they recognize the popular appeal of casual, informal worship and expert preaching, especially when it purports to champion "traditional values" in an age that seems to have lost its moral moorings.

The weakness for celebrity, the affinities between evangelicalism and the medium of television, and the tendency of evangelicals to gravitate to charismatic leaders, leave the subculture vulnerable to self-aggrandizement and egomania. "Nobody wants to play rhythm guitar behind Jesus," as the Oak Ridge Boys say, "everybody wants to be the lead singer in the band."[4] But there are other ways in which American culture and the evangelical subculture have fed off each other. Prosperity theology, which amounts to a baptism of American materialism and consumerism, is all the rage in evangelical circles these days, as I discovered in my travels. Jesus will save your soul and your marriage, make you happy, heal your body, and even make you rich. Who wouldn't look twice at that offer? Even if you drop a twenty in the collection plate every Sunday, it's still cheaper than a therapist. Surely such a message has an obvious appeal to the middle-class aspirations of many American evangelicals, but I had been unprepared for how thoroughly the God-will-make-you-rich-and-happy pablum has pervaded evangelicalism, especially among people who pride themselves on biblical literalism. Whatever happened to the scandal of the gospel, to Jesus' invitation to forsake everything—family and fishing boats, beachhouses and BMWs—to follow Him?

Returning to the subculture after several years' hiatus, moreover, I was astounded at how the media, especially television, have permeated evangelical worship. Soloists and musical ensembles gyrate to "canned" orchestra music from cassette tapes played over elaborate sound systems. Applause regularly punctuated Sunday morning services almost everywhere I went, as though each congregation was a studio audience. God apparently likes applause, a fact that had eluded me as I grew up within the evangelical subculture.

Television, furthermore, only exaggerates the evangelical weakness for charismatic leaders and the cult of personality. Lacking an overarching organization, distinctive polity, authority structure, or liturgical rubric, evangelicals generally galvanize around a personality who articulates—and even defines—the faith of his followers according to his own idiosyncratic reading of the Bible. Indeed, what an evangelical leader does—be he Jimmy Swaggart or Robert Schuller or

Neal Frisby or Jack Wyrtzen—is to construct a reality for his follow-ers. Word of Life Island in the Adirondacks, Dallas Theological Semi-nary, the Capstone Cathedral in Phoenix, Camp Freedom in Florida, and even Donald Thompson's films are all socially constructed uni-verses, full of symbols and invested with meaning.[5] In Phoenix, Neal Frisby has contrived a world of divine healing and deliverance in which Frisby himself, the Rainbow Prophet and former alcoholic, provides a symbol of hope for people who clearly do not share in the good life of this world. The Capstone Cathedral, replete with pro-phetic and dispensational symbolism, offers a retreat from that out-side world.

Other structured realities may be less bizarre, but they also offer a retreat and regular commerce with others who share similar views of the world. The peculiar and highly regimented theology of Dallas Theological Seminary is at odds with the prevailing currents of the broader society, and yet there in the heart of Texas a group of white male seminarians dressed in yuppie suits can gather around a table in the student center to discuss the nuances of their eschatology without fear of challenge, or they can chortle about a professor's masterful, ugly put-down of a female student. The structured reality of Voice of Calvary in Mississippi represents a nobler vision, to be sure—one of racial harmony and social justice—but it is no less illu-sory, no less incongruous with the larger world. In the contrived uni-verse of Jack Wyrtzen's ninety-acre island, the girls are modest, the boys chaste, and everyone is a "Christian" (or soon will be). Douglas Frank's community, cradled in the Cascade Mountains, is also quite insular, try as he will to ensure that theirs is a geographical isola-tion and not an intellectual one. In the celluloid world of Donald Thompson's films, righteousness prevails over godlessness, and the meek finally inherit the earth, albeit after an apocalyptic struggle.

In the larger universe, of course, the meek do *not* inherit the earth any more than teenagers wear bathing togs that reach beyond their fingertips or a majority of Americans subscribe to dispensationalism. All of these socially constructed realities, then, offer an alternate, idealized view of the world, a place of retreat and escape, no less than the utopian communities that dotted the American landscape in the nineteenth century. Indeed, the entire evangelical subculture itself is a socially constructed reality, a place of retreat built primarily after the Scopes Trial of 1925, when fundamentalists became convinced that the larger American culture had abandoned them. Nestled safely within the subculture for most of the twentieth century, evangelicals smugly contrasted their world with the outside world in a kind of orgy of dualistic rhetoric: good *versus* evil, sacred *versus* secular, righteous *versus* unrighteous, saved *versus* damned. Evangelicals felt secure within the cocoon of this contrived universe of churches, summer camps, Bible institutes, colleges, and seminaries. Only in the mid-to-late 1970s, when a conservative mood swing looked congenial and when politicians promised, in effect, to impose the ethos of the evangelical subculture on *all* of American society, did evangelicals begin to venture outside the cocoon.

SINCE UNDERTAKING THIS PROJECT, I have been asked countless times for my opinions about the future of evangelicalism in America. The question invariably comes from nonevangelicals who have little appreciation for the history of evangelicalism and who clearly are skittish about the influence of fundamentalists in politics. Although I am more comfortable as a historian than as a prognosticator, I generally respond that we can look for some mitigation of fundamentalist ardor in the coming years—it's difficult, after all, to sustain religious fervor for a long period of time, and even more difficult to pass that piety along to the next generation—but that evangelicals will continue to make their presence felt in American culture, just as they have (more or less visibly) throughout American history.

If my peregrinations taught me nothing else, they showed me that the evangelical subculture is broad and deep in the United States, and it is sustained by numberless institutions—churches, missions, camp meetings, publishing houses, colleges, seminaries, Christian schools, Bible camps—that often escape the notice of the casual observer.

This network of institutions provided the foundation for the evangelical return to the public arena in recent years.

Evangelicalism will also persist, I think, because of its timeless appeal. It promises intimacy with God, a support community, an unambiguous morality, and answers to the riddles of eternity. It offers eternal life, and nothing frightens us mortals more than death. The evangelical theology of conversion and assurances of a reward in heaven appeal to Americans, who have always nurtured the illusion that they control their own destinies. Many evangelical preachers have added still other enticements: the promise of deliverance from sickness, suffering, and pain, and, more recently, the prospect of material prosperity.

Evangelicalism simply will not go away. In the 1920s H. L. Mencken, no friend of evangelicals, remarked that if you tossed an egg out of a Pullman window almost anywhere in the country, you would hit a fundamentalist. Pullman cars are obsolete in America today. Fundamentalists are still around.

No pilgrim returns from his journey unchanged. Myself, I shall long remember the energy and self-assurance of Donald Thompson, the resilient faith of Jacob and Ada Sollenberger, and the quiet determination of Innocent Good House, fighting to reconcile his faith with his heritage, straining to see signs of hope among his beleaguered people. I recall Neal Frisby, the Rainbow Prophet of Revelation, as a pathetic figure, although I am confident he would refuse my sympathy. I shall also remember Frisby's followers who, night after night, bring their sad, broken lives to Jesus. If Douglas Frank is right, however, we all have sad, broken lives, and all our self-righteous moralizing serves only as an artifice to shield us from that awful truth. I recognize myself in the adolescent struggles of Amy Durkin, Candy Schroeder, and Carl Watkins. I wonder where their pilgrimages will lead. Will they stumble by the way or somehow, through persistence or fate or even the grace of God, claim the faith of their parents as their own? I won't soon forget the dolorous strains of "Seek Ye First the Kingdom of God" in Santa Ana, California, the triumphalism of "Mine Eyes Have Seen the Glory" in Concord, New Hampshire, or singing "We Shall Overcome" on the anniversary of Martin Luther King's birth with the folks of Mound Bayou, Mississippi, who still have so much to overcome.

I think I heard the gospel in those hymns. I heard the gospel at various discrete moments in my travels and certainly in Douglas Frank's sad yet insistent quarrel—a lover's quarrel, really—with evangelicalism. Those small epiphanies affected me, evoking as they did the religion of my childhood. That the evangelical gospel can still be heard at all above the din of what passes for evangelicalism in America today is miracle enough, perhaps, to capture the attention of even the most jaded observer. What it all means I'm not yet sure, but I now find it less easy to dismiss the preposterous evangelical claims about a God of amazing grace who, despite our bumbling and nonsense and hoary theological schemes, saves us from ourselves.

No pilgrim, after all, returns from his journey unchanged.

Afterword: Twenty-five Years Later

TWENTY-FIVE YEARS AGO, I opened *Mine Eyes Have Seen the Glory* with a survey of license plates and bumper stickers in the parking lot of Calvary Chapel. As I provide an update on some of the people and the places that have appeared in successive editions of the book, that same parking lot seems as good a place to start as any.

ETERNITY: SMOKING OR NON-SMOKING? read one bumper sticker, and another: CHRIST HAS SET US FREE. A California tag read NGODS CO. Another tag apparently refers to the owner's favorite Psalm: PS 107. These days, people adorn their bodies with slogans as well, and the worshipers at Calvary Chapel sport plenty of tattoos—crosses, Bible references, the Holy Spirit dove that is the symbol of Calvary Chapel. Lots of jeans and sandals and tee-shirts, one of which read JESUS FREAK, a reference, intentional or not, to the origins of Calvary Chapel in the Jesus movement of the early 1970s.[1]

The Sunday morning service opened with a praise song, "The Air I Breathe." Calvary Chapel is arguably the fount of "praise music," the lilting melodies that have become ubiquitous in evangelical worship. According to an oft-told story, a band of ex-hippies who called themselves Love Song auditioned for Chuck Smith, the pastor, on a Monday afternoon in 1969. Accompanied by guitars, they sang a simple, mesmerizing tune, "Welcome Back." Smith was hooked. "I was so touched," he recalled, "their music moved my heart." Smith asked if they could perform at seven o'clock that evening.

Chuck Girard, the leader, tentatively said yes. Their lead guitarist was spending weekends in jail on a marijuana charge. "But he was due to be released at 6 P.M.," Girard recalled, "so we pulled it off."[2]

Calvary Chapel still occupies the same sprawling campus on the corner of Sunflower and Fairview in Santa Ana, California, and worshipers still mill about during the Sunday services. Some are inside the auditorium, and others sit in overflow rooms with large television screens. Still others lounge in the courtyard, occasionally checking their smartphones, or remain in their cars. Smith, now in his mid-eighties, had been recently diagnosed with lung cancer (he died a few days before I completed this Afterword). Although he continued as senior pastor, he ceded many responsibilities to his associate pastor, Brian Broderson, who delivered the sermon on the morning of my visit. "The word of God is the final authority," Broderson said in something very close to a monotone. "A disciple is someone who takes the word of God seriously." The woman next to me took copious notes.

With his shiny pate and decidedly un-hip demeanor, Chuck Smith represented a kind of anti-charisma to the hippies who flocked to Calvary Chapel in the early 1970s; they responded to his simple, straightforward, no-frills teaching. Broderson takes aversion to charisma to new extremes, but the church still draws the crowds, especially the younger generation. Hunter Smith, a tall, gangly teenager carrying a Bible, told me that he had been attending for a couple of years. "I like it," he said. "It provides fellowship with the Lord." The Winter 2013 issue of *Calvary Chapel Magazine* ran an article entitled "Break Free: Breakdancing Ministry Reaches Young People with the Gospel."

The morning of my return visit to Calvary Chapel, the real-estate section in the *Orange County Register* carried a piece about the demand for megachurches in southern California. Calvary Chapel in La Habra, one of the featured congregations, was looking for larger facilities to accommodate its growing numbers.[3] Calvary Chapel has replicated its success globally; over fifteen hundred congregations around the world claim to be members of the Calvary Chapel Association. But is the Calvary Chapel Association a denomination, similar to, say, the Evangelical Lutheran Church of America, the Presbyterian Church U.S.A., or the Southern Baptist Convention? The Calvary Chapel website insists that "Calvary Chapel is a non-denominational church movement," and the weekly bulletin distributed to worshipers says that it "is not a denominational church."

I was in Des Moines, Iowa, in June 1993 for the celebration of my parents' fortieth wedding anniversary when I received a telephone call from Daniel Matthews, rector of Trinity Church, Wall Street, in New York City. Matthews was head of a cable channel that offered free access to Protestant denominations. Calvary Chapel had applied to put its programming on the channel, and Matthews, knowing my interest in the movement, was calling to ask if the Calvary Chapel Association was a denomination. I quoted Smith, who in conversation with me a year or so earlier had insisted emphatically that Calvary Chapel was *not* a denomination. Just out of curiosity, I asked, what did Smith say? Matthews reported that Chuck Smith, apparently willing to recalibrate his assessment in light of the possibility of access to television, had told Matthews that the Calvary Chapel Association was indeed a denomination.

Between services at Calvary Chapel, I decided to embark on what I knew was a fool's errand. During my first visit to Calvary Chapel in 1987, Smith had refused to see me. I returned with a colleague several years later to write a scholarly article on Calvary Chapel. We waited in the receiving line after church and were able to ask a couple of questions, but once again he declined our request to schedule an interview, protesting that he didn't grant interviews. In the summer of 1991, however, when we came to southern California to film the documentary version of *Mine Eyes Have Seen the Glory*, Smith was available and gave us an extended interview.

On this Sunday, however, with no camera crew in tow, I knew I didn't have a, well, prayer. I stopped by the church office between services, explained my mission, and left a business card with my cell number. I'd be happy to come back any time later today, I said. Just have him give me a call.

The phone never rang.

I WAS UNABLE TO REVISIT all of the people and places I wrote about in earlier editions, but I do have intelligence on some.

In 1993 Multnomah School of the Bible, in Portland, Oregon, became Multnomah Bible College and Seminary. The school won accreditation from the Northwest Commission on Colleges and Universities in 2005 and took the name Multnomah University in 2008, thereby replicating in a few short years the evolutionary process of other Bible institutes—the same process that many of the founders of such schools believed would compromise their doc-trinal purity. Garry Friesen, one of my informants all those years ago, volunteered to be one of two faculty members cut from the Bible department; he headed to Rwanda to teach fulltime at the Africa College of Theology. Daniel Scalberg, whom I characterized as edgy by the standards of Multnomah because of his affinity for jazz, is now dean of the College of Arts and Sciences. When I asked him if the institutional changes at Multnomah had placed the school on a slippery slope toward liberalism, Scalberg said no, although he acknowledged that some of the school's fundamentalist allies had withdrawn their support. The Bible College at Multnomah is still there, although its enrollment has been declining in favor of degree programs in fields like counseling, business, and global develop-ment. Scalberg believes that Multnomah has moved away from the isolation so characteristic of fundamentalism and has largely shed what he called its "bunker mentality."[4]

While shooting the documentary in the early 1990s, the director and I entertained the possibility of a segment about Innocent Good House and Standing Rock Indian Reservation. When I called to explore the prospect, however, Edna Good House informed me that her husband, the rector of St. Luke's Episcopal Church in Fort Yates, North Dakota, had died.

I feared that St. Luke's had since fallen on hard times and might even have closed its doors, but that is not the case. In June 2012 the Niobrara Convocation, a more-or-less annual gathering of Episcopalians in the Dakotas, was held in Fort Yates. At the noonday prayers on June 15, Michael Smith, the Episcopal bishop of North Dakota, wearing an Indian feather headdress, together with other clergy processed at St. Luke's to a Lakota "calling song" performed by Cedric Good House: "I am coming from above, grandfather told me to come." With sage burning, the clergy encircled a barrel and removed a rolled-up buffalo skin painted with seventy-two pictographs of the life of Jesus as recorded in the Gospel of Luke. The Sioux call this a Winter Count, a way of telling a community's story and carrying on the oral tradition. "I declare this buffalo robe, as a sacred expression of this culture, be restored as it was used in former generations to give honor, that it may honor Jesus and make his story known in and through his people," the bishop said.[5]

Innocent Good House would have been proud.

In 2005, Michael Clancy, a reporter for the *Arizona Republic*, contacted me to say that Neal Frisby, the "Rainbow Prophet," had died. Clancy thought I would want to know, and he in turn wanted a quote. During a visit to Phoenix some years earlier, I had stopped by the Capstone Cathedral, near the corner of Tatum and Shea, for a Sunday evening service. Brother Frisby was not present; I assumed that he was in a back room somewhere working on another of his prophetic scrolls.

A couple of months before his death, the reclusive Frisby deeded the Capstone Cathedral and surrounding property, which included Frisby's home, to Robert Brooks, a former player for the Green Bay Packers. Brooks had experienced a vision that he would one day preach at the Capstone Cathedral. Years later, Brooks met one of Frisby's sons, who then arranged a meeting with the Rainbow Prophet himself; Frisby in turn had a dream in which he was told to turn the property over to Brooks. Following Frisby's death, the football player-turned-preacher tore down Frisby's home—there's some

dispute about whether the Rainbow Prophet had wanted it razed—
and renamed Capstone Cathedral the Capstone Center; the odd,
pyramid-shaped building now serves as headquarters for Brooks's
ministries.[6]

One of the most riveting segments of the *Mine Eyes Have Seen the
Glory* documentary, in my opinion, is the bit on Word of Life Camp,
the place I wrote about in the "Adirondack Fundamentalism" chapter. (I've received more mail about that chapter over the years than
anything else I've ever written.) Jack Wyrtzen, the camp's founder,
who died in 1996, was warm and welcoming when we showed up for
filming, although he wondered why I hadn't spent more time talking
with him during my initial visit. I've since forged a friendship with
his son, Don Wyrtzen, and Jack Wyrtzen's delightful grandson Josh
was a student in several of my courses when I was a visiting professor at Yale Divinity School.

I revisited Camp Freedom in April 2011 while I was in town to
do some lectures for the Columbia alumni/ae association. The imposing white sign on Fifty-fourth Avenue North still advertises You
ARE WELCOME! and DELIVERANCE FROM SIN IN CHRIST, just as it did
in 1988, but now a smaller sign warns PRIVATE PROPERTY...TRES-
PASS PROHIBITED. Go figure. It was off-season for camp meetings,
and so I saw no signs of life other than a couple of salamanders that
skittered away as I walked past.

I've thought many times over the years about "Roger," the tor-
mented gay man I met at Camp Freedom. I identified him as in
his late sixties then, and I suspect he is now deceased. Attitudes
toward homosexuality have shifted dramatically over the past several decades, even (though to a lesser degree) among evangelicals.
The topic itself was still considered a bit edgy in the late 1980s; I
remember that when I submitted the book manuscript, I called my
editor's attention to the passage about Roger and wondered if she
wanted me to cut it. Happily, she didn't.

I'd like to think that Roger found some peace about himself, that
the self-loathing so evident in our conversation had abated, even if

only a little. The chapter concluded with Roger's observation that "one little sin may keep you out of heaven." I'm not well connected enough to know where Roger is now, but somehow I doubt that he found much surcease for his pain among the folks at Camp Freedom.

ON JUNE 24, 2012, A SMALL GROUP of people gathered in a newly completed building in Lincoln, Oregon, for the dedication of the Harry Evans Prayer Chapel. The central space is circular, constructed of blue pine, with a bank of windows providing a lovely and tranquil view of the woods. The ceiling arches gently, gracefully toward a large, circular skylight, and the room is bathed in a lambent glow. Directly beneath the skylight, a low table, the cross-section of a large tree, its concentric rings recording the passage of time, serves as a communion table when the occasion warrants. The chapel was designed by Phil Kling, an alumnus of the Oregon Extension who, along with his wife, Alison, an alumna, has lived and worked there for a couple of decades now. Kling, together with Sam Alvord and a succession of volunteers, hewed and sawed and mitered and crafted the wood into a lovely, contemplative space.

Harry Evans, for whom the chapel is named, was there. Evans, long retired, was president of Trinity College and Trinity Evangelical Divinity School in the 1970s, and it was during his watch that the Oregon Extension came into being. The OE, as it is affectionately known to the scores of students who have passed through Lincoln, has been a place where young, intellectually restless evangelicals have come to study, walk in the woods, and consider their faith—or, at times, their lack of it.

The dedication of the Evans Chapel came at a transitional moment for the Oregon Extension. Several years earlier, Alvord had decided to retire from teaching at the OE, although he and his wife, Pat, still live on the property; Sam works full time as an administrator for the Pinehurst School District, with offices a few steps down Greensprings Highway from the OE. When Alvord stepped aside, other faculty looked at the dates on their Medicare cards and decided it was time to consider the future of the Oregon Extension.

After much discussion—apparently, *very much* discussion—the faculty, who jointly held title to the residential portion of the property, decided to sell the OE to a group of former students. Two discrete groups had made bids, and the choice of one (a group financed by the inventor of Clif Bars) over the other engendered some tension among the retiring faculty.

Douglas Frank and I found a few minutes early on Sunday morning. We grabbed coffee in the cookhouse and settled into a corner of the library. In addition to the chapel dedication later that day, Doug and his wife, Marj, were packing up their belongings in preparation for a move down the mountain to Ashland the following day. Frank was ambivalent at best about leaving the place where for the past thirty-seven autumns he had invested himself, heart and soul, in the lives of the thirty or so students who came to study at the Oregon Extension. "I'm not exactly sure what I'm going to do with myself," he said.

Not surprisingly, at this transitional moment his own mortality was weighing heavily, but his comment caught me off guard. Invoking one of Frank's favorite books from years past, *Escape from Evil,* by Ernest Becker, I tried feebly to assure him that his legacy endures in the students whose lives he had touched over the years, but the bromide sounded tinny and inadequate even to my ears. Do you still consider yourself an evangelical, I asked. He looked briefly over his shoulder and out the window, sighed heavily, and turned back. "No," he said. "Not in anything but a metaphorical sense." He'd seen too much over the years, he added, kids emotionally battered and broken over their attempts to live the godly lives that their parents—and the entire subculture—expected of them. Too often the God of evangelicalism, Frank had concluded some time ago, was demanding and punitive, even vindictive, and until evangelicals caught sight of Jesus, in all of his humanity, younger evangelicals—many of them, at least—would succumb to despair.

Thomas Kinkade, the "Painter of Light," died on April 6, 2012. Good Friday. The cause of death was an overdose of alcohol and Valium. In 2010 Kinkade had separated from his wife, Nanette, in whose honor he had embedded "N"s in his paintings. Rumors of misconduct had been trailing Kinkade for several years: drunkenness, public urination, groping a woman's breasts at an event in one of his galleries. In 2010 he was arrested in Carmel, California, and convicted of driving under the influence of alcohol. When he died, he was living with his girlfriend, Amy Pinto, who told the press that Kinkade "died in his sleep, very happy, in the house he built, with the paintings he loved and the woman he loved."

Nanette, traveling in Australia with the couple's daughters, didn't exactly care for Pinto's characterization. She sought a restraining order (doubtless in part to protect business interests) to prevent Pinto from releasing any photographs or information that "would be personally devastating" to Kinkade's wife. A probate battle ensued—Kinkade had handwritten a couple of wills that gave Pinto some of his estate—but the matter was settled out of court.

While I interviewed Kinkade in his studio in Monte Sereno, California, in 2000, the artist asked me to write his biography, promising that I would sell millions of copies. I demurred. But the book would have had a helluva conclusion.

Another Californian has fared better, although his family too was touched by tragedy. Rick Warren, pastor of Saddleback Church, held a presidential candidates' forum on August 16, 2008. Barack Obama, the Democratic nominee, and John McCain, his Republican opponent, appeared sequentially at Saddleback, and Warren quizzed them about various issues, including abortion and the composition of the Supreme Court. Following Obama's historic election, Warren was invited to give the invocation at the inauguration on January 20, 2009.

Shortly before the 2008 election, Warren had endorsed a ballot initiative, Proposition 8, that aimed to reverse the California Supreme Court's ruling that allowed same-sex marriage. Many people, including me, were disappointed. Citing the Baptist tradition (Saddleback is part of the Southern Baptist Convention), I called on Warren to reconsider. "Warren and all people of faith have every right to hold to their religious views about homosexuality," I wrote for Huffington Post. "But to insist that those standards must be observed by everyone in a pluralistic society is—well, it's not Baptist. Rick Warren knows better." Appearing on CNN the following April, Warren seemed to deny that he had endorsed Proposition 8. "I am not an anti-gay or anti-gay marriage activist," he told Larry King. "Never have been, never will be."

Tragedy struck the Warren household in April 2013 with the suicide of their youngest son, Matthew, twenty-seven years old. The Warrens received an outpouring of sympathy but, sadly, some of Rick Warren's critics used the occasion to gloat. "Grieving is hard," Warren said. "Grieving as public figures, harder. Grieving while haters celebrate your pain, hardest." Several months later, while I was changing planes in Atlanta, I caught a snippet of a television interview with Warren and his wife, Kay. Both were still clearly distraught over their loss, although Kay's responses struck me somehow as more visceral, more honest. Rick Warren told the interviewer that he had repeatedly assured Matthew, in the midst of his son's despair, that there was "a purpose to our pain," and part of Warren's strategy for dealing with his own grief was to encapsulate the stages into one of his schemes: shock, surrender, sanctification.

I WAS, I CONFESS, a tad hesitant about visiting Stan White in Valdosta, Georgia. Easter Sunday evening, 1990, was still fresh in my mind—the music, the enthusiasm, the air of expectation as more than two hundred pentecostal congregants were received into the Episcopal Church, queuing up before five bishops. By the close of the service, everyone—everyone—was exhausted. Stan White was still a postulant then, not yet ordained an Episcopal priest, but he articulated eloquently the case for evangelical and pentecostal fervor within the rubric of the *Book of Common Prayer* and the historical rootedness of the Episcopal Church.

Why was I hesitant? I was afraid, frankly, that the journey from Assemblies of God to Episcopal Church might have been a bridge too far, that pressures from within and without might have triggered a conservative backlash. I knew that the congregation's name had changed from Church of the King to Christ the King, but that was a minor matter. The Episcopal Church has been buffeted over the past decade by controversies over homosexuality and the consecration of an openly gay bishop. Many congregations chose to abandon the Church for one or another schismatic group, and I feared that Christ the King might have jumped ship.

I couldn't have been more wrong.

When I caught up with Stan White at Christ the King, our conversation turned almost immediately to that Easter evening in 1990. "It's pretty hard to sustain something like that," he said. His smile was almost wistful. "We've gone through some changes," he added. "But we're in a good place."[7]

Their physical place has changed. About a decade ago, as the parishioners of Christ the King were contemplating a move from the boat showroom they had adapted for worship, they briefly considered buying property and constructing a building. They concluded, however, that a better use of resources, both financial and natural, would be to purchase a four-story building in downtown Valdosta, just across the street from the Lowndes County courthouse. The move was transformative, both for the parish and for downtown itself. The bottom floor, called Hildegard's, functions as a parish hall, complete with a glassed-in chapel with windows opening to the street. Hildegard's (named for Hildegard of Bingen, a medieval mystic) was also a coffee house, bookstore, and improvisational theater; earlier during the weekend of my visit, the parish had mounted a performance of *The Laramie Project*. Hildegard's quickly became a hive of activity, drawing students from nearby Valdosta State University and luring suburbanites downtown. The parish organized art walks, shops and restaurants moved in, and the tax base increased substantially with the sale and refurbishing of nearby buildings.

A county official, however, took it upon himself to close down the coffee house. (White suspects it has something to do with observing pierced and tattooed college students working behind the counter.) But clearly Christ the King has exerted a salutary influence in downtown Valdosta.

The Sunday worship opened with "Morning Has Broken," accompanied by organ, trumpet, drums, guitar, bass, and piano. The enthusiasm was a bit more muted than what I recalled, but no less affecting. The space is warm, with hardwood floors, warehouse-style light fixtures, and a brick wall behind the altar flanked by shutters. White's sermon touched on several themes, including the biblical notion of jubilee, the year after the seventh cycle of sabbatical years when debts are forgiven and servants freed. "I'm not sure there's any other gospel," White said. "That's the one we're authorized to preach."

During the announcements, White welcomed another gay couple as new members of Christ the King. The congregation ranged from suburban matrons and businessmen to college students and elderly folks, some of whom I recognized from my visit long ago. Stan White's parents, Ann and James (Jimmy) are still active parishioners. "We're just enjoying the ride," Jimmy White, former pastor of Evangel Assembly of God, said. "We just love this church," Ann added. "Every step was directed by the Lord." Bob Elder and his wife, Linda, are relative newcomers. "We didn't think we'd find a place like this in Valdosta," he said.

Stan White told me later that one of the challenges of ministry in a place like Valdosta, a mid-size city, was turnover. When people get promoted, he said, they move on to places like Atlanta and Jacksonville. In addition, the ranks of leadership in the parish had been depleted by the large number of priests—fifteen or sixteen, by his count—who had been ordained from the parish and who now serve parishes elsewhere. At times during our conversation, I sensed a weariness in White's voice. It's impossible to sustain a high level of religious fervor over a long stretch, he said, and the day-to-day responsibilities of being a rector take a toll. "I think being a parish priest is really quite monastic in many ways."

What I did not know until my return to Valdosta was that my chapter all those years ago had sparked a flurry of interest in White and his congregation. He received letters and fielded phone calls both from pentecostals and from evangelical Episcopalians around the country. The head of one "renewal" group, for example, flew to Valdosta, promised to set White on a fast track to becoming bishop, and then promptly ran through a checklist to be certain that White was up to code on a range of theological and ideological matters. Biblical inerrancy, right? And then a litany of Religious Right political issues. White protested: "I became an Episcopalian in part to move away from such litmus tests."

And how comfortable is White with the label *evangelical* these days? "I would consider myself an evangelical," he said, "because I really love Jesus." He regularly preaches strong repentance sermons, and many of them culminate in altar calls. "I have a real appreciation for Holy Scripture, though not in the literalistic sense of my Baptist colleagues," he said. "I think we need to let it breathe." White paused and looked out the window. "The power of preaching the word is what keeps Christ the King alive," he added. "We have the experiential element, but the preaching promotes substance."

I MET DONALD THOMPSON for a Sunday morning breakfast in Des Moines, Iowa, forty years after the release of *A Thief in the Night*, his signature motion picture that scared the bejesus out of a generation of evangelical adolescents. My former Sunday school teacher handed me a book, *My Friend Jesus, Me and the Movies*, billed as "a biography of Donald W. Thompson as written by J. Howard Sloan." He paused. "I think you're in this book," Thompson said uncertainly.[8]

The book is studded with exclamations like "God is so awesome" and "there is no such thing as a coincidence."[9] The narrative strings together many anecdotes from Thompson's varied and illustrious career—stock-car driver, actor, radio personality, filmmaker—many of which I had heard before, some of them several times. But it also records his bouts with depression, which became so severe that he received shock treatments some years back. I had seen him during what was likely the manic phase that preceded his slide into depression and was dimly aware of some rumors to the effect that he had been hospitalized. Still, it had been several years since I'd seen Thompson or even been in contact. Some time ago, he'd invited me to write his biography, and I considered the possibility, but I concluded that the portrait I'd written for *Mine Eyes Have Seen the Glory* was probably as far as I wanted to go.

Over breakfast, Thompson seemed slightly less ebullient than I'd remembered him from encounters over the years; I couldn't decide at the time if it was simply his age (seventy-five) or the rumored shock treatments. Still, he is clearly a person of considerable energy, especially when he slips into his raconteur persona, although some of the dates and stories have begun to blur. He still punctuates his speech with declarations like "the Lord is good" and "I'm so grateful to Him for opening doors and closing doors." He recounts conversations with Jesus as casually as some people would recall an exchange with a real-estate agent or a clerk in the grocery store. "Jesus, what do you want me to do?" To which the Lord replies, "I want you to quit your job." In another exchange, the Almighty entertained Thompson's preferences for a new automobile: "Lord, I sure would like to have that Eldorado."

Although any conversation with Don Thompson is an exercise in free association, pin-balling from topic to topic, I learned that he no longer attends Westchester Evangelical Free Church, the congregation my father led from 1968 until 1979, because the current pastor "preaches a political agenda." As a member of Westchester in the 1970s, Thompson had forged friendships with many of the people who helped him produce *A Thief in the Night*, which *Time* magazine once described as a "church-basement classic." Some of the church members invested financially in the shoestring production, others helped logistically with production and distribution, and a few appeared as actors or extras in the film. In the course of writing the script and planning the production, Thompson frequently stopped by the pastor's study to seek counsel and encouragement from my father, who played the "good" preacher in *A Thief in the Night*. Thompson, in fact, credits my father with inspiring the idea. After hearing one of my father's many sermons about the "end times," Thompson vowed, "I'm going to make a movie about that." With evident sincerity, he described my father as "such a good pastor and a good friend."

Despite his protestations to the contrary, Thompson remains bitter about Mark IV Productions, the entity that produced that film and several others and which owns all the rights. I don't pretend to know the entire story, but Thompson claims that his erstwhile partner, Russell Doughten, unfairly, perhaps illegally, forced him out. "That company is worth millions, and I got nothing," Thompson told me. "Not a nickel." I'd heard variations of this account many, many times, but they were invariably followed by a declaration of forgiveness. This time, pointing to the book, Thompson said, "I don't say anything about Russ because I've forgiven him." Later in the conversation, Thompson pointed in the direction of the Mark IV offices, just a few blocks away. "They are so into money over there," he said, referring to Doughten, and added, with no apparent sympathy, "After he screwed me, his house burned down."

Still, Thompson says he derives satisfaction from the fact that "three hundred people a day come to Christ" through seeing his films, many from viewing them online. "It just breaks my heart to know that there are people who don't know Christ," he said.

As we headed to the parking lot, I asked casually if he still lived on Shawnee Place, a question that triggered another free association. "I had this thing one day where the Lord told me to go next door and tell my neighbors about Christ," he said. "One guy just laughed at me, and the other got so mad. He still won't talk to me. I guess he thinks I'm one of those religious nuts."

Thompson paused and headed for his car. He turned back, and a big grin suddenly enveloped his face. "When the tribulation comes," Thompson said about his neighbor, "he'll be singing a different tune."

HAVING TRACKED SOME OF THE CHANGES in the people and places I wrote about over the past twenty-five years, I would be disingenuous if I didn't say something about some of the changes in *me* over the same interval. The writing of *Mine Eyes Have Seen the Glory* evoked many sweet and powerful memories from my childhood, and the depiction of American evangelicalism that emerged in the book was—overall, I think—an appreciative, soft-focus portrait. That's not to say that my assessments were universally positive. Not at all. Evangelicalism is, as I tried to demonstrate, a vast and internally diverse movement, and those searching for either heroes or villains will find representatives of both species. But the general tenor of the book—and most readers agreed—was warm, at times elegiac.

My attitudes toward evangelicalism are considerably more complicated today than they were in 1989, and they were plenty complicated even then. A part of me desperately wants to cling to my evangelical identity—out of loyalty to friends and family, especially to the memory of my father, who was an evangelical minister for forty years until his death in 1997. When I construct a case for remaining in the movement, I generally summon the folks in Mississippi or Valdosta or friends like Tony Campolo and Jim Wallis, who encourage me not to succumb to despair about the state and the future of evangelicalism.

But, much as I admire their tenacity, there is reason for despair. The biggest change in evangelicalism over the last twenty-five years, in my view, is that so much of evangelicalism has become coarse and vitriolic. I abhor the political agenda now commonly associated with evangelicalism: the warmongering, the indifference toward God's creation, the callousness toward those Jesus called "the least of these." The glass-is-half-full evangelicals claim, with some justification, that those attitudes are changing, especially as a younger generation moves into positions of leadership and as Latino evangelicals find their political voice. But the fact remains that many, perhaps most, evangelicals over the past several decades registered no dissent when their leaders denigrated women or minorities, demonized gays and lesbians, or supported reckless military engagement that wouldn't meet even generous interpretations of just war criteria. Such positions, in my view, utterly disregard the teachings of Jesus; they also default on what I consider the noble legacy of nineteenth- and early twentieth-century evangelicalism, which invariably took the part of those on the margins of society.

The conviction that inspired this book was a belief in the goodness and integrity of ordinary, grassroots evangelicals, and here is where I pin my hopes for the future. Having tired of the media portrayals of evangelicals during the televangelist scandals back in the 1980s—they seemed to assume that all evangelicals were the moral equivalent of Jim Bakker, Jimmy Swaggart, and Jerry Falwell—I wanted to depict the real character of evangelicalism at the grass roots. Twenty-five years later, my slim confidence in evangelical leaders is, if anything, even more diminished, especially because of their misbegotten politics. Reclaiming the prophetic voice of American evangelicalism will require more than a little exertion, especially in the absence of responsible leadership, but the prospect of evangelicals energized once again by the gospel and inspired by the benevolent impulses of nineteenth-century evangelicalism would be (to use one of evangelicals' favorite words) awesome.

Evangelical worship could use some refurbishing, too, though I acknowledge that, in part at least, is a matter of taste. As I noted in the new chapter, virtually every evangelical gathering opens these days with what evangelicals call "praise music." Many people love it—obviously—but I've encountered it often enough, in venues as varied as Santa Fe, New Mexico, and Evart, Michigan, to see it as contrived and formulaic. I guess I'm too much a traditionalist. Well, yes, I am a traditionalist; I might as well confess to that. And I've also become a sacramentalist. I believe that a central element of worship—*the* central element of worship—is not the sermon or praise music but the Eucharist, where we gather in the communion of the saints to meet Jesus himself in the bread and wine of Holy Communion.

Most evangelicals, however, have little patience for the sacraments. Most take a "memorialist" view of Holy Communion—the bread and wine of the Lord's Supper merely *remind* us of the death of Jesus—and so many evangelical churches observe Holy Communion only once a month or even once a quarter. And most places use *grape juice* rather than wine, a hangover from the Temperance Movement in the nineteenth century. (When I visited Sarah Palin's church in Wasilla, Alaska, on a communion Sunday, the deacon's wives distributed the bread of Holy Communion wearing the plastic gloves worn by workers in fast-food restaurants.) If you believe, as I do, that we meet Jesus himself at the Lord's Table, then what passes for evangelical worship is impoverished by the absence of a robust sacramental theology.

THROUGHOUT AMERICAN HISTORY, evangelicalism has flourished because of its uncanny ability to speak the idiom of the culture, from the open-air preaching of George Whitefield and other itinerants in the eighteenth century, the camp meetings and colporteurs of the nineteenth century, to the stadium crusades and suburban megachurches in the twentieth century. Although it is still far too early to ascertain the shape of evangelicalism in the twenty-first century—and I'm a historian, not a prognosticator—I feel confident in predicting that evangelicalism, America's folk religion, will outlast the twenty-first century in some form or another.

The relationship between evangelicalism and popular culture, however, is more fraught than it appears. It's not a matter simply of evangelicals appropriating mass media or the internet or coffee houses or breakdancing in order to propagate the gospel. In many ways, the link between evangelicals and the culture resembles an intricate dance. Sidelined by my fundamentalist scruples, reduced to the status of observer, I don't a whole lot about dancing, but I do know that one partner typically leads and the other follows. The analogy here is that, at various points in American history, evangelicals have led the dance with culture, especially in the antebellum period and for much of the nineteenth century when evangelicals set about to reform society and devised extraordinarily creative and energetic ways to address the plight of those on the margins. In recent decades, however, evangelicals have ceded that lead to a culture shifting decidedly toward the political right—and they were pulled along.

The sad consequence is a diminution of the gospel, a departure from the capacious words of Jesus, who invited all who labor and are heavy laden to come and find comfort. Any movement preoccupied with judgment and excoriation will begrudge grace, and without grace, at least as I read the New Testament, there is no gospel, no "good news." In the words of the apostle, without love, we are only a "resounding gong or a clanging cymbal."[10]

Will evangelicalism ever extricate itself from the mire of reactionary politics and once again reclaim its prophetic voice? To do so, evangelicals must reconsider the words of Jesus and reappropriate the agenda of evangelicals who have gone before, including their calls for economic justice, peace, and equality, especially for women and minorities. In other words, recovering an evangelical prophetic voice would entail once again assuming the lead in the dance with culture.

No easy task, but that would be a dance worth watching.

Notes

A Word about Words

1. *Oxford English Dictionary* (1971), s.v. "Evangelical."

2. Quoted in Hugh T. Kerr and John M. Mulder, eds., *Conversions* (Grand Rapids: Wm. B. Eerdmans, 1983), p. 59.

3. I'd like to add here a parenthetical note about pronunciation. Almost everywhere I traveled, evangelicals pronounced the word *evangelical* with a short *"e"* (the first two syllables rhyme with "leaven" or, perhaps more appropriately, "heaven"). Almost all the people I encountered who could *not* be described as evangelicals pronounced the first syllable with a long *"e"* (*ee*-van-gel-i-cal; similar to the way Britons pronounce *economic*).

Chapter 1: California Kickback

1. Everyone is casual here. I sat in on a seventh-grade algebra class at Maranatha Christian Academy (Calvary Chapel's grammar school), where the students addressed their teacher, a man in his late thirties, as "Randy."

2. Singing is an important element in the worship at Calvary Chapel; every service or meeting I attended during my visit opened with a long period of congregational singing.

3. Estimates vary. One pastor quoted the figure at twenty thousand. A 1979 article in the *Los Angeles Times* put the number at twenty-five thousand; see Russell Chandler, "Cleric Finds Success Serving Hippie Needs," *Los Angeles Times*, July 5, 1979, pt. 2, pp. 1, 8.

4. Other examples: Robert Schuller's Crystal Cathedral in Garden grove, Vineyard Christian Fellowship in Anaheim, headed by John Wimber, and the First Evangelical Free Church in Fullerton, led by Chuck Swindoll.

5. Chuck Smith, *The History of Calvary Chapel* (Costa Mesa, Calif.: Word for Today, 1981), p. 3.

6. Ibid., p. 6. For a description of Calvary Chapel in its early years, see Ronald M. Enroth, Edward E. Ericson, Jr., and C. Breckinridge Peter, *The Jesus People: Old-Time Religion in the Age of Aquarius* (Grand Rapids: Wm. B. Eerdmans, 1972), ch. 4.

7. Oden Fong, interview, May 11, 1987.

8. L. E. Romaine, interview, May 11, 1987.

9. Fong interview.

10. Smith, *History of Calvary Chapel*, pp. 9–10.

11. Quoted in Richard Dalrymple, "Beach Baptism Helps Save the Young," *Los Angeles Herald-Examiner*, October 24, 1970, p. A–7.

12. Romaine interview.

13. See Acts 2.

14. These, I recognize, are generalizations. Pentecostals will protest that doctrine and theology are indeed quite important to them, while fundamentalists will insist that they value religious affections.

15. This is a reference to Isa. 55:11.

Chapter 2: Dallas Orthodoxy

1. Dallas Seminary's statement of purpose reads in part: "The Seminary is committed to the primacy of the authoritative, inerrant Scriptures. Its instruction, which includes teaching, defending, and applying the truths of the Christian faith, is given within the framework of evangelical, premillennial, dispensational theology."

2. Quoted in William G. McLoughlin, ed., *The American Evangelicals, 1800–1900: An Anthology* (New York: Harper & Row, 1968), p. 184.

3. Grace Union Presbytery, "Position Paper on Employment of Seminary Students" and "Policy Regarding Reception of Ministers." I am grateful to Carrie Washington, executive presbyter of the Presbytery of Newark and a former resident of Texas, for pointing this out to me.

4. John D. Hannah, "The Early Years of Lewis Sperry Chafer," *Bibliotheca Sacra* 144 (January–March 1987): 21, 22.

5. Records are incomplete, but Donald Kraus, Bibles editor at Oxford University Press, estimates that the press has sold anywhere from thirty to fifty million copies since 1909. According to Jonathan Weiss, sales manager at Oxford, the Scofield Bible has sold more than 4.2 million copies since 1967, 85 percent of them leatherbound editions, an indication of the Scofield Bible's continued popularity as a devotional tool.

6. Quoted in John A. Witmer, "'What God Hath Wrought'—Fifty Years of Dallas Theological Seminary, Part I: God's Man and His Dream," *Bibliotheca Sacra* 130 (October 1973): 295.

7. Whitmer, "'What God Hath Wrought,'" p. 292.

8. The divinity degree awarded at Dallas is the Master of Theology (Th.M.), the requirements for which include writing a thesis. Most seminaries offer the Master of Divinity (M.Div.) as their basic divinity degree and the Th.M. after another year of specialized study.

9. Henry Bettenson, ed., *Documents of the Christian Church* (New York: Oxford University Press, 1947), p. 165.

10. James H. Thames, ed., *Dallas Theological Seminary: 1986–87 Catalog* (Dallas: Dallas Theological Seminary, 1986), p. 161.

11. Charles C. Ryrie, "What Is Dispensationalism?" rev. ed. (Dallas: Dallas Theological Seminary, 1986), [p. 5].

12. Norman Geisler, interview, April 1, 1987.

13. Several months after my visit, Dallas Theological Seminary dismissed three members of the faculty because of their apparent sympathies with charismatic theology; see Randy Frame, "Three Professors Part Paths with Dallas," *Christianity Today*, February 5, 1988, pp. 52–53.

14. Although he breezily dismissed the woman's query, Pentecost readily fielded questions from male students. Later in the lecture, seeking to illustrate the meaning of the term *leaven*, Pentecost asked: "Any of you girls bake bread?"

15. Typically, the biblical references cited against the ordination of women are 1 Tim. 2:11–12 and 1 Cor. 14:34. Those in favor of women's ordination point to Gal. 3:28, where Paul insists that in Christ there is "neither Jew nor Greek, there is neither slave nor free, there is neither male nor female; for you are all one in Christ Jesus" (RSV). Pentecost's reference to "ask their husbands at home" comes from 1 Cor. 14:35 (RSV).

16. Roy B. Zuck, academic dean at Dallas, interview, April 2, 1987; Ari L. Goldman, "As Call Comes, More Women Answer," *New York Times*, October 19, 1986.

17. Barbara A. Peil, "A Seasoned Approach," *Kindred Spirit* 11 (Spring 1987): 12, 13.

18. Geisler interview.

19. Herb Bateman and Jimmy Carter, interview, April 3, 1987.

Chapter 3: On Location

1. Nick Lamberto, "Frail Heart Tom by Blow, Boy Needs Transplant," *Des Moines Register*, September 26, 1986, p. A1; idem, "Boy's Final Plea: 'Please Don't Let Me Die,'" ibid., September 27, 1986, p. A1.

2. "I Wish We'd All Been Ready," words and music by Larry Norman © 1969, 1971 Beechwood Music Corp. and J. C. Love Publishing Co. All rights administered by Beechwood Music Corp. Used by permission.

3. Mark 13:32. (KJV). The final message on the screen reads: "The End…is near!"

4. Harry Bristow, June 24, 1983, in International Cinema Artists Corporation booklet; idem, telephone conversation.

5. Jack Thompson, telephone conversation, January 12, 1987; James L. Berry, interview, September 12, 1986.

6. James Manilla, "Making Miracles in the Heartland," *Industrial Photography* (April 1986): 20, 53.

Chapter 4: Phoenix Prophet

1. This account derives from impressions gathered over the course of several meetings during the February 1987 crusade.

2. On the design of the Capstone Cathedral, see "Glass-Dome Capstone Believed Largest Phoenix Church," *Arizona Republic*, February 21, 1971; Henry Fuller, "Capstone Cathedral Rises from the Desert," *Arizona Republic*, July 11, 1971.

3. W. V. Grant, *Creative Miracles* (Dallas: Faith Clinic, n.d.), pp. 17, 18. This booklet, purportedly written by W. V. Grant, a fellow evangelist, actually consists of three chapters: the first is a kind of introduction by Grant; chapters 2 and 3 are first-person, autobiographical narratives by Frisby.

4. Frisby's unusual theology has prompted David Edwin Harrell, Jr., to dub him the "most bizarre prophet of the 1970s" (*All Things Are Possible: The Healing and Charismatic Revivals in Modern America* [Bloomington: Indiana University Press, 1975], p. 221).

5. Neal Frisby, *The Revelation of the Written Scrolls and the Word of God as Given to Neal Vincent Frisby* (Phoenix: n.p., n.d.), pp. 183–84. Frisby also refers to the building as the Lord's "holy Temple" (p. 210).

6. See Fuller, "Capstone Cathedral Rises from the Desert."

7. Frisby clearly believes we are living in the seventh age, but although this idea of church ages is a tenet of dispensational theology, I ran across no reference to the term *dispensation* in his writings.

8. Frisby claims to have seen visions of Branham's death in advance; see Frisby, *Revelation of the Written Scrolls*, p. 54. Regarding Paul as the first messenger, see *Revelation of the Written Scrolls*, p. 111. On William Branham, see Harrell, *All Things Are Possible*, pp. 159–65; C. Douglas Weaver, *The Healer-Prophet, William Marrion Branham: A Study of the Prophetic in American Pentecostalism* (Macon, Ga.: Mercer University Press, 1987).

9. Frisby, *Revelation of the Written Scrolls.*, p. 149; cf. p. 191. Frisby often stops just short of making this claim explicitly, but it is surely implied in his writings. See, for example, *Revelation of the Written Scrolls*, p. 127. He also uses his birthdate (in logic I cannot decipher) to confirm this; see *Revelation of the Written Scrolls*, p. 134. At the conclusion of Scroll 57, Frisby responds to queries about the identity of various prophets mentioned in previous scrolls. He says, "The last one mentioned is the writer of scrolls" (p. 189).

10. Frisby, *Revelation of the Written Scrolls*, pp. 111, 173. For further significance of the rainbow motif, see *Revelation of the Written Scrolls*, p. 169.

11. Frisby, *Revelation of the Written Scrolls*, p. 183; see also p. 194.

12. Grant, *Creative Miracles*, pp. 10, 21, 11, 23.

13. Frisby, *Revelation of the Written Scrolls*, pp. 12, 26.

14. Frisby, *Revelation of the Written Scrolls*, p. 133. It has always intrigued me that God speaks seventeenth-century English.

15. Grant, *Creative Miracles*, pp. 18, 19. *Shekinah* means divine presence.

16. Frisby, *Revelation of the Written Scrolls*, p. 83.

17. Frisby, *Revelation of the Written Scrolls*, pp. 5, 89. Even the compilation of the scrolls has significance: "The Lord shows Bro. Frisby the hour has arrived to put the Scrolls in Book Form to reveal to his special partners and Crusade friends

some remarkable prophecy visions God gave him personally of the future of the world!" (p. 7). Later, he writes: "The significance of what I have been writing is a final message to the Bride [Church]-and pronouncing judgment on the nation" (p. 158).

18. Rev. 8:1; 10:1–11 (RSV).

19. Frisby, *Revelation of the Written Scrolls*, p. 152; Frisby uses the designations "Rainbow Prophet" and "Rainbow Angel" interchangeably and says that the Rainbow Angel "will be transformed into a prophet" (p. 168). The designation "mighty rainbow cap angel" occurs on p. 227.

20. Frisby, *Revelation of the Written Scrolls*, pp. 110, 111, 149 Frisby, a diffident man, is careful to shrug off any divine infallibility, even as he professes to speak the mind of God: "I want to make this plain, I am no special person because I am used in writing the scrolls. But Jesus is the special one" (p. 112). Regarding the dollar bill, Frisby holds that God "put all this on a dollar instead of a 20 or 100 dollar bill, being (one) would be seen or handled more as a greater witness! Also the USA currency is in almost every nation witnessing this very thing" (pp. 149–50). I am quoting Frisby verbatim throughout, including his erratic spellings and syntax.

21. He writes: "The U.S.A., Israel and England will go through great tribulation for being involved with Babylon (Catholics) at the end" (Frisby, *Revelation of the Written Scrolls*, p. 59). During one meeting he charged that music videos provided "a wellrounded Satanic education."

22. Frisby, *Revelation of the Written Scrolls*, pp. 55, 56.

23. Frisby, *Revelation of the Written Scrolls*, p. 69.

24. Frisby, *Revelation of the Written Scrolls*, pp. 73, 75, 92, 95, 106, 148. Of Reagan, Frisby wrote that "Ronald Reagan could cause an upset for the presidency" (p. 87). The scrolls in the printed collection are undated, but this one also included prophecies for the late 1960s and early 1970s. Frisby later altered his prediction for atomic destruction and spoke of the neutron bomb (p. 155).

25. Frisby, *Revelation of the Written Scrolls*, p. 146.

26. Rev. 21:1 (RSV). On the exclusiveness of the elect, Frisby says, "The world will have to except the 'Capstone Ministry' of the last message or they will have to except the brimstone message of the lake of fire!" But later in the same paragraph he hedges: "I am not saying this will be the only work of God, but it is an Elect major work of His!" (Frisby, *Revelation of the Written Scrolls*, p. 161).

27. Frisby, *Revelation of the Written Scrolls*, p. 137. At times Frisby seems to equate Armageddon with some sort of atomic destruction; see *Revelations of the Written Scrolls*, p. 141.

28. Frisby, *Revelation of the Written Scrolls*, pp. 78, 108, 131. Elsewhere, he writes: "According to Gods true time it would almost seem impossible for the world to continue after 1986" (p. 137).

29. Frisby, *Revelation of the Written Scrolls*, pp. 162, 113, 66, 67. Frisby concluded this section: "And I, Neal, understood and wrote these things and worshipped Him who is the beginning and the end, standing beside me. Amen" (p. 68).

30. Frisby, *Revelation of the Written Scrolls*, p. 63.

31. Frisby, *Revelation of the Written Scrolls*, pp. 105, 159, 215, 217–18. Frisby devotes an entire scroll (no. 68) to the importance of numbers; *Revelation of the Written Scrolls*, pp. 226–28.

32. Frisby, *Revelation of the Written Scrolls*, p. 203.

33. Frisby, *Revelation of the Written Scrolls*, pp. 221, 234–35.

34. Frisby, *Revelation of the Written Scrolls*, p. 205. He writes: "The Temple here is just full of the power of God, a thick presence is in it! There is only one life to live, and everyone should see Capstone before His return. We want all to come and be healed, no disease can stand here. When a person lines up with the Headstone, diseases and devils fall like the lightning!"

35. Frisby, *Revelation of the Written Scrolls*, p. 145.

36. Frisby, *Revelation of the Written Scrolls*, p. 155.

37. From transcript of court records, quoted in Tom Fitzpatrick, "Bombing Case Intriguing, But Suspects' Ties Blew It Out of Water," *Arizona Republic*, August 29, 1985; see also idem, "Gun Case Involving Officer's Son, Preacher's Nephews Inspires Questions," ibid., September 5, 1984; Susan Leonard, "2 Brothers Held In Blast at Home of Police Official," ibid., August 30, 1984; "Phoenix Man Pleads Guilty in Threat Case," ibid., December 20, 1984; "Defendant Admits Bombing at Phoenix Lawman's Home," ibid., March 5, 1985.

38. A newspaper article written in 1973 put the congregation at eight hundred; Max Jennings, "Hallelujah! Ailments Vanish at Revival," *Arizona Republic*, February 23, 1973.

39. The figure of twelve million was quoted to me several times, although one person indicated that the active list was eight million. Given the attendance at the crusade, these figures seemed exaggerated.

40. Frisby, *Revelation of the Written Scrolls*, p. 162.

Chapter 5: Adirondack Fundamentalism

1. *Word of Life 1987 Annual* (Schroon Lake, N.Y.: Word of Life Fellowship, 1986).

2. Chaim Potok, *The Chosen* (New York: Simon & Schuster, 1967).

3. This is a composite description taken from the observation of several evening rallies at the Pine Pavilion during the summers of 1984 and 1987.

4. *Word of Life 1987 Annual*. 1 Tim. 2:9 reads: "women should adorn themselves modestly and sensibly in seemly apparel, not with braided hair or gold or pearls or costly attire" (RSV). These rules apply to all campers in all the Word of Life camps, including the adults at Word of Life Inn.

5. This account of the campfire is entirely fictionalized—the only such passage in this book. It is based, nevertheless, on conversations with campers and counselors at Word of Life Island as well as on observations of meetings there. It is also based on personal experience and reminiscences from many summers at several different Bible camps.

Chapter 6: Georgia Charismatics

1. Quoted in Barbara White, "Pastor, Congregation Find Their Roots," *Florida Times-Union*, April 14, 1990, Religion section, p. 4.

2. Quoted in "Rector and a Rumpus," *Newsweek*, July 4, 1960, p. 77.

3. Quoted in ibid. See also "Speaking in Tongues, *Time*, August 15, 1960, pp. 55, 57.

4. See Mark A. Noll, "Evangelicals on the Canterbury Trail," *Eternity* 29 (March 1978): 14–19ff. Robert E. Webber (also of Wheaton College) appropriated Noll's title for his own book, *Evangelicals on the Canterbury Trail* (Wilton, Conn.: Morehouse, 1989).

5. For a treatment of Episcopalians' outsized influence in American culture, see Kit and Frederica Konolige, *The Power of Their Glory: American's Ruling Class: The Episcopalians* (New York: Wyden Books, 1978).

6. Lyrics by Phil Driscoll and Lari Gass, Mighty Horn Music.

Chapter 8: Campaign Journal

1. From the 9:00 a.m. service, February 7, 1988; see also William Simbro, "Robertson to be Target of Sermon," *Des Moines Register*, February 6, 1988, p. 8A.

2. From the 10:15 a.m. service, February 7, 1988.

3. From the 6:00 p.m. service, February 7, 1988.

4. Alexis de Tocqueville, *Democracy in America*, ed. Henry Steele Commager, trans. Henry Reeve (New York: Oxford University Press, 1947), p. 199. On nineteenth-century femininity and domesticity, see Colleen McDannell, *The Christian Home in Victorian America, 1840–1900* (Bloomington: Indiana University Press, 1986); Ann Douglas, *The Feminization of American Culture* (New York: Knopf, 1977).

5. Barbara A. Peil, "A Seasoned Approach," *Kindred Spirit* 11 (Spring 1987): 13.

6. A good example of this genre is Peter Marshall and David Manuel, *The Light and the Glory* (Old Tappan, N.J.: Revell, 1977). For an evangelical response to this revisionism, see Mark A. Noll, Nathan O. Hatch, and George M. Marsden, *The Search for Christian America* (Westchester, Ill.: Crossway Books, 1983).

7. Douglas Frank started me thinking about the fetus as symbol. I am grateful to him for allowing me to develop this idea here.

8. Quoted in Michael Oreskes, "Almost 'Got to Give God Credit,' Robertson Says in Thanking Staff," *New York Times*, February 9, 1988, pp. A1, B7.

9. Tuttle was referring to a passage found in 2 Cor. 6:14.

10. On the social concerns of evangelicals in the nineteenth century, see Timothy L. Smith, *Revivalism and Social Reform in Mid-Nineteenth-Century America* (Nashville: Abingdon Press, 1957); Charles C. Cole, Jr., *The Social Ideas of the Northern Evangelists, 1826–1860* (New York: Columbia University Press, 1954).

Chapter 9: Mississippi Missions

1. "Ross Barnett, Segregationist, Dies; Governor of Mississippi in 1960s," *New York Times*, November 7, 1987.

2. From *Eyes on the Prize*, six-part television documentary, episode 2: "Fighting Back, 1957–1962."

3. John Perkins, *Let Justice Roll Down: John Perkins Tells His Own Story* (Ventura, Calif.: Regal Books, 1976), p. 25. Much of the ensuing account of Perkins's life relies on this book.

4. Ibid., p. 72.

5. Perkins, in fact, views his mission work as a response, or at least an alternative, to the tenets of the Nation of Islam. See John Perkins, "Mendenhall Model Answers the Black Muslims," *Christianity Today*, January 30, 1976, pp. 8–13.

6. After Perkins shifted his attentions to Jackson in the mid-1970s, the programs in Mendenhall took the name Mendenhall Ministries.

7. For a brief sketch of Perkins's life, see Will Norton, Jr., "John Perkins, the Stature of a Servant," *Christianity Today*, January 1, 1982, pp. 18–19.

8. John Perkins, telephone interview, North Pasadena, Cal., June 8, 1987.

9. Milton C. Sernett, ed., *Afro-American Religious History: A Documentary Witness* (Durham, N.C.: Duke University Press, 1985), p. 310.

10. Sernett, *Afro-American Religious History*, p. 241.

11. John Perkins, *With Justice for All* (Ventura, Cal.: Regal Books, 1982), p. 98.

12. Perkins, *With Justice for All*.

13. Perkins, *With Justice for All*, p. 99.

14. Perkins, *With Justice for All*, p. 102.

15. Perkins, *With Justice for All*, ch. 9, 14, 18; Lem Tucker, "The Desire of My Heart," *Inter Varsity* (Summer 1984): 10–13.

16. "We're not teaching people how to live with rats and roaches," D. L. Govan, a member of the pastoral team at Voice of Calvary Fellowship, said, "we're teaching them to live with dignity." Perkins is not at all averse to free enterprise. During an interview in 1982, he said, "I believe in stewardship that is expressed in capital ownership," but he added, "The weakness of our system is that capitalists believe that the church should not speak against capitalism, but only against socialism, communism, and fascism" (Will Norton, Jr., "An Interview with John Perkins, the Prophet," *Christianity Today*, January 1, 1982, p. 20).

17. Statistics from "John M. Perkins Christian Community Development Institute Workshop Manual," pp. 57–60.

18. See Perkins, *With Justice for All*, ch. 7.

19. Perkins interview.

20. Joseph Parker, interview, January 18, 1987.

21. Perkins, *Let Justice Roll Down*, p. 220.

22. Perkins interview.

Chapter 10: *Bible Bazaar*

1. For an excellent treatment of the various—and contradictory—ways in which Americans have used the Bible throughout history, see Nathan O. Hatch and Mark A. Noll, eds., *The Bible in America: Essays in Cultural History* (New York: Oxford University Press, 1982).

2. Walter A. Elwell, "Belief and the Bible: A Crisis of Authority?" *Christianity Today*, March 21, 1980, pp. 20–23.

3. Isa. 55:11.

4. Mark A. Noll et al., eds., *Eerdmans' Handbook to Christianity anity in America* (Grand Rapids: Wm. B. Eerdmans, 1983), p. 488.

5. George W. Cornell, "Christian Book Business Booms," Rockford (Ill.) *Register Star*, July 24, 1988, p. 8C (this story was picked up from the Associated Press).

6. In 1987 Zondervan had a net income of $859,000 on sales of $105.8 millon; see "Murdoch Buys Bible Printer," *New York Newsday*, July 14, 1988, p. 49 (this story was picked up from Reuters).

7. Cornell, "Christian Book Business Booms," p. 8C.

8. Ibid.

9. Quotations taken from VALdyme promotional literature.

10. Quotations from a conversation with Max Greiner, Jr., and from his promotional literature.

11. From the ad copy of Sonshine Graphics's advertisement in *Bookstore Journal* (July 1988): 16.

12. Art Levine, "The Devil in Gorbachev," *Washington Post*, June 5, 1988, pp. C1, C4. Faid says that the biblical reference to Satan as a red dragon with a trail of stars is Rev. 12:3–4.

13. Luke 16:13 (TLB).

Chapter 11: *Episcopal Indians*

1. Acts 1:8 (NIV).

2. By some estimations, the Indian population of central Mexico declined from twenty-five million in 1519 to just over one million in 1605; see Charles Gibson, *Spain in America* (New York: Harper & Row, 1966), p. 63.

3. Jay P. Dolan, *The American Catholic Experience: A History from Colonial Times to the Present* (Garden City, N.Y.: Doubleday, 1985), p. 24.

4. This is the general conclusion of Henry Warner Bowden in *American Indians and Christian Missions: Studies in Cultural Conflict* (Chicago: University of Chicago Press, 1981). His argument is considerably more nuanced than what I've summarized here, but he finds generally that the stronger and more stable the native culture, the better those Indians withstood the assaults of Christian missionaries.

5. See Neal Salisbury, "Red Puritans: The 'Praying Indians' of Massachusetts Bay and John Eliot," *William and Mary Quarterly*, 3rd ser., XXXI (1974): 27–54.

6. I am grateful to Virginia Luger of Fort Yates for pointing this out to me.

7. This was the unemployment rate as of January 1987. I am grateful to the staff of Senator Daniel Patrick Moynihan (New York) for supplying me with this information.

8. Despite his representation at the dedication, Daschle has opposed efforts in the U.S. Senate to restore 1.3 million of the 7.3 million acres that the U.S. government wrested from the Sioux in 1877.

9. See, for example, Robert S. Ellwood and Harry B. Partin, *Religious and Spiritual Groups in Modern America*, 2d ed. (Englewood Cliffs, N.J.: Prentice-Hall, 1988), pp. 168–70.

10. John and DeVonna Bush interview, July 26, 1987.

11. For a fuller description of the Sioux Sun Dance, see Royal B. Hassrick, *The Sioux: Life and Customs of a Warrior Society* (Norman: University of Oklahoma Press, 1964), pp. 239–47; see also Bowden, *American Indians and Christian Missions*, pp. 215–20.

12. From *The Hymnal* 1982, © 1985 The Church Pension Fund. Used by permission.

Chapter 12: Camp Meeting

1. *The Camp Meeting Challenge* 10 (Spring 1987): [2–7].

2. Matt. 5:48.

3. The references here are, respectively, 2 Cor. 6:17 and 1 Sam. 16:7.

4. This scruple derives from 1 Cor. 11:15.

5. See W. J. Rorabaugh, *The Alcoholic Republic: An American Tradition* (New York: Oxford University Press, 1979) regarding alcohol consumption in the early nineteenth century.

6. The most popular camp-meeting manual of the nineteenth century was B. W. Gorham, *Camp Meeting Manual: A Practical Book for the Camp Ground* (Boston, 1854).

7. Most of this information comes from Dickson D. Bruce, Jr., *And They All Sang Hallelujah: Plain-Folk Camp-Meeting Religion, 1800–1845* (Knoxville: University of Tennessee Press, 1974).

8. See Randall H. Balmer, "From Frontier Phenomenon to Victorian Institution: The Methodist Camp Meeting in Ocean Grove, New Jersey," *Methodist History* 25 (April 1987): 194–200.

9. This "altar" nomenclature, which is quite common in evangelical churches, raises an interesting issue. Although evangelical preachers make "altar calls" and invite the true believers to "lay their all on the altar," there is, technically, no altar in the vast majority of evangelical churches. An *altar*, of course, is a place of sacrifice; in Roman Catholic churches, it is the place where the "sacrifice of the Mass" is performed, when the bread and wine of Holy Communion *actually become* the body and blood of Christ, even though they retain the outward appearance of bread and wine. The "sacramental" theology of most evangelicals, however, is *memorialist*—that is, the elements of Holy Communion serve merely to remind us of the death of Christ; there is no objective partaking of grace, as Catholics and others believe, nor is there,

properly, an altar where the eucharistic rite is performed. Evangelicals have instead spiritualized the notion of altar to mean, roughly, the surrender of the individual to the will of God. They persist in using the terminology of the altar, however.

10. These scruples about feminine attire derive, in part, from 1 Tim. 2:9–10.

11. I have altered some of the details of this story in order to disguise the identity of the person involved.

Chapter 13: City Crusade

1. Jacob A. Riis, *How the Other Half Lives: Studies Among the Tenements of New York* (New York: Charles Scribner's Sons, 1890), p. 210.

2. Quoted in Selwyn Rabb, "Taking on Tammany, 100 Years Ago," *New York Times*, February 14, 1992, p. B3.

3. Lyrics by Charlotte Elliott, 1834.

Chapter 14: Oregon Jeremiad

1. Since my visit, the Oregon Extension has become affiliated with Houghton College, a Wesleyan school in western New York, rather than Trinity College. A new president at Trinity College, eager to placate some of the more insistent fundamentalists within Trinity's supporting denomination, the Evangelical Free Church of America, severed the college's ties with the Oregon program.

2. From "A Proposal for a Trek Curriculum," photocopy.

3. Douglas W. Frank, *Less Than Conquerors: How Evangelicals Entered the Twentieth Century* (Grand Rapids: Wm. B. Eerdmans, 1986).

Chapter 15: Prime Time

1. Jimmy Swaggart, with Robert Paul Lamb, *To Cross a River*, 3rd ed. (Baton Rouge, La.: Jimmy Swaggart Ministries, 1984), p. 30.

2. Swaggart, *To Cross a River*, p. 35.

3. Rodney Clapp, "Swaggart's Worst Enemy," *Christianity Today*, June 17, 1988, p. 17.

4. "Swaggart Responds," *Christianity Today*, December 11, 1987, p. 46.

5. Swaggart, *To Cross a River*, pp. 92, 93.

6. Swaggart, *To Cross a River*, p. 93.

7. Swaggart, *To Cross a River*, pp. 35, 42.

8. Swaggart, *To Cross a River*, pp. 54, 92.

9. Swaggart, *To Cross a River*, p. 100.

10. Swaggart, *To Cross a River*, p. 193.

Chapter 16: Sound Check

1. "Liquid," lyrics by Dan Haseltine, © 1995 Pogostick Music (BMI)/Bridge Building Music (BMI). All rights administered by Brentwood Music Publishing, Inc. Used by permission.

2. April Hefner, "Boys 2 Men," *CCM Magazine*, October 1997, p. 32.

3. Kent Zimmerman, review of Jars of Clay, *Much Afraid, Gavin Report*, September 5, 1997.

4. Lucy Diaz Kurz, "Mainstream Biz Can Gain Much from Gospel." *Bill board*, April 24, 1999, p. 4.

5. "Boy on a String," lyrics by Dan Haseltine, © 1995 Pogostick Music (BMI)/Bridge Building Music (BMI). All rights administered by Brentwood Music Publishing, Inc. Used by permission.

6. Ibid.

7. "Worlds Apart," lyrics by Dan Haseltine, © 1995 Pogostick Music (BMI)/Bridge Building Music (BMI). All rights administered by Brentwood Music Publishing, Inc. Used by permission.

8. Ibid.

9. Quoted in Hefner, "Boys 2 Men," p. 38.

10. "Much Afraid," lyrics by Dan Haseltine, © 1997 Bridge Building Music/Pogostick Music (BMI). All rights administered by Brentwood-Benson Music Publishing, Inc. Used by permission.

11. "Fade to Grey," lyrics by Dan Haseltine, © 1994 Bridge Building Music/Pogostick Music (BMI). All rights administered by Brentwood-Benson Music Publishing, Inc. Used by permission.

12. "Liquid," lyrics by Dan Haseltine, © 1995 Pogostick Music (BMI)/Bridge Building Music (BMI). All rights administered by Brentwood Music Publishing, Inc. Used by permission.

13. "Fade to Grey," lyrics by Dan Haseltine, © 1994 Bridge Building Music/Pogostick Music (BMI). All rights administered by Brentwood-Benson Music Publishing, Inc. Used by permission.

14. Quoted in Hefner, "Boys 2 Men," p. 32.

15. "Love Song for a Savior," lyrics by Dan Haseltine, © 1995 Pogostick Music (BMI)/Bridge Building Music (BMI). All rights administered by Brent wood Music Publishing, Inc. Used by permission.

16. Quote taken from Jars of Clay biographical statement (n.d.).

17. "Hymn," lyrics by Dan Haseltine, © 1997 Bridge Building Music/Pogostick Music (BMI). All rights administered by Brentwood-Benson Music Publishing, Inc. Used by permission.

18. Haseltine, "Hymn."

19. Haseltine, "Hymn."

Chapter 17: Kinkade Crusade

1. A profile of Calvary Chapel appears as chapter 1 of this book.

2. Letter to the author, August 17, 2000.

3. Quoted in Tessa DeCarlo, "Landscapes by the Carload: Art or Kitsch?" *New York Times*, November 7, 1999.

4. Quoted in Brenda L. Moore, "'Painter of Light' Sketches New Role: Self-Help Guru," *Wall Street Journal*, March 24, 1999.

5. Quoted in DeCarlo, "Landscapes by the Carload: Art or Kitsch?"

6. Philippe de Montebello, "Making a Cause Out of Bad Art," *New York Times*, October 5, 1999.

7. Quoted in DeCarlo, "Landscapes by the Carload: Art or Kitsch?"

8. Quoted in DeCarlo, "Landscapes by the Carload."

Chapter 18: Purpose Driven

1. Bad architecture is a holdover from when evangelicals believed in the imminent Second Coming of Jesus. The rationale was, "Why spend good money on buildings when Jesus will return soon?" Evangelicals still ostensibly hold to the imminent, premillennial return of Jesus (a topic addressed in chapters 2 and 3 of this book), but they—upwardly mobile suburbanites in particular—have become more and more comfortable in this life, so they speak less frequently of the life to come. The message seems to be, "Yes, come, Lord Jesus, but take your time."

2. A profile of Calvary Chapel appears as chapter 1 of this book. The precise definition of "megachurch" has been the subject of some debate. Originally, it referred to a congregation of a thousand or more, but with the proliferation of megachurches, many observers raised the threshold to two thousand.

3. The PBS companion version of this book, *Mine Eyes Have Seen the Glory*, opens with a profile of Willow Creek: *Mine Eyes Have Seen the Glory*, 3-part PBS Series, 1993.

4. For a profile of Bellevue and an example of its militarism, see Randall Balmer, *Grant Us Courage: Travels Along the Mainline of American Protestantism* (New York: Oxford University Press, 1996), chap. 7.

5. In an odd and (I'm sure) unintended way, the plethora of weekend services at megachurches represents a restoration of sabbatarianism (by which I mean, in this context, worship on Saturday) to Christianity. The early church, an out-growth of Judaism, worshiped on Saturday until the conversion of the emperor Constantine to Christianity at the Battle of Milvian Bridge in 312 c.e. At that point, Constantine, still loyal to the Sun God, decreed that the Christian day of worship would be Sunday, not Saturday, a practice generally followed by Christians to this day, except for Seventh-day Adventists.

Chapter 19: Latino Evangelicals

1. The description of New Life Covenant Church offered here is a conflation of three Sunday morning services on June 30, 2013. My interview with De Jesús took place in the interval between the second and third services.

2. Elizabeth Dias, "¡Evangélicos!" *Time*, April 15, 2013, pp. 20–28; "The 100 Most Influential People in the World," *Time*, April 29–May 6, 2013, p. 66.

3. Wilfredo De Jesús, *Amazing Faith: How to Make God Take Notice* (Springfield, Mo.: Influence Resources, 2012), p. 15.

4. De Jesús, *Amazing Faith*, p. 18.

5. Quoted in Cara Davis, "Wilfredo De Jesús: The New Face of Social Justice," Charisma News, http://www.charismanews.com/us/39000-wilfredo-de-jesus-the-new-face-of-social-justice (accessed July 4, 2013).

6. Quoted in Davis, "Wilfredo De Jesús."

7. Hebrews 13:2 (NLT).

8. *Windy City Live*, April 29, 2013.

9. *Windy City Live*, April 29, 2013.

10. *Windy City Live*, April 29, 2013.

11. Quoted in Davis, "Wilfredo De Jesús."

Epilogue

1. Acts 16:31 (KJV), italics mine.

2. This is the conclusion—that mainline churches are losing members because of their inchoate theology—of Wade Clark Roof and William McKinney, *American Mainline Religion: Its Changing Shape and* Future (New Brunswick, N.J.: Rutgers University Press, 1987).

3. I owe this idea of America as a nation of talkers to Harry Stout.

4. The refrain from "Rhythm Guitar," by T. A. Hill.

5. On the social construction of reality,. see Peter L. Berger and Thomas Luckmann, *The Social Construction of Reality: A Treatise in the Sociology of Knowledge* (Garden City, N.Y.: Doubleday & Co., 1966).

Afterword: Twenty-five Years Later

1. This visit to Calvary Chapel took place on February 3, 2013.

2. Debra Smith, "A God-Inspired Musical Revolution," *Calvary Chapel Magazine*, Summer 2013.

3. Richard Clough, "Moves of Faith," *Orange County Register*, February 3, 2013, Real Estate, pp. 1, 9.

4. Garry Friesen, e-mail to the author, October 9, 2013; Daniel Scalberg, phone conversation, October 14, 2013.

5. Mary Frances Schjonberg, "'Winter Count' Brings Indigenous Story Telling Method to the Gospel," Episcopal News Service, June 25, 2012.

6. Michael Clancy, "Neal Frisby: Eccentric Evangelist Touched Followers' Lives," *Arizona Republic*, May 15, 2005.

7. I visited Stan White and Church of the King on September 22, 2013. A portion of these observations appeared in an article I wrote for The Living Church: "Pentecostals on the Original-Blessing Trail." *The Living Church*, November 24, 2013, 4–7.

8. My breakfast with Thompson took place on September 23, 2012, in Des Moines, Iowa. Turns out (as I found months later) he was right about my cameo in the book; Donald W. Thompson with J. Howard Sloan, *My Friend Jesus, Me and the Movies* (Bloomington, Ind.: Wordclay, 2008), pp. 254–55.

9. Thompson, *My Friend Jesus*, pp. 128, 90.

10. 1 Corinthians 13:1 (NIV).

Index

Abolitionism, 34–35

Abortion: anti-abortion movement and, 46, 161; arguments and opposition to, 160–61, 237, 350; on demand, 147–48; legalization of, 156

Academy of Traditional Art, 320

Acts of the Apostles (book of), 129

Adam, 157, 203, 324

Adams, Dennis, 181

Adams, Judi, 181–82

African Methodist Episcopal Church, 188–89

Agee, Bedsaul, 226–28

AIDS, 239–40

Alcohol, 231; dependency, 73, 150; evils of, xvii, 30, 45, 82, 92; Sioux and, 214, 215, 217, 222. *See also* Behavioral standards

Aldersgate Street, xvi

Aldrich, Joseph, 138–39, 141

Allen, Richard, 188

Allen, Tom, 155

Altar, 388n9; calls, 62, 109, 123, 372; during service, 120–21, 222, 234–35, 371

Alvord, Patsy, 270, 366

Alvord, Thomas (Sam), 259–60, 267, 270–71, 366–67

American Bible Society, 196

American Catholicism, 114. *See also* Roman Catholicism

American Civil Liberties Union, 162–63

American Civil War, 35, 176, 247

American Indians and Christian Missions: Studies in Cultural Conflict (Bowden), 387n2

American Media, 67–68

Amish, 229

Anaheim Stadium, 332

Anderson, Frank, 168

Anderson, Melvin, 188

Anti-abortion movement, 46, 161

Antioch School, 130

Architecture, 15, 32, 133, 326, 337, 391n1

Arizona Republic, 364

Armageddon, Battle of, 83, 383nn26–27

Arminianism, 241

Arminius, Jacobus, 241

Art Center College of Design (California), 313

Art curriculum, 127, 133, 318

Art Hall of Fame, U.S., 314

Artist's Guide to Sketching, The (Kinkade, William Thomas), 314

Asbury, Francis, 328

Assemblies of God, xvii, 79, 108, 283–84, 344, 346

Augustine, St., 26, 34

Automobile culture, 13–14

Baker, Kenneth, 322

Bakker, Jim, ix, 9, 191, 283, 292, 376

Bakker, Tammy, 191
Baptism, 210; at Calvary Chapel, 23–25; experience of, xvii; Jesus movement and, 23–25; at Saddleback Church, 337–38. *See also* Conversion; Salvation
Barnett, Ross, 176
Barry, Dave, 336
Barth, Karl, 41, 268–69
Bateman, Herb, 46–47
Battle of Milvian Bridge, 391n5
Bauer, Arthur, 67–68
Bawden, Paul, 155
Bay Psalm Book, 300
Beauty, 5, 210, 313, 315, 319, 322–24. *See also* Modernism
Becker, Ernest, 268, 367
Beecher, Lyman, 173
Beeson, Robert, 306
Behavioral standards, 7, 28, 75, 239
Bellevue Baptist Church (Memphis, Tennessee), 327, 328
Benedict, St., 38
Bennett, Dennis J., 113
Berger, Peter, 268
Bergman, Ingmar, 34
Berry, James, 66
Berry, Wendell, 268
Bible, 4, 263, 286, 313; apocalypse in, 33; arrays, types and versions of, 193–94, 198–99; as big business, 196–99; in Christian bookstores, 199; demand for, 198; evangelical and, 194–95; Gospel of Luke in, 17; inerrancy and, xvi, 26, 32, 40, 128–29, 265; infallibility and interpretation of, xvii, 25–28; languages of, 38; New International Version of, 197; proliferation of, 194; prophecies of, 33; teaching of, 22; Word of God and, 41, 159, 195–96, 242. *See also* New Testament; Old Testament

Bible: literal interpretations of, xvi, 81; model of, 129–30; Scriptures and, 9, 17, 33–35, 37, 135, 194; Thompson, D. W., on, 57–58
Bible camps: movies at, 64; summer, 104–6. *See also* Word of Life Fellowship
Bible Institute of Los Angeles, 37, 133
Bible institutes, 37; appeal and subculture of, 130–31, 274; curriculum and respectability of, 132–33; isolation of, 131; relocation of, 133–34. *See also specific institutes*
Bible Methodists, 227
Billboard, 303
Biola College. *See* Bible Institute of Los Angeles
Biola University. *See* Bible Institute of Los Angeles
Black, Ed, 117
Black, Jane, 117
Black Muslim, 255
Blacks: leaders among, 187–89; plight of, 191–92; punishment of, 176–77; religion and, 179–80
Blood on the Mountain, 51
Bloy, Francis Eric, 113
Blue Highways: A Journey into America (Moon), 10
Blume, Peter, 321
Book of Common Prayer, 110, 111–12, 122, 352, 369
Bookstore Journal, 199
Bowden, Henry Warner, 387n2
Branham, William, 77–78, 382n8
Branstad, Terry, 153
Brethren in Christ, 227, 230
Bristow, Harry, 66
Bronleewe, Matt, 297–98
Brooklyn Museum, 320
Brooks, Robert, 364
Brown, William Wells, 180
Bryan, William Jennings, 349
Bull, Harold Eagle, 223

Bush, DeVonna, 219–20
Bush, George H. W., 163, 165, 168
Bush, George W., 348
Bush, John, 219–20, 223
Butcher, Blaine, 137

Cafeteria Christianity, 328
California, 177–78, 368–69. *See also*
    specific churches
Calvary Baptist Church (Jackson,
    Mississippi), 187
Calvary Chapel (Santa Ana, California),
    11, 40, 301, 314, 360–62, 390n1, 391n2,
    392n1; associations and fellowships
    with, 27–28; baptism at, 23–25; *Bible*
    and, 14; complex and location of,
    15–16, 21; congregation of, 17–23,
    28–31, 379n3; events, services and
    studies at, 18, 25–28; hippies and,
    20–23; Jesus movement and, 20–23,
    28–31; parking lot at, 13–14, 16; radio
    station, conference and retreat
    centers of, 18–19; routinization and,
    28–31; singing and, 15, 16, 379n2;
    statement of faith at, 27; worship
    services at, 14–17, 379n2. *See also*
    Maranatha Christian Academy;
    Smith, Chuck
Calvary Chapel Association, 362
Calvary Chapel Magazine, 361
Calvin, John, 240–41, 300, 307
Camp Freedom (St. Petersburg,
    Florida), 244–46, 365–66; gatherings
    and services at, 226–31, 234–36;
    preachers at, 236–42; property,
    233–34, 388n9; rising bell at, 226
Camp meetings, 11, 226; manual of,
    388n6; tradition of, 231–33. *See also*
    Camp Freedom
Campolo, Tony, 281, 375
Capitalism, 82, 190, 386n16
Capital punishment, 161

Capstone Cathedral (Phoenix, Arizona),
    364; building, construction and
    symbolism of, 71–72, 77–79, 84–85,
    382nn7–9, 384n34; congregation of,
    71, 72–76, 87–89, 381n1, 384nn38–39.
    See also Frisby, Neal Vincent
Card-playing, xvii, 45, 230. *See also*
    Behavioral standards
Carmel-by-the-Sea, California, 318, 368
Carmichael, Ralph, 301
Carter, Jimmy (president), 73, 349
Carter, Jimmy (student at Dallas
    Theological Seminary), 46–47
Cashulines, Juanita, 170
Cason, J. M., 281–82
CBA. *See* Christian Booksellers
    Association
CCM Magazine, 298
Central Park (New York), 246–57
Chafer, Lewis Sperry, 37–38
Charisma. *See* Cult of Personality
Charismata (spiritual gifts), xvii, 26, 77
Charismatic, 26, 28, 112, 114; beliefs of,
    xvii, 40–41; as term, xv, xviii
Charismatic movement, 121, 211; growth
    of, 113–14, 116; leaders of, 124–26, 268,
    328, 353, 355; Roman Catholicism
    and, 114, 125–26; roots of, xvii
Chautauqua Institution, 295, 296
Chicago Public School System, 346
Chicago Tribune, 343
Children, 274; evangelical and, 130,
    156; fundamentalists and, 45;
    schooling of, 156, 172, 174
Chosen, The (Potok), 91–93
Christ, Jesus: personal relationship with,
    58, 379; return of, 33, 59; sharing, 28–31
Christian Booksellers Association
    (CBA), 11–12; convention, 193,
    196–97, 200–201; merchandise
    and vendors at, 201–8; offices,
    publications and seminars of, 199;
    political bias at, 205–6

Christian bookstores, 199–200

Christian Film Distributors Association, 66

Christianity: conversion to, 51; evangelical, 179–80, 189–90; Native American religion and, 210–14, 219–22

Christianity Lite, 328

Christianity Today, 279, 284

Christians, 3–4, 7; history of, 158; Israel and, 42; Jews and, 41–42; origins of, 159

Church Age, 42

Church of God (Anderson, Indiana), 227

Church of God in Christ, xvii

Church of the King (Valdosta, Georgia), 107, 370–72, 392n7; confirmations and services at, 117–18, 120–25; congregation of, 110–12, 119–26; decor of, 118–19; Episcopal Church and, 111–26; first gathering of, 111

Church of the Nazarene, 227, 313, 348

Church of the Redeemer (Houston, Texas), 114

Church of the Reformation (Washington, D.C.), 339

Cimino, Richard, 22

City, evangelical attitudes toward, 246–57

City of God, The (Augustine), 34

Civil rights, 149, 176, 182, 340

Claassen, Howard, 271

Clancy, Michael, 364

Cloud, Vernon Iron, 217

Colacuori, Mike, 198–99, 203

Collector's Corner Gallery, 312

Collins, Mary, 213

Commodification, 324

Common Sense Realism, 26, 129

Communion. *See* Lord's Supper

Communism, 82

Community Law Office (Mendenhall, Mississippi), 181–82

Comprehensive Bible Correspondence Course, 37

Compton, Philip, 237

Concerned Women for America (Iowa chapter), 157, 162

Concerned Women for America (New Hampshire chapter), 166–75

Confession, 264–65, 352

Confirmation, 117–18, 120–25

Constantine, 391n5

Consumerism, 262, 278, 321–22, 329, 355

Contemporary Christian music, 201, 298

Conversion, 26, 51–52, 62, 91–92, 97, 105–6, 189, 211–12, 227, 229, 243–44, 308, 351. *See also* Baptism; Salvation

Conwell, Russell H., 327

Cooperation, 142, 182, 250, 334

Copeland, Kenneth, 191

Cosmetics, xvii, 45. *See also* Behavioral standards

Covenant theology, 33, 41–43. *See also* Dispensational premillennialism

Creative Miracles (Grant), 382n3

Cross a River, To (Swaggart), 281–82

Cross of Christ, The (Stott), 143

Crystal Cathedral (Garden Grove, California), 15, 379n4

Cult of personality, 8, 292, 355

Cultural bias, 213

Culture, 211, 213; automobile, 13–14; of evangelical, 131–32; fundamentalist on, 93; popular, 377–78

Cupples, Justin Charles, 51

Dakota. *See* Sioux

Daley, Richard M., 348

Dallas Theological Seminary, 11; campus of, 32; classes and faculty at, 38–41, 381n13; divinity degree at, 380n8; founding of, 32; Multnomah School of the Bible and, 128; statement of purpose by, 380n1; theology at, 356; women at, 43–46, 381nn14–15

Dancing, xvii, 45, 88, 102, 109, 119, 143, 216–17, 219, 230. *See also* Behavioral standards

Daniel (book of), 33–34, 58, 60

Daniel (prophet), 84

Darby, John Nelson: background of, 34–35; ideas and interpretations of, 33–37, 275

Dartmouth Area Christian Fellowship (Hanover, New Hampshire), 171–75

Darwin, Charles, 35

Darwinism, xvi, 265

Daschle, Tom, 216, 388n8

Davis, John, 254

Decentralized worship, 331

De Jesús, Elizabeth, 342

De Jesús, Wilfredo: on immigration, 346–47; leadership of, 342–48, 350; preaching of, 344–45

Democratic Party, 148, 150–51

Denominations, xvii, 19, 27, 93, 96, 115, 131, 209, 227

Detroit Bible College. *See* William Tyndale College

Devil. *See* Satan

Dinkins, Carolyn, 116–18, 122

Dinkins, Robert, 117–18, 122

Disease, 177, 212, 236, 248–49, 334

Disestablishment, religious, 354

Disneyland, 330

Dispensation. *See* Church Age

Dispensational premillennialism, 128, 275; doctrines and theology of, 33–41, 46–47; implications of, 35–36; successive covenants of, 41–43

Distant Thunder, A, 63–64

Divorce, 139, 238, 328

Dole, Elizabeth, 155

Dole, Robert, 155, 163, 165, 168

Domesticity, ideal of, 158–59, 385n4

Donne, John, 310

Doughten, Russell, 60, 62, 64, 67

Drinking. *See* Alcohol

Drugs, 29, 73, 82, 92, 214, 222, 289, 345, 346. *See also* Behavioral standards

Drye, Margaret, 172

Drye, Rob, 172

Dualism, 263

DuBois, W. E. B., 180

du Pont, Pete, 163

Durkin, Amy (fictional character), 102, 105, 358

Durland, Gwen, 137–38

Eddy, Maker Baker, 77

Eden, 157, 325

Edwards, Jonathan (sheriff), 183

Eliot, John, 196, 212

Eliot, T. S., 310

Eller, Vernard, 268

Ellul, Jacques, 267–68

Emanuel, Rahm, 348

England, 383n21

Engle, Jacob, 229

Enlightenment, 353; influences, 265; standards, 135, 272–73

Enlightenment Rationalism, xi, 265, 321

Episcopal Church, 222, 369; Church of the King and, 111–26; establishment of, 116, 385n5; evangelicalism and, 209, 220

Episcopalians, 209, 224

Escape from Evil (Becker), 268, 367

Eschatology, 35; comprehension of, 129–30; course on, 38–41; doctrine of, 33–34; quarrels over, 36–37

Evangel. *See* Gospel

Evangel Assembly of God (Valdosta, Georgia), 108; congregation of, 110, 126; history of, 109

Evangelical, 265; beliefs of, 352–53;
Bible and, 194–96; children and, 130,
156; Christianity, 179–80, 189–90;
connotations and definition of, xv–xvi;
culture of, 131–32; modem-day,
xv–xvi; music, 299–311; preachers,
37; pronunciation of, 379n3; reform
movements, 34–35; social concerns
of, 385n10; spiritual piety and, xvi; as
term, xv, xviii; theology, 32; worship,
376–77; writing on American, ix–xi
Evangelical Free Church of America,
389n1
Evangelical Immigration Table, 339
Evangelicalism, 6, 8, 353–54; changes in,
375–76; characterization of, xvi, 192,
351–52; doctrines of, 26; Episcopal
Church and, 209, 220; future of,
357–59; popular culture and, 377–78;
as quilt, 353–54; rational, 264–66;
twentieth-century, 131
Evangelical Lutheran Church of
America, 362
Evangelical Lutheran Free Church, 336
Evangelical Theological College,
37. *See also* Dallas Theological
Seminary
Evangelism. *See* Proselytizing
Evans, Harry, 366–67
Eve, 157, 203, 324
Evers, Medgar, 177
Existentialism, 41

Faid, Robert, 206
Faith healers, 76–77
"Faith of Our Fathers," 180
Falwell, Jerry, xviii, 8, 173, 263, 302,
349, 376
Family Life Center (Baton Rouge,
Louisiana): compound, 284–85;
congregation of, 282–83, 290–91;
leadership of, 278–80

Farmers Home Administration
(FHA), 179
Fasting, 20, 112
Female space, 324
Feminism. *See* Women, evangelical
views of
Ferriday, Louisiana, 286–87
Fetus, 160, 385n7
FHA. *See* Farmers Home
Administration
Fiddler, Mary, 220–21
Findlayter, Orlando, 340
Finney, Charles Grandison, 65, 349
Fiorimonti, Gloria, 48–50
First Congregational Church (Dallas,
Texas), 37
First Evangelical Free Church
(Fullerton, California), 379n4
First Federated Church (Des Moines,
Iowa), 155, 156
First Thessalonians (book of), 10, 61, 63
Fish symbol (ichthys), 313
Fitz, Ida, 198–99, 206
Flagg, Madeline, 168
Fletcher, Artis, 188
Flying Bye, Joe, 216
Fong, Oden, 20–24, 27
Franciscans, 211
Frank, Douglas, 12, 259–61, 264–65,
269–70, 356, 359, 367, 385n7; on
Bible, 262–63, 271–73; interests of,
266–67; observations of, 274–77, 305
Franklin, Benjamin, 327
Friesen, Garry, 138, 363
Frisby, Curtis, 71
Frisby, Neal Vincent, 10, 356, 358,
364–65; background of, 79, 85–87;
healing powers of, 73–76, 87–89,
382n3; prophecies of, 77, 79–85,
382n4, 382n9, 382n17, 383n24,
383nn19–21, 383nn27–29, 384n31;
sermons of, 72–73. *See also*
Capstone Cathedral

Frost, Ronald, 127–28, 138
Fuller, Charles E., 65
Fundamentalism, 90, 138, 142;
    American, 11; brand of, 307
Fundamentalist, 5, 128; on culture, 93;
    on liberalism, 96; origins, doctrines
    and teachings of, xvi–xviii, 26–27,
    380n14; as term, xv, xvi
Fundamentals, The, xvi–xvii

Galatians (book of), xv, 240
Gallup, George, 195
Gangs, 346
Gangsta' rap, 319
Gardner, Randy, 39
Geisler, Norman, 40–41, 45–46
General Association of Regular
    Baptists, 307
Genesis (book of), 35, 45, 60, 81, 129, 266
Genesis One School (Mendenhall,
    Mississippi), 181
Gibbons, Harry E., 205
Gideons, 196
Gilbert, Mary Ann, 151
Gilley, Mickey, 286, 287, 293
Giovenetti, Leo, 324
Girard, Chuck, 361
Gladden, Washington, 36
Global religious networks, 334
Glossolalia: Episcopal Church
    and, 113–14; outbreak of, 113–14;
    pentecostalism and, xvii, 26–27, 109
God: existence of, 135; grace and, 115,
    262–63; providence and will of,
    52–57, 126; Word of, 41, 159,
    195–96, 242
Good House, Edna, 214, 217, 224, 363
Good House, Innocent, 210–18, 220,
    222–25, 358, 363–64
Gorbachev, Mikhail, 206
Gorham, B. W., 388n6
Gorman, Marvin, 283

Gornell, Barbara, 174–75
Gornell, Dan, 174
Gospel (evangel), xv, 379
Gospel Music Association, 306, 309
Gospel Music Association Spotlight
    Competition, 297
Gospel Music Week, 307
Govan, D. L., 386n16
Grace, 342; experience of, 104–5; God
    and, 115, 262–63
Grace Presbytery (Texas), 36
Graham, Sylvester, 76
Graham, William Franklin (Billy), 8,
    15, 123, 202, 247–57, 327–28
Grant, Amy, 302, 303, 308–9
Grant, W. V., 382n3
Grassley, Charles, 155
Great Awakening, 65
Greater Bethel A. M. E. Church
    (Mound Bayou, Mississippi),
    189, 359
Greek (language), 38
Greenville College, 297
Greiner, Max, Jr., 203
Grindstone, 213
Griswold, Kelly, 170
Guggenheim Museum, 322
Guilt, 5, 255
Gutenberg, Johann, 193, 207
Gutenberg Bible, 193
Gutenberg press, 334

Hagin, Kenneth, 202
Hahn, Jessica, 283
Haig, Alexander, 148, 168
Hallof, Duane, 128, 137, 141
Hankins, Holly, 44–45
Harper & Row, 197
Harrell, David Edwin, Jr., 77, 382n4
Harry Evans Prayer Chapel, 366–67
Hartley, Brian, 310
Haseltine, Dan, 297–98, 303–6, 308–10

Healing: as charismata, 77; divine, 285–86; powers of Frisby, Neal, 73–76, 87–89, 382n3; services, 234–36

Heaven, 33–34, 36, 39, 65, 70, 81, 221, 242–45; hell and, 4, 91, 101, 251; kingdom of, xviii, 42, 63; way to, 29, 83, 101, 173

Hebrew (language), 38

Hebrews (book of), 33

Hell, 283, 293; heaven and, 4, 91, 101, 251; torments of, 29, 96, 103, 242–45

Henry, Carl F. H., 268

Herbert, George, 310

Herrara, Carlos, 336

Hicks, Greg, 142

High Church, 5, 114, 116, 118, 121, 124, 314. *See also* Liturgy

Higher criticism, xvi, 35, 45

Hill, E. V., 281

Hippies, 20–23

Hispanics, 340–41

Hobe Sound Bible College, 237–39, 389n10

Holiness movement, 227, 230–31, 234, 237–39

Hollerud, Helge, 336

Hollywood, California, 54, 62, 64, 68, 229, 329

Holy Communion, 123–24, 195, 377, 388n9

Holy Spirit: blessing and filling by, xvii, 26–27, 31; inspiration of, 32; peacemakers and, 154; reality of, 109; second blessing of, 227, 242

Homestead Act of 1862, 213

Homosexuality, evangelical attitudes toward, 82, 243–45, 348, 365–66, 389n11

Hope Chapel (Hermosa Beach, California), 327

Houghton College, 389n1

Howard, Beverly, 319

Howe, John, 121

Howie, Don, 184–85, 187

How the Other Half Lives (Riis), 247

Humanitarianism, 332

Hunger, 222, 334

Hurst, Jacoba, 112, 120–21

Hybels, Bill, 340

Ichthys (fish symbol), 313

Image of the Beast, 63, 202

Immigration, 341, 346–47, 350

Impressionism, 312–13, 320. *See also* Painting

Inchoate theology, 392n2

Indian Department, U.S., 213, 388n6

Indian River Camp Meeting (South Carolina), 233

Indians. *See* Native Americans

Infanticide, 147

Ingram, Bobby, 124–25

Inspiration Books East, Inc., 252

Institutional church movement, 130

International Church of the Foursquare Gospel, xvii, 19. *See also* McPherson, Aimee Semple

Internet, 334, 337

Iowa Methodist Hospital (Des Moines), 50, 53–54

Iowans for Israel, 151

Iowa precinct caucuses: candidates during, 147–48, 163–75; convening of, 163; developments during, 147–49, 150–56; Robertson during, 147, 163–67

Iowa Right to Life Committee, 146, 152–53

Iranian Revolution, xvi

Israel, 151, 383n21; Christians and, 42; dietary and moral standards of, 33

Ives, Gaius, 151

Jackson, Jesse, 205

Janway, Cecil, 288

Jars of Clay, 390n16; albums, lyrics and songs of, 296, 298–99, 303–11; performances of, 295–96; success of, 298–99

Jehovah's Witnesses, 178, 223

Jepsen, Roger, 153

Jerusalem, 39, 77, 82, 142

Jesuits, 211

Jesus Movement, 150, 301, 360; baptism and, 23–25; Calvary Chapel and, 20–23, 28–31

Jesus people. *See* Jesus movement

Jewett, Alice, 218

Jews: Christians and, 41–42; salvation for, 42

Jews for Jesus, 42

Jews in America, 352

Jimmy Swaggart Bible College, 285

Jimmy Swaggart Ministries, 278, 284, 289

Johnson, Joyce (fictional character), 100

Johnson, Lyndon, 171

Joyce Meyer Ministries, 343

Judaism, 391n5

Kellogg, John Harvey, 77

Kemp, Jack, 147, 151, 155, 159, 163–65, 168–69

Kemp, Joanne, 155

Kennard, Gregg, 119

Kennedy, John F., 177

Kierkegaard, Søren, 268

Kindred Spirit, 44

King, John, 125

King, Martin Luther, Jr., 176, 178, 281, 359

King Philip's War, 212

Kinkade, Nanette, 313–14, 316, 368

Kinkade, William Thomas, 368, 390n1; childhood of, 313; education of, 313–14; faith of, 314; genius of, 312; lithographs and works of, 312–15, 318–20, 322–25; modernism and, 319; publishing house and warehouse of, 315–17; success of, 317–18. *See also* Thomas Kinkade Collectors' Society; Thomas Kinkade Foundation

Kraus, Donald, 380n5

Kroc, Ray, 324

Kruger, Barbara, 320, 321–22

Kuhlman, Kathryn, 77

LaHaye, Tim, 263

Lakewood Church (Houston, Texas), 328

Lamb's Church (Manhattan, New York), 348

"Lamplight Bridge" (painting), 312

Lamplight Village, 316

Land, Richard, 340

Latin America, 341

Latino evangelicalism, x, 375–76; growth of, 339, 340–41; potential of, 349–50

Lausuén, Fermin F., 212

Law, 263

Lawrence, John, 129–30

Lee, Robert E., 176

Lehman, Simon, 236–37, 243

Leon, Lee de, 340

Leslie, Lynn, 151–52

Leslie, Sarah: background of, 147, 149–50; children of, 151–53; as political activist, 147–49, 150–54, 161, 163–65

Less Than Conquerors: How Evangelicals entered the Twentieth Century (Frank), 275

Leveraged giving, 318

Lewis, C. S., 114–15

Lewis, Elmo, 287–89

Lewis, Jerry Lee, 286, 287, 293

Lewis, Sinclair, 5

Liberalism, 5, 154, 189–90, 363;
    fundamentalist on, 96; institutions
    and, 130, 132, 141; Protestant, xvi,
    125, 190, 256; theological, 32, 38, 93,
    134. *See also* Modernism
Liberals, xvi, 5, 36, 96, 125, 190, 256
Liberation theology, 32, 169, 224
Liberty Counsel, 339
Licensing, 316, 319
Life Flight, 48–50, 56–57, 68
Light, 313–14
"Light of the World, 1932" (painting), 321
Lightpost Publishing, 314, 317
Lincoln Christian Church (Lincoln,
    Oregon), 270–73
Linton, John, 267, 269, 271–73
Literalism. *See* Bible: literal
    interpretations of
Little Eagle Holiness Church,
    219–20, 223
Liturgy, 8, 114–15, 352. *See also* High
    Church
Living Bible, 207–8
Lonsdale, Marty, 318
Lord's Supper, 109, 111, 115, 293, 377.
    See also Sacramentalism
Los Angeles Times, 379n3
Lowell, Charlie, 297–98
Luger, Virginia, 388n6
Luke (book of), xv, 17, 364
Luther, Martin, 240–41, 244, 334; on
    doctrine of transubstantiation, 115;
    theology of, xv–xvi, 25, 35, 104–5,
    194. *See also* Protestant Reformation
Lutherans, 101, 110, 115, 151, 240, 352

Madison, James, 155, 159–60
Magoun, Caroline, 287
Mainline Protestantism, 209, 392n2
"Main Street at Dusk-Placerville"
    (painting), 314
Manilla, James, 66

Mapplethorpe, Robert, 320
Maranatha Campus Ministries
    International, 202
Maranatha Christian Academy:
    classrooms at, 16; students and
    studies at, 18; teachers at, 379n1
March on Washington (1989), 321
Mark IV Pictures, 67–68
Mark of the Beast, 61, 206
Marsh, Cherry, 166–69, 170–75
Marsh, Hannah, 166
Marsh, Keith, 166–69, 170–75
Martin, Paul, 236
Mason, Stephen, 297–98, 308–9, 311
Matthew 5:16, 314
Matthews, Daniel, 362
McCain, John, 368
McPherson, Aimee Semple, xvii, 19, 329
Media Arts Group, Inc., 314, 317, 323
Megachurches, 391n2; flourishing
    of, 327–28; pastors of, 326–27; in
    southern California, 19, 379n4.
    See also specific churches
Mencken, H. L., 5, 358
Mendenhall (Mississippi): housing in,
    179; Perkins, John, in, 178–84
Mendenhall Cooperative Health
    Center, 181
Mendenhall Ministries, 178–81, 190,
    386n6
Mennonites, 229
Meredith, James, 177
Messiah College, 185–86
Methodism, 227
Metropolitan Museum of Art (New
    York), 322
Mexico, 212, 387n2
Millennium, 318
Minasian, Raffi, 36
Missionaries, 211–13, 220, 287, 387n4
Missionary Baptist, 108
Mission for the Coming Days, 253
Mission Portland, 142

Missions, 209–10, 224
Mission Valley Christian Fellowship
    (San Diego, California), 324
Mississippi, 187, 189; programs in, 179,
    181–82; racism in, 176, 182–85.
    See also Mendenhall; Voice of
    Cavalry Fellowship
Mitchell, Janice, 253
Mitchell, John G., 128
Modernism, xvi–xvii; Kinkade,
    William Thomas and, 319;
    theological, 32, 38, 93; threats of,
    130; with moral overtones, 65.
    See also Liberalism
Montebello, Phillippe de, 322–23
Moody, Dwight Lyman, 35, 37, 130,
    249, 275
Moody Bible Institute, 37
Moody Press of Chicago, 200
Moon, William Least Heat, 10
Moralism, 264
Morality, 274
Moral Majority, xviii, 173, 191, 302
Mormons, 223, 274
Motion Pictures, 45, 230. *See also*
    Behavioral standards
Moynihan, Daniel Patrick, 388n7
Multnomah Bible College and
    Seminary, 363. *See also* Multnomah
    School of the Bible
Multnomah Press, 141
Multnomah School of the Bible
    (Portland, Oregon), 363; campus
    of, 127, 143–44; curriculum and
    programs at, 128–29, 134, 138–41;
    Dallas Theological Seminary and,
    128; ethnic groups at, 142–43;
    founding and motto of, 128, 130;
    social values and theology at,
    134–36, 138–41; students and faculty
    of, 127–28, 136–38, 140–45; women
    and, 139–40
Murdoch, Rupert, 197

Music, 201, 297–98; evangelical,
    299–311; groups, 301, 302; rock, 82;
    Swaggart, Jimmy, and, 287–88

Nahum (prophet), 82
National Association of Limited
    Edition Dealers, 314
National Council of Churches, 250
National Hispanic Christian
    Leadership Conference, 346
National Latino Evangelical Coalition,
    340, 348
Nation of Islam, 178, 186n5
Native Americans, 209; culture, language
    and traditions of, 211, 213; decimation
    of, 212, 387n2, 387n4; kinship of, 211;
    religions of, 210–14, 219–22
Neel, Alice, 320, 321
Nelson, Craig, 151
Nelson, John, 275
New Age, 41, 200, 303
New Hampshire, 166–75
New Hope Christian Fellowship
    (Brooklyn, New York), 340
New Jersey Right to Life, 151
New Life Covenant Church (Chicago,
    Illinois), 341–45, 392n1
New Testament, 196, 211, 266; Daniel
    in, 33, 58; Greek, 128; parables of, 42
New York Times, xiv, 66, 322–23
Niebuhr, Reinhold, 42
Ninety-five Theses (Luther), 25
Nordhoff, Charles, 10
North Central Bible College, 346
Norwegian American Hospital, 343
Novelty, 115, 333
Numerology, 384n31

Obama, Barack, 348, 368
Odmark, Matt, 298, 307, 308
Ofili, Chris, 320

Old Glory: An American Voyage
   (Raban), 10
Old Testament, 42
Oneida Community, 34
Orange County Register, 361
Oregon Extension (Lincoln, Oregon),
   366–67, 389n1; community at,
   261–62; property of, 258–59
Original sin, 337
Origin of Species, The (Darwin), 35
Ortega, Daniel, 156
Oxford English Dictionary, xv
Oxford University Press, 37, 380n5

P. E. A. C. E. plan, 335
Painting, 152, 179, 312–19, 321–24, 368
Palin, Sarah, 377
Palmer, D. D., 77
Papacy, xvi. *See also* Roman
   Catholicism
Parham, Charles, 121
Parker, Joseph, 188–89
Parkhurst, Charles H., 248
Patriotism, 162, 328
Patti, Sandy, 247, 302
Paul (apostle), 77, 240–41, 262–63,
   264, 307
Paul, St., xv, 42, 140, 381n15
Payne, Daniel Alexander, 180
PBS. *See* Public Broadcasting Service
Peete, Nan, 124
Peil, Barbara A., 44
Pentecost, J. Dwight, 41–43, 381nn14–15
Pentecostalism: beliefs and worship
   of, 26–27, 40, 380n14; charismata
   and, xvii, 26; definition of, xv, xvii;
   glossolalia and, xvii, 26–27, 109;
   ordinances of, 109; as term, xv, xviii
Pentecostals, 136, 287
People for the American Way, 162–63
Pepsico, 343
Perkins, Clyde, 177

Perkins, John, 386n16; beating,
   economic boycott and, 182–84; in
   California, 177–78; childhood of,
   177; faith of, 178, 186n5, 189–91; in
   Mississippi, 178–88
Perkins, Vera Mae, 178
Pettit, Warren, 298–99
Pew Forum on Religion and Public
   Life, 340
Pharisees, 266
Philadelphia College of the Bible, 37
Philippians (book of), 262
Phillips, Sam, 287
Picasso, Pablo, 319
Piety, xiii, xvi, 4, 9, 11, 91, 104, 136, 159,
   180, 276, 300, 324, 351
Pilgrim Holiness Church, 227
Pilgrim's Progress, The, 213
Pinto, Amy, 368
Pirsig, Robert, 10
Placerville, California, 313–14
Pledge of Allegiance, 162, 164
Popular culture, 377–78
Populism, 324
Pornography, xv, 237
Postmillennialism, 34–35
Potok, Chaim, 91
Pott, Jon, 207
Prayer, 157
Premillennialism. *See* Dispensational
   premillennialism
Presbyterian Church U.S.A., 362
Presbyterianism, 352
Prestonwood Baptist Church (Plano,
   Texas), 327
Price points, 316
Prison reform, 35
Procedural grounds, 352
Prodigal Planet, 63, 202
Prodigal son (parable of), 91–92
Pro-life, 147, 161
Proselytizing, 30, 42
Prosperity theology, 262, 355

Protestantism: American, 36, 130, 241, 256; authority structure within, 26
Protestant liberalism. *See* Liberalism
Protestant Reformation, 194; launch of, xvi; theology of, xv, 267. *See also* Second Reformation
Psalter (Watts), 300
Public Broadcasting Service (PBS), x, 391n3
Purification, 210–11
Puritans, 34, 91, 212, 300
Purpose Driven Life, The (Warren, R.), 333–34
Purpose driven movement, 326, 333–35

Quilt, evangelicalism as, 353–54

R. A. Buckley Christian Youth Center, 181
Raasch, Ken, 314
Raban, Jonathan, 10
Rainbow Angel. *See* Frisby, Neal Vincent
Rainbow Prophet. *See* Frisby, Neal Vincent
Rapture: belief in, 33, 35–36, 39, 59, 61, 83, 173, 253; life on earth after and during, 63, 65, 78, 83, 214, 253
Rationalism, 265–66
Rauschenbusch, Walter, 36
Read, Cynthia, x, xiv
Reagan, Ronald, 82–83, 139, 173, 302, 349, 383n24
Rededication, 102
Reeves, Ken, 117–18, 122
Reeves, Rachel, 117, 122
Reformation. *See* Protestant Reformation
Religious Right, 333, 349–50, 372
Republican Party, 148, 205
Revelation (book of), 33, 58, 60, 83; dismissal of, 34; study of, 18, 25

Revisionism, 159–60
Rice, John R., 281
Riggs, Stephen Return, 213
Riis, Jacob, 247–48
Rissinger, Homer, 226–28
River Brethren, 230
Riverside Book & Bible House, 198–99, 206
Roberto Clemente High School, 341, 344, 345–46
Roberts, Oral, ix, 8, 9, 77
Robertson, Pat, xvii, 263, 349; during Iowa precinct caucuses, 147, 163–67; as New Hampshire candidate, 166–75
Rock music, 82
Rockwell, Norman, 323–24
Rojas, Eddie, 254
Rojas, Richard, 254
Romaine, L. E., 21, 24–25
Roman, Efraim, 254
Roman Catholicism, xvii, 35, 82, 194, 252, 340–41, 388n9; charismatic movement and, 114, 125–26; doctrine of transubstantiation and, 115, 195–96; theology of, xv–xvi, 25, 337
Romans (book of), xv–xvi, 229, 240, 263
Rosenberry, John, 234, 238
Rosenblum, Robert, 322
Routinization, 28–31
Rutberg, Jack, 322
Ryrie Study Bible, 95, 194

Sabbatarianism, 391n5
Sacramentalism, 115, 293
Saddleback Church (Lake Forest, California), 324, 344, 368; baptism at, 337–38; campus of, 337; services and worship at, 329–32, 337–38; venues at, 330, 334–37
Salguera, Gabriel, 340, 348–50
Salters, John, 136–37

Salvation, 62, 104, 123, 229, 266,
   272–73, 289; earning, xv–xvi, 4,
   42, 240–42; for Jews, 42; spiritual
   rebirth and, xvi, 30–31, 307.
   See also Baptism; Conversion
Salvation Army, 227, 248
Sams, W. Birt, 125
Sanctification, 77, 227, 229, 242, 369.
   See also Second blessing
Sanders, Denise, 315–16, 324
San Francisco Chronicle, 322
Satan, 150, 206, 241; politics and,
   165; Saturday evenings and, 17–18;
   women and, 157–58; worship, 29
Scalberg, Daniel, 363
Schlafly, Phyllis, 159
Schmalenberger, Jerry, 154
Schmul, H. E., 239–41
Schroeder, Candy (fictional character),
   100–101, 358
Schuller, Robert, 15, 169, 191, 328, 355,
   379n4
Scofield, Cyrus Ingerson, 37, 275
Scofield Memorial Church. *See* First
   Congregational Church
Scofield Reference Bible, 37, 194, 380n5
Scopes, John T., 45
Scopes Trial, 45, 93, 130, 173, 357
Scriptures. *See* Bible
"Seasoned Approach, A," 44
Second Awakening, 231
Second blessing, 227, 242.
   See also Sanctification
Second Coming, 33, 36, 63, 391n1
Second Great Awakening, 34, 231–32
Second Reformation, 334–35.
   See also Protestant Reformation
Secular humanism, 134, 160
Secularism, 256
Seventh-Day Adventists, 77, 391n5
Seventh Seal, The (Bergman), 34
Sex trafficking, 346
Sexuality, 300

Shakers. *See* Society of Believers in
   Christ's Second Appearing
Shaw, Luci, 207
Shea, George Beverly, 257
Shepherd, Paul, 198–99
Shepherd, The, 72
Shipps, Harry W., 112, 120, 122–23,
   125–26
Shipps, Louise, 125
Sieleman, Maxine, 156–58, 160, 161–62
Sikes, DeAnne, 161–63
Silage, 296
Simon, Paul, 150–51
Sin, 242–43, 245, 251
Sinfulness, xvi, 3–4, 36, 91, 104, 240,
   255–56, 262–65, 273, 306
Sioux, 209, 211; alcohol, drugs and,
   214, 215, 217, 222; heritage and
   traditions of, 215–19; lands of, 88n8,
   213. *See also* Standing Rock Indian
   Reservation
Sioux Sun Dance, 221–22
Sitting Bull, 213, 225
Slater, Philip, 268
Slings, Melissa, 312–13
Smith, Chris, 151
Smith, Chuck, 17–18, 301, 326, 360–63;
   acceptance, compassion and
   message of, 21–23; career of, 19–20;
   as co-founder, pastor and preacher,
   14–17; studies and teachings of,
   17–19, 21–23, 24, 26–28.
   See also Calvary Chapel
Smith, Michael W., 303
Smoking, 102, 360. *See also* Behavioral
   standards
Snyder, Paul (fictional character),
   101–2
Social Gospel, 36, 38, 190, 249
Society Hill (Philadelphia,
   Pennsylvania), 327
Society of Believers in Christ's Second
   Appearing, 33

Sojourners, 339
Sojourners (magazine), 263–64
Sojourners Community (Washington, D.C.), 263
Sollenberger, Ada, 229–30, 235, 358
Sollenberger, Jacob, 229–30, 235, 358
Sound systems, 94, 143, 155, 326, 337, 355
South, Robert, 124
South Dakota American League, 216
Southeast Christian Church (Louisville, Kentucky), 328
Southern Baptist Convention, xvii–xviii, 301, 337, 362
Southern Baptist Ethics and Religious Liberty Commission, 340
South Park, 319
Southwestern Baptist Theological Seminary, 331
Speaking in tongues. See Glossolalia
Spiritual gifts. See Charismata
Springs of Living Water Church (Winnipeg, Manitoba), 327
Sproul, R. C., 202
St. Anne's Episcopal Church (Tifton, Georgia), 112
St. John's Catholic Church (Valdosta, Georgia), 126
St. John's Lutheran Church (Des Moines, Iowa), 153–54
St. Luke's (Seattle, Washington), 114
St. Luke's Episcopal Cemetery (South Dakota), 214–15
St. Luke's Episcopal Church (Fort Yates, North Dakota), 210, 222–24, 363–65
St. Mark's Episcopal Church (Van Nuys, California), 113
St. Paul's Episcopal Church (Darien, Connecticut), 114
Standing Rock Indian Reservation, 209–10, 224, 363; alcohol and drugs at, 214, 215, 217, 222; Little Eagle powwow at, 215–19; unemployment rate at, 213, 388n7

Steinbeck, John, 10
Stevens, Mark A., 203–4
Stewart, Lyman, xvii
Stewart, Milton, xvii
Stewart, Potter, xv
Stott, John R. W., 143
Stout, Harry, 392n3
Strelecki, Stanley, 3–4
Stringfellow, William, 268
Strouse, Larry, 228–29
Stubbs, Brian, 137
Suburbia, 329
Sun Dance, 221–22
Sunday, Billy, 249, 268, 327
Sunday school, 16, 18, 194, 295
Sun Records, 287, 293
"Sunrise: A Prayer of Hope for the Millennium of Light," 318
Supreme Court, California, 368
Swaggart, Donnie, 279–80, 282, 284, 289–90
Swaggart, Frances, 281, 287
Swaggart, Jimmy, 9, 15, 268, 279, 355, 376; autobiography of, 281–82; music and, 287–88; preaching of, 288–90, 293–94; scandal involving, ix, 278, 282–84, 291, 293–94. See also Family Life Center (Baton Rouge, Louisiana)
Swindoll, Chuck, 15, 268–69, 379n4; books by, 95; sermons of, 22

Tag-team preaching, 336
Talmud, 92
Tammany Hall, 248
Taylor Woodrow Homes, 316
Technology, evangelical attitudes toward, 316, 321, 334–35, 353
Televangelists, ix, 8–9, 18–19, 65–66, 195, 261, 280, 283, 293, 354; leaders amongst, 191; scandals involving, ix, 173, 202, 247, 292, 300, 376–77

Television, 354–56
Temperance, 35, 76. *See also* Alcohol
Temple University, 327
Templo Calvario, 340
Tennent, Gilbert, 328
Thagard, Bennett, 117, 122
Thagard, Patricia, 117, 122
Thief in the Night, A, 58–63, 372
Thomas, Lorraine, 291
Thomas Aquinas, St., xv, 26
Thomas Kinkade Collectors' Society, 317
Thomas Kinkade Foundation, 319
Thomas Nelson Publishers, 197–98
Thompson, Donald W., 11, 356, 358,
    372–75, 392n8; awards of, 66–67;
    characteristics and personality of,
    50, 52–53, 66; faith of, 50–56, 66–70;
    vocations and works of, 48–52, 56,
    58–70, 147–49, 151, 202
Thompson, Jack, 66
Thompson, Meldrim, 170
Time, 345
Tithing, 334
Titus, Jim, 259, 267
Tocqueville, Alexis de, 159
Transubstantiation, 115, 195–96
Trauten, Edsel, 242
Travels with Charley (Steinbeck), 10
Trek Inc., 259–60
Tribulation, 35–36, 39, 47, 63–64, 83,
    253, 374–75, 383n21
Trinity Church (Wall Street), 362
Trinity College, 134, 259–60, 346, 389n1
Trinity Evangelical Divinity School,
    134, 263
Trinity Seminary and Bible College.
    See Trinity College
Trotter, A. N., 281
Tsunami relief, 332
Tucker, Lemuel, 186, 190
Turner, Nat, 188
Tuttle, Beverlie, 168, 385n9
Tyndale House Publishers, 207–8

United States (U.S.), 383n21; currency,
    82, 383n20; doctrine of manifest
    destiny of, 213; established religion
    of, 115–16
United States Army Corps of
    Engineers, 210
University of California, Berkeley, 313
University of Notre Dame, 114

Vallejo, California, 325
Vesey, Denmark, 188
Vietnam War, 51, 131, 260
Vineyard Christian Fellowship
    (Anaheim, California), 326, 327, 379n4
Virgin birth, xvii
Voice of Cavalry Fellowship (Jackson,
    Mississippi), 182; evolution of,
    186–87; programs of, 184–86,
    190–91, 386n16; reality of, 356
Voice of Cavalry Ministries, 186–87.
    See also Mendenhall Ministries

Walker, Ralph, 291–92
Wallis, Jim, 375
Wall Street Journal, 322
Warren, Kay, 369
Warren, Matthew, 369
Warren, Rick, 328, 330, 331–35,
    368–69
Watkins, Carl (fictional character),
    103–5, 358
Watts, Isaac, 300
Weary, Dolphus, 188, 190
Weber, Max, 268
Weiss, Jonathan, 380n5
Weisser, Blake, 117
Weisser, Gordon, 117
Wesley, Charles, 300
Wesley, John, 300; conviction of, 27;
    evangelical experience of, xvi, 27
Wesleyan Church, 227, 242

Wessells, Glenn, 313

Westchester Evangelical Free Church (Des Moines, Iowa), 155, 373

Western Health Reform Institute, 77

Westminster Confession of Faith, 36

Wheaton College, 275

Wheeler, Dale, 129

White, Ann, 117, 371

White, Ellen Gould, 76–77

White, James (Jimmy), 108–10, 126, 371

White, Stan J., 369–72, 392n7; characteristics of, 108; as pastor, 108–10, 116, 118–26. *See also* Church of the King; Evangel Assembly of God

Whitefield, George, 65, 327–28, 377

Whites, 189, 212; flight of, 184; racism and, 183–84

Whitney Museum of American Art, 320–22

Whittenberg, Vickie, 291–92

Wicca, 29

William Tyndale College, 134

Willingdon Church (Vancouver, British Columbia), 328

Willow Creek Community Church (South Barrington, Illinois), 327, 340

Wilson, Bill, 280, 289

Wimber, John, 326, 379n4

Windy City Live, 347

Witmer, John A., 38–40

Witnessing. *See* Proselytizing

Women, 218–19, 328; at Dallas Theological Seminary, 43–46, 381nn14–15; Multnomah School of the Bible and, 139–40; Satan and, 157–58

Women, evangelical views of, 11, 15, 29, 128, 167, 228–29, 231, 238; domesticity, femininity and, 158–60; piety as, 300

Women's ordination: opposition to, 43–44, 381n15; seminary movement and, 35, 44

Women's rights, 154, 321, 349, 378

Word, Inc., 197

Word of knowledge, xvii, 27

Word of Life Fellowship (Schroon Lake, New York), 356; bible camps at, 90–106, 365; campfire at, 99–104, 384n5; courtships and romance at, 97–99; establishment of, 90; Pine Pavilion at, 93–97, 384n3; rules of, 95, 384n4

Works, theology of, xv

World Christian Fundamentals Association, 37

Worldliness, xvii, 93, 130, 137, 236–37

World Vision, 318

Wyrtzen, Don, 365

Wyrtzen, Jack, 90, 93, 95–97, 365, 384n4

Wyrtzen, Josh, 365

Young Men's Christian Association (YMCA), 248–49

Zen and the Art of Motorcycle Maintenance (Pirsig), 10

Zimmerman, Kent, 298

Zondervan Publishing House, 197, 387n6

Zwingli, Ulrich, 115, 194